MW01199911

homi
bhabha
and the
computer
revolution

Homi Bhabha (extreme right) with Albert Einstein,
Hideki Yakawa, and John Wheeler (from left to right)
at the Institute for Advanced Study, Princeton, 1948.
Photograph courtesy AIP Emilio Segrè Visual Archives

homi bhabha and the computer revolution

edited by
R.K. Shyamasundar
M.A. Pai

OXFORD
UNIVERSITY PRESS

OXFORD
UNIVERSITY PRESS

YMCA Library Building, Jai Singh Road, New Delhi 110 001

Oxford University Press is a department of the University of Oxford. It furthers the
University's objective of excellence in research, scholarship, and education
by publishing worldwide in

Oxford New York

Auckland Cape Town Dar es Salaam Hong Kong Karachi Kuala Lumpur
Madrid Melbourne Mexico City Nairobi New Delhi Shanghai Taipei Toronto

With offices in

Argentina Austria Brazil Chile Czech Republic France Greece Guatemala
Hungary Italy Japan Poland Portugal Singapore South Korea Switzerland
Thailand Turkey Ukraine Vietnam

Oxford is a registered trademark of Oxford University Press
in the UK and in certain other countries

Published in India
by Oxford University Press, New Delhi

© Oxford University Press 2011

The moral rights of the author have been asserted
Database right Oxford University Press (maker)

First published by Oxford University Press in 2011

ISBN-13: 978-0-19-807246-1
ISBN-10: 0-19-807246-5

Typeset in 10.5/13.2 Adobe Garamond Pro
by Excellent Laser Typesetters, Pitampura, Delhi 110 034
Printed in India by DeUnique, New Delhi 110 018
Published by Oxford University Press
YMCA Library Building, Jai Singh Road, New Delhi 110 001

To R. Narasimhan (1926–2007),
the doyen of Indian computer science

Homi Bhabha, N.B. Prasad, and Jawaharlal Nehru (from left to right) at AEET, 1958. *Photograph courtesy TIFR*

Contents

part IV future perspectives

Figures, Tables, and Boxes

figures

tables

boxes

Homi Bhabha (third from right) showing a model of the new TIFR building to Jawaharlal Nehru (extreme left), S.S. Bhatnagar (second from left), and Morarji Desai (extreme right), 1954. *Photograph courtesy TIFR*

Foreword

This book is part of the birth centenary celebrations of the founder of the Tata Institute of Fundamental Research (TIFR), Homi J. Bhabha. Bhabha's visionary role in the development of diverse branches of science and technology in India, most notably nuclear technology and molecular biology, is well known and documented. This volume focuses on a not so widely known or acknowledged contribution of Bhabha which has been of great significance—the role of TIFR in the creation and evolution of India's computer industry, where India's prowess is recognized globally today.

Right from the inception of TIFR, Bhabha had been aware of the key role of electronics and instrumentation, not only for nuclear electronics but also for a wide spectrum of applications ranging from the space programme to health physics. He was among the early ones to recognize that electronics was one of the most vital and essential branches of modern technology that India needed to master if it was to become self-reliant.

The imperatives of conducting research at TIFR also acted as a spur in furthering Bhabha's involvement with the then nascent field of digital computers. The workforce of high calibre that Bhabha put together at TIFR, expectedly, created a robust demand for instrumentation for scientific experiments at a time when the institute was still dependent mostly on analogue computers. In response, Bhabha, drawing on his personal knowledge of the work being done in overseas universities in building computers for physics research, set up a special group committing TIFR to build its own digital computer.

Tata Institute of Fundamental Research Automatic Calculator (TIFRAC), India's first full-scale digital computer, made its debut in 1960, and TIFR scientists became among the early users to use computers and its applications for a large-scale professional effort. Tata Institute of Fundamental Research Automatic Calculator came to be subsequently widely used by the atomic energy establishment, defence sectors, educational institutes, etc., as these users learnt to trust the ability of TIFR to build large and complex systems with simple and basic components.

Tata Institute of Fundamental Research Automatic Calculator was followed by the setting up of the National Computation Centre at TIFR in 1964 when it imported the then state-of-the-art CDC 3600 160A. Around that time, IIT Kanpur, set up with the help of the US, also became a hub for the new and exciting world of computers. Thus it was through their academic work and the creation of a critical mass of computer scientists in the country that TIFR and IIT Kanpur sowed the seeds of excellence in electronics and computer technology in India, contributing to making India a global force in the computer industry.

This book, jointly edited by R.K. Shyamasundar of TIFR and M.A. Pai of the University of Illinois, is a fitting tribute to Bhabha for his role and vision in sowing the seeds of the IT industry in India. The volume also traces the subsequent developments in indigenous efforts in India's telecom revolution and concludes with an overview of some key fields in computer science and IT that have potential applications in the betterment of society. I am pleased to commend this welcome addition to the corpus of Indian books on the role of science and technology in improving our quality of life.

Chairman, Tata Sons

Message from the Director, TIFR

In the year following the centenary of Homi J. Bhabha's birth, as we look back at all he accomplished, we are struck by the fact that the impact of Bhabha's work is as broad as it is deep. Thus if we ask for the constituency that remembers him today, there is no single answer. One may say that Bhabha's constituency is India, as he helped shape national policy and founded institutions of national importance. On another scale, his constituency is the Department of Atomic Energy, which today is taking forward Bhabha's dream of self-sufficiency in energy for the country. Or one may argue that his constituency is the Tata Institute of Fundamental Research (TIFR), Bhabha's earliest initiative, from which sprang all the others. Tata Institute of Fundamental Research scientists will testify that Bhabha's imprint is felt as much in the practices and scientific culture of the institute as in the research programmes themselves.

How did Bhabha manage to accomplish so much in a span of a little more than twenty years? Two contributory factors were: one, a rare ability to spot talent, and, two, equally an ability to recognize new fields whose importance would grow in time. Bhabha's model of institution-building rested on identifying exceptional people. He emphasized that people came first, buildings later. The growth of computer science and molecular biology, for instance, had much to do with Bhabha's identification of exceptionally talented individuals.

The growth of computer science and allied areas at TIFR has seen several landmarks. These include the commissioning in 1960 of Tata Institute of Fundamental Research Automatic Calculator (TIFRAC), India's first indigenously designed computer, and in the 1970s, the establishment and nurturing of the National Centre for Software Development and Computing Techniques which branched off into an independent existence. In the 1960s and 1970s, researchers from all over the country were provided computing facilities and support at TIFR, thereby introducing them to the use of modern computational methods and tools. Tata Institute of Fundamental Research also played a major role in initiating the indigenous national effort in electronics, which Bhabha recognized as 'one of the most vital and essential branches of modern technology'.

Given this background, and the promise that computer science holds for the future, it is entirely apposite that a volume such as this appear in the Bhabha birth centenary period. R.K. Shyamasundar and M.A. Pai have done a commendable job of conceiving this compilation, and translating the concept into reality. The articles that appear here will remain a valuable resource for future researchers who would like to know about the beginnings of the field in the country, its status, and, most of all, about the visionary who started it all.

Mumbai   MUSTANSIR BARMA
January 2011   Director
                              Tata Institute of Fundamental Research

Acknowledgements

Many in the media and general public attribute the information technology (IT) revolution in India to the process of liberalization in the 1990s. Those familiar with the science and technology scene in post-Independence India, however, have a different take on this issue, as well as on other issues such as the Green, Milk, and Telecom revolutions that took place in the first three–four decades after the Independence. These contributed significantly to the success of India's economic reforms in the 1990s.

The information technology revolution began in the late 1950s in India when Homi J. Bhabha saw the need to develop the knowledge of computer and its scientific usage in the country. Commemorating Homi Bhabha's birth centenary, this book is a tribute to his vision of changing the science and technology landscape of India. We thank Mustansir Barma, Director, Tata Institute of Fundamental Research (TIFR) who liked the idea and readily promoted the effort initiated by M.A Pai through an email to the TIFR colloquium coordinator, B. Sathyanarayana. In this effort, we received strong support and encouragement from TIFR at every step of the way. We thank him for bringing us together for the endeavour. We also thank the faculty and staff of the School of Technology and Computer Science, TIFR, for extending all the assistance towards this initiative.

For a book that covers such a wide span of topics ranging from history to a futuristic look on the role of computers in science, technology, and society, we owe a special debt of gratitude to all the contributors. It is a tribute to Bhabha that all of them readily agreed to contribute to the book, and kept up with the tight timeline in spite of their busy schedules. Our profuse thanks to all of them who made the book possible. Our special thanks to Ratan N. Tata for readily agreeing to provide a Foreword in a short time.

We thank S. Biswas, G. Siva Kumar, and S. Ramesh for their valuable inputs while reviewing the outline and structure of the book at a short notice. Thanks to Sunanda Vittal for editing some of the articles and giving valuable suggestions. We thank the TIFR archival group, particularly Ananya Dasgupta who was of great help in providing us with the quotes and the dates of Homi Bhabha's speeches and images from the TIFR archives.

We dedicate this book to the memory of R. Narasimhan who led the team that developed India's first digital computer at TIFR, which marked the beginning of India's long journey in computer science and IT. The technical design of this computer is described in his paper, 'On the System and Engineering Design of the General Purpose Electronic Digital Computer at TIFR', which appeared in the *Proceedings of Indian Academy of Sciences*. The paper has been reproduced in the Appendix. We thank the Indian Academy of Sciences (IASc) for giving us permission to reproduce the article in this volume. We also thank National Institute of Science Communication and Information Resources (NISCAIR), CSIR, Government of India, for allowing us to reproduce a few passages from a special issue of *Science Reporter* that bring to light their research study on the evolution of IT in India.

Finally, our special thanks to the editorial team at Oxford University Press India for providing excellent editorial input and support.

January 2011   R.K. Shyamasundar and M.A. Pai

Bhabha, 'Big Science', and the IT Revolution in India

During its long history reaching back to thousands of years, India has given birth to some of the world's greatest teachers, scientists, mathematicians, and philosophers who shone brilliantly and left the mark of their genius through path-breaking inventions and ideas. In post-Independence India, Homi Jehangir Bhabha (1909–1966) stands out as one such luminary who not only did great science but also paved the way for founding science and technology institutions in India. Though known by many for his seminal contribution in the atomic energy sector, Bhabha had a much broader vision as can be seen from his personal interest in nurturing diverse areas like molecular biology, developing India's first digital computer, and laying down the blueprint for the development of the country's electronics and space programmes. He created a broad canvas of science and technology missions with immense passion and commitment. His 'Big Science' approach to the country's development has today made India a proud nation and an emerging global economic power.

One might wonder what inner urgings drove Bhabha to such a mission. The evidence of his indomitable spirit can be found from his lecture to the International Council of Scientific Unions at Mumbai on 7 January 1966, prior to his unfortunate death in an air-crash. Bhabha said:

What the developed countries have and the underdeveloped lack is modern science and technology and an economy based on modern technology. The problem of developing the underdeveloped countries is therefore the problem of modern science in them and transforming their economy to one based on modern science and technology. An important question which we must consider is whether it is possible to transform the economy of a country to one based on modern technology developed elsewhere without at the same time, establishing modern science in the country as a live and vital force ... the problem of establishing science as a live and vital force in society is an inseparable part of the problem of transforming an industrially underdeveloped to a developed country.

One can see in these words Bhabha's conviction about the impact of science on society and at the same time the enormous task ahead of realizing this mission. He was internationalist in his outlook, while at the same time extremely focused on achieving excellence domestically. His sincere passion for achieving things is best described in his own words:

I know quite clearly what I want out of my life. Life and my emotions are the only things I am conscious of. I love the consciousness of life and I want as much of it as I can get. But the span of one's life is limited. What comes after death no one knows. Nor do I care. Since, therefore, I cannot increase the content of life by increasing its duration; I will increase it by increasing its intensity. Art, music, poetry and everything else that I do have this one purpose—increasing the intensity of my consciousness of life.*

One way to understand this is to see how Bhabha went about realizing that each country has its own trajectory of development. Unlike countries that benefitted from the industrial revolution, countries that gained independence post-World War II had to tread a different path. While a large majority of these nations succumbed to authoritarian or dictatorial rule, India alone stood as a large country that took a different route. The non-violent approach of Mahatma Gandhi and the democratic impulses of the country's first Prime Minister Jawaharlal Nehru paved the way for a unique model of governance, perhaps unparalleled in the world. When he took the reins of a newly independent India in 1947, Nehru believed that democracy and a mixed economy would be the ideal formula for nation-building. Lacking in capital and human resources at that time, he believed correctly that with its rich heritage

* Homi J. Bhabha in a letter to Jessie Maver, 1934.

and excellent scientists available at the time of independence, though small in number, India could build a self-reliant economy based on democracy, secularism, and a scientific outlook. That he succeeded in this effort is now a matter of history. Those who differ with this idea would do well to look at other nations who gained independence after World War II.

Among the small cadre of scientists in India at the time of independence was Homi J. Bhabha, who after his return from Cambridge in 1939, decided to stay back in India although he had lucrative employment offers from some of the most reputed schools in the UK. He worked at the Indian Institute of Science (IISc), Bangalore for a few years and pursued a research project in cosmic rays under the supervision of Nobel Laureate C.V. Raman, who was the Director of IISc at that time.

Bhabha received his bachelor's degree in mechanical engineering from Cambridge University in 1930, and went on to pursue PhD from the same university. It was his love for Physics that drew him into the circle of great minds of Cambridge University. Introducing Bhabha at the meeting of the Indian Academy of Sciences in 1941, C.V. Raman said that Homi Bhabha '[is] the modern equivalent of Leonardo da Vinci'. This is not only a testimony of Bhabha's scholarship but also reveals C.V. Raman's expectations from him.

Between his return to India and the end of World War II, there was a distinct change in Bhabha's perception of the country. With India becoming independent, he also developed a unique personal rapport with Nehru. Both believed that the development of science and technology was the only means to eliminate poverty in India. They shared a common philosophy as to how an impoverished country like India should develop with a great degree of self-reliance. Bhabha believed that if India cultivated a critical mass of scientists within the country, then it could forge ahead in science and technology, almost like the western nations had done.

In a letter to the Tata Trust in 1944, Bhabha outlined the need for a school of excellence in the fundamental sciences (of mathematics, physics, and chemistry) in Bombay (now Mumbai).[†] As he developed the idea of the need for India to become self-reliant in science and its applications, he wrote, 'I have recently come to the view that provided

[†] See Appendix.

proper appreciation and financial support are forthcoming, it is the duty of people like us to stay in our own country and build up outstanding schools of research such as some other countries are fortunate enough to possess'.[‡] Bhabha argued that investment in science had a longer pay-off time. His education at Cambridge University left a deep impression on his mind; he was fascinated with the energy problem. Looking at the Indian landscape and the finite coal resources the country had, Bhabha realized that nuclear power was India's salvation for energy independence. He was passionate about energy and nuclear energy in particular as India's answer to the energy problem and its road to industrialization. He mentioned this in his letter to the Tata Trust. When viewed in the context of the current global energy scenario, his views and actions seem nothing less than prophetic.

Bhabha's passion for developing the energy sector saw him championing the cause of nuclear energy much before the Hiroshima and Nagasaki bombings. He chaired the first international conference on peaceful uses of nuclear energy in 1955. Vienna was chosen as the headquarters, and Bhabha had a prominent role in this. Moreover, the visit to Vienna allowed him to indulge in his second passion—his love for western art and music. He fervently believed that science had no boundaries, and if science had to have any meaning in India, its fruits must trickle down for the benefit of the common man.

Bhabha was the recipient of several prestigious awards and honours. At the age of thirty-two he was elected Fellow of the Royal Society in 1941. He was awarded the Adams Prize in 1943 by the Cambridge University for his work on cosmic rays, and in 1948 the Hopkins Prize of the Cambridge Philosophical Society. In 1963, he was elected Foreign Associate of the US National Academy of Sciences and Honorary Life Member of the New York Academy of Sciences. He was conferred the title of Padma Bhushan in 1954.

TATA INSTITUTE OF FUNDAMENTAL RESEARCH— THE BEGINNINGS

Tata Institute of Fundamental Research (TIFR) started functioning in Mumbai in 1945 in a modest temporary building. Bhabha was determined to take on a new approach to the development of science

---

[‡] Homi J. Bhabha in a letter to S. Chandrasekhar, 20 April 1944.

in India. Structurally, TIFR was slightly different from the Council of Scientific and Industrial Research (CSIR), which was established immediately before independence (in 1942). Council of Scientific and Industrial Research had adopted a centralized model. Bhabha instead opted for intense and systematic investments in basic sciences by identifying the best and brightest talents. This signalled a new paradigm for science and technology growth in India, which reaped unparalleled benefits in new thinking and directions.

Initially, there was no organizational chart for the development of TIFR. However, Bhabha chose to follow the model created by the Max Planck Institute in Germany, that is, first, he would select qualified people and then he would build departments around them. In his presidential address at the annual meeting of the National Institute of Sciences of India (later renamed Indian National Science Academy) in October 1963, he expanded on this philosophy of developing institutions:

I feel that we in India are apt to believe that good scientific institutions can be established by Government decree or order. A scientific institution, be it a laboratory or an academy, has to be grown with great care like a tree. Its growth in terms of quality and achievement can only be accelerated to a very limited extent. This is a field in which a large number of mediocre or second rate workers cannot make up for a few outstanding ones, and the few outstanding ones always take at least 10–15 years to grow.

While atomic energy research was an integral part of CSIR's portfolio, Bhabha insisted and convinced Nehru that there should be an independent entity for developing atomic energy resource in India. Initially, Bhabha's priority was to develop atomic energy at TIFR. For this purpose he conducted a survey of natural resources, particularly materials of interest to atomic energy programmes, such as uranium, thorium, beryllium, graphite, etc. For this purpose, a special unit, named the Rare Minerals Division was created in Delhi. Bhabha was thus able to lay the foundations of a long-term strategy for the development of atomic energy in India.

With the establishment of its first nuclear reactor Apsara in 1954 in Trombay, India entered into a full-fledged atomic energy programme. Given the unique nature of the Apsara project, it was required to bring a pool of brilliant workforce based on a thorough screening process. Subsequently, each fresh recruit had to undergo rigorous training in nuclear science and technology. This later became a model replicated in institutions such as the Indian Space Research Organisation (ISRO). Unfortunately, in other sectors such as electric power this practice was not followed, with the result that today the country is facing a perennial energy crisis. In addition to shaping a high calibre workforce, TIFR also created a great demand for instrumentation for scientific experiments, including balloon experiments. This led to the setting up of the instrumentation unit, which was later shifted to the atomic energy facility site.

It was at this time that Bhabha was keen to acquire modern digital computers that needed to be developed for the large number of users at TIFR, who at the time were mostly dependent on analogue computers. This became a reality under the leadership of R. Narasimhan, who had joined the institute in 1954. His team fabricated the first digital computer in India in 1960, which was widely used by the atomic energy establishment, defence sectors, educational institutes, industries, and so on. The electronics production unit that started in TIFR became the nucleus of the large corporation known as the Electronics Corporation of India Ltd. (ECIL) at Hyderabad. Bhabha also initiated a plan for semiconductor manufacturing in Punjab. Unfortunately, after Bhabha's death in a plane crash in 1966, this activity did not take off.

Bhabha had definite inputs for the Industrial Policy Resolution of 1956, which focused on attaining industrial self-reliance for the development of the country. While there was ample scope for the private sector to grow, it did not fill the space adequately, thus leaving India open to the charge of being branded a 'socialistic' state, which did not seem to be a proper interpretation of the policy. Interestingly, India was moving towards a mixed economy, which was largely responsible for creating the basic contours of institutions like banking, insurance, IITs, etc.—all of which helped to usher in the Green, Milk, and Telecom (GMT) revolutions of the modern era.

In fact, the beginnings of IT revolution in India were spawned by the efforts at TIFR in 1955, resulting in India's first indigenously developed digital computer (commissioned five years later, in February 1960). At the same time, P.C. Mahalanobis imported the country's first digital computer—a Hollerith computer for performing statistical calculations at the Indian Statistical Institute (ISI). The Hollerith computer was also used by the Planning Commission of India. In addition, it played a vital role during India's first general elections. Later, ISI, in association with Jadavpur University, came up with a machine based on transistors, known as the Indian Statistical Institute Jadavpur University (ISIJU) computer, which was specifically used for research purposes.

FIRST INDIGENOUS COMPUTER AT TIFR—
THE EARLY YEARS

By the 1950s Bhabha was globally recognized as a physicist of great repute. Through his frequent travels abroad he would keep himself up to date with the latest developments in science and technology. On a visit to Princeton University, Bhabha came to know about the pioneering computer design of John von Neumann (1903–1957). Neumann's design captured Bhabha's attention, and he brought a copy of Neumann's report. He was keen to start a concurrent effort in India, and was searching for expertise. R. Narasimhan had just returned to India after completing his PhD in mathematics from Indiana University. Since Narasimhan was also familiar with Neumann's report, he presented a special seminar about designing a computer at TIFR. There was already some work being conducted in logic circuits at TIFR, and therefore Bhabha became convinced that India needed to build a computer of its own. Thus began the journey—of making the first state-of-the-art digital computer in India. It took seven long years to complete the project. There was no supervision by Bhabha as such. It was largely due to his guiding principle to have faith in the individual's ability to work independently and give her/him freedom with excellent logistical support—from the people working in the workshop to scientists and engineers. However, the internal memory of the TIFR computer consisted of a three-dimensional ferrite-core matrix (made up of 40 planes). Therefore, the matrix assembly had to be purchased from Mullard and Co., England.

While the project was initiated in 1955, the computer became functional only in 1959. The physics group at TIFR and several scientists from Chennai and Bangalore used it extensively. What was important, however, was a group of TIFR scientists were the first to use computers and its applications for a large-scale professional effort. During the inauguration of the new building of TIFR in 1962, Nehru named the computer Tata Institute of Fundamental Research Automatic Calculator (TIFRAC). It included 2,700 vacuum tubes, 1,700 germanium diodes, and 12,500 resistors. It had 2,048 40-bit words of memory. The design of TIFRAC by Narasimhan was first published in the proceedings (Section A, 52, pp. 47–57) of Indian Academy of Sciences (IASc).[§] TIFRAC was supposed to have been donated to IISc, but this never took place. It is a tragedy that such a great testimonial of India's scientific history was never preserved.

The scientists at TIFR had extensively used TIFRAC for their daily computation. It had no higher level of language other than the machine language. This was indeed the main problem for its usage. A separate article discusses TIFRAC in some detail. Comparing TIFRAC with other contemporary machines, Narasimhan says:

The pilot machine, except for its size, was quite in pace with the state of the art in 1954. The design of TIFRAC (named only in 1962 after it had been operational for a few years) in 1957 was still not very much behind what was being attempted at that time elsewhere. But by the time it was officially commissioned in 1960, computer technology had surged ahead leaving our machine behind as an obsolete first generation machine.

Meanwhile, technological advancements were rapidly taking place in the western countries that led to a spectrum of computer applications in business, academia, and industry that relied on user-friendly software. Realizing that TIFRAC could not be upgraded for the next generation (it was the same case with the Princeton-type computers), and that manufacturing one's own computer would not satisfy the requirements of scientists and engineers, TIFR decided to import CDC 3600 (of Control Data Corporation) in 1962, which after being operational in 1964 became a national computation centre. It is interesting to note that a Time-Sharing Operating System (TOPS) was designed and implemented on CDC 3600-160A using a large disc file to allow users to edit files, debug programs, and work on remote typewriter terminals.

While TIFRAC was operational, it was mainly used for a variety of offline applications. Tata Institute of Fundamental Research took up the design and implementation of Online Data Processor (OLDAP) to answer the need for a minicomputer for online control of nuclear physics experiments, in particular the analysis of bubble chamber photographs. A second objective was to examine and evaluate the feasibility of designing a fairly large and complex digital system primarily using Indian components, which were then available. Such an effort, apart

[§] Reproduced in Appendix with permission from IASc.

from its relevance from the point of view of national self-sufficiency, was also intrinsically challenging. Finally, it was expected that such a professionally worthwhile design effort would yield valuable experience in terms of indigenous design capability and generation of manpower.

The Online Data Processor incorporated several novel and state-of-the-art design features. The first specifications of this machine were drawn up in mid-1965. System designing took a little more than a year. Fabrication was started in mid-1967, and OLDAP was ready in 1969. The experimental physics groups started using it from the early 1970s. Many of these activities provided a strong interaction between TIFR and ECIL, but the institute itself did not go further on such ventures as the technologies had advanced drastically and the activities had become widespread across industries worldwide.

Over the years at TIFR, Bhabha took an increasing interest in developing institutions in many other spheres of science activities including molecular biology, radio astronomy, and space and electronics. Due to his global exposure to science and technology issues, he was in a sense a science and technology gatekeeper for India. He would send his staff abroad for training in specific areas since he was well known around the world. While at TIFR, he started the molecular biology unit, which has an outstanding facility in Bangalore in the form of the National Centre for Biological Sciences (NCBS). The radio telescope unit at Ooty was yet another remarkable initiative. He also initiated space research activity, which then became the sole responsibility of Vikram Sarabhai (1919–1971).

BEYOND TIFRAC

The success of TIFRAC gave scientists at TIFR the necessary confidence to use computer as a tool for advanced research in the sciences. As mentioned already, TIFR became a national computation centre with the import of CDC 3600-160A when the computational needs of the institute and the country grew in leaps and bounds. A systematic effort to spread computer software education and training, while it had its genesis in TIFR, also began to spread elsewhere in the country.

The arrival of IBM 1620 at IIT Kanpur in 1963 under the Indo-American US AID programme marked the next important milestone along with TIFR's initial entry into the computer field. Initially headed by H.K. Kesavan and then by V. Rajaraman, the IIT computer centre became an instant hub of activity for students and industries around the country. A separate article highlights these efforts. The Kanpur Indo-American programme was a consequence of the visit of Prime Minister Nehru to the US to meet President Kennedy. In the words of the Late John Galbraith, former US Ambassador to India, 'Of all the developments in India during the last few decades, Kanpur must have had the highest multiplier effect. The arrival of IBM 1620 was a great event.'

Both TIFR and IIT Kanpur were emblematic of Nehru and Bhabha's forward thinking and computer technology aspirations for India. Particularly, after the 1962 war with China, both leaders were cognizant that India could not go very far without the growth and development of the electronics industry. Thus, a roadmap for the development of electronics was initiated and pursued by Bhabha in the form of a TIFR committee report. Unfortunately, Bhabha died before he could present the report to Nehru. In 1964, after Nehru's death, the report was revisited by Indira Gandhi, who offered full support for its implementation with the establishment of the Department of Electronics (DoE) within the Government of India under the leadership of M.G.K. Menon, the then Director of TIFR.

EFFORTS AT TIFR IN CREATING SOFTWARE EXPERTISE

With the emergence of the DoE in 1970, the Electronics Commission was set up in 1971. The commission played a decisive role in disseminating the know-how developed at the TIFR Computer Group. One of the focused efforts towards realizing this goal was the opening of the National Centre for Software Development and Computing Techniques (NCSDCT) as part of TIFR. Initially, NCDSCT was supported through assistance from the United Nations Development Programme (UNDP) and focused on software development and computing techniques. It shared its resources with practically every interested research and development (R&D) institution in the country. Perhaps the most valuable contributions of the group were in the form of sharing the know-how with other institutions. It also ensured the R&D leadership for the future. A detailed account of this is given in the essay by S. Ramani.

One of most important programmes whose impact was seen for a long time was the organization of advanced R&D in computer science.

Eminent personalities from abroad were invited to TIFR, particularly to help researchers to keep themselves up-to-date with the latest frontiers in research. These research efforts had a far-reaching effect including the nurturing of computer scientists, new generation projects, and attracting talent. In 1981, NCSDCT also set up the now well-known conference series, 'Foundations of Software Technology and Computer Science', creating the first peer-reviewed forum for interaction among researchers, initially led by R.K. Shyamasundar and Mathai Joseph. This has now become a well-recognized international conference.

On another front, when Indo-US relations deteriorated during the early 1970s, multinational computer giants such as IBM exited India. This opened up a tremendous opportunity for Indian science and technology developers, unleashing India's latent talent in logic and mathematics that eventually manifested itself in a flurry of software development. Computer Maintenance Corporation Ltd. (CMC) was born to cater to the maintenance of computers in India. This institution provided the much needed indigenous maintenance support and also offered the impetus and backbone for several R&D activities, which paid rich dividends during the Y2K transition. In retrospect, many consider the exit of IBM to be a blessing in disguise for the Indian software industry. An important byproduct was the railway reservation system—a combined effort of CMC and NCSDCT.

Another turning point in India's quest for computer self-reliance was the creation of ECIL, which ostensibly prevented a takeover of the Indian TV industry by multinational corporations. Similarly, the Centre for Development of Telematics (C-DOT) later prevented the establishment of an outdated model of telecommunication development in India, particularly when C-DOT founder, Sam Pitroda saw telephone access as more important than telephone density. Thus, India's forward march in the telecom revolution began as a result of C-DOT, which had the full support of the then Prime Minister Rajiv Gandhi. Separate essays discuss the contributions of ECIL, CMC, and C-DOT.

LIBERALIZATION AND IT IN INDIA TODAY

The first four decades after India's independence represented an extraordinary period in modern Indian history. Fervent efforts were devoted to develop and create core strengths in basic industries such as steel, heavy machinery, and advanced computer technology. In addition, India's two remarkable success stories, namely the Green and the Milk revolutions consolidated the foundation of self-reliance in food supply. It is natural to consider all these historical events as a given, just as we take for granted the benefits of democracy and freedom. Many would also forget how these were accomplished against heavy odds.

The reform era started in the 1980s with the opening up of the economy in a measured way. Just as the Green and the Milk revolutions made the country self-sufficient in food, the C-DOT revolution made communications ubiquitous and heralded an unprecedented growth of the telecom industry. Consequently, we saw the beginnings of the IT industry flourish in the form of three major technology giants—Infosys, Tata Consultancy Services (TCS), and WIPRO—which led to the creation of a number of software start-up companies to continue the effort.

It was only after the economic liberalization of the 1990s initiated during Prime Minister P.V. Narasimha Rao's time by the then Finance Minister Manmohan Singh that the IT industry really began to gain momentum. India took on monumental challenges on the global scene in defusing the Millennium Bug (Y2K), followed closely by the growth of the BPO services sector. By this time heading into the twenty-first century, the IT industry in India had developed the confidence to move up the value chain in terms of corporate consulting and software exports, and had developed an indelible global footprint. Separate articles discuss these issues in depth. Today, India is recognized globally as an IT hub of exceptional talent and for her command over the IT know-how.

The principle on which the TIFR was founded has been vindicated by the results that we see today in the science and technology landscape of India. As Bhabha said, 'there is no genuine knowledge of the universe that is not potentially useful for man, not merely in the sense that action may one day be taken on it, but also in the fact that every new knowledge necessarily affects the way in which we hold all the rest of our stock.'[¶]

Today, as in the 1950s, India requires a Bhabha-like figure to solve her problems in several areas of infrastructure. As growth and

---

[¶] 'Allocation of Scientific Research to the Universities' by H.J. Bhabha (27–8 September 1943).

innovation continue to thrive in the areas of hardware, software, and computer applications, computer science and IT can help in the efficient management of the country's development. However, in the twenty-first century, innovations in science and technology must soar to even greater heights in discoveries, inventions, and technological solutions that touch the lives of the masses in meaningful ways as Bhabha envisioned it. His strongest belief was that science should filter down to common people and work to improve their lives.

Bhabha's 'Big Science' approach fostered the blossoming of indigenous talent and cemented our global presence as an IT powerhouse. Today, it also serves as a powerful reminder of what India can accomplish in decades to come given its vast reservoir of human talent and resources. India has the unique advantage of a sizeable young population often referred to as 'the demographic dividend sector'. The potential here is enormous and still waiting to be tapped into. This book includes essays ranging from the historical evolution of the computer in India to current trends in IT, and finally looks ahead at the future possibilities. A brief overview of the essays follow.

Part I provides a historical perspective on computer technology and how over the years it has been developed in the country. The technical details of India's first computer TIFRAC is ably chronicled by P.V.S. Rao who was intimately associated with the TIFRAC project. At that time it was a state-of-the art computer in India.

In the appendix, the original article on its design and implementation authored by R. Narasimhan has been reproduced with permission from Indian Academy of Sciences. The article clearly provides beginnings of the effort with appropriate credits for the persons concerned.

Since India could not gear up with semiconductor chip manufacture after Bhabha's death, attention was focused on software. The genesis of today's software capabilities can be traced to the establishment of NCSDCT. S. Ramani provides an excellent account of the R&D activities that were initiated through NCSDCT/NCST and outreach activities.

Bhabha was also responsible for the creation of ECIL which produced minicomputers and also developed TV technology. S.R. Vijayekar and Y.S. Mayya describe the effort on building computers in India—both hardware and software. In an effort to make e-governance possible, National Informatics Centre was established; N. Seshagiri piloted this important effort over the years. The effort of IIT Kanpur in computer science education is discussed by V. Rajaraman who played a major role in this area.

Part II is devoted to self reliace in electronics and telecommunication. The first essay by M.G.K. Menon emphasizes the guiding principle of Bhabha about achieving self-reliance by nurturing indigenous talent. He traces the actions of Bhabha towards making India self-reliant in electronics. Sam Pitroda's essay traces the creation of C-DOT and its impact on the Indian masses, which ultimately paved the way for more than half the country's cell phones. Centre for Development of Telematics was the brainchild of Sam Pitroda. The article by him and M.V. Pitke (his colleague in C-DOT) describes this work. They trace Bhabha's effort to achieve self-reliance in electronics for the newly independent country. It may also be noted that efforts on building supercomputers when India was denied its import, was also initiated during this time. This aspect is also touched upon in the article by Sam Pitroda and M.V. Pitke. It is easy for India to ignore this principle in the era of globalization with the result that we will fail to cash in on the demographic dividend.

Part III talks about the rise of the software industry with the emphasis on its future by N.R. Narayana Murthy who steered Infosys to global heights, and also showed an ethical model of building an ideal corporation. Alongside was TCS where the genius of F.C. Kohli made it the leading software company in India. S. Ramadorai narrates how TCS was a game changer in establishing a global footprint for itself. The next essay by Nandan Nilekani is on creating a unique identity number for each of the 1 billion people in India which will affect the country in all walks of life in the future.

Bhabha also created the space programme for India, which was later headed by Vikram Sarabhai. This singular achievement of ISRO, which made India a major power in space research, is well documented by U.R. Rao, former Chairman of ISRO.

The final part deals with emerging technologies where computer plays a vital role. While some of the essays may not be related to Homi Bhabha, they bring to light his philosophy of encouraging highest levels of contemporary and even speculative science and technology. Peter Hofstee provides a coherent travel from von Neumann (the story goes that Homi Bhabha was in touch with him) architectures to multicore architectures and beyond. While R.K. Shyamasundar looks at how software has evolved from a craft form to a well-grounded science through academic discipline and touches upon the efforts on these aspects at TIFR, A. Paulraj describes the state of wireless technology both in India and abroad, and how India can leapfrog in this area with proper policies. Rahul Jain, J. Radhakrishnan, and Pranab Sen provide a detailed survey on quantum computation. While this article may not be exactly related to the main theme, it provides a link to a quality interdisciplinary science and speculative technology which Bhabha had always relished and would have gone a step ahead in its promotion had he been alive. Bud Mishra outlines an India-specific agenda in bio-computing and narrates how India can make advances in computational biology. Again, keeping the openness of Homi Bhabha, we have two essays on applications of IT on infrastructures (or in general cyber physical systems): Jay Giri narrates the application on power infrastructure and Parvin Varaiya and Alex A. Kurzhanskiy narrate applications on transportation infrastructure.

We hope this collection of essays will serve both as a historic documentation of India's dominance as an IT superpower and indicate how far IT can serve her common people, which was the dream of Homi Bhabha.

January 2011   M.A. PAI and R.K. SHYAMASUNDAR

part I
historical perspectives

Homi Bhabha and J.R.D. Tata in discussion, 1960s. *Photograph courtesy TIFR*

P.V.S. RAO

1 Homi Bhabha and Information Technology in India
TIFRAC—India's First Computer

Tata Institute of Fundamental Research Automatic Calculator (TIFRAC), the first electronic digital computer designed and built in India marked the first significant step the country took towards self reliance in information technology (IT). It is a tribute to Homi Bhabha that he had the vision that India must have the expertise in this vital area.

The impact of this activity went far beyond the immediate one-time benefits that accrued from the availability of such a machine. It influenced the growth of computer technology, computer awareness, and utilization over a much wider field. In addition, it enabled the building up of a strong group of competent first-generation computer professionals in the country. As a result, the 'TIFRAC spirit' characterized nearly all subsequent activities of the group and influenced the subsequent development of computer technology in India.

This essay describes some of the unique features of TIFRAC. It traces how the technological know-how developed, the role it played in facilitating scientific and technological research, and also the multiplier effect it had in all aspects of IT.

THE BHABHA PHILOSOPHY

Tata Institute of Fundamental Research Automatic Calculator was the first digital computer to be built in India. It exemplifies Bhabha's approach to develop facilities, infrastructure, and competence in areas of sophisticated technology which were of vital interest to the country: (a) anticipate the directions in which science and technology are likely to move, (b) initiate well in advance the steps necessary to achieve proficiency and self-dependence in these areas, and (c) institute institutional structures to make this possible. He believed that if a certain sophisticated instrument or system was required for this effort, it was not proper to import it if it could be developed within the country—the spirit of self reliance.

THE EARLY DAYS OF COMPUTERS IN INDIA

To achieve the objective of developing computer technology expertise, a small computer section was formed in the mid-1950s as part of the Electronics Instrumentation Group of Tata Institute of Fundamental Research (TIFR). P.C. Mahalanobis also appreciated the importance of computers for the development of science in India. In 1956 he decided to import a computer for the Indian Statistical Institute (ISI) which he headed. It was a Hollerith HEC 2M computer. Its specific use was for the Planning Commission in developing the five year plans for India's development, as well for the purpose connected with holding the country's first general election. This was a 24-bit, serially accessed machine with a magnetic drum memory—a Hollerith card reader for input and a modified Hollerith card tabulator for output. It was not an easy machine to use. Indian Statistical Institute's second computer, the 'Ural', a Russian machine, was acquired in 1959. It was a binary, fixed point, single address, 36-bit, 1024-word, magnetic drum memory, vacuum tube machine with an operating speed of 100 operations per second. It had paper tape and 'key printing device', input/output (I/O) and external storage in the form of magnetic tape and paper tape.

TIFRAC AND APSARA

Tata Institute of Fundamental Research Automatic Calculator was taking shape at about the same time as India's first nuclear reactor, Apsara (both so named by Jawaharlal Nehru). The Apsara and TIFRAC design teams were working together and interacting regularly. There was much jubilation when Apsara went critical for the first time. There was similar excitement when all the subunits—the arithmetic, memory, control, and display units operated in synchrony and the first program could be run on the system which consequently became a TIFR-designed 'computer'. It was a small machine language program cumulatively adding one number to another; it looped a number of times and stopped after a specified number of cycles. To the design team, the first Indian computer running a 'stored program' was as much a milestone as the first Indian reactor sustaining a chain reaction of nuclear fission!

TIFRAC DESIGN*

The Early Stages

Tata Institute of Fundamental Research Automatic Calculator was intended to be a full-blown, powerful computer, and was meant to meet the computing needs of groups in the various units of the atomic energy establishment. In addition, it was expected to provide a stimulus for the use of computers in the field of research in Indian universities and government-funded science and technology establishments. Even its use in the commercial institutions was not ruled out.

When the computer section was formed as part of the Electronics Instrumentation Group of TIFR in 1955, it consisted of a handful of fresh postgraduates in physics (with specialization in electronics) and supported by a few radio engineering diploma holders. The seniormost member of this group was R. Narasimhan, who joined TIFR in 1959 after he had completed his PhD from the Indiana University.

Globally, the basic techniques of computer design began to be understood and developed at a few universities and by some active computer manufacturers at that time. Much of the work done at these places remained largely unknown to others because of lack of communication.

Tata Institute of Fundamental Research group had access to some minimal information about the Ordnance Discrete Variable Automatic Computer (ORDVAC) designed at the University of Illinois. However, this information was sketchy and fragmentary. There was hardly any source of information to help the beginner to get started. Therefore, one

---

* The major contributors to the development of TIFRAC are: R. Narasimhan, B.K. Basu, P.V.S. Rao, T.R.N. Rao, M.M. Dosabbhai, and V.K. Joglekar (arithmetic and control); S.P. Srivastava, R.N. Neogi, and B.B. Kalia (memory); K.L. Bhakhru (input output); D.S. Kamat (magnetic drum); P.V.S. Rao and R.R. Nargundkar (text and graphics display); M.M. Farooqui and D.F. Cooper (power supply); and K.S. Kane (software).

had to 'learn on the job'. Lack of information forced the TIFR design group to do most of their design independently, ab initio and in vacuo, rather than copy from other computers. This was as much a handicap as it was a challenge. Also, it was an excellent opportunity to innovate.

To design a full-scale computer straightaway could well have been a daunting challenge, especially for a group of novices. Hence, rather than developing a full-fledged machine at one go, the group decided to work on a 'pilot model' of the computer in the first instance. This pilot model was completed in less than two years, that is, in late 1956. With the skill and self-confidence gained in that exercise, the group could design and build a full-fledged machine in about three years. Later, Prime Minister Jawaharlal Nehru named it TIFRAC in 1962.

TECHNICAL SPECIFICATIONS

The design of both the pilot model and TIFRAC was based on the general principles enunciated in the classic von Neumann report of the Institute of Advanced Studies at Princeton. The basic components of this machine were the arithmetic unit, the memory unit, I/O unit, and the control unit. Each of this unit contained subunits and complex

FIGURE 1.1   TIFRAC being named and inaugurated by
Prime Minister Jawaharlal Nehru

subsystems consisting of registers for holding numbers, adders, counters, selectors, decoders, and encoders, and other functional digital circuitry such as flip-flops, gates, and drivers. These in turn were built out of vacuum tubes, resistors, and other components with a total of over 20,000 individual pieces of electronic hardware.

The pilot model was a parallel, asynchronous, fixed point, and single address machine with a word length of 12-bits and a two-dimensional ferrite core memory of 256 words. Input and output were accomplished via paper tape and teletype. The total power consumption of this machine was about 10 kw.

The full-scale system (of TIFRAC) (Figures 1.2–1.4) had a 40-bit word length and a three-dimensional ferrite core memory of 2,048 words. With a cycle time of 15 microseconds (μs), it was better than the IBM 701. In fact, it had a state-of-the-art three-dimensional magnetic core memory system, which was designed and put together in TIFR. Largely due to the Rao-Basu carry bypass adder, the addition took only a few microseconds; multiplication and division took much less than a millisecond (ms) each. Input and output were by paper tape and a standard teletype unit running at 50 baud (7 characters per second). It had 2,700 vacuum tubes, 1,700 germanium diodes, and 12,500 resistors. It occupied a floor area of approximately 4,000 square feet and had a power consumption of well over 20 kW.

Figure 1.2   TIFRAC with doors removed

FIGURE 1.3   Plug-in units of TIFRAC

FIGURE 1.4   TIFRAC power supply

Since the memory could not accommodate a compiler, the group implemented a three-address interpretive routine for floating point arithmetic. This incorporated several features which were especially useful for inversions of large matrices.

INNOVATIONS IN TIFRAC

Since not much literature was available, much innovation was required, including the memory unit, adder, and the electronic display, each of which is briefly described here:

The Memory Unit

Since magnetic core memories had just become available, the TIFR group opted for it. But the readymade memory assemblies were not available at that time. Tata Institute of Fundamental Research group procured the miniscule magnetic cores from abroad and built its own memory system using them. Kalia and his team actually strung the memory matrix together, designed the special plexi-glass frames, and threaded the hair-thin enameled wires through the sub-millimeter magnetic ring cores—eighty thousand of them. Each core carried four wires! It was the combination of careful design, engineering skill, and dexterity of this team that accomplished this challenging task.

The Rao-Basu Adder

The time required for the addition of two numbers is an important factor that determines the speed of operation of computers. When two numbers are added, bit-wise addition can be performed in parallel but the sum can be determined only after the completion of serial propagation of carry through the bit stages. In the worst case, carry has to propagate from the least to the most significant bit. This delay can be considerable for long word length machines. Tata Institute of Fundamental Research Automatic Calculator implemented a simple and ingenious scheme for minimizing carry propagation time.

Theoretically, there are numerous methods of reducing carry delay. A brute force solution is to eliminate carry altogether and compute the sum output of each bit stage independently as a direct function of the addend and augend bits of this stage and of all less significant bit stages. Such an implementation would be very complicated and need a different circuit for each bit stage.

Carry storage adders save time when several numbers have to be added in sequence. They store the carry generated during each addition step and add it to the next bit stage only during the next addition. The sum obtained will have to be corrected; hence there has to be a final carry assimilation step after all the additions have been carried out. This is known as the Rao-Basu adder which is described in the literature.

Electronic Display of Text and Graphical Information

Computers of that period (including TIFRAC) used slow electrome-chanical devices such as teletype writers as the standard output medium. Tata Institute of Fundamental Research Automatic Calculator had a very futuristic visual display with textual and graphical output. Such displays became available in commercial machines only much later. It also used a very original (flexible and line segment based) display strategy for alphanumeric characters.

Fully implemented in 1960, this system had several innovative features (Rao 1959, 1963). Instead of dot matrix display, individual characters and letters were formed out of line segments, giving much more clarity for the same amount of information and making the text significantly easier to read (See Figure 1.5). Eight types of basic lines were used (four

FIGURE 1.5   All the characters that could be displayed in TIFRAC
(A mathematical equation displayed by the system is shown in Figure 1.6)

along the axes and four diagonals). Information required to trace these lines was represented as two ternary sequences of X and Y displacements (+1, 0, and –1): equally spaced pulses of either polarity. This information was contained in an easily modifiable form, in pulse transformers with multiple secondary windings. These secondary windings had to be connected in series in the right polarity, two such connections being needed for each character (for X and Y displacements). Extra windings were provided for future use. Character shapes could thus be changed and even new characters added without circuit modifications, simply by altering or adding to the existing wiring. Interfacing with the computer was extremely simple and straightforward. There was a single display instruction which conveyed the character display specifications through the Q register. Display was initiated by means of a start pulse from the computer; a 'display on' pulse signalled the completion of operation.

Figure 1.7 shows an equation and the corresponding plot along with the X and Y axes and calibration markings. In all likelihood, that was the first text and graphics display of computer outputs anywhere on a cathode ray tube (CRT) screen. A 'memotron' memory display tube was used that could retain the image and did not require to be refreshed frequently. The display tube was circular in shape and 4″ in diameter.

The futuristic features of this design became evident in 1962 in a very refreshing manner. During the evaluation of CDC 3600 computer (of Control Data Corporation) for purchase by TIFR team, they also saw the ongoing development of CDC 6600. The display system for CDC

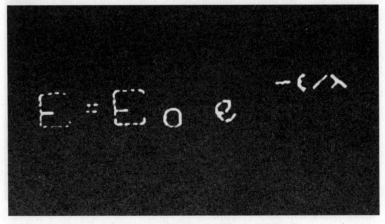

FIGURE 1.6   CRT textual display in TIFRAC

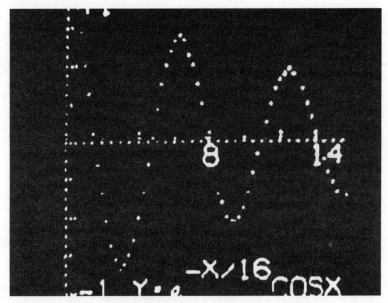

Figure 1.7   Textual and graphical display in TIFRAC
(probably the earliest such display ever done by anyone)

6600 machine also had a CRT display facility with line segment display for text characters—a feature that was a matter of immense pride and happiness for the CDC team. After a fruitful interaction between the TIFR and CDC teams, it was gratifying to realize that TIFR's design was almost at par with, if not ahead of, one of the leading computer design teams in the world.

COMPUTER LITERACY AND COMPUTER AWARENESS—ROLE OF TIFRAC

Tata Institute of Fundamental Research played a significant role in disseminating the importance of computer literacy in India. Initially, academic institutions and research organizations were reluctant to use computers. This was largely due to the fact that it was very expensive to import computers from abroad and difficult to access and use. Under these circumstances, rather than remaining as a captive facility, TIFRAC was made available to any organization that wished to use it. This was a major factor responsible for spreading computer awareness and the culture of using computers for scientific research as well as in governance.

Tata Institute of Fundamental Research Automatic Calculator served the widely dispersed scientific community in the country well. To facilitate this, TIFR teams ran special computer programming courses in a number of centres for a variety of user groups. With the availability of TIFRAC, scientists in India were essentially at par with their counterparts in other parts of the world in terms of scientific computing infrastructure. These were the early years of the atomic energy training school. The students of this school (who were later to occupy important administrative and research positions in TIFR, the Atomic Energy Establishment, and a number of other leading institutions) had their first introduction to and opportunity for using computers using the TIFRAC. Packages developed at TIFR were being widely used in the oil companies and the naval dockyard laboratories. Research and development centres of the power and space agencies and state governments as well as town planning organizations were using the TIFR facility.

Tata Institute of Fundamental Research Automatic Calculator, which was operational by early 1960 continued to remain heavily used till 1965. Within a year or two of TIFRAC's operation, it was clear that demand for its use was growing so fast that it was estimated that in next five years it would exceed its capacity of commissioning—both in terms of volume and speed. The machine was put on two-shift operation to meet this demand.

A decision was then taken to commercially acquire rather than build TIFR's second machine. The institute also launched the design and fabrication of a minicomputer out of Indian components. In subsequent paragraphs, I have briefly discussed this machine and its impact on computer technology and use in India.

To appreciate the reasons for this apparent departure from the earlier policy of local design, it is necessary to understand the manner in which computer technology evolved over the years. I attempt this in the following sections.

Evolution of Computer Technology

In most of the developed countries, the first step towards designing and building computers was taken in their universities. Even the most advanced computers were designed at academic institutes and research organizations. The ideas developed there (such as pipelining, cache systems, and virtual memories) were adapted by the leading computer manufacturers.

The first few decades also saw major advances in component technology. With the advent of integrated circuits, circuit design moved away from the research laboratories and the computer manufacturer into the domain of the integrated circuit (IC) manufacturer. With the advent of large-scale integration, increasingly complex functions could be implemented within a single chip, and even innovations in computer architecture now had to happen within the chip itself. Consequently, circuit, logic, and system design all came into the domain of the chip manufacturer. Small-scale operations for computer manufacture were becoming increasingly less viable. Due to economics of scale, even with today's worldwide proliferation of computers, there are only a handful of computer chip manufacturers worldwide.

Even within a short span of seven years or so that elapsed after the start of the TIFRAC venture, computer technology and the art of making computers advanced very significantly. Manufacturers such as IBM and Burroughs were still holding on to discrete component technology. However, they adopted sophisticated packaging and assembly techniques which were largely impractical in an academic institution.

In India too, as in the advanced countries, the first steps towards designing and building computers were taken in academic and research institutions. Tata Institute of Fundamental Research was the first to start their computer design and implementation in 1955. It was largely due to Homi Bhabha's philosophy of self-reliance. There was no technological infrastructure in India at that time. The Indian Statistical Institute and Jadavpur University started their own joint design of a transistorized computer (the ISIJU) in the 1960s. These efforts were credit-worthy and successful. Even today, they continue to be significant in a historical perspective.

Tata Institute of Fundamental Research Automatic Calculator's accomplishment carved an important place for India in the field of IT and computer science. In fact, the effort established a lasting culture of self-confidence, self-dependence, and daring innovation which qualitatively influenced the progress of IT development in India during the following decades.

The design effort for TIFRAC was ambitious, innovative, and fully state of the art. It was very successful. Although implementation was a difficult task in the restrictive Indian milieu and numerous problems arose, yet the machine was ready in time and performed well both in terms of design objectives and reliable operation. Good software support was provided, including a very widely used three address interpretive routine that facilitated operations such as inversion of large matrices.

Tata Institute of Fundamental Research Automatic Calculator was maintained by teams headed by some of its designers. It could be operated without any problems and had high up-time for several years. It was used extensively by research groups in TIFR, Bhabha Atomic Research Centre (BARC), and many other government laboratories, educational institutions, as well as public and private industry. Over fifty organizations were regular users.

The TIFRAC spirit was manifested in almost all subsequent activities of the group. It played a very important role in the development of computer technology in India. When the time came for augmenting the computer facilities, the group took the decisive step of selecting a machine which was still on the drawing boards (in preference to importing a tried and tested but hence obsolescent machine). Rather than leaving the maintenance of this complex system to the manufacturer, TIFR team took the responsibility on its own shoulders and excelled even here. In fact, when a problem would baffle the manufacturer, the group wpi;d come up with a workable and innovative way to work around it. Moreover, the team provided high quality consultancy and software support to the large user community. It organized countrywide courses and played an active, in fact vigorous, role in spreading computer awareness and usage across the country.

Tata Institute of Fundamental Research group found niche areas that were ideally appropriate, given India's needs, strengths, and weaknesses. It worked on the design of a minicomputer for online applications, using Indian components. This project was also completed in time. Open lightweight directory access protocol (OLDAP), the computer that was so designed, was used by the experimental physics groups of TIFR. It opened up a new vista—computers could be used for real-time and online applications. In parallel, the OLDAP design group also developed the nascent computer design efforts of the electronics division of the BARC which led to the Trombay Digital Computer (TDC) series. There is a separate article on the role played by Electronics

Corporation of India Ltd. (ECIL) in the manufacture of computers. When Prime Minister Indira Gandhi decided that the county needed to have a complete air defence data handling system, the TIFR computer group took up the challenge and spearheaded an inter-institutional design. Importantly, the implementation team built this system without any foreign collaboration, know-how purchase, or external consultancy. This system, in addition to exacting technical requirements, also had the responsibility to fulfil very tough mechanical and environmental specifications. Tata Institute of Fundamental Research shared the knowledge for this system with ECIL, which successfully manufactured and delivered it in large numbers to the Indian Air Force, adding substantially to the country's defence readiness.

REFERENCES

Basu, B.K. and P.V.S. Rao (1957), 'A Fast Logical Adder', TIFR Internal Report, TIFR: Bombay.

_____ (1957), 'A Modified Gating Logic to Improve the Speed of Operation of Double Rank Counters', *Proceedings of Indian Academy of Science*, vol. 46, August, pp. 354–9.

Narasimhan, R. (1960), 'On the System and Engineering Design of the General Purpose Electronic Digital Computer at TIFR', *Proceedings of Indian Academy of Science*, A 52.

Narasimhan, R. and P.V.S. Rao (1984), 'Computer Science and Technology in India: A Critical Assessment', *Sadhana*, vol. 7, part 3, November.

Rao, P.V.S. (1959), 'Character Display System for Use as Digital Computer Output', *Rev. Sci. Instr.*, vol. 30, August.

_____ (1963), 'Cathode Ray Display of Digital Computer Outputs', *Proceedings of Indian Academy of Science*, vol. 57, April, pp. 121–34.

Rao, P.V.S., V.K. Joglekar, J.G. Nemivant, and M.N. Cooper (1965), 'An Online Data Processor with Real-time Input-output and Control Facilities', *Ann. Conv. Comp. Soc. Ind.*, Kanpur, December.

S. RAMANI

2 R&D in Software Technology at the National Centre for Software Technology, 1960–2001[*]

National Centre for Software Technology (NCST) was born out of the pioneering efforts at the Tata Institute of Fundamental Research (TIFR) in the area of computer science and technology. This paper describes the origin of the Centre, the supporting entities and individuals, the major areas of work and the scientists who led the teams in these areas, and the work done and its significance.

It starts with a brief reference to the creation of a prototype of a digital computer by the Electronics Group of TIFR, and the later development of the full-fledged Tata Institute of Fundamental Research Automatic Calculator (TIFRAC). It covers the growth of a part of the TIFR computer group into the National Centre for Software Development and Computing Techniques (NCSDCT) and the work carried out by this Centre. However, the main focus is on the autonomous NCST created in 1985, staffed by a core team from the NCSDCT. This essay describes the key roles played by the Department of Electronics (DoE), Government of India, the Electronics

* I would like to thank P. Sadanadan, S.P. Mudur, Raman Chandrasekar, K.S.R. Anjaneyulu, and George Arakal for their helpful comments and suggestions on the draft. A few other colleagues have also given me feedback, but it is not possible to list them here.

Commission, and the United Nations Development Programme (UNDP) in these developments.

The essay goes on to describe the objectives of setting up the NCST, the work done by it, and the significance of its work in the very early phases of the Indian software research and development (R&D). The work done by different divisions of the NCST is covered in some detail. Collaborations between NCST on one hand and other national organizations and companies are highlighted. The growth and development of NCST over a two-decade period are given due coverage. So are the educational roles played by NCST during the early years when Indian industry adopted computer and software technologies, and the fledgling years of the Indian IT industry. The essay also reflects on the characteristic features of NCST, including what it inherited and what it added.

This is an informal report of my experience with NCST and what I have learnt from it. It is not a complete record of events, which is available in the annual reports of the institution. The achievements of the NCST were due to the talents, sincerity, and commitment of staff at all levels, starting with that of the leaders of the divisions and groups. However, reports like this are written by individuals at the risk of the author's views being of a subjective nature. Another limitation is that I have largely desisted from commenting on developments after my retirement in February 2000. These developments are best covered elsewhere by those who were involved after that date.

The heads of divisions at the time of starting the Centre were Minoo Dosabhai, Sudhir P. Mudur, P. Sadanandan, and myself, and the Head of Administration was G.N. Phatak. Annexed at the end of this essay is a partial list of staff members who were on NCST's roster at that time.

The rapid development of India and increased focus on R&D has led to the creation of hundreds of new institutions concerned with higher education and research. My hope is that a report like this would be of use to those involved in shaping these institutions.

NCST'S SEEDBED—THE TIFR COMPUTER GROUP

Tata Institute of Fundamental Research under the leadership of Homi Bhabha had recognized from the very beginning that science and technology go hand in hand. One of the technologies that the institute chose to work on was that of digital computers. Tata Institute of Fundamental Research created its computer team (one of the earliest in India) in the mid-1950s as a part of its Electronics Group and charged it with developing a prototype of a digital computer. D.Y. Phadke was in charge of the Electronics Group at that time. This Group spawned a section that eventually became the TIFR Computer Group, headed by R. Narasimhan, and went on to develop a digital computer when the technology was at a nascent stage all over the world. This computer was formally dedicated to the nation in 1962 by the then Prime Minister, Jawaharlal Nehru, and was named TIFRAC. Tata Institute of Fundamental Research appreciated the valuable support that this Group offered to research in general. When a technology and related science are in their formative stages, there are significant opportunities to do pioneering work, an important one being support-ing research in other sciences. In the case of TIFR, it was physics that utilized computers the most, with impressive results. Tata Institute of Fundamental Research was also driven by a vision that the science and technology of computers would develop considerable scientific, economic, and strategic significance over the years.

An important component of the TIFRAC was an 'intangible' item named its assembler, designed and implemented by R. Narasimhan and Kamalakar S. Kane. It was almost certainly the first item of system software to be implemented in India. As against an application program, which has specific uses, system software is an essential part of a computer system that is necessary to implement the very complex functionality that computer systems need to provide. It is not practical to substitute system software by hardware. Clearly, the TIFR computer group had recognized in 1959–60 the importance of software; this was a time when the term 'computer software' meant nothing to anyone outside a small community of specialists in the world.

The presence of a reasonable number of scientists in the TIFR com-puter group made it possible for a part of the group to grow into the relatively more autonomous entity and to address big challenges in the field. This has been discussed in detail in the next section.

THE ELECTRONICS COMMISSION'S ROLE IN THE CREATION OF NCSDCT

The Government of India created the DoE in 1970 and the Electronics Commission in 1971. One of the many initiatives of the commission aimed at ensuring national-level utilization of the computing infrastruc-ture and know-how that the TIFR computer group had developed. This initiative resulted in the creation of a unit named the NCSDCT as a part of TIFR with a high level of autonomy and its own budget supported by the DoE. The purchase of an up-to-date computer, a DEC-1077, along with other equipment in 1972, under assistance from the UNDP, made it possible for this unit to focus on software techniques. National Centre for Software Development and Computing Techniques shared its resources with practically every interested R&D institution in the country. The most valuable contributions of the Group were in the form of know-how that the Group shared with other institutions and the R&D leadership for the future that it nurtured.

M.G.K. Menon, the then Chairman of the Electronics Commission, and R. Narasimhan, Director, NCSDCT, played key roles in these developments. B.V. Sreekantan, who succeeded Menon as the Director of TIFR, fully supported the growth and development of NCSDCT.

NCSDCT

The support by DoE made it possible for NCSDCT to develop R&D teams in a number of important areas: computer graphics, computer networks, database technology, systems software, and theoretical computer science. National Centre for Software Development and Computing Techniques adopted the practice of TIFR and that of most renowned institutions in the world, first identifying leadership for each of the areas it wanted to develop, and then giving them the necessary freedom to define scientific objectives of proposed research in these areas and to recruit staff. Some of the early members of the research teams were Mathai Joseph, Srinivasan Ramani, P. Sadanandan, Sudhir P. Mudur, Kesav Nori, and R.K. Shyamasundar.

These were the salad years for all the areas that NCSDCT had chosen to work on. Interesting challenges were taken up by NCSDCT, for instance, creating software for TDC316 computers designed and built in India by the Electronics Corporation of India (ECIL). The objective here was to carry out R&D and innovate in a nationally relevant context, and not merely to produce software. One of the projects taken up was the design and implementation of an Operating System that created a close-coupled network of several minicomputers. Another was on computer-networking software to link computers separated by long distances. National Centre for Software Development and Computing Techniques and ECIL collaborated to ensure the success of these projects.

The earliest efforts in India in the field of computer graphics and in using Indian scripts on the computer were launched. Work on developing a compiler to support concurrent programming was undertaken. The future potential of relational database technology was recognized before it became popular; some of the earliest projects in this area were carried out. There was research on the foundations of software technology and in theoretical computer science. Part-time courses in the computer area were initiated. A link was established with the Victoria Jubilee Technical Institute (VJTI), 15 km away, using the communication software developed by NCSDCT running on a TDC316 computer. This link enabled the NCSDCT staff to start a rigorous part-time course at VJTI in 1977.

The review mechanism of UNDP permitted the NCSDCT to have pioneers like Maurice Wilkes and William Wulf on the review committee. Their comments on work plans and on work carried out gave valuable feedback to the young teams. A number of PhD projects were undertaken and completed. A book was written, based on the work done at NCSDCT, and was brought out by an international publisher.

The scientists of NCSDCT ran a number of training programmes to disseminate the know-how they were gaining. Training in programming was in much greater demand than it had been in the TIFRAC era. Computational activity had spread into most branches of science and technology, and computer technology itself had advanced very significantly. Each one of the R&D teams pitched in with courses in its area of interest. These were usually short courses, typically spread over three to ten working days. These courses were of significant value to a number of professionals, who went on to occupy leadership positions in Indian software companies.

An important contribution of UNDP was to provide for visits by eminent academics and professionals from all over the world. Almost every year there was a winter school on a selected topic. This brought an average of three eminent scientists every year to spend one or two weeks at the Centre to lecture on advanced topics and to interact with researchers from different R&D groups in India. Fellowships by UNDP supported travel by researchers of the Centre to leading laboratories in the world, for a few months of work there. United Nations Development Programme also paid for specialized state-of-the-art equipment necessary for the research teams at NCSDCT.

An annual conference 'Foundations of Software Technology and Theoretical Computer Science (FST&TCS)' was started by NCSDCT scientists. It has sustained itself and grown significantly over the years.

An interesting aspect of computer-related work at TIFR and NCSDCT was that the Hardware Section carried out in-house maintenance of all computing equipment, including imported computers. Based on this experience, Menon and Narasimhan had worked to create a public sector company, the Computer Maintenance Corporation Ltd. (CMC), in 1975, to ensure continued maintenance of imported computers in India. Narasimhan was the founding Chairman of the company and Prem Prakash Gupta was the first Managing Director. Some of the R&D at NCSDCT was carried out in cooperation with CMC and for CMC, a major supporter of development of IT in India. The staff of NCSDCT played a variety of other important roles outside the Centre. Narasimhan was the founder-President of the Computer Society of India (CSI); practically every senior member of the NCSDCT served the CSI in some capacity or the other during the first two decades of its existence.

The Space Applications Centre (SAC) in Ahmedabad invited NCSDCT's collaboration in the area of satellite-based data communication in 1978. Soon, a collaborative project was defined between these two centres and the Telecommunications Research Centre (TRC), Delhi. This project used packet switching software developed by the NCSDCT team, running on small, dedicated real-time computers assembled by the same team, using a satellite communication terminal[†] designed by SAC and a 32-kbps modem designed and built at TRC. This experimental network, named COMNEX, used the satellite APPLE and was operationalized in 1982.

The staff of NCST played key roles in creating and running national and international conferences in India; for instance, Networks 80, the first conference in India sponsored by the International Federation for

---

[†] The technology used was essentially what was later developed by companies worldwide to create Very Small Aperture Terminals (VSATs) for computer networking. However, the antenna used by the NCSDCT team was 20 feet in diameter, as the electronics available in India at that time necessitated this. Team members were later to joke that this had been the world's largest VSAT! A small octagonal building designed to accommodate this antenna on its roof was a prominent feature on the TIFR lawns for a long time.

Information Processing (IFIP). This conference brought around twenty leaders in computer networking from a number of countries to India, and provided a significant stimulus to work in this area. Prem Gupta recognized the importance that this new technology would have in the IT scene in India and played a role in organizing Networks 80 as a major step towards adopting the technology of computer networks in India.

An operational email system was designed and implemented on NCSDCT's DEC 1077 computer system by 1980. This was the first email system to be operated in India and it served a couple of hundred users on one computer. A prototype multi-city Railway Passenger Reservation System was planned, discussed with the Railways, and a prototype was implemented by NCSDCT for demonstration at Networks 80. This work provided the basis for continued championing of the concept by Prem Gupta. Later, the NCSDCT scientists contributed to CMC's planning for Project Interact,[‡] which would focus on software design and development for dedicated systems and international cooperation in training in the field. Under this project, CMC built on the concepts of the 1980 efforts and created an advanced prototype of a Railway Passenger Reservation System. So, when the Railways did place an order for such a system on CMC Ltd., there was know-how in the company to design and build an impressive system and succeed in the first attempt. Over the next decade this system and its successive versions made a big impact on the Indian IT scene. It combined real-time systems with computer networking to make nationwide online reservations possible. This was the first IT project which met a significant need of a large segment of the Indian population.

The graphics team developed an item of software named Indo GKS, which was picked up by CMC Ltd. for marketing to end users. Another major activity with a software development dimension was the message switching system created by a joint team of NCSDCT and CMC Ltd. Press Trust of India (PTI) provided the test bed for this system and made available its nationwide communication network. This work resulted in full-fledged activity in this area within CMC Ltd., leading to several commercial projects. One of these projects, utilizing software

[‡] The United Nations Fund for Science and Technology for Development approved this proposal and funded it to the extent of about USD 2 million. The project was carried out during 1981–4.

designed and developed jointly by NCSDCT and CMC Ltd., created an operational network for PTI. As CMC Ltd. was getting more and more involved with systems development, Prem Gupta decided to change the company's original name 'Computer Maintenance Corporation' to CMC Ltd., signifying its transformation into a total services company in the computer field. Collaboration between NCSDCT and CMC Ltd. in the above-mentioned projects had contributed to making this transformation possible.

The approach of NCSDCT to the design and development of message switches was based on the recognition that the arrival of affordable and powerful minicomputers was opening a new opportunity: systems development in India for imported minicomputers could achieve a lot that had earlier required very expensive systems. National Centre for Software Development and Computing Techniques had used a state-of-the-art real-time operating system on an inexpensive minicomputer as well as the high level language Pascal to implement the message switch. Earlier generation systems had been programmed in assembly language which made them difficult to extend and maintain. Soon after the NCSDCT–CMC message switch became operational, a leading multinational in the field of message switching systems approached Tata Consultancy Services (TCS) for designing a new generation message switch. F.C. Kohli, the founder of TCS, who was then in charge, was aware of NCSDCT's work in the field. He decided to have TCS benefit from NCSDCT's infrastructure and know-how created for this work. Tata Consultancy Services won the contract, with the help of NCSDCT's cooperation, and went on to create a new generation message switch of its own design to meet the multinational's requirements. The software development environment of NCSDCT was used during the implementation of TCS's system.

Origin of NCST

The Department of Electronics constituted a committee in 1983 to plan for the creation of an autonomous national laboratory in software technology, drawing upon NCSDCT to provide the core. Prem P. Gupta was then the Secretary to the Government in the DoE, and launched a number of initiatives in the computer area to build up Indian competence. One of these initiatives was the effort to create the above-mentioned laboratory. The author was given the responsibility of planning for the proposed autonomous institution, working with his colleagues, P. Sadanandan and S.P. Mudur. The three of them served on the Committee, working with the Chairman S. Krishnaswamy, Nitin Desai, and J.C. Khurana. The Committee made recommendations in favour of setting up a Centre named the NCST, defining its goals as follows:

- Function as a pace-setter in software technology;
- Keep track of significant developments worldwide;
- Carry out self-motivated R&D to remain at the leading edge of a carefully identified subset of the rapidly developing software technology;
- Generate and spin off high technology software products and services in selected sub-areas;
- Give a place of pride to high quality continuing education and training programmes for software specialists.

The Government of India accepted the report of the Committee and a budget was allocated for the financial year 1984–5. The launch of NCST was very timely, as the growth of software technology in India accelerated manifold in the following decades.

The approved plan for the creation and development of NCST provided for the institution's growth over the next few years, for acquiring a laboratory building and residential premises of its own, and for growth of its staff strength. An autonomous scientific society was registered under the Societies Act and the Public Trusts Act, to work under the auspices of the DOE of the Government of India. The author was appointed Director of NCST in October 1985; P. Sadanandan and S.P. Mudur were appointed Heads of Divisions.[§] The staff members of NCSDCT who had a software technology orientation were transferred to NCST, and new staff members were recruited to take on the increased responsibilities. Minoo Dosabhai, a senior engineer on the rolls of TIFR, also joined the leadership team at NCST. One of the many responsibilities he undertook was looking after the planned acquisition of a large time-sharing system. G.N. Phatak headed the Administration Group.

[§] Subsequently they were promoted as Associate Directors.

NCST Activities

Laboratory premises at Juhu and residential premises at Bandra Reclamation were acquired from the Maharashtra Housing and Area Development Authority (MHADA) in 1985. A Vax 8600 running Ultrix was ordered. This was the first powerful system purchased by India at that time running any version of Unix.

The growth of the software industry required a large number of talented and knowledgeable professionals. There were few degree-granting programmes in the institutions of higher professional education. There were only a few research groups of any significant size in this field in India. Regular recruitment of a significant number of young scholars by NCST and their induction into R&D made a major impact on the scene. Dozens of these scholars would spend a number of years at NCST, participate in R&D, and move on to industry or to academia. The following sections offer brief reports on the work of the different teams at NCST. Many of these activities are best described as R&D projects. National Centre of Software Technology was not to become a software house; the focus was on absorbing and creating new ideas in the emerging technology and exploring them by creating prototypes and tool kits.

Database and Office Information Systems Division

This Division, headed by P. Sadanandan, had a focus on the technology that was changing office environments everywhere by eliminating drudgery and by supporting decision-oriented activities. It worked on integrating database management as well as messaging and conferencing, forms management and document preparation in a unified framework, starting with the formal specification of the model and the primitive operations supported by it using Z. 'Intelligent forms' was one of the topics of interest.

Over the years, the Division developed interests in a number of other areas as well. It conducted research and ran courses in areas such as database management, object oriented systems, client server computing, data warehousing, data mining, decision support and knowledge management, workflow computing, and enterprise computing. It also developed expertise in the areas of benchmarking, quality planning, and team development.

This Division carried out extensive consulting work in the above-mentioned areas, playing a key role in the adoption of these technologies by business and industry in India, for instance, those in the steel sector, communication sector, and in e-governance, at a time when the Indian IT sector was itself working to acquire the necessary expertise. One example of this type of work was a database review of a mission-critical application of a power company. The staff of NCST carrying out this work presented to them suggestions for major design alterations and for improvements.

The Division also carried out projects for early adopters of the technologies it was interested in; some of these projects were carried out in cooperation with an external software team, to ensure effective transfer of responsibilities after a formative phase. The Division also conducted short-term professional education courses for the IT industry on a scheduled basis as well as on request.

Members of this team played a seminal role in running the International Conference on Management of Data (COMAD) over a number of years. P. Sadanandan played a major role in bringing the International Conference on Very Large Data Bases to India. This conference was held in 1996 in Mumbai for the first time.

Graphics and CAD Division

S.P. Mudur headed this Division. Early work included the development of a graphic designer's workbench named Cuneiform, shape representation and analysis, a font generator, a Devanagari font, image processing, and a geometric library. This Division continued work on Indo-GKS mentioned earlier, creating a new 3D version named Indo GKS-3D. The fact that this software was based on an ISO draft standard, GKS-3D, demonstrates the leading-edge nature of the work at that time. Research in the graphics and CAD areas resulted in a number of doctoral dissertations.

Interaction, Simulation, Rendering, and Visualization

One of the many activities of this Division was the development of tools, techniques, and software to enable application programmers to develop graphical interfaces. This included the development of a toolkit named Houdini for providing higher-level abstractions in comparison to the

X/Motif tool kit. It was built as a C++ class library, and provided for specifying 3D interactions and 3D view modification. Additional classes were added to Houdini for rendering of 3D shaded objects represented using triangulated mesh structure.

Later on, this team developed a software package named VolGrid for discretising complex volumes and for volume grid generation. Facilities provided by the system included visualization using external tools such as VRML[5] viewers. The Division also developed a mechanical simulation system named Clodion under the sponsorship of the Mechanical Engineering Department of the Indian Institute of Technology (IIT), Bombay.

The Division developed a class of software components for dealing with multimedia and virtual reality environments. It also carried out R&D on stick figure animation.

Computer Aided Design

Zeus, an interactive system for complex surface design, was developed by this Division. It used Fortran and GKS or PHIGS for graphics support. This system for rapid design and fairing of surfaces relevant to aircraft, automobile, and ship-building industries was developed under the sponsorship of the Aeronautical Development Agency (ADA), Bangalore, and completed in 1992. It provided for the creation and interactive editing of geometrical elements including curves represented as B-Splines, piecewise linear curves, B-Spline surfaces, as well as surfaces of rotation with B-Spline profile curves. The system was installed on ADA's IBM hardware. Converting user-designed doubly curved surfaces into a polyhedral representation, Zeus provides for computational fluid dynamics analysis, structural analysis, and global illumination computations. It provides for grid generation using the advancing front technique and for determining an optimal set of equilateral triangles. Later work also used Energy Minimization Techniques for generating optimally structured grids on surfaces.

Planar Development of Complex Aircraft Surfaces

This work dealt with planar development of shallow doubly curved surfaces such as the wing surfaces of an aircraft. Such surfaces can be

---

[5] Virtual Reality Modeling Language.

developed into a plane only approximately. This has to be done under the constraints unique to the manufacture of wings.

A second phase of this project involved redesign and integration of a large number of modules developed by several groups: ADA, NCST, Indian Institute of Science (IISc), Bangalore, and IIT Kanpur. A system for use in detailed 2D skin engineering for the manufacture of composite laminate components was developed subsequently.

Handling Indian Scripts and Languages on the Computer

The Division had long-term collaboration with R.K. Joshi of the Industrial Design Centre, IIT Bombay, a well-known calligrapher and font designer. This mutually beneficial collaboration resulted in a number of published insights related to handling of Indian scripts and languages on the computer. It also resulted in a novel design for an Indian language keyboard layout that was easy to learn and efficient in use.

Another project of this Division focused on creating a set of tools for multilingual text processing named Vividha. This set of tools was handed over to CMC Ltd. as Beta level software in 1992.

The Division also developed early expertise in India in the design and implementation of graphical user interfaces for different applications. It played a pioneering role in getting Indian fonts on to the early Windows environment and developed a Windows 95 word-processor named Darshan. Later, it carried its work to the Win32 environment. In 1997, the division developed a Win32::GUI for an Indian language editor. This editor had the look and feel of all standard applications, and included special features such as script detection based on TrueType font, and What-You-See-Is-What-You-Get (WYSIWYG) support for printing.

The group identified an interesting problem while working with Indian languages and scripts: Indian names were difficult to enter into a database, as they are best written in a phonetic script like Devanagari, and linear representation/coding of text did not do full justice for handling such scripts. Creation of bilingual records and searching for a name were often required but frustrating on a computer. The team formed to address this problem had staff members from the Graphics Division and the SPC (Software Promotion Centre). Members of this team came up with algorithms to translate names entered using the Roman script into printable Devanagari form acceptable to native speakers. This involved use of a set of translation[**] rules to account for phonology, and table look-up techniques for speeding up the translation. This work resulted in the adoption of this technology by the Bombay University for printing of over forty thousand bilingual[††] degree certificates per year. Later, NCST worked with the Mahanagar Telecommunication Nigam Ltd. (MTNL) to handle its massive bilingual telephone directory printing activity covering nearly 1.3 million customers. An even bigger challenge met by this project was the preparation of the huge bilingual voters list of the Mumbai collectorate on a very demanding time schedule. The challenge was in taking on these tasks at a time when the technology then available was inadequate and needed to be developed.

Projects undertaken by this Division included one on a leading edge graphics research activity[‡‡] using a parallel processing system; exploration of distributed computation for complex 3D visualization, technology transfer in Indian languages (partly transferred to Microsoft); international software education; and activity-driven multimedia-based training for trainers of school teachers (for Intel).

The Division also carried out very significant consultancy activities. Notable was S.P. Mudur's work as a UN consultant to the Department of Arts, Government of India, on the multimedia documentation requirements of the Indira Gandhi National Centre for Arts (IGNCA). He also worked as a member of the UNDP team for the mid-term evaluation of a major UNDP project called 'Modern Cartographic Centre', carried out by the Survey of India.

The Graphics and CAD Division played a key role in organizing the International Conference on Computer Graphics, ICCG '93, and the International Conference on Visual Computing, ICVC '99. Team members, particularly S.P. Mudur, played a significant role in conference organizing activities of Eurographics and presented several papers at these events.

[**] This term is used consciously as the task involved is more than mere transliteration.

[††] In Marathi and English. This involved the use of specially designed Marathi font.

[‡‡] This had come out of a research proposal that won an award and a financial grant.

Real-time Systems and Computer Networks Division

The author headed this Division. Its work ranged over packet switching networks, use of satellite channels for computer networks, packet broadcasting applications, and security of computer communications. The Division developed a real-time monitor for supporting dedicated controllers and an X-25 PAD during its first few years of work, but moved on to focus on computer networking more and more. Research work produced a number of ideas that were published: a low-altitude data satellite for handling email, pseudo-random generation of pairs of function that were inverses of each other, provable ciphers, new hashing algorithms, and analysis of their computational complexity. Three of them led to doctoral dissertations.

The author had proposed an academic network for India in 1983. Based on this proposal and other inputs from academic groups in India, the DoE started advance planning for a project in this area, which was launched during 1985–6 under the name ERNET (Education and Research in Computer Networking).[§§] This division contributed significantly to this project, playing a lead role in creating an email network to start with, followed by an IP-based network for Indian academic and R&D institutions.

National Centre for Software Technology team brought a number of assets to the ERNET project: early experience in building a satellite-based computer network, know-how related to communication capabilities of available computers including the VAX 8600 running Ultrix, an implementation of Unix. Ultrix came with reliable email-relay software and an efficient UUCP[¶¶] protocol implementation that supported development of an email network. It also had an implementation of the TCP/IP protocol that has played a central role in the development of what we now call the internet. The team put these assets to good use. The first step was to acquire a few dial-up modems—the only ones available in India were 1,200 bps modems—and try them out. Only a

---

[§§] ERNET had a team each at the DoE, five IITs, IISc, Bangalore, and the NCST working in a collaborative mode. The DoE node, headed by S. Ramakrishnan, played a technical as well as a coordinating role.

[¶¶] Unix-to-Unix Copy Protocol.

few years earlier, use of dial-up modems had been forbidden*** in India. A dial-up email link was established in 1986 between NCST and IIT Bombay using the UUCP protocol—the first email link between two Indian institutions! Dozens of users at the two ends started using the link soon. The network then added IIT Madras and IIT Delhi in 1987; other nodes followed soon after. The Vax 8600 became the email hub, shakti.ncst.ernet.in. Import of high-speed modems vastly improved traffic capacities at this stage. Telecommunication was not in too happy a state in the country at that time and there was frustration in places such as IIT Kanpur. So, quietly, a very peculiar email link was established between NCST and IIT Kanpur. Email files for IIT Kanpur were copied into a floppy and sent out by speed-post! Similarly, Kanpur would send back floppy mail for relay to networked locations.

National Centre for Software Technology started dialing out CWI††† in 1988 in Amsterdam, which offered email relay to other locations around the world. Email coming from India aroused considerable interest around the world. National Centre for Software Technology started posting on the internet selected news stories from the PTI with their consent, as they arrived over the wire. This caused considerable excitement abroad and soon UUNET groups were abuzz with discussions of Indian developments stimulated by the email feed of news. The IIT Kanpur alumni abroad, who were happy to communicate with their professors over email, noticed the sluggish communication and soon discovered the secret of floppy mail. This created a furore, and soon enough the project was given a telecom connection to IIT Kanpur! ERNET teams at other locations—Delhi, Madras, and Kharagpur—quickly set up email hubs and started providing service to institutions in the region. The international email gateway continued to be shakti.ncst.ernet.in for many years. Originally, the CWI connection had used a dial-up link. This had later become a TCP/IP over X.25 link. Dial-up connections between Bombay and the other ERNET hubs were replaced by analogue leased lines, which were the

---

*** A senior administrator had explained at the Networks 80 symposium that the Department of Telecom did not want its revenues from the Telex service being threatened by dial-up modem traffic. A few years later we were told that TCP/IP would not be allowed as CCITT protocols were the only ones that were recognized as international standards!

††† Centre Wiskunde Informatik.

only ones available in 1988. Soon, routers were installed at all ERNET hubs and (analogue) leased lines were used to create a TCP/IP network. Subsequently, analogue leased lines were replaced one by one as digital links became available. The Indian academic network had come of age! ERNET had become the first Internet Service Provider (ISP) in India, even though it focused mostly on the education and research community. The fledgling software industry of India got its first set of email accounts from ERNET.

A 9600 bps analogue leased line was set up in 1989 to connect shakti with the UUNET hub in Falls Church, VA in USA, to replace the connection to CWI. The link to UUNET was changed to a 64 kbps digital connection in 1992, and moved to higher and higher data-rates as traffic built up. It is worth noting here that the first commercial ISP, Videsh Sanchar Nigam Ltd. (VSNL), entered the market in 1994.

Given its experience with satellite communication during NCSDCT days, and the difficulty of getting leased landlines and maintaining them, the NCST team successfully championed the cause of a satellite communication network for ERNET. The project acquired and commissioned a hub for this purpose in 1994 at the Software Technology Park (STP) in Bangalore, and a set of VSATs were located wherever a good leased line was not available. This system was of considerable value to institutions in cities and towns outside metropolitan areas.

By this time the ERNET TCP/IP hubs at the major communication nodes—Delhi, Bombay, and Delhi—had been upgraded. Gradually, the ERNET team at DoE in Delhi took over the bulk of the administrative load and a lot of the operational responsibility. The ERNET Hub at IISc Bangalore got a digital link with adequate capacity from the satellite communication hub in the same city.

While it had started with a focus on the needs of a few institutions of higher learning and research, the ERNET was keen to extend its services to all universities. A subscription model was developed for this purpose and any college or university could get ERNET services on payment. A major step was taken when the University Grants Commission (UGC) asked ERNET to help it set up the University Grants Commission Network (UGCNET) to serve all universities funded by it. The two networks went on to work closely together. A significant role was played in this cooperation by the Information Library Network (INFLIBNET), a unit of the UGC, which was charged with the creation of the UGCNET.

The author served as the Honorary Chairman of INFLIBNET for three years.

In view of the fact that NCST was the first entity in India to set up an internet node, the UUNET, which was coordinating domain name registration activities around the world, had asked NCST to function as the Domain Registrar for India's top level domain '.in'. National Centre for Software Technology has been doing this for well over a decade.

A number of industries and businesses discovered the necessity of IP-based networks in the 1990s. This included financial service institutions such as banks and stock exchanges, the oil industry, and the communications industry. Networking and modernization of computing facilities went hand in hand. Research institutions, such as laboratories of the Indian Council of Agricultural Research (ICAR), also required networking. Communication Service Providers were discovering the need to become ISPs. National Centre for Software Technology played an important role as the consultant for setting up many corporate networks in all these sectors and in planning for a new generation of computing equipment. It also played the role of the consultant when MTNL decided to become an ISP.

National Centre for Software Technology ran a project named the Bombay Library Network (Bonet) with funding from the Department of Science and Technology, Government of India. Since its inception in 1992, Bonet provided a service to library professionals and academics in library science, offering them training and cooperation in the area of internet connectivity and applications.

Software Engineering Division

P. Sadanandan headed this Division as well, and his teams played a significant role in the Juhu as well as Bangalore campuses. Research and Development focused on new modeling techniques in Executive Information Systems (EIS) and in Decision Support Systems. Scientists on these teams met a timely need of the Indian IT industry for training, consultancy, and training materials at a time when courses in software engineering were quite rare. This Division organized several in-depth courses to serve the needs of the industry; for instance, in 1994, it conducted five intensive training programmes, each a month long, for middle and senior level officers of a large company. The Division offered consultancy to a major public sector organization on the development of an EIS. It also organized a ten-week training programme 'Software Engineering: Technology and Management' for participants from sixteen commonwealth countries. The programme covered the management aspects of handling the development of very large software systems and the use of state-of-the-art CASE tools.

The creation of course materials on different subjects of technological relevance for use by institutions in education and training is now recognized as an important activity. This Division had initiated work on this as early as 1998. The first product was a complete package covering twenty sessions in Database Management, completed that year. It was used by ten faculty members at seven locations almost immediately. Another package on Object Oriented Programming was also developed.

Knowledge Based Computer Systems Division

The author headed this Division. This group worked with other like-minded groups in India and with the DoE to plan a nationwide project named Knowledge Based Computer Systems (KBCS),[‡‡‡] under the auspices of the DoE. This project was launched in 1986. Research interests pursued by this Division and the systems/tools developed are described in this section.

Product Tanker Scheduling System for the Oil Industry

This work was sponsored by the Oil Coordination Committee (OCC). It used expert systems techniques to carry out near optimal scheduling of oil tankers, using a variety of inputs such as production and consumption figures as well as inventories at different ports. It used expert knowledge collected by interaction with professionals involved, to reduce the heavy costs of hiring and operating oil tankers.

A scheduling system for oil pipelines was also developed, using expert system techniques and interaction. It was tested successfully by use in

---

[‡‡‡] Both ERNET and KBCS were supported by UNDP, which played the critical role of offering these two projects a window to the world. This brought eminent international visitors to run one- or two-week courses for project staff as well as invitees from selected institutions all over India. UNDP also gave fellowships to project staff to visit major centres of research in their respective areas.

scheduling the Mathura-Jalandhar pipeline for a few months. Later on, the Division also did some work on oil tanker scheduling for the import and domestic movement of crude.

Knowledge Based Aircraft Scheduling Support System

This system named Sarani was developed in the 1990s under the sponsorship of Air India. It used expert system techniques to provide for human-aided creation of efficient airline schedules. It was successfully concluded with satisfactory results, though it did not go into regular operation. It resulted in a doctoral thesis.

AI Applications in E-learning

One of the driving perceptions of the team working in this area was that online and computerized offline testing is valuable even when separated from online instruction. Much of computer-based instruction is too expensive for widespread use in developing countries where access to a personal computer (PC) is very limited for most students. This perception led to the development of an online system, named Veda, for educational testing meant to give performance feedback to learners along with diagnostic help, identifying concepts that had not been learnt well. Veda was used to conduct one of the first online tests in India for admission to NCST courses, testing up to 2,000 candidates a year. Novel techniques were developed and tested at the research level. One of these, inspired by binary search, was that of presenting questions at different levels of difficulty in an adaptive sequence, to measure the candidate's level of proficiency. The team also worked with large-scale educational testing and used mark-sense readers for quick and inexpensive offline testing of thousands of candidates at a time. This experience encouraged NCST staff to propose and contribute to the creation of the series of tests under the name 'National Standard Test of Programming Competence' (NSTPC) for the CSI. The Department of Electronics funded CSI for running these tests for a few years and then established the Department of Electronics and Accreditation of Computer Classes (DOEACC) to run them on a large scale.

Another project involved the design and implementation of Vidya, a multimedia tutor for the Hindi language, based on the immersion principle: teaching a language without using another as a medium of communication. This work, carried out in 1993, gave an opportunity to the team to work on student modeling. A team member of the group worked on Explanation Based Learning during his visit to the University of Saskatchewan. He also worked on Learning by Teaching, based on the idea that a student's learning is enhanced while playing the role of a teacher. Another group member worked on different types of collaboration in the context of a training system named Sherlock, during his visit to the Carnegie-Mellon University.

One doctoral dissertation in this Division dealt with a testing and remediation system for high school mathematics. Another explored the area of visual programming. An experimental system was designed, implemented, and tested. It was designed for use in teaching programme design to students.

Team members working in this area took part in an international competition organized by Global Information System Technology, Inc., a US company. The competition had been announced over the internet, and there was a five-member panel of eminent scientists to select the winning entries. This involved creating domain-independent strategies that could be used in computer-based training. Members of the team won the first, second, and third prizes in this competition.

Natural Language Processing and Machine Translation

There was strong interest within this group in natural language understanding and natural language processing. The work included intelligent categorization, archiving and retrieval of information, and used the text of news items from PTI acquired online.

A machine-aided translation system for news stories was developed in 1993, using a variety of techniques such as automatic topic identification, stochastic part-of-speech tagging, user-assisted structural analysis, and parameterized generation of text in the target language. The technique of using heuristic transformations to break long sentences into two simpler sentences was developed as a part of this work. This made the parsing of the input much more reliable. The work in this area led to a doctoral thesis by one of the team members. The domain in which this system was tested was one of machine-aided translation of news stories. The vision was that of taking PTI news stories from a real-time feed in English and translating them into Hindi.

There was also work on categorization, archiving, and retrieval of news. Early work on a system named Quest developed into a more ambitious effort named Glean, carried out by a group member during his visit to the University of Pennsylvania.

Expert Systems

Building on its experience with expert systems techniques, the Group went on to design and implement an expert system shell named Vidwan (in 1992), which was made available to users on PCs and Unix machines. Improved versions followed in subsequent years. The team experimented with and implemented a copy-protect mechanism for discouraging software piracy. The PC version of Vidwan was protected with this mechanism and was sold to users. Several user groups used this shell to implement their own expert systems. Vidwan was also used in an off-campus course on Expert Systems that NCST ran at that time. Members of the team authored a book on Expert Systems in 1993.

Publishing a Quarterly

The Knowledge Based Computer Systems team initiated a low-cost quarterly, *Vivek*, in 1987. This was designed to be of use to AI researchers. It had a magazine format, but carried serious papers. It served for a long time as an important communication vehicle for researchers in this field in India.

KBCS Conferences

National Centre for Software Technology played a key role in creating this series of conferences in 1987. The Knowledge Based Computer Systems groups in India have all contributed to the success of this series of conferences, though the events were largely held in Bombay.[§§§] This momentum led to a proposal by the team to hold the International Joint Conference (IJCAI) in India. The first attempt to compete for the conference did not succeed but building on that effort, India succeeded in getting IJCAI-2007 to Hyderabad.

Software Promotion Centre and Hardware Division

Minoo Dosabhai headed this Division during the formative years of NCST. He went beyond the responsibilities of this Division and played the role of chief engineer, handling all engineering responsibilities of

---

[§§§] Since renamed as Mumbai.

NCST including campus developments as well as maintenance. S.B. Patankar headed this Division after Dosabhai's retirement; Bharat Desai took over as Head when Patankar retired.

With improved availability of computers, the 'computer centre' was no longer an appropriate name. The staff who handled the systems comprised of system, database, and network administrators, and were knowledgeable about a variety of software. Their consultation was necessary for efficient functioning of anyone who was in software R&D. National Centre for Software Technology had recognized this from the very beginning, and created a 'software promotion centre' in 1985. The staff of this unit was free to pursue interests of their own in addition to their primary responsibilities and to contribute to software development as well as training.

The Hardware team handled acquisition of new equipment, installation, operations, and maintenance. Gradually, hardware maintenance effort reduced due to worldwide changes in computer technology. Instead, there was a major increase in the efforts involving installation of software, 24×365 operations of equipment, management of systems and networks, and consulting. Over the years this Division installed and maintained a number of large computers spread over a few generations. It also developed expertise in planning and setting up and maintaining large Local Area Networks (LANs), involving a couple of hundred client machines ranging from terminals, workstations, and PCs. This team developed over the years an interest and expertise in performance measurement and benchmarking as well. Members of this Division made significant contributions to consulting activity.

A special mention needs to be made of this Division's contributions to ERNET operations, which served a nationwide need for 24×365 operation of a high-capacity network hub.

Administration

Phatak headed this Division in the first few years of NCST and George Arakal took over the responsibility following Phatak's retirement. The Division enabled NCST to follow the TIFR principle that excellence in administration is necessary to support excellence in scientific and technical activities. Its major responsibilities included campus development and maintenance, major equipment and software purchases, recruitment, government liaison, and the operation of a library and a cafeteria that have traditionally been available for long hours during weekdays and for one shift on weekends. The secretarial support extended to technical divisions by the administration also played a crucial role in the efficiency of the organization.

Postgraduate Diploma Courses at NCST

National Centre for Software Technology had initiated a part-time postgraduate course in Software Technology while it was at TIFR, in anticipation of the setting up of NCST. This was one of the earliest courses of this type in India. This effort was scaled up in 1985 and the course was redesigned as a part-time Postgraduate Diploma course in Software Technology (PGDST). The result was impressive: there were nearly 2,000 applications for 100 seats. This was a time when there were few university programmes leading to a degree in computer science or engineering. Just about every professional in the industry had earned a degree in some other field. Many of them occupied senior positions in their companies/organizations and were keen to undergo formal education in the field. Therefore, NCST's PGDST activity grew over the years, attracting as many as 8,000 applicants per year in some years. Many professionals who completed this programme went on to lead departments/units in their companies. The course was different from other similar courses because of its emphasis on rigour. The motto was that 'a part-time course can reach the same level of rigour as any other full-time course'. The PGDST effort met the need for conversion-education of otherwise well-educated candidates to make them software professionals. These ideas enabled NCST to make a very important contribution to human resource development for the software industry in the critical first two decades of this industry in India. This initiative of NCST served as a model for many courses all over India.

Associated with the PGDST course was the Competence in Software Technology (CST) Examination, which had grown out of admission tests held in the early years. This examination served multiple purposes: admission test for PGDST, selection test for a small number of full-time research associates for NCST, and an examination that set standards for recruitment of entry-level employees for the IT industry. Companies and organizations that had become members of the 'Technical Affiliate' (TA) programme of NCST could recruit successful CST candidates who were willing to have their contact information given to technical affiliates. This programme also provided for a number of other privileges at NCST, including preferred admission to professional education programmes for their staff, use of the library, and access to specialized software development environments.

Taking note of the wide recognition that the PGDST course had earned, NCST followed this up with an Advanced PGDST programme (APGDST) for graduates in the IT field, and for those who had qualified to receive the PGDST diploma. Variants of the PGDST course have been run for varying periods of time focusing on specific areas, for instance, software engineering and internet technology. The most successful of these variants is discussed later on in the section on NCST's Bangalore campus.

Cooperation with International Organizations

National Centre for Software and Technology organized several international conferences and publications. Noteworthy were conferences organized by it under the banners of the International Federation for Information Processing (IFIP) and the International Council for Computer Communication (ICCC). A series of conferences named 'Computer Communication for Developing Countries' was originated by NCST and conducted in cooperation with ICCC in India as well as in a couple of other developing countries over a period of several years. Its role in bringing in high quality international conferences enhanced the national and international visibility of NCST. Members of the Centre's team also played leadership roles in selected international professional societies.

National Centre for Software and Technology made significant contributions to the worldwide Sustainable Network for Development Programme (SDNP) of the UNDP. The Ministry of Environment, Government of India, had appointed the author as the National Project Advisor of SDNP. The Centre organized two-week international training programmes for SDNP staff drawn from all over the world in 1993 and 1994. Its staff also contributed to a feasibility study (in 1994) of the Small Island Developing States Network, visiting and interacting with government entities and NGOs in four countries. The Centre also had cooperative arrangements with the Commonwealth Network of IT for Development (COMNET-IT), having played the role of a founder in its formation, and was recognized as one of its two Operational Centres in the world. It organized a number of training workshops for delegates from member states of the Commonwealth all over the world. The *Journal of IT for Development* initiated by COMNET-IT was edited at NCST during the first five years of its founding.

. The United Nations University based in Tokyo considered the possibility of creating a Centre in Macau in the area of computer science and technology, and a feasibility study was launched in 1989. The author was asked to Chair the Committee. This feasibility report was well received; the International Institute for Software Technology (IIST) came into being in 1990.

The United Nations created a Panel of Experts in 2000 to assist the then proposed UN ICT Task Force. The author was invited to be a member of this Panel, which went on to consider the proposal and make recommendations to the UN Economic and Social Council. The ICT Task Force was created the same year and the author served on this panel for a three-year term.

The Bangalore and Navi Mumbai Campuses

National Centre for Software and Technology acquired a plot of land in the Electronic City in Bangalore in 1991. P. Sadanandan moved to Bangalore on a permanent basis to begin activities in the same year, using premises leased from the Karnataka government, without waiting for the campus. One of the activities started at the leased premises was the PGDST course.

It took several years to find the necessary funds to create a campus, for which work began in the late 1990s. Sadanandan played a major role in the development of this campus, supported by George Arakal and K.S. Krishnakumar. The buildings on the campus became ready for occupation in 2000. Facilities at the campus enabled NCST to start the Full-time PGDST course (FPGDST).

Another NCST campus was created in Navi Mumbai. Work for this had begun in 1998, and buildings on the campus became ready for occupation in 2001. S.P. Mudur had played a major role in the creation of this campus, with the support of Bharat Desai, George Arakal, and K. Chandran.

Well-designed and well-maintained office premises are important; they make a statement about the institution's concern for the welfare and morale of its staff and the respect it gives to high standards in everything it undertakes. The Governing Council of NCST has always supported the Centre in its efforts to follow this principle; all three campuses have benefited from this.

MY EXPERIENCE WITH NCST

It is worth standing apart from the record of events at NCST and looking at it at some level of abstraction. I will frame a few questions at an institutional level, and try to answer them.

Why is it necessary to start with good culture?

After running NCST for a few years and listening to the compliments that people gave us, I became acutely aware of the culture and traditions we had inherited from TIFR consciously as well as unconsciously. It was the greatness of the founders of TIFR that they had imbibed the culture and traditions of the international labs they had worked at, and used them as a point of departure to create the soul of TIFR. That, more than anything else differentiates great institutions from the labs that are created ignoring good examples elsewhere!

We had been fortunate to imbibe some of the culture and traditions of TIFR and, therefore, had the organizational capital to start with, and used it as well as we could. As biology shows, nature as well as nurture are both important. We recognized from day one, that we differed from TIFR in one important aspect: we were a technology lab, not a fundamental research lab. Some of us had a great deal of interest in fundamental research, but we knew we had chosen to be a technology lab. This did not stand in the way of inheriting a number of good traditions from TIFR. One of them was building activities around leaders. The leaders come first; constituent labs, buildings, growth, etc. come later. If you do not have a good leadership team at the start, you have nothing to begin with.

What is the role of the Governing Council?

In the absence of the right governing council, autonomy for the organization has little meaning. Over the years, NCST has had men of eminence and standing from outside the government; to name a few: Narayana Murthy, F.C. Kohli, R. Narasimhan, V. Rajaraman, and Prem Gupta. Equally important were secretaries to government in the DoE; to name a few: S.R. Vijayakar, Shyamal Ghosh, R. Rajamani,

Ravindra Gupta, and N. Vittal. The value systems of these professionals and administrators, their insight and their commitment to the good of the institution and its reputation acted as a protective shield. Under these circumstances, it was easy to make decisions in Governing Council meetings at the Lab jointly with the persons who enhance the credibility of the institution and at the same time ensure its accountability. The Lab did not have to be a small cog in a big machine.

One needs far-sighted members on the Governing Council to encourage and support passion for R&D among the scientific and technical staff, giving them the necessary autonomy in selected matters. Effective autonomy cannot be created by a formula. It can only be created by the respect and authority one gives to a set of eminent people who have proved their worth in national life, after appointing them to the Governing Council.

How do we ensure institutional governance?
We need to pay equal attention to other aspects of institutional governance, such as having the leadership team meet frequently and deliberate on all decisions. The director should be responsive to the opinions expressed in these meets.

External experts are necessary in selection and promotion committees. They help us ensure merit-based decisions. These in turn set up standards for the institution, creating brand value.

We need to be uncompromising in resisting external pulls and pressures that might mar the standards of an institution. It is better to break than bend when any vested interest puts pressure on the institution.

Discipline versus Administrative Power

We need to be conservative in the exercise of administrative power. I remember the time when a Chairman of the Governing Council suggested a change in the purchase procedure we had proposed. 'You ought to increase the limit for purchase without tenders by a factor of five', he said, citing some other labs. We politely said, 'No, thank you; we are a small lab and would rather have more discipline than less.' A credible institution has to ensure total integrity in financial matters, but that is not enough. Its procedures have to be seen to be systematic and respected.

Special Features of NCST

Having discussed what we had inherited, I must also discuss what we consciously added. Some of these had very much been there at NCSDCT. Some were not new to TIFR either. Some were unique to NCST. Together, they became the defining characteristics of NCST as an institution.

Development Orientation

Why did the UNDP assist in the creation of NCSDCT? As its name indicates, UNDP's focus is on development. In some of the projects it has run worldwide, UNDP has assisted the creation of high technology labs, though this has been more an exception than the rule. In these cases, it has satisfied itself that the lab being created would contribute to developmental activities, educate and train a large pool of knowledgeable professionals where necessary, and focus the lab on problems of socio-economic significance.

Recognizing the need for creating a sustainable institution, UNDP was fully with us till the formation of NCST. The institution's leadership team adopted the development orientation of the UNDP as a permanent feature, irrespective of any assistance from UNDP.

Software Development

There is such a thing as pure science, but there is no pure technology. Work in technology is motivated by the desire to make a practical impact. Therefore, one's ideas have to reach the level of proof-of-concept, and have some application(s) in sight. In the field of software technology, this is best done by creating prototype software. Sometimes one goes beyond this and creates software developed well enough to transfer to real users in the outside world. But, invariably, creation of prototype software results in the kind of know-how and experience that is highly valued by industry. The best technology transfer occurs when the developers of an item of prototype software move to industry where they can go on to create software products.

National Centre for Software and Technology avoided duplicating any work that other groups in India were doing well, particularly in the creation of software and choosing to stay at the leading edge. It also avoided doing classified work, despite a few opinions to the contrary expressed in the Governing Council.

Postgraduate Courses and Courses for Working Professionals

We had tried running part-time postgraduate courses at NCSDCT, and gave such courses a very significant place in our activities at NCST. The interior of the building was in fact designed taking into account the needs of courses that had been planned. We scaled up our education and training activities substantially to meet a part of the growing IT sector's tremendous need for well-educated professionals. We also placed great importance on short courses for professionals already in the industry. These were usually one- or two-week courses.

Service Orientation

National Centre for Software Development and Computing Techniques had charged for the computer facilities it had offered to users from outside TIFR. This cost-recovery had been enough to sustain the Centre and there was no need to ask for a government grant for 'recurring expenses'. However, the environment was changing rapidly; minicomputers were making computing facilities more widely available, reducing to a great extent the dependence on big, expensive computers. The PC was on the Indian horizon in 1985. A lab such as NCST could not, therefore, plan to depend upon on this source of income for long. However, the idea could be and was generalized. Making a technology lab depends upon its beneficiaries for its recurring expenses was seen as a sure way of ensuring the external orientation of its scientific teams. The courses, software development, and consulting were seen as possible sources of income. What we did not realize at the start but were to learn later, was that consulting was not merely giving the benefit of our expertise to external organizations. It was also the surest way of developing links to business and industry and learning from them. We learnt as much as we gave. This helped the development of the careers of R&D team members, giving them opportunities to work more and to learn from the real world. The ambitious goal of meeting all recurring expenses from the institution's earnings was in fact realized.

The Value of a Make-do Campus

Not every institution can have its own campus to meet all its needs. The Juhu building of NCST was too small to provide for even a few guest rooms, leave alone a hostel for young researchers. So, the Centre adopted the second best solution. A separate residential building

6-7 km away from the Juhu campus and a bus service that provided for flexible travel to the labs and back even at odd hours and holidays gave NCST a virtual campus.

Role of the Administrative and Support Staff

Institutions have traditionally valued their scientific and technical staff, but not all have recognized the importance of administrative and support staff. Their cooperation, commitment, and sense of belonging are essential for the scientific and technical staff to do well in their own work. This requires that every employee of the institution is valued.

What I Wish had been Different

Provision for Significant Recruitment at Senior Levels

Restrictions on recruitments are not unique to government institutions and are common in corporate labs as well. These restrictions apply even if the authorized budget is adequate to cover the proposed appointments. Obviously, appointments create a continuing future commitment and are therefore tightly controlled. Unfortunately, however, the restrictions at NCST more or less limited us to recruitment at relatively junior levels, including the case of scientific and technical staff. Further, the availability of affordable accommodation in Mumbai made it difficult to attract professionals at higher levels. We thought we could rectify this by acquiring a campus at Navi Mumbai and in Bangalore. It was possible to get government funding for creating a campus and buildings, but restrictions in force from the beginning prevented lateral entry of professionals with external education and experience beyond that required for the lowest salary grades. There was an exception for the position of Director, but faculty-level positions were effectively restricted to promotions from within.

Recognition as a Degree-granting Institution

I would have preferred to see NCST go on to become a degree-granting institution focused on the postgraduate level, but rules governing the creation of such institutions made this impossible in the 1990s. Work at NCST had resulted in over fifteen doctoral dissertations and more than thirty Master's dissertations. Some of the doctoral work was carried out by faculty members of university departments who spent varying periods of time working at NCST. As a degree-granting institution, NCST could have gone on to support a lot more of such activity at a time when there was acute shortage of PhD level faculty.

Young scientists who had worked for a number of years at NCST largely moved on, a number of them to work at labs and universities abroad. Some went on to industry. Many of them have done remarkably well, becoming professors, CEOs, entrepreneurs, directors of companies, and so on. This was of value to them, their universities, and companies. An institution should be happy to make contributions by enabling such career development. But this movement of talent compounded the problem of increasing NCST's staff size at the faculty level. The loss of experienced staff was very much accentuated by the remarkable growth of the education sector and of the software industry, starting from the 1990s.

Merger of a Number of Scientific Institutions

A few scientific institutions funded by government in the field of information technology were merged in December 2002. The biggest of them in this category was the Centre for the Development of Advanced Computing (C-DAC); the entity resulting from the merger was also named C-DAC. Should NCST have been covered by this merger? This is an interesting question, best discussed by colleagues who were on the scene when this merger took place, or just prior to it.

What was NCST's contribution?

- Papers arising from R&D;
- Doctoral theses;
- Prototypes of advanced software;
- Education and leadership development;
- Contributions to the adoption of software technology, with a development orientation.

It was a combination of all these. The two decades of NCST as an independent institution saw a dramatic growth in the software industry and in the adoption of IT in India. At the beginning there were very few degree-level courses in computer science and technology, serving a few hundred entrants every year. Doctoral level research in these disciplines was far scarcer. The Centre, as a new generation national laboratory, was there to serve the nation during those demanding and exciting years.

Now, well over 3,00,000 students enroll in degree-level courses in these areas annually all over India. This demonstrates the importance of the tasks which NCST had taken on decades earlier, and the role it had played.

ANNEXURE

PARTIAL LIST OF STAFF OF NCST DURING 1985–6

This listing does not include the Heads of Divisions mentioned earlier, to avoid redundancy in the text.

Database and Office Information Systems: S.M. Desai, T.M. Vijayaraman, K. Suresh Babu, P.C. Banthia, Lavina Bhatnagar, S.N. Pal, K.T. Sridhar

Graphics and Computer Aided Design: P.K. Ghosh, P.A. Koparkar, S.J. Nath, Laxmi Parida, S.N. Pattanaik, H.S. Ravi Shankar

Real Time Systems and Networks: A.G. Joshi, K. Vinod Kumar, R. Bharadwaj, A.K. Garg, S.P. Joshi, A.R. Madan Mohan

Knowledge Based Computer Systems: K.S.R. Anjaneyulu, Sudeep Bharati, R. Chandrasekar, Madhavan Mukund

Software Promotion Centre: Alka Irani, V.S. Rao, G.R. Baliga, Jitendra Loyal, Alaknanda Rao

Hardware: S.B. Patankar, B.N. Desai, J.D. Deshmukh, D. Jagadish, S.H. Pathak, D.S. Rane

Administration: George Arakal, S.H.K. Iyer, K. Chandran, Sushma Samarth

S.R. VIJAYAKAR and Y.S. MAYYA

3 Towards Indigenous Computer
Role of ECIL

The success of indigenous development and commercialization of Trombay Digital Computer (TDC) series by Electronics Corporation of India Ltd. (ECIL) was a remarkable outcome of Homi J. Bhabha's (1909–1966) visionary efforts. Today it reads like a dream—a saga of sheer audacity of a few individuals. The achievements of these early years of computerization in India are formidable—design and production of world-class computers in India, their deployment in a variety of applications in nuclear, aerospace, and defence sectors, and building a brilliant team of hardware and software professionals within the country who could stand shoulder to shoulder with the best in the world.

The investment on computers was truly an 'investment on people' as Vikram Sarabhai (1919–1971) prophesied way back in 1971. Computers and Information Technology (IT) are areas wherein the contributions of ECIL had a nationwide impact in terms of skill generation, technology base creation, and nurturing of high calibre techno-managerial talent, which played a pivotal role in the IT revolution in the country. The synergy among the research labs, educational institutions, and the industry that everybody is advocating today was pioneered by ECIL exclusively in the field of IT, right in its formative years. In perfecting this chemistry and seeding a large base of applications, products, technologies, and talent pool, ECIL seems to have contributed more to the industry as a whole than to corporation's top and bottom lines. Electronics Corporation of India Ltd. generated several top notch computer professionals who went on to lead the nascent computer industry in India and abroad. Apart from scoring several 'firsts' in the country in terms of computer hardware development, the team at ECIL pioneered development of System Software and Application Software.

THE EARLY YEARS

The development of the first of the TDC series of computers, TDC12, was the task undertaken by a team of engineers and scientists at Bhabha Atomic Research Centre, Bombay (BARC). It is important to understand that 21 January 1969 was a red-letter day in the annals of Indian science and technology as it was on this day that the first Indian-built electronic digital computer was commissioned by Vikram Sarabhai at BARC. It was a historic occasion not only for the development team at BARC but for the entire nation. There was wide coverage of the event in the national media. All the national newspapers carried details of the fabulous achievement. Sceptics were silenced with the path-breaking achievement of the development team.

The TDC12 system had 4k ferrite core memory, 12-bit processor, and a teletypewriter as the input/output (I/O) device. Although the capability of the machine was modest in comparison to today's computers, the achievement of the team was path-breaking. A small band of young engineers and scientists, fresh from the colleges, without any previous knowledge of computers or guidance from people with hands-on experience in the field, succeeded in designing, engineering, and pro-ducing a computer which worked! Their only inputs were the trust and confidence that their superiors reposed in them. The key figure was Sivasubramanian Srikantan, a 'veteran' of 36 years then! He returned from the US and proposed to A.S. Rao to design digital computers in India. Rao had his own views about the feasibility of this ambitious, if not a mad, dream. But he was not a man to discourage the daring. He gave the go ahead.

The political and economic scenario in the country in the early and mid-1960s was very grave. The war with China in 1962 had shaken the nation. Food items were being rationed. The economic strength of the country was miserable. Foreign exchange for imports was scarce to come by and strictly controlled. Every effort in the country was to conserve foreign exchange. The focus of the country was to develop everything indigenously and make the country self-sufficient. Department of Atomic Energy (DAE) pioneered the indigenous development of high technology areas such as nuclear energy and electronics. Electronics Corporation of India Ltd. was created by DAE as an effort towards making the country self-sufficient in electronics, namely, in electronic components, semiconductors, instruments, and systems. Many of the research and development (R&D) people were able to take up the development of less complex items. But indigenous development of computer systems was considered a gigantic and almost impossible task.

It was in such an environment that Srikantan made the proposal to build computers within the country. All that he had with him were a few handbooks on computers pertaining to Programmed Data Processor (PDP), Hewlett Packard (HP), and Honeywell and Nova series. There were no other resources worth mentioning for a task of the kind and size that he had undertaken. The training school recruits were few and in great demand for several programmes of BARC. The strongest resources Srikantan could boast of were an indomitable zeal and belief in his own ability to organize and manage the huge development task.

For a long time, the only places where computer activity was being pursued were Tata Institute of Fundamental Research (TIFR) (which developed the Tata Institute of Fundamental Research Automatic Calculator [TIFRAC] computer in the 1950s), Jadhavpur University (which developed the ISIJU computer in association with Indian Statistical Institute), and Indian Institute of Technology, Kanpur (where computer science was being taught). Electronics Corporation of India Ltd. had significant linkages with all these eminent institutes. The relationship with TIFR was close and deep since the pioneers shared a common origin—DAE. The computer gurus at TIFR acted as friends, philosophers, and guides. A.S. Rao, while personally not very conversant with computers, was certainly a very perceptive and sensitive manager of technologies and a great judge of people. He requested Narasimhan of TIFR to oversee the computer activity at BARC.

Before taking up the development of TDC12 digital computer, Srikantan had built an Electronic Analog Computer (EAC) facility, and work was on for developing a 60-amplifier EAC 62 machine indicating the year of commencement of work. The machine was brought out in 1964 and about ten were sold to various engineering colleges in the country. One of the very interesting applications for which this computer was put to use was the design of the fly-over bridge at Kemps Corner, Mumbai (then Bombay), in association with Roorkee and Osmania universities. The system was also employed for the simulation of control systems of CIRUS reactor.

The computers of 1960s would consist of a dozen varieties of logic circuits totalling 200 printed circuit boards (PCBs). The central processing unit (CPU) occupied about 100 PCBs while the memory and teleprinter interfaces needed 50 and 20 PCBs respectively. PDP 8 computer of the Digital Equipment Corporation (DEC) was the most famous online computer of those days. In terms of power and technology, the TDC12 was just 3–4 years behind.

FORMATION OF COMPUTER DIVISION AT ECIL

As an offshoot of the R&D work done at BARC, ECIL was established in 1967 by DAE at Hyderabad as a public sector company to specialize in development and manufacture of electronic equipment in India. The computer development team of BARC was shifted to ECIL in 1969 with a view to scale up the computer programme in the country, with Srikantan as the head of the computer division at ECIL.

The First Five Year Plan of the Computers in India (1971–6) was a remarkable document and reflects the vision of the computer team. It is really breath-taking, considering the limitations of knowledge and exposure of the people engaged in the activity in those times. The products identified included TDC12, TDC312, TCD16 and TCD332. The plans included the analogue and hybrid range of AC-20, AC-80, AC-20H and AC-80H. The application products covered systems for business, real-time, process control, and scientific applications. The document envisaged a manpower intake of 2,000 in the five-year period.

The vision of Srikantan, A.S. Rao, and DAE, and their courage to embark on an ambitious programme to develop a series of digital computers at ECIL along with associated system software and a variety of applications development indigenously in India created such an aura in the country that one could see a reverse brain drain from reputed foreign companies in the US and the UK to India. Bright and talented engineers migrated to ECIL from leading academic institutes in the country and abroad. It is predominantly because in ECIL they

FIGURE 3.1   H.N. Sethna, Chairman, AEC, during his visit to the
computer division, ECIL

found a place that gave them the opportunity to work on cutting-edge technologies.

The printed circuit board (PCB) is the basic building block of any electronic system and the country had only two facilities—both in Bangalore. It was deployed for the fabrication of single-sided and double-sided PCBs in those days. Computer division had to set up its own small PCB facility, more to telescope the development cycle time than to make a large number of PCBs.

One could see bright young faces all over with lot of enthusiasm and initiative to achieve something very fulfilling for themselves and for the organization. The technical challenges were of the highest order and spurred them to give their best intellectually and also emotionally.

The creation of infrastructure for R&D and manufacture of sophisticated electronic systems like computers was as challenging a task as the design and development of the computer itself. However, the support industry to develop and manufacture complex equipment was almost non-existent during the 1960s and 1970s.

With respect to availability of manpower, the situation at that time was that, except at IIT Kanpur, computer science was not taught in any engineering college in the country. Electronics Corporation of India Ltd.

FIGURE 3.2   J.R.D. Tata, doyen of Indian Industry, keenly looking at
the PCB facility at ECIL with A.S. Rao

had to organize internal training programmes to generate the required
number and quality of computer engineers and scientists.

Converting R&D expertise into something good enough for manufacturing, namely, reliability engineering to improve the know-how, was
a great effort put forth by ECIL.

In fact, ECIL's major contribution to the country was that it had
proved how it was possible to successfully productionize the locally
generated R&D knowledge, and in the process, given confidence to the
Indian electronic industry.

This capability of ECIL had attracted many industry stalwarts in the
country and abroad. Many were keen to participate with ECIL in building electronic equipment in India.

THE GLORIOUS DAYS

The period 1971–4 was very challenging in the Computer Group as
development programmes related to the commercial exploitation of
TDC12, development of TDC16 computer for deployment in the Air
Defence Ground Environment System (ADGES) Project, development
of Analogue computer AC-80 for use by the Indian Space Research
Organisation (ISRO) at Thumba, and a host of other activities related

to software development in both the domains, namely, system software development as well as application development, were in full swing. The commercial exploitation of TDC12 was aimed at realizing a number of business oriented applications and implied development of peripheral equipment interfaces and other associated hardware. In order to ensure compatibility of usage with a number of 1401 systems that were in use in the country, ECIL took up the development of 1401 auto coder, cross assembler. The IC version of TDC12 and TDC312 was also on the anvil of development. Concurrent with these hardware development programmes, especially ambitious projects were also taken up for the indigenous development of peripheral devices. Important amongst these were the card reader and magnetic tape.

The first dispatches of computers took place in the year 1971. Two TDC12 systems were sent to Gas Turbine Research Establishment (GTRE) and Electronics Process Engineering Lab (EPEL) at BARC. In addition, a few AC-20s were supplied to some laboratories and universities.

Electronics Corporation of India Ltd. came out with several firsts like TDC12 for scientific real-time and business applications which was followed by TDC312, TDC316, TDC332, AC-20, AC-20H, AC-80, and AC-80H.

FIGURE 3.3   Analogue Computer AC-20

The first microcomputer in the country, developed by ECIL, was released in the year 1978. It was called Micro 78. Electronics Corporation of India Ltd. received orders from sixty customers who had not even seen how the product looked like.

FIGURE 3.4   TDC316

FIGURE 3.5   TDC332

SOFTWARE R&D AT ECIL

Today India plays a major role in exporting computer software. This is a developmental activity subcontracted to India by many foreign companies with no Intellectual Property Rights (IPR) to the Indian companies.

Many would find it difficult to believe that in India ECIL had developed many system software and application software packages during the 1970s and 1980s with its own IPR.

Electronics Corporation of India Ltd. had developed assemblers, cross assemblers, compilers for Fortran, Cobol, Basic, etc., simulators, operating systems on to run on its own TDC12, TDC312, and TDC316 machines.

Electronics Corporation of India Ltd. was the first to introduce microprocessor-based computer systems in the country.

In this context ECIL had taken full advantage of the expertise available at various R&D organizations like TIFR, academic institutes like IITs and IIMs. It is worth mentioning that the Basic compiler of ECIL was developed by Narayana Murthy (presently the mentor of Infosys) while he was at IIM Ahmedabad.

A large number of system software and application software packages were developed at ECIL during a time when software activity was not still recognized as industry. At many computer science seminars during 1970s, whether software can be an industry or not, used to be an important topic of discussion.

DEVELOPMENT OF COMPUTER-BASED APPLICATIONS

Electronics Corporation of India Ltd. had developed many computer-based applications in commercial and real-time areas. It had developed many application-specific software packages for a variety of applications with all the IPRs with ECIL. Department of Science and Technology recognized ECIL's contributions to software and during 2004 (during a time when software industry in India is on a boom) gave ECIL an (R&D) award in the area of software development.

Concurrent with the numerous development programs outlined earlier, ECIL also took on a complex mission—a critical project called Automatic Data Handling System (ADHS) for the Air Defense Ground

Environmental System (ADGES) project. This system was meant to be an online and real-time system to enable the authorities of the Indian Air Force to identify the nature of the aircraft hovering on the Indian skies and take appropriate counter-measures if the aircraft cited belonged to the 'enemy'. The actions included taking stock of the counter-measures available and deploying the most appropriate ones as the situation warranted.

It is a matter of great pride to ECIL that these systems supplied in the 1980s are still operational in the country. Tata Institute of Fundamental Research and Radar Communication Project Office (RCPO), ECIL, were the core development agencies for this project.

The computer applications covered a wide range of applications related to defence, police, the department of telecommunications (DoT), process industries like steel and cement, transmission, distribution of power and load balancing, civil aviation, systems for laboratory automation, especially for the DAE like nuclear diffractometers and X-ray diffractometers, and seismic analysis systems are among the host of products and systems taken up for development.

The Store and Forward Telegraph Systems for use by DoT, the Automatic Message Switching System for use both by Defence and DoT, and the Message Retransmission Systems for use by the Overseas Communication Services of those days (present VSNL), were all systems developed internally.

FIGURE 3.6   Flight data analyser for airbus—TDC316

FIGURE 3.7   Fast Breeder Test Reactor (FBTR computer)

FIGURE 3.8   LIC Computer System

Subsequently, there had been significant developmental work carried out at ECIL in the field of computer-based systems, especially in the field of telecommunications. The excellent work done in respect of Store and Forward Telegraph Systems (SFT), Message Retransmission

FIGURE 3.9   Police Computer System for Chennai Police

FIGURE 3.10   Automatic Message Switching System

Systems, etc. have given ECIL a very respectable status in the field of telecommunications for computer-based systems.

Another major telecom project undertaken and very successfully executed by the then computer group at the express request of DoT was the Operations and Maintenance Centre (OMC) project. The indigenous development of this project had to be taken up on priority basis because of the obsolescence and withdrawal of the MITRA computers of France used for the OMC purpose in the electronic E10B telephone exchanges.

The Operations and Maintenance Centre project developed by ECIL is one of the outstanding contributions of the organization towards telecommunications in India. Behind every E10B telephone exchange operational in India there is one ECIL-designed OMC. During the year 2000 approximately 200 ECIL-designed OMC systems were operational at various telephone exhanges of BSNL. In addition, 197 Directory Enquiry Services was another innovative application developed by ECIL for the first time in the country for use by DoT/BSNL.

Besides the work done in the telecom area, the group has rendered yeomen services through its pioneering work in areas like insurance, banking, education, process control, laboratory automation, space applications, police applications, defence applications, and so on and so forth. The front-office automation in banking was carried out for the first time in the country by ECIL. Same is true in respect of insurance-related applications. Crime and criminal data processing systems developed by ECIL were used by the state governments and police forces.

Rapid changes in technology, slow adaptation to environmental changes, putting in position appropriate business models, inability to overcome the inherent rigidities in compensation structures of a government company, and the software boom and erosion of talent, are among the important contributing factors for the decline of the computer activity at ECIL.

The work done at ECIL in the field of computers cannot be gauged by the present generation in its true perspective. The 'firsts' scored in the field of software indeed are to be more admired than the 'firsts' achieved in the field of hardware, which were spectacular in themselves. In addition to the stupendous volumes of system software generated encompassing operating systems, language processors and compilers, and utilities and library routines, the application software developed for several applications stands out for its variety and excellence.

Looking back, it has been such a glorious journey. Electronics Corporation of India Ltd. has set a trend, blazed a trail, and moved on. Its major contributions were in the areas of skill-building, technology development, applications engineering, and nurturing techno-manage-rial competence. The role played by ECIL, TIFR, and BARC in trig-gering the IT industry of the country deserves to be written in golden letters in the history of the highly successful IT industry of India.

N. SESHAGIRI

4 National Informatics Centre
Evolution and its Impact

National Informatics Centre (NIC) evolved as an offshoot of the Informa-tion, Planning and Analysis Group (IPAG) of the Electronics Commission of the Government of India, and outgrew it by over a hundred fold within a decade and half, for giving information, analysis, and planning support to every ministry/department of the central government, all secretariats of the thirty-five state governments and union territories (UTs), and eventually over 600 district collectorates in India. By setting up National Informat-ics Centre Network (NICNET), a Very Small Aperture Terminal (VSAT) based computer-communication network spanning all these offices as well as several attached offices in the public sector and utility sector, a pervasive and integrative connectivity was established to assist in the streamlining of the functions of the government.

As a novel experiment with Information and Communication Technol-ogy (ICT) as well as with the evolution of strategies for progressive conversion of conventionally oriented officers and staff in government, NIC took on the role of a change agent, and embedded itself in the governmental structure to strive to become the harbinger of modernity, efficiency, timeliness, trans-parency, and change. The successes and failures, impacts and pitfalls, and diagnoses and prognoses are given here illustratively.

EVOLUTION OF NIC

The Nucleation Phase

Recognizing the paramount importance of information on the electronics industry, on becoming the founder chairman of the Electronics Commission in 1971, M.G.K. Menon gave priority for the setting up of the IPAG which inter alia functioned as the technical secretariat of the commission, initially benefiting by the administrative infrastructure of the Tata Institute of Fundamental Research (TIFR). The Information, Planning and Analysis Group, while developing an extensive computer-based database on all aspects of the electronics industry relevant to decision making at the Electronics Commission, guided the entrepreneurs with industry-related analysis, made available to them through the journal *Electronics Information and Planning*. The Information, Planning and Analysis Group was also the technical secretariat for coordinating the funding in research and development (R&D) and academic institutions as well as some development-oriented industries through Technology Development Council (TDC).

When IPAG was relocated in 1974 from Mumbai (then Bombay) to New Delhi, under a recommendation of Parliament, it became the progenitor of a wider concept of the NIC for information, analysis, and planning services to the central government at Delhi, through a successful pilot demonstration of the usefulness of information technology (IT) in a few ministries.

With the successful implementation of a rudimentary intracity and intercity computer-communication network, and hosting and servicing databases on games information system on it for the Asian Games 1981, NIC made IT visible not only to the political echelon and the bureaucracy in government, but also to the Indian public, the games participants, and the press in general. Thereafter, the United Nations Development Programme (UNDP) and the Planning Commission gave adequate financial support for propelling NIC on a growth path.

The Formal Constitution

Formally constituted in 1975 with the approval of the Electronics Commission, NIC received the status of a Five Year Plan project in 1977 with the long-term objective of setting up a computer-based informatics network for decision support to the ministries/departments and the development of databases relating to India's socio-economic development, assisting in the monitoring of projects and schemes, and playing a catalytic as well as a participatory role in creating informatics awareness, systematizing the data collection, collation, processing, and analysis in government and facilitating its online availability. From 1985, NIC extended its informatics support services to state administrations and signed memoranda of understanding (MoU) with all state governments/UTs of the Union of India. By a Presidential notification, dated 14 March 1988, NIC was transferred to the Planning Commission. When a separate Ministry of Communications and Information Technology (DIT) was formed in 1999, NIC was transferred to this ministry with autonomous powers delegated to it.

Since its formation in 1975, NIC was functioning with considerable autonomy as a service unit with a broad set of terms of reference given by the Electronics Commission.

The major objectives of NIC for e-governance in government are the following:

• Development of necessary and appropriate computerized information systems/data bases in various sectors of the economy for interactive use;

• Promotion of informatics culture at district, state, and central levels;

• Improvement of the analytical capacity and quality of presentation of statistics for decision making and planning at various levels;

• Development of modeling and forecasting techniques that is required for optimal planning for economic development;

• Establishment of computer network with necessary communication equipment for ensuring easy access of information across the nation and ensuring reliable, timely, and accurate information, enabling optimal use of resources;

• Evolution of standards for data collection, compilation, and dissemination with the cooperation of the stakeholders at district, state and central levels;

• Creation of a dedicated training school with branches in all parts of the country for extensive training of existing government personnel and NIC users; and

- Provision of value-added services on NICNET to the users in public and private sectors.

IMPROVISATION OF PRODUCTIVITY IN GOVERNMENT FUNCTIONING

The impact of NIC on productivity in governmental functioning is being increasingly realized by various departments of the Government of India. Principally, this impact arises from the following methodologies adopted.

- Interactive Management Information System (MIS): The Management Information System in an interactive mode within and between various ministries/departments. It has helped the timeliness, quality, and coverage of information, leading to better decision making. A reduction in ad hoc decision making has been observed in several departments.
- Processing at the data sources: For various reasons, those who are in charge of certain data sources are reluctant to part with their information. Through the network concept, terminals are increasingly being located at data sources with required processing capability to carry out preliminary data validation at the source itself. This has helped the pooling of information which otherwise was difficult.
- Standardization in coding and formats: By bringing together several departments on a common platform, standardization in coding and data formats is being evolved. Standardization helps in better exchange of information between ministries/departments and their associated organizations. It also facilitates a network-based query system.
- Correlatory databases: India has a long history of collection of statistical information. These largely remained as manual databases in the form of files and other documents. Consequently, making correlatory studies on data in more than one database was not easy. Distributed databases on a distributed computer network has facilitated correlatory analysis of several databases.
- Spreading the effects of innovation: By making NIC a dynamic showpiece of new innovation in informatics, and providing the prime movers of such innovation through well trained human resource (HR), the NIC concept is being propagated to the state governments.
- National Informatics Centre as an agent of transformation of work culture: When a ministry/department links up with NICNET, a

series of transformations take place in the method of functioning. A cardinal principle adopted by NIC is to train existing government staff in handling various levels of computer-based information handling systems, analysis, programming, coding, key punching, and routine logistics of information processing. This changes the quality of work of the government employees without causing any reduction in employment or in many cases, without inducting a large number of computer specialists.

Enhancement of productivity in information processing itself is made possible by adopting the following pooling concepts implemented by NIC (Seshagiri 1993):

• Hardware pooling: The computer network with a large host system and several terminals has the advantage of bringing the power of a large system to the locations of each ministry/department.

• Software pooling: A number of computer programme packages and modules are common to different departments. By judicious planning it is possible to create a library of software modules of common utility in the various departments. Development of a special package for a particular department can be considered as an exercise in writing programmes maximally utilizing such modules and software components.

• Specialists pooling: There are so many different specializations in informatics, for example, databases, optimization, operations research, systems analysis, format design, simulation, computational econometrics, Geographic Information System (GIS), Management Information System (MIS), Decision Support System (DSS), etc. that HR productivity can be maximized only by creating a central pool of specialist HR. When any department has an informatics project to be implemented, a team is constituted with some specialists from the HR pool of NIC and some officers/staff from the user ministry/department. After the project is implemented, the NIC specialists may return to the pool. In certain cases, specialists may be assigned at the same time to more than one project on a time-sharing basis. When continuity of dual specialization of IT and the domain experience is essential, the specialist may continue with the project/department/state. All these are planned in such a manner as to maximize specialist HR productivity within government.

• Pooling of delivery means: Generally, the dissemination of information processed in NICNET is the responsibility of the user department. Of late, a number of users are increasingly requesting NIC to organize dissemination. For this, NIC has a central computer-aided document preparation facility, computer output photo offset master, and websites for increasing the productivity of the dissemination.

• Pooling of training: Different departments project at various times requirements for training in various aspects of informatics. National Informatics Centre Training Wing helps plan the training programme of various departments by indentifying the commonalities and differences in the requirements, and prepares the course content to specially meet the requirements over a specified duration ahead. In this way, efficiency of training is increased.

• Pooling of experience: One of the most important contributions of NIC is to carry the experience or software developed at one project in one department to another project in the same or another department, or from one state to another, so that one derives maximum benefit from past experience. The experience pool which is obviously cumulative in nature makes NIC progressively more and more competent to handle the problems that may be faced by governments in future.

Central Government Informatics

National Informatics Centre gives comprehensive turn-key informatics support to a majority of ministries/departments except the maintenance and utilization of the created databases for which special training is given to the users. This necessitated the creation of over fifty technical divisions in NIC in domain areas like agriculture, commerce, chemicals and petrochemicals, cooperatives, customs and excise, energy, external affairs, finance, financial resources, health and family welfare, home affairs, land records, legislature, human resources, fertilizer, legal resources, parliament, personnel and public grievances, rural development, social welfare, steel and mines, transport and highways, tourism, urban development, water resources, and women and child welfare (Seshagiri 1988, 1989).

While providing macro-level information in the respective sectors for assisting planning and project monitoring, these divisions also develop special domain databases or analytics identified by the users.

The databases so created are owned by the user ministry/department, which have the ownership for use and dissemination, for which NIC provides only infrastructural and software development support. With specialized training given by NIC, if they show initiative to develop software and databases by themselves, or through outsourcing to realize better economy and quality, NIC has a step-by-step strategy to recede from that area and move support to other areas of priority which require hand-holding.

Informatics Support to State Governments

State government informatics evolved in a direction similar to that of the central government. From massive awareness creation on the benefits of IT in early years, to setting up of IT units in some of the important departments such as finance, planning, agriculture, and rural development among others, NIC has come a long way to undertake contract projects on a semi-commercial basis. Beginning with Karnataka, Kerala, and Haryana in 1985, all states and UTs have been covered by the mid-1990s, knitting all states and the capital into one large integrated system, with essential messages and other information going back and forth over NICNET's mail and other transaction services.

Within the ambit of an MoU, the National Informatics Centre-State Coordination Committee (NSCCs) under the chairmanship of the respective chief secretaries, have been set up in all the states, with NIC State Informatics Officer as the convenor. National Informatics Centre-State Coordination Committees review the informatics development at the state level. The state governments are using NICNET facilities for online monitoring of various sectors of the economy and social development on a regular basis, and also for data development and transactions for administration and development planning. Training provided by NIC to officers at all levels has made the states more and more self-reliant. Further, where economically, time wise, and quality wise justified, NIC encourages outsourcing of projects to other institutions in the public and private sectors. For greater economy, NIC promotes pooling of IT resources of several states with common problems by transferring the experience gained and software developed by one state to another (NIC 1999).

The following are the typical illustrative projects implemented in various states: land records, municipal property tax, commercial and road transport tax, personnel management, accounts consolidation, financial accounting, insurance, social welfare schemes, household survey data, health databases, small savings schemes, local rainfall data, old age pension disbursement, public grievance redressal, employee census, MIS for chief minister and other ministers, governor's office management, and budget processing in local language, among numerous others.

A few of the more important areas, where NICNET is being routinely used to transmit data from the states to the centre are

• Agricultural and civil supplies commodity prices data on a weekly basis;

• Centrally sponsored and central sector schemes monitoring data on monthly basis. For example, Universal Immunization, Integrated Child Development Services (ICDS), Jawahar Rojgar Yojana (JRY), Integrated Rural Development Programme (IRDP), Public Distribution System (PDS), etc.;

• Reservoir data;

• Construction data on power and other large projects.

A strength of NIC lies in its vast geographical spread with trained technical HR in all its over 600 sub-centres, which has bestowed a unique position to handle information on a national scale, including for the Accountant General's Office, Central Excise Collectorates, Passport Offices, Central Pay and Accounts Offices, Regional Provident Fund Offices, Press Information Bureau Offices, Food Corporation of India (FCI), District Court Information System, National Literacy Mission, Sample Surveys, Economic Census, Agricultural Census, etc.

Support to District Collectorates

Every one of the over 600 districts in India has an NIC centre with computing facility and a Very Small Aperture Terminal (VSAT) or fibre optic connectivity to NICNET. Each such office has at least two well trained IT specialists with additional HR trained by NIC and sponsored by the state government in some of the important districts. National Informatics Centre acts as a facilitator of information flow from the micro (district and below), meso (state), and macro (national) levels.

Recognizing the importance of information as a vital resource at the grassroots, with applications in rural development and agricultural development, NIC launched its District Information System (DISNIC) programme in 1987 with specific objectives like

- Providing MIS and DSS for the collector and his functionaries;
- Developing necessary databases in various sectors of the economy for planning;
- Promoting information culture at the district level;
- Improving local statistics and analytics;
- Developing local-level modeling and forecasting;
- Promoting micro-level Geographical Information System (GIS), including natural resource management.

Many states have taken the implementation of District Information System of National Informatics Centre (DISNIC) on a priority basis and have used it beneficially in applications like agriculture, land records, industry, educational statistics, transport, primary health care, treasury, revenue, administration, civil supplies, animal husbandry, decentralized planning, project implementation and monitoring, and block development among others.

Evolution of Nationwide NICNET

Metropolitan Area Network (MAN) and several Local Area Network (LAN) services to over fifty departments of the central government were provided by 1985 (Seshagiri et al. 1985). National Informatics Centre Network expanded to include regional centres at Hyderabad, Pune, and Bhubaneswar through direct intracity links with the setting up of large computer centres around four NEC SX-1000 large mainframe computers by 1986. When demand for NIC services from every state capital mounted, a decision was taken to set up a national Wide Area Network (WAN) connecting not only all state capitals but also all the then over 430 districts.

The events that led to this expansion are worth recording as it has certain lessons for the future:

In 1985, there was an embargo on procurement of large mainframe computers by India from the US and allied countries. Japan was then outside the purview of this. The government directed urgent procurement of large mainframes from Japan before they joined the embargo. National Informatics Centre staked a claim for importing four systems. The government negotiated with Japanese companies for not only the transfer of the complete maintenance and minor repair know-how to NIC but also uninterrupted supply of spare parts for the life time of the systems. A very high end system was installed in New Delhi for the NIC headquarters to serve all central government departments and other attached offices as the main hub as well as the northern and central regions. Three others were installed to serve state governments from regional centres at Pune for western states, Bhubaneswar for eastern and north-eastern states, and Hyderabad for southern states respectively.

By 1986, every state government wanted to have their own centres from NIC, and made strong representation to the central government with offer of adequate office space to NIC in their secretariat buildings. This required a major decision for wide area computer-communication connectivity. Rajiv Gandhi, the then prime minister of India, decided that it would be advantageous to expand NICNET, giving not only connectivity to state capitals but also to all district collectorates in one step instead of two.

National Informatics Centre made in-depth technology status and forecast analysis in the spirit of IPAG and searched for a technology which should

• Take the load of a predominantly sparse and infrequent information flow between districts, and between the district and the state capital;
• Be achieved at the lowest possible cost for installation and maintenance at the districts;
• Be capable of seamlessly connected to indigenous computers/ personal computers (PCs) to be installed in the district headquarters;
• Give the lowest possible total system cost for the vast geographical spread of the country while giving high uptime with viable support staff.

National Informatics Centre discovered that there was a promising satellite earth station technology, still in the beta stage, requiring more development efforts to confidently deploy it for a large wide area network. When NIC approached the company, Equatorial Inc. of the US, it refused to sell the product. It was largely due to Equatorial's lack of confidence to sell them to India as only a rudimentary network was operational in the US itself. National Informatics Centre technically had examined their product, then called 'Very-low-aperture Earth

Stations', and found that it ideally suited the NICNET requirements, if NIC could import and deploy these in several districts along with the design know-how, superpose NIC's own R&D in communication software, and spread the network to the rest of the districts.

Department of Telecommunications (DoT) opposed the proposal of NIC and contended that their terrestrial telecom network should be utilized for district-level network at a cost of nearly Rs 5,000 million, as against NIC's proposal for the satellite-based network of Rs 900 million, on the ground that the proposed technology is not proven. However, Rajiv Gandhi and the then finance minister V.P. Singh were confident of NIC's ability to make the new technology work in India. Further negotiations with Equatorial Inc. resulted in their decision to not only sell the product to NIC but also transfer know-how for manufacture to a new joint venture partnership with them through a joint sector company to be called 'ITI Equatorial Satcom Ltd.' (IESL). The entire production for the first three years was solely purchased by NIC for setting up the district-level NICNET.

National Informatics Centre set up a full-fledged R&D unit for developing the communication software needed to install and manage such a nationwide network. It became a 'win-win' proposition for NIC, IESL, and Equatorial Inc. Technical experts from West Germany and Australia came to study the successful implementation by NIC and later set up similar satcom networks in Europe and Australia. Thereafter this technology, renamed VSAT, spread worldwide. Thus India became the second country after the US to build a VSAT network, and for some-time NICNET was the largest nationwide government VSAT network in the world. Again, in the first half of the 1990s, India (through NIC) scored a first in the country to set up a high bandwidth Ku-band VSAT network with a purchase-cum-technology arrangement with Gilat of Israel and Hughes of the US.

For handling hardware and software, as a guiding philosophy, NIC adopted a well tested method originally promoted by Homi Bhabha in atomic energy—assimilate the latest know-how obtained from developed countries, modify them to suit Indian requirements, and superpose local R&D continuously thereafter to keep it contemporary and even excel, all the while keeping cost minimization in purview.

By the year 2000 (Seshagiri 1993), NICNET had a high capacity master earth station and an international gateway at Delhi, lower capacity gateways at Mumbai, Bangalore, Chennai, and Calcutta, 800 C-band C-200 VSATs, 32 high speed C-band SCPC VSATs, 250 GILAT Ku-band Frequency and Time Division Multiple Access (FTDMA) VSATs, 150 Hughes Ku-band Time Division Multiple Access (TDMA) VSATs, and numerous Direct PC broadcast Ro-VSATs. By then a host of application enabling software, many of them indigenous, were hosted, including mail service, directory service, Electronic Data Interchange (EDI), intercity simultaneous point-to-point and multipoint video conferencing, web services, authorization and authentication software, and web directory user agent service among several others. Network decentralization was achieved by installing bhawan-wise LANs in Delhi, secretariat LANs in state capitals, and hub-based wireless MANs. Over 2500 IT specialists developed thousands of application software packages and databases for domain information access, MIS, DSS, GIS, and analytics for the central, state, and district offices, and some public sector units like FCI. To administer and obtain feedback corrections on the system, National Informatics Centre-Ministerial Coordination Committees (NMCCs), NSCCs, and National Informatics Centre-District Coordination Committees (NDCCs) numbering over 600 were set up which set goals and priorities. and also monitor and make mid-course corrections apart from spreading the IT-based work culture. To give promotional and commercial impetus to the activities of NIC, the following organizations were created:

- NIC Services Inc (NICSI), a section-25 company;
- National Centre for Trade Information as a joint venture with India Trade Promotion Organization (ITPO);
- Regional Computer Centres (RCCs) as autonomous societies for training and related academic work;
- Research and Educational Network of NIC (RENNIC) to support academic/research work of many organizations under Indian Council of Medical Research (ICMR), Indian Council of Social Science Research (ICSSR), Indian Council of Agricultural Research (ICAR), and Department of Biotechnology (DBT), Government of India. Council of Scientific and Industrial Research (CSIR), and University Grants Commission (UGC);
- National IT Promotion Units (NITPUs) with strong network based EC/EDI facilitation for supporting exporters at seventy major cities and towns.

In the following decade, the momentum of growth and innovations continued. By 2005, gateway nodes were established in fifty-three central departments, thirty-five state secretariats, 602 district collectorates, and over 1000 blocks. They provided various ICT services, VSAT-based broad band facilities, extensive video conferencing to 400 cities/towns, terrestrial fibre optic leased line circuits up to 34 mbps (E3), up to 5.8 Giga band terrestrial Radio Frequency (RF) circuits, Web- (Virtual Private Network/Secure Socket Layer) VPN/SSL, Multi-protocol Label Switching (MPLS) Layer S3 and S2, smart card facilitation, and disaster recovery centres superposed on NICNET.

Projects on Government Informatics

In over 3,000 projects on government informatics—big and small—implemented by NIC, over a thousand had substantive impact. A tiny fraction of these are given here as illustrations:

• Beginning with the 1991 general election, the election results were carried online from every constituency via NICNET and the running status was conveyed to the public by Doordarshan and Press Information Bureau. Every Lok Sabha election since then, as well as many assembly elections of states, was similarly broadcast online supported by a web-based newsmagazine. For Lok Sabha and Rajya Sabha a detailed MIS and a query based parliament information system is in operation with a store of millions of pages of classified parliament information on details of proceedings of committees, house debates, and FAQs among numerous others[*]. Similar support is given to several state legislatures including a model state-of-the-art reporting system for Gujarat Vidhan Sabha.

• National Informatics Centre set up computer centres linked to NICNET in the Supreme Court by 1991, all eighteen high courts and their benches by 1997, and over 430 district courts by 1999. Project COURTIS has implemented the List of Business Information System (LOBIS), filing counter computerization, pending case status, Judgement Information System (JUDIS) cause lists, Daily Orders Web DBs, and Citation Information of Reported Cases (SUPLIS) among others, providing access to judges, lawyers, litigants, and the public through e-kiosks, and the internet via NICNET. Video conferencing systems are

---

[*] http://parliamentofindia.nic.in and http://rajyasabha.nic.in

being installed to speed up justice. According to the statement of one of the chief justices of India this had helped the reduction of pending cases with Supreme Court from 1,80,000 to 16,000 within three years.

• For promoting transparency and receptivity in administration, as recommended by Department of Administrative Reforms and Public Grievances, an online public grievances monitoring system was developed and implemented in most of the central ministries/departments.

• 'India Image' website on internet presents the latest perspective of India and its government on internet.[†]

• Since 1990, on an annual average, 1,00,000 man weeks of training at various levels was imparted to officers and to the staff of the central and state governments to make them maximally self-reliant in IT applications in their domains areas. Training programmes were also customized to suit the requirements of individual central departments and state governments.

• On the recommendation of the Prime Minister's IT Task Force, NIC along with the Government of Maharashtra and the Warana Vibhag Shikshan Mandal implemented the 'Warana Wired Village Project' as a real life demonstration of integrated development of the Cooperation Movement at grassroot level through IT tools and NICNET. A measurable impact on the socioeconomic development over a networked cluster of seventy contiguous villages around Warana in the Kolhapur and Sangli districts were observed. With facilitation booths, RF networking, and substantive training of the more educated villagers in the seventy villages, the area got exposure to world knowledge, implementation of a local MIS and GIS in Marathi, and supplementing with tele-education at primary and higher levels. The success led the Pravara Cooperative at Shirdi to implement, with initial NIC technical assistance, the networking of about 200 villages with their own funding and initiative. This IT-led grassroot-level development model has begun spreading to other parts of the country.

• Seventy percent of the treasuries in the country were computerized by the year 2000 and over 15 per cent additionally by 2010. With online budget control of treasuries along with IT tools for state budgets, a significant impact on monitoring of state financial system has been realized.

[†] www.nic.in

• For urban planning, a GIS-based utility mapping project has been established for Delhi, including roads, water lines, sanitary lines, and cable routes. The success has prompted several states like Tamil Nadu to initiate implementation of similar projects in their capital cities replete with cadastral mapping.

• General Information System Terminal (GISTNIC) provides wide-ranging information to the government and the public on various aspects of the Indian economy, including the monthly review, tourism, hotel guide, polytechnic guide, census, and village amenities. Data warehousing facilitates in-depth analytics.

• Jointly with Ministry of Rural Areas, NIC has implemented or supported the land records computerization in 514 districts by the year 2000, and almost all districts subsequently. For example, the software of the highly visible project of Karnataka called 'Bhoomi' was basically developed by NIC but its high degree of success is due to the visionary implementation by the officers of the state itself. Training was imparted to over 3000 personnel in the revenue departments of states/UTs.

• By the year 2000 the Indian Customs EDIF Act-based EDI system (ICES) and a system for excise revenue and monitoring (SERMON) were implemented in most of the main centres, including customs linkage with DGFT, seaports, airports, and banks through EDI.

• Jointly with the Finance Ministry, a computerized Central Pension Accounting Office (CPAO) was set up, completely eliminating manual registers and thereby creating a model 'paperless office' with full NICNET connectivity with administrative departments and access through internet. For the benefit of all government personnel a standardized composite payroll system has been implemented. Along with the office of the Controller General of Audit, Project (Pay and Accounts Office) PAO-2000 was implemented to utilize IT with the business rules of PAOs so as to make the work of PAOs more efficient and timely; this is a culmination of a comprehensive support to the entire accounting system of all the ministries/departments and attached offices of the government.

• Project 'Yojana' affords real-time monitoring for plan expenditure by NCT of Delhi. Similar systems for several other states are also in place.

- Project 'e-Tender' gives a comprehensive web-based solution for publishing any tender launched by government to increase transparency, efficiency, and fairness in government purchases.

- With agriculture still having a high impact on the Indian economy, very comprehensive network-based databases and analytics have been put in place jointly with the Ministry of Agriculture. These have been supporting MIS and DSS in the central ministry of agriculture and those in several states on a regular basis, many since the year 1990. These include Agricultural Resources Information System Network (AGRISNET) up to block level offices for facilitating agricultural extension services and agribusiness; AGMARKNET rapidly growing towards a target to network 7000 agricultural produce wholesale markets and 32,000 rural markets; Agricultural Marketing Information Network (ARISNET) supporting agriculture research; SEEDNET for Seed MIS; COOPNET for enabling access eventually to 93,000 Agricultural Primary Credit Societies (PACS) and Agricultural Cooperative Marketing Societies; HORTNET for horticulture; FERTNET for facilitating the integration of nutrient management at the farm level; PPIN for plant protection; APHNET for animal production and health; FISHNET on fisheries; AFPINET on Agricultural and Food processing industries; and ARINET on agricultural and rural industries. This coverage is regarded as one of the more extensive ones in Agri-ICT even compared to more developed countries.

- For supporting decentralized development initiatives of the Panchayati Raj Institutions (PRIs) initiated in 1992, a Panchayati Raj Administration Software called 'Priasoft' was developed as an umbrella software catering to the administrative needs as well as for monitoring the accounts of PRIs by the state departments of rural development and the Comptroller and Auditor General (CAG) Office, and published on the web for transparency. Priasoft is adopted by several states like Orissa, Karnataka, Tamil Nadu, Madhya Pradesh, and Andhra Pradesh.[‡]

Projects on Security Related ICT

Over the past two decades NIC was called upon to assist with special security related ICT projects mainly concerning ICT security, Food

---

[‡] panchayat.nic.in; ori.nic.in/priasoft; and sio@ap.nic.in

Security, Financial Security, Environmental Security, Border Security, and National Security. One illustrative project in each of these six areas is outlined here.

ICT Security

National Informatics Centre's extensive networking of the north-eastern states invited the attention of some extremist groups. National Informatics Centre Net was subjected to repeated cyber attacks defacing the north-eastern websites and databases. Forced by necessity, some innovative cyber security software were developed, which later helped to combat other cyber offensives from some inimical countries.

Food Security

Since 1995, NIC has been giving high-end ICT support to the Public Distribution System (PDS) (Seshagiri 1996). By the dawn of the new millennium these massive efforts were consolidated into an 'Integrated Information System for Foodgrain Management (IISFM)' with the on-line integration of workflow of FCI from their geographically distributed depots with the MIS and DSS at the headquarters by networking nearly 700 depots, district offices, regional offices, zonal offices, and head office. FCI mobilized massive human resources exceeding 2,000 personnel who were well trained in ICT.[§] In addition, most of the organizations involved in the procurement, distribution, and management, including Confed and Hindustan Warehouse Corporation (HWC), have been networked through this project.

Financial Security

Emergency requests and directives often posed challenging problems and resulted in rewarding innovations. A case in point is the Harshad Mehta financial fraud case investigated by a special court in Mumbai. The court issued a directive to NIC to break the security codes on several computers seized without losing any substantive information buried within. There were security barriers built presumably with special assistance. National Informatics Centre developed innovative security code breaking techniques and unearthed the cache of information that helped as an important input to the special court to bring the culprits to justice.

[§] http://iisfm.nic.in

Environmental Security

National Informatics Centre's Pune regional centre reacted with humanitarian instinct when the Latur earthquake devastated a vast area, by positioning a portable VSAT van at the epicentre with in a short time of getting the information. Messages were relayed on VSATs about the post-disaster needs of the local people to all neighbouring districts and Mumbai as one of the inputs to rush food, medical supplies, and other requirements. Similar assistance was given during some cyclone disasters in Orissa, Tamil Nadu, and Andhra Pradesh.

National Security

In the wake of the Kargil conflict, the Army Head Quarter and Airforce Head Quarter through signals-in-charge sought the installation of a subnet of NICNET in Kargil with links to their headquarters in Delhi. With efficient support of the air force, NIC created a multi-node VSAT subnet in Kargil along with a special software developed within a short time. The successful deployment served a tactical move of the defence forces. National Informatics Centre, out of dire necessity, developed the concept of 'reusable software components' ab initio to meet such emergency security requirements, long before such a software technology concept became popular in the IT industry.

Special Research & Development Projects

As a human resource policy, NIC consciously implemented several frontline R&D projects to inculcate an ambience of innovation even in service functions. Some illustrative projects are outlined here.

Nonlinear SESAM Project

Between the mid-1970s and mid-1980s, there was a total embargo from the US and allied countries on India importing large and sophisticated Computer Aided Design (CAD) software. This affected the design and development of engineering structures even by the civilian sector. To overcome this, NIC launched a CAD project under the Norwegian Programme 'NORAD' in 1981 and negotiated with a Norwegian company for acquiring high-end CAD software. The package 'Sesam', which was extensively deployed in the design of the North Sea Oil Platform, was identified as best suited. Sesam was powerful on the linear CAD but weak on many nonlinear capabilities. National Informatics

Centre offered to develop the nonlinear system to higher sophistication on commercial terms in exchange for the willingness of the Norwegian company to make available the complete source code of the Sesam software.

This created a 'Win-Win' situation for both. The entire nonlinear package so developed at a low cost, with over a million lines of code, gave to India access to total solution of one of the field-tested high-end CAD software. National Informatics Centre assisted several organizations with their CAD problems, including Oil and Natural Gas Commission (ONGC) and Handicraft Design Centres.

•   With the experience of Sesam and other related software, NIC developed ab initio a Computer Aided Design/Computer Aided Manufacture (CAD/CAM) software called 'Collab CAD' with collaborative facility, Finite Element Analysis, Virtual Reality, and other features, which has assisted some design efforts in Bhabha Atomic Research Centre (BARC), Vikram Sarabhai Space Centre (VSSC), Aeronautics Development Agency (ADA), National Aeronautics Laboratory (NAL), National Petrochemicals India Ltd. (NPCIL), and many other high-tech organizations. To meet the increasing demand, a consortium of some of the above mentioned organizations and a few private industries has been set up.

•   Distributed Geographical Information System has been developed for applications like the National Natural Resources Informatics system. Other GIS initiatives include a web-based coastal regulation system.

•   In the first half of the 1990s, 'CAPES', which is a web-based computer-aided paperless examination system, was developed and initially utilized successfully by the Union Public Service Commission (UPSC) for an examination of over 10,000 candidates. Since then it has helped Steel Authority of India (SAIL), DOEACC-CCC, and several other organizations with their all-India examinations.

Platform for Governmental Promotion of the ICT Industry

In 1984, IPAG, NIC, Computer Division, and Appropriate Automation Promotion Centre (AAPC) were consolidated into a wing under the of DoE called Computers, Communication and Instrumentation wing (CCI-Wing) under the director general of NIC. The CCI-Wing was also given the responsibility for the promotion of the ICT industry. The technical secretariat for this was IPAG/NIC/Computer Division from 1984 to 1988.

The liberalized IT policy for computer hardware, software, and applications of 1984 and the 1986 policy on software export, development, and training emanated from CCI-wing by providing technical support. When NIC was transferred from DoE to the Planning Commission, it was again called upon to coordinate the Prime Minister's IT Task Force of 1997 to put in place an extensive set of policies to give a boost to the IT industry through further liberalisation and globalization. In the Appendix, an in-depth citation analysis by *Science Reporter* of NISCAIR is given with excerpts referring to NIC/CCI-Wing (Editorial Staff, *Science Reporter* 2007).

National Informatics Centre nurtured the concept of government-facilitated Software Technology Parks (STPs) using satellite earth stations to promote small and medium software export companies who later became significant players in the Indian software export growth. From 1979, NIC successfully promoted the concept of software and database export and import 'double funneling' between developed and developing countries as well as among developing countries using satellite earth stations through UN forums like UNESCO (Final Report of Advisory Group of Experts 1979), UNIDO (UNIDO Secretariat, 1994), UNESCAP, and United Nations Centre on Transnational Corporations (UNCTC).

A United Nations Centre on Transnational Corporations report recommended:

External gateways can be given to competent software export houses to link up with such nascent systems installed in the location of the competitors abroad ... By stationing their manpower in India itself software export houses can maximize the advantage of low labour costs in India. This will also help the manufacturer abroad to minimize his cost on the development of system and utility software .... (Seshagiri 1984)

The chairman of the Electronics Commission, who sponsored the participation of the representative of NIC in the preparation of the above report, suggested that the above recommendation be reflected in the New Computer Policy of 1984. Between 1984 and 1988 CCI-Wing in general and NIC in particular evolved the concept of STPs as government-facilitated promotional entities in various cities. However, with the transfer of NIC to the Planning Commission in September

1988, the CCI-Wing was disbanded and the creation of the first two STPs at Bangalore and Bhubaneswar, for which approvals of ministries concerned were either obtained or were in an advanced stage, got shelved until their resurrection in 1990. Thereafter DoE constituted a National Advisory Board for STPs with the director general of NIC as chairman.⁵

IMPACT ASSESSMENTS

Both internal and external assessments of the impact of NIC have been made. The project-wise internal assessment of the impact is submitted to Parliament annually as 'Performance Budget'.

The main conclusions of assessment made by external agencies are given below.

Assessment by the Standing Committee on IT of Parliament

In December 2003, the standing committee submitted a report to the Thirteenth Lok Sabha (fifty-sixth report) whose main conclusion is reproduced here (Standing Committee-Loksabha, 2003):

NIC was created way back in September, 1976 with an allocation of meagre Rs 3.44 crores plus a UNDP contribution of USD 4.4 million for funding the activities set for it. Over the last about two and a half decades of its existence, NIC has crossed various landmarks towards providing common IT infrastructure, creating vast wealth of sustained domain and IT knowledge, spanned throughout the country and has built up wherewithal except financial strength to provide the basic e-governance vehicle. The committee feels that the requirements and expectations have grown substantially for moving to new Information age. Therefore, NIC as the nodal organization for e-governance has to gear up itself to face the challenges. This includes upgrading of NICNET up to each block level and ultimately up to the village Panchayat level with a view to provide reliable and safe information backbone, sustain different applications, interface with industry for building their effective participation and lead the e-governance through R&D initiatives. These tasks for NIC to usher in new Information Age will not be easy unless it is given the flexibility and freedom as provided to some of the other organizations and scientific departments like Indian Space Research Organisation (ISRO), BARC, and DRDO.

⁵ For an in-depth analysis of the history of STPs one may refer to Dinesh Sharma's *The Long Revolution: The Birth and Growth of India's IT Industry*.

Assessment by Ernst & Young

Ernst and Young, a private consulting company, made an analysis of the existing structure of NIC. Their report of January 2005 suggested, among others, appropriate outsourcing models relevant to NIC which are practical in the contemporary context of government organizations and the existence of a vibrant private IT industry (Ernst & Young, 2005).

Assessment by Administrative Reforms Commission (Report on E-Governance-ARC, 2008)

In 2008, the Administrative Reforms Commission has submitted to the Government of India, a 'Report on e-Governance'. Concerning NIC, some of the observations and recommendations are given below.

The efforts of the National Informatics Centre (NIC) to connect all the district headquarters during the eighties was a very significant development. From the early nineties, IT technologies were supplemented by ICT technologies to extend its use for wider sector wise applications with policy emphasis on reaching out to rural areas.

An analysis of NIC's strengths and weaknesses (refer Annex 5) helps bring out the role that NIC needs to play under the NeGP. The Committee feels that the only way NIC can scale up its involvement and help meet expectations is by expanding its current role as a technology service provider to that of a technology manager for systems across all levels of Government. Para 7 has clearly brought out the imperative of retaining certain critical capabilities within the Government. NIC, as a manager of technology has an important role to play in assisting Departments retain strategic control of e-governance systems while leveraging private sector to the extent necessary to address capacity gaps...

Existing resources within NIC should be better utilized by focusing them on high priority areas and projects. To the extent possible multiple versions and implementations of the same project should be avoided so as to rationalise the resources and spread them across more initiatives.

A strong interface for project implementation should be worked out between the government agencies like NIC and the private sector.

For supplementing its resources for application development and for rollout of large projects, NIC could empanel a set of private Application Service Providers (ASPs).

REFERENCES

Administrative Reforms Commission, Government of India (2008), 'Report on E-Governance', New Delhi: Administrative Reforms Commission, Government of India.

Editorial Staff, *Science Reporter* (2007), 'A Citational Milestone History: Information Technology in India', in *Science Reporter*, Special Issue on 60 Years of Indian Science, 44(8), New Delhi, August, pp. 30–7.

Ernst & Young Consulting Team (2005), 'National Informatics Centre: Technical Services', *Report to DOE*, New Delhi: Ernst & Young.

NIC (1999), 'Sector-wise Details of Software Packages Developed for State Governments: Horizontal Transfer Plan', NIC Printed Report, New Delhi: NIC.

Seshagiri, N. (1983), 'Improvisation of Government Productivity: A Case Study of NIC', International Symposium on Electronics for Productivity, New Delhi: Electronics Commission.

———— (1984), 'Transborder Trade in Data Services and Information Flow', Consultant Report, New York: United Nations Centre on Transnational Corporations, April.

———— (1988), 'The Role of Information Systems in Development Planning in India: A Case Study of DISPLAN of NICNET', mimeo, Singapore: Expert Group of Integrating Information Systems, Technology in Local/ Regional Development Planning.

———— (1989), 'IT as a Tool for Development: Experience with Computer Communication Network and Future Vision', mimeo, APO Workshop on IT, Kuala Lumpur: Asian Productivity Organization.

———— (1993), 'Road Map of Evolution of NICNET towards Globalisation of Computer-Communication', *Electronics Information and Planning*, New Delhi: Electronics Commission, pp. 595–608.

———— (1996), 'Information System for Safety Net Implementation', in N. Seshagiri, J. Salmona, I.P. David (eds), *Information Systems for Electronics in Transition (ISET-IC)*, New Delhi: Tata McGraw-Hill, pp. 362 –77.

Seshagiri, N., K.K.K. Kutty, N. Vijayaditya, Y.K. Sharma, D.P. Bobde, and M. Moni (1987), 'NICNET: A Hierarchic Distributed Computer-Communication Network for Decision Support in Indian Government', *Proceedings of the International Conference on Computer-Communication for Developing Countries (CCDC-87)*, Geneva : International Council for Computer Communication.

Sharma, Dinesh (2009), *The Long Revolution: The Birth and Growth of India's IT Industry*, New Delhi: HarperCollins, pp. 303–57.

Standing Committee on IT, Thirteenth Lok Sabha (2003), 'Working of National Informatics Centre (NIC)', New Delhi: Lok Sabha Secretariat.

UNESCO (1979), Final Report of UNESCO Advisory Group of Experts in Information, Paris: UNESCO, September, p. 50.

UNIDO Secretariat (1994), 'Globalization of IT and Computer Communication in India', based on Consultant (N. Seshagiri) Report, 1993, Geneva: UNIDO, IPCT. 198 (Spec.), January.

Annexure*

A Citational Milestone History—Information Technology in India

Information Technology has carved for itself a steadily growing niche in the industrial, social, economic and export landscape of India. Science Reporter *presents its history through link-annotations of Citations of Indian and International industry watchers and economic, organizational and policy analysts. India's IT miracle is the result of a consciously planned unfolding of liberalization and globalization, where each of the milestones outlined here contributed substantially to create the conditions necessary for the achievements of the next and other milestones.*

THE ELECTRONICS COMMISSION

Pursuant to the major recommendations of the Bhabha Committee Report, a need was felt to crate a single-point regulatory and promotional authority for Electronics and Computers that could create nationwide ambience for their growth without being unduly subject to the inelastic rules of the Government and guide the industry in the shortest possible time and the best possible manner.

* *Science Reporter*, a reputed popular science magazine under the National Institute of Science Communication and Information Resources (NISCAIR), CSIR, Government of India, in the round up of sixty years of Indian Science, in their August 2007 special issue, published their research study of the evolution of Information Technology in India (Vol. 44, No. 8, pp. 30–7). NISCAIR has given permission to reproduce here the following excerpts verbatim from this article. For a fuller account, see the entire article.

The Electronics Commission was set up in February 1970 under the Chairmanship of M.G.K. Menon. The DOE was set up on 26 June 1970, with Menon as the Secretary of the Department. The Department functioned directly under the PM. It was considered a 'scientific department'.

The Electronics Commission under M.G.K. Menon gave a strong focus and visibility to the Electronics and Computer technology industry and applications through the creation of numerous promotional bodies: The Information, Planning and Analysis Group (IPAG), Technology Development Council, National Informatics Centre, Appropriate Automation Promotion Programme, Radar Development Council, Computer Maintenance Corporation, Electronic Trade and Technology Development Corporation, Semi Conductors Ltd., among others. These organizations, in turn, crated a positive ambience and buoyancy that was taken for granted during subsequent growth of the industry.

The regulatory role of the Electronics Commission, however, had to contend with the overall national ethos of the time when 'profit was broadly regarded as a sin and private initiatives were tolerated as necessary appendages'. In spite of this, the Commission steered the best permissible via media between the Public and Private Sectors.

PRIVATE INITIATIVES THAT REWROTE THE ETHOS

The credit for changing such negative ethos goes to a handful of Indian companies whose sustained achievements have bestowed on them a lead position to this day, standing up to international competition.

TCS was the first Indian software services company to exploit the tremendous opportunities in the export market. In the 1980s, TCS was joined in this segment by several companies like Hinditron, Patni Computer Systems, Datamatics, Infosys, Wipro and Tata Burroughs Limited.... (*Courtesy:* N.R. Narayana Murthy, Ref. 2)

THE 1985 LIBERALIZATION POLICY

A turning point for the computer industry came in the wake of a tech-savvy Prime Minister Shri Rajiv Gandhi coming to power in 1984.

• Seshagiri had been one of Rajiv Gandhi's 'Computer Boys'... Rajiv's patronage encouraged Seshagiri to modify the computer policies that were being debated by the Electronics Commission and adapt them to the urgent need for the computerization of the government, industry and business, and to set a new tempo for the country to move forward...

The new computer policy was announced on 19 November 1984.

(*Courtesy:* C.R. Subramanian, Ref. 1)

• Within the formation of the Software policy, one of the dominant features is that a single person, Seshagiri, the DoE Additional Secretary, during a crucial part of the 1980s played such an important role. It it Seshagiri who is credited with being 'the architect' and 'the moving spirit' behind the 1984 and 1986 policies and he argued in favour of liberalization not because any interest group wanted it, but because it was his personal conviction. (*Courtesy:* Richard Heeks, Ref. 3)

THE 1986 PROTO-GLOBALIZATION POLICY

With TCS having demonstrated the feasibility of software exports from India, strong demand arose from a number of big, medium and small companies to create a policy framework that would encourage the creation of Software Export as a high-thrust industry.

• The software import provision linked with Seshagiri's theory of 'flood-in, flood-out' evoked a mixed response. Well-entrenched companies like TCS welcomed the proposal. But the smaller companies were afraid that the domestic software industry would be killed. Seshagiri maintained that by importing international software, the local industry could add value and re-export, and this was better than trying to develop afresh what had already been done elsewhere. (*Courtesy* : C.R. Subramanian, Ref. 1)

• After the computer policy was announced on 19 November 1984, the growth of computer production went up within a year to about 100 per cent in physical terms and 65 per cent in monetary terms and the prices declined by 50 per cent. During the same period the average added value of indigenous manufacture increased by about 15 per cent. This accelerated growth of the computer industry had posed numerous problems for the software activities calling for rationalization of the policy for import and manufacture of software and using this base for promoting software exports. ...The Seventh Plan target for Software export is USD 300 million, which is less than 0.6 per cent of the inter-country trade in software. This clearly underlines the need for formulating a software policy along a liberal framework conductive to long-term growth in software development and exports.

(From the Preamble to the policy on computer software export, software development and training—*Gazette of Indian Notification*, Part I, Section 1, pp. 807–10, dated Dec. 27, 1986, signed by N. Seshagiri, Additional Secretary to GOI; Ref. 10).

• The 'software import-against-software export' policy of 1986 created a win-win situation for both software companies and the end-users. This policy made available world-class imported software, hitherto practically a banned item, to end-users. (*Courtesy* : N.R. Narayana Murthy, Ref. 2).

IMPACT OF FINANCIAL LIBERALIZATION & ECONOMIC REFORMS

• Prime Minister P.V. Narasimha Rao and Finance Minister Manmohan Singh bestowed the chance to succeed on the 'prepared minds' of the leaders of Indian software export companies. Since then, successive finance ministers and commerce ministers strengthened the reform process. (*Courtesy*: N.R. Narayana Murthy, Ref. 2).

SOFTWARE TECHNOLOGY PARKS

The 1984 and 1986 policy on Computer Software, Export Software Development and Training outlined the procedural and institutional mechanisms for utilizing satellite communication and promoting software exports as well as Government organized facilities for assisting small and medium companies in this effort. The Software Technology Parks were conceived in pursuance of these cabinet approached policies.

• Access to computers abroad through satellite links is a technically sound approach for export of software … We envisage exports to the tune of at least $ 100 million per year within the next 3 to 4 years through this alone. (*Courtesy*: Interview of N. Seshagiri by Sunil Agarwal, 'Rationale of the New Computer Policy', Ref. 7, Dataquest, December 1984)

• In his tenure, he (N. Vittal) realized that an inexpensive satellite data communication facility, easy access to world-class technology, zero or low tariffs, an increase in the technical talent pool, and creation of branch equity abroad were necessary if Indian software export companies were to show high growth rates using the offshore development model … (*Courtesy*: N.R. Narayana Murthy, Ref. 2)

CATALYTIC ROLE OF NASSCOM

• A privately managed association called National Association of Software and Services Companies (NASSCOM) was founded in 1988 with 38 members. By 1999 it had 464 members representing 95% of the software industry revenues…. NASSCOM's leaders interact continually with politicians and policymakers, and the association is represented on many influential committees of the Government of India…. NASSCOM is also the sole source of IT industry data in India. Its annual Strategic Review provides the only detailed and up-to-date figures on employment revenues, exports, and market share for the software and other IT industries … (*Courtesy*: Anna Lee Saxenian, Ref. 4)

IT ACTION PLAN: BOOSTER DOSE OF POLICIES

To give a boost to the IT industry, the GOI set up an IT Task Force with J. Singh as Chairman, N. Chandrababu Naidu and M.G.K. Menon as Co-Chairmen and N. Seshagiri as Member-Convenor.

• The Task Force moved extremely quickly—far more so than is the norm in India—and released its information Technology Action Plan a year after the group was convened. The Task Force also developed an unusually open and transparent process for collecting information and formulating recommendations, a process that involved consultation with an unusually wide variety of public and private sector actors.... The IT Action Plan is the most ambitious IT-related policy proposal in India since the Computer Policy of 1984 and the Software Policy of 1986. The Plan lists 108 recommendations of 'revisions and additions to the existing policy and procedures for removing bottlenecks and achieving a preeminent status for India.' And it sets as targets for 2008, $ 50 billion in software exports and 'IT penetration for all.' (*Courtesy:* Anna Lee Saxenian, Ref. 4)

SUSTAINED MOMENTUM THROUGH SELF-PROPELLED GROWTH

Since 1984, the quest has been: What policies are to be made, enacting which no more policies are necessary. This evolution broadly led to the IT Action Plan 1998 and the National Telecom Policy—1999 and positive action-oriented steps in subsequent years.

Growth of Indian Software Industry (in $ million)

Year	Exports	No. of Firms	Av. Revenue	Exp/T. Revenue
1980	4.0	21	190,476	50
1984	25.3	35	722,857	50
1990	105.4	700	150,571	N/A
2000	5287	816	7,598,039	71.8
2004	12200	3170	7,003,154	73.9

(*Courtesy:* Based on compilation and estimation of Rafiq Dossani, Ref. 12)

The citation milestone history of the IT Industry in India is charted through a linked-presentation of the analysis and findings of reputed IT specialists of high national/international standing: CEOs of Companies (C.R. Subramanian, N.R. Narayana Murthy), IT economists (Richard Heeks, Anna Lee Saxenian, World Bank specialists) and technologists (S.K. Mathur, R. Dossani). Such a presentation brings together the importance of events and identification of milestones as perceived by leading analysts at the epochs when they actually transpired, instead of looking back at earlier milestones from the present vantage of much higher IT development and trade.

REFERENCES

Agarwal Sunil, (1984), 'Rationale of the New Computer Policy', Interview of N. Seshagiri on 22, 23 and 24 November 1984, in *Dataquest*, pp. 39–58 (December).

Dataquest Staff (1985), 'The Policy Revisited', Interview of N. Seshagiri in *Dataquest*, pp. 41–8, (December).

Government of India Gazette Notification dated 27 December 1986, pp. 807–10, on, 'Policy on Computer Software Export, Software Development and Training' signed by N. Seshagiri, Additional Secretary to GOI.

Govt. of India extraordinary gazette notification, Part I–Section 1, No. 160 pp. 1–44, dated 25 July 1998, on 'IT Action Plan' signed by N. Seshagiri, Special Secretary to GOI.

Heeks, Richard (1996), *India's Software Industry: State Policy, Liberalization and Industrial Development*, Delhi: Sage Publications,.

Lee Saxenian, Anna (2001), 'Bangalore: The Silicon Valley of Asia', in *Center for Research on Economic Development and Policy Reforms*, February, Stanford University: USA.

Mathur, S.K. (1984), 'Indian IT Industry: A Performance Analysis', in *MPRA*, March, no. 2368, Munich personal RePec Archive, *Govt. of India Notification* on 'New Computer Policy' 19 November.

Malhotra, S. (1987), 'The New Software Policy—Seshagiri Clarifies,' *Dataquest*, pp. 82–95, (January).

Narayana Murthy, N.R. (2000), 'Making India a Significant IT Player in INDIA-Another Millennium', in *India Another Millennium?* Romila Thapar (ed.), New Delhi: Viking-Penguin Books.

Rafiq, Dossani (2006), *Origin and Growth of the Software Industry in India'*, *Asia-Pacific Center*, Stanford University: USA.

Subramanian C.R. (1992), *India and the Computer: A study of Planned Development*, New: Delhi: Oxford University Press.

V. RAJARAMAN

5 Impact of Computer Science Education
IIT Kanpur on Information Technology in India

The significant contributions of IIT Kanpur was spreading computer education to working professionals in mid-1960s and early 1970s, integrating computer science in all undergraduate educational programmes and developing human resource which contributed to the development of information technology (IT) industry in India in the 1970s and 1980s. The faculty members of computer science at IIT Kanpur also participated as consultants in developing IT industry and as policymakers in government bodies which enabled the growth of IT industry.

THE BEGINNING

Computing at IIT Kanpur began with the arrival of IBM 1620 in August 1964. IIT Kanpur was set up with the assistance of the United States Agency for International Development (USAID) which channeled the funding through the Kanpur Indo-American Programme (KIAP). KIAP was a consortium of nine major US universities which assisted IIT Kanpur by deputing visiting faculty members and by assisting in purchase of equipment (Subba Rao 2008). One of the major decisions taken by KIAP was to install a computer at IIT Kanpur. In 1964

IBM 1620 was a popular computer used by several universities in the US. It was a small digit-oriented computer with 60K digit main memory, three tape drives, and a punched card reader/writer. It had no disk and printer. Along with IBM 1620, IIT Kanpur also received twenty card punching machines to prepare programs and an IBM 407 accounting machine to print the punched card programs for IBM 1620 as well as its output punched cards. These machines were installed by Indian IBM engineers trained abroad. IBM 1620 had a Fortran II compiler, which in hindsight was the most important feature of the machine. Even though other computers were installed in India in 1964 such as the home-built Tata Institute of Fundamental Research Automatic Calculator (TIFRAC) at Tata Institute of Fundamental Research (TIFR), Mumbai, Russian Ural at Indian Statistical Institute (ISI), Kolkata, and IBM 1401s and ICL 1900s in some companies, unlike the IBM 1620, none of them had a high level language such as Fortran. As they used assembly language, very few specially trained programmers could use them. Further, their primary purpose was not education, whereas IBM 1620 was predominantly used for academic purpose. A number of initiatives in computer science education were taken for the first time in India at IIT Kanpur which had far reaching consequences on the development of IT in India. The most significant initiatives were:

• Developing and organizing ten-day' intensive residential courses in computing with hands-on training in programming computers. This course was taught thrice a year between 1964 and 1973 to scientists, engineers, and teachers from all over India. Over 1500 professionals were trained to program computers in these courses. This was instrumental in several organizations installing computers and using them productively.

• Developing a core course on computing which was made compulsory for all undergraduate students at IIT Kanpur. This pioneering initiative led several students to migrate to the IT industry later in their career. Several graduates used computers in their own engineering and scientific work.

• As affordable textbooks in computing were not available, several textbooks were written by IIT Kanpur faculty to be used both in the intensive courses and in the core course on computers (Rajaraman 1969, 1971b). These books on computer programming using Fortran and on computer-oriented numerical methods were widely used by students/ professionals in India. Over 50,000 books were sold between 1969 and 1976 spreading computer education.

• An M.Tech and PhD programme with computer science as major subject was initiated within Electrical Engineering Department encouraged by H.K. Kesavan, the then Head of Electronic Engineering Department in 1965–6. The students with M.Tech joined the emerging IT industry—Tata Consultancy Services (TCS), Electronics Corporation of India Ltd. (ECIL), and HCL, and later started their own IT companies. N.R. Narayana Murthy and Narendra Kale are notable alumni of this M.Tech programme. A doctoral programme in computer science was also started in 1966. Students who obtained PhD went to other IITs and started computer science programmes there. Several PhDs also joined the government (Department of Electronics) and were instrumental in implementing government policies in IT.

• A separate computer science programme awarding M.Tech degree was started in 1972 and this increased the number of M.Techs available to industry in India. Almost all IT companies such as TCS, HCL, Infosys, WIPRO, DCM, and ORG Systems which were then growing had M.Techs from IIT, in leadership positions in their design and development wings.

• In 1976 a B.Tech course in computer science was started, the first IIT to start such a course. The popularity of this course persuaded other IITs to start B.Tech course in computer science.

In the rest of this article we will expand on these initiatives and their impact on the development of Information Technology in India.

INTENSIVE COURSES IN COMPUTING

Prior to the arrival of IBM 1620 three professors led by Harry D. Huskey of the University of California, Berkeley, came to IIT Kanpur to prepare the ground work to receive the computer and train the IIT Kanpur faculty to run it and use it. After the computer started working reliably and the required system software and Fortran were installed, the first task was to recruit and train system programmers to maintain the software. The second task was to train IIT Kanpur faculty to program the computer and use it in their teaching and research.

The number of faculty at IIT Kanpur was quite small in 1964. H.D. Huskey took a proactive step and instead of restricting the course on programming to IIT Kanpur faculty, he planned it as a ten-day intensive course in computing to which scientists, engineers, and academics from various laboratories of Council of Scientific and Industrial Research (CSIR), Indian Agricultural Research Institute (IARI), Defence Research & Development Organisation (DRDO), and Indian Space Research Organisation (ISRO) and several universities were invited. No fee was charged. The programme was residential with all the participants staying in IIT Kanpur visitors' hostel. The course was intensive and required all the participants to program ten problems using Fortran, punch them on cards, execute the programs, correct errors and re-run programs until they executed successfully giving correct results. The course not only taught programming but also numerical methods appropriate for use of computers and the basics of logical operation of computers. Each course was attended by around fifty participants. Lectures were in the morning, followed by three laboratory sessions in three shifts. As we had twenty key punch machines, each laboratory group had twenty participants. Each laboratory session was of four hours and thus the last laboratory shift ended at midnight. By the end of the course each participant had written at least ten programs in Fortran. From the feedback received from participants it was clear that by the end of the course they had a good appreciation of computing and how the learning could be applied in their own scientific work. The visiting professors from the US left after a year. This course was so popular that it was given thrice a year from 1964 to 1975 by IIT Kanpur faculty. A total of over 1500 scientists and engineers were trained in these courses. This had a tremendous impact in spreading computer awareness and their applications to all the CSIR, DRDO, ISRO and IARI laboratories, and several universities and industries. This resulted in many of the participants initiating steps to install computers in their own institutions. These courses spread the reputation of IIT Kanpur as the centre of computer education.

The success of these courses made the IIT Kanpur faculty realize the pent-up demand for computer education for engineers/scientists working in various laboratories and industries, and led to the development of several short-term courses. Some of the courses given were Operations Research and Computer Methods (in collaboration with IIM Calcutta),

Assembly Language Programming and Real-time Systems, Decision Tables and their Applications, and Analogue and Digital Simulation.

In early 1965 H.D. Huskey arranged an International Conference on Computing (with funding from USAID) and persuaded several eminent professors to come to IIT Kanpur to share their thoughts on developments in computing and its role in education. About fifty participants from various organizations in India attended.Among those present from India, besides IIT Kanpur faculty, were A. Balasubramanian of DRDO, B. Nag of Jadavpur University, P.P. Gupta (then with International Computers Ltd. or ICL), S.R. Thakore (of Pysical Research Laboratory, Ahmedabad), and P.V.S. Rao (of TIFR). Invited lectures were given by M. Wilkes of Cambridge University, J. Bennet of Sydney University, A. Beltran of Mexico, and S. Barton of Control Data Corporation (CDC). One of the significant decisions taken at the end of the conference was to convert the IBM Computer Users Group (which was formed in 1964) to a professional society which was anointed Computer Society of India. It was registered later at DRDO, Hyderabad, where A. Balasubramanian was employed. The premier Society of Computer Professionals of India had its genesis at IIT Kanpur.

CORE COURSE IN COMPUTING

The undergraduate course at IIT Kanpur was of five years duration in 1964. The course had a common 'core curriculum' of three years and specialization of two years. The core curriculum had besides Physics, Chemistry, Mathematics, and Humanities and Social Sciences, a set of courses in engineering science and technical arts. Technical arts were practical courses in workshop and surveying. Computing was introduced in the curriculum as a technical arts course (numbered TA306) even though it should have been an engineering science course. This was a course with three lectures a week and a three-hour laboratory session. Students, however, were permitted to use the computer at any time as the computer centre functioned 24 hours a day, 7 days a week. The laboratory time was primarily used to guide students with their debugging problem. The course consisted of computer programming using Fortran and numerical methods necessary to solve engineering/science problems using computers. Besides these, simulations of some engineering problems using analogue computers were also part of the course. The course had one instructor-in-charge who delivered the lectures and several tutorial instructors, one per batch of twenty-five students. Tutorial instructors were teachers drawn from all departments who were interested in computing. The course was given every semester with 150 students and six instructors and was very popular. All students who graduated with a B.Tech had thus a good working knowledge of how to program a computer. Many students used the computer in their B.Tech project. Students of IIT Kanpur, when they joined industries, knew how to use computers and several migrated to their IT departments or were able to use computers in their design work. Several top managers in IT industry today did their B.Tech degree in mechanical, metallurgy, and chemical engineering, etc. All of them had their initiation in computing as students of TA 306. Notable among the early batch of B.Tech students of IIT Kanpur who went on to pioneer the IT industry in India and abroad are Som Mittal (currently president of National Association of Software Companies (NASCOM), Bhaskar Pramanik (Ex-CEO of Sun Microsystems), Saurabh Srivastava (CEO, IIS Infotech/Xansa), Prabhu Goyal (CEO, Dual Technologies), and Pradeep Sandhu (CEO, Juniper Systems) (Rajaraman 1969).

Another impact of this course as well as the intensive courses was the effort to write good textbooks in this subject. In 1965 there were no books published in India on computers. In fact, there were very few publications on computing. Notes on computer programming, numerical methods, and analogue computing were written by me and distributed to the students of intensive courses on computing and of the core course on computing (TA 306). They were printed in the Graphics Arts Centre of IIT Kanpur and sold at its book store. Later in 1969 a commercial publisher published *Principles of Computer Programming* after a lot of hesitation as publishers felt there was no market for books on computer programming (three publishers had declined to publish the book). I insisted on the price being kept low (Rs 15) so that it was affordable to students in India. To my surprise and that of the publisher 6,000 copies were sold in the first year. This demonstrated the pent-up demand to learn about computers in India. This was followed up by textbooks on *Computer Oriented Numerical Methods* (Rajaraman 1971a) and Analog Computation and Simulation (ibid.). These books had an important role in spreading IT education in India as they were low cost, easy to understand, and widely available.

POSTGRADUATE COURSE IN COMPUTER SCIENCE

In 1965, IIT Kanpur initiated postgraduate courses in engineering. H.K. Kesavan, who was the then head of the electrical engineering department, encouraged us to introduce a computer science option in the M.Tech programme in electrical engineering. This option started with a very small number of students (around eight). We were also encouraged to start a PhD in computer science. The primary aim of starting a doctoral programme was for the faculty to do research to improve their teaching and to train a pool of persons who could later take up academic position in Indian Institute of Technology and universities in this emerging area of computer science. Another aim was to strengthen and grow our own programme. Indian Institute of Technology Kanpur was the only place where a student interested in computer science could do an M.Tech during the mid-1960s. We got very good students from all over India. These students were well trained in computer science, particularly in systems programming and digital logic design. The unique aspect of the course at IIT Kanpur was the equal emphasis it gave to both software and hardware resulting in well-rounded engineers. Information technology industry was just starting in India and trying to build minicomputers. Several companies such as ECIL, WIPRO, HCL, ORG Systems, DCM Data Systems, and PSI were in hardware design and TCS was in software design. Indian Institute of Technology Kanpur's M.Tech students joined these companies and were pioneering in designing machines as well as in designing software systems. As pointed out earlier, some of them started their own IT companies later, the notable among them being N.R. Narayana Murthy (of Infosys) and Narendra Kale (of Kale Consultants).

PhDs from IIT Kanpur spawned computer science departments at IIT Delhi and IIT Madras. Several PhDs also joined the then department of electronics and attained positions of responsibility in guiding the growth of IT industry in India.

By the mid-1970s a thriving school of computer science was active at IIT Kanpur with around a dozen PhD students and around twenty-five postgraduate students and half a dozen faculty members specializing in computer science. Indian Institute of Technology Kanpur had a policy of encouraging faculty to provide consultancy to industry and to spend extended periods during the summer vacation with industry.

Several faculty members were consultants to companies such as ECIL, TCS, TELCO, and L&T.

In the early days of TCS (1970) a large number of IIT Kanpur students joined it. The in-house training programme of TCS for fresh graduates was planned by IIT Kanpur's computer science faculty and was also conducted by them. This was a trendsetter for other IT companies which were recruiting B.Techs in all engineering disciplines and training them in-house.

 With the growing popularity of the computer science course and its recognition by industry in India, the senate of IIT Kanpur approved in 1972 the starting of an independent computer science programme not coupled to the electrical engineering department. This was the first postgraduate computer science programme in India and gave further impetus to the growth of IT in India.

UNDERGRADUATE COURSE IN COMPUTER SCIENCE

Computer science as a discipline was growing and there was a need to introduce it as an undergraduate course. After a long debate in the IIT Kanpur senate it was decided to begin a B.Tech programme with a small enrollment of twenty students. The support of A. Bhattacharya, who was the director of IIT Kanpur at that time, was vital in initiating this visionary programme. The first batch of twenty students were admitted in 1978. To the surprise of the IIT faculty, the last student admitted to this programme was the 40th-ranked student in the All India Joint Entrance Examination (JEE) held by IITs. Thus we got very bright students in the first batch of B.Tech computer science. The curriculum was well planned and sustained the interest of students, and they became leaders in the profession in later years. The success of the B.Tech (computer science) programme was a trendsetter. All other IITs soon started computer science departments admitting undergraduate students. Today all engineering colleges have computer science departments and this discipline is one of the most popular ones.

COMPUTER CENTRE AND COMPUTER SCIENCE SYNERGY

Indian Institute of Technology Kanpur was the first to start an academic computer centre and was a trendsetter in several ways. Computer Centre was a central facility available to all students and faculty of IIT Kanpur for their academic work. It also allowed industries, research laboratories, and universities to use its facilities on concessional payment. The centre was operated 24×7 as an 'open shop' allowing interested students free access to facilities. M.Tech students in computer science were required to assist computer users with their programming problems (as consultants) and thereby understood users' problems. Being in close contact with computers and being able to go through the systems manuals, they were able to understand how computers are architected. They were also able to take up challenging problems in systems programming. This synergy of Computer Centre and computer science programme was a very important reason for IIT Kanpur students becoming leaders in the profession later in their career.

ROLE OF IIT KANPUR IN POLICYMAKING IN INFORMATION TECHNOLOGY

The expertise of IIT Kanpur faculty in computer science was well recognized, and led to their being members of several policymaking bodies of the Government of India. In 1978 I was invited to be a member of the Electronics Commission whose chairman was B. Nag and later P.P. Gupta. I was a member for four years. I chaired two important committees set up by the commission. One was the Software Export Promotion Committee (SEPC) and the other Manpower Development Committee. India was undergoing a severe foreign exchange problem and import of several goods was restricted. Computers were associated with automation and their impact was discouraged due to the fear of reducing employment. One of the important decisions taken by the SEPC was to allow import of computers by software industry if they committed to export software and earn foreign exchange equal to double the foreign exchange outflow for buying the computer. This decision allowed the fledging computer software services companies to import computers and begin export of software services. The fact that India could compete with the rest of the world and export software was an eye-opener. This decision to allow import of computers for software export led to India later becoming a leading software exporter (Parthasarathy 2009).

It was also evident that with the growth of IT industry there will be difficulty in employing appropriate persons in this new technology. The B.Tech courses were primarily designed to educate students to design computer hardware and systems software. The need of the IT industry was to design information systems to manage organizations. The type of education needed had to have both the breadth of general knowledge and the specialized knowledge to analyse and design operational and management information systems. The Manpower Development Committee's task was to propose programmes to develop human resource for IT industry and plan their implementation. One of the major recommendations in the report (Banerjee 1996) was to start a new academic programme called master of computer applications (MCA). This was designed as a three-year programme after B.Sc or B.Com degree with emphasis on designing information systems for organizations. An important aspect of the proposal was practical project training of six months in an IT industry. This programme was unique in India. Initially the Department of Electronics of the Government of India in cooperation with the University Grants Commission (UGC) aided a dozen educational institutions to start this course. Information Technology industry welcomed this initiative. The MCA programme also provided a professional growth path for B.Sc, BA, and B.Com degree holders. MCA degree programme was started at a large number of colleges. In fact, it was one of the initiatives which led to the explosive growth of IT services export industry as a large number of MCA graduates were available to the IT industry when it needed them.

In retrospect, IIT Kanpur became a trendsetter in India in computing and computer science due to the visionary initiatives taken in its early days. Academic debates in the senate, as well as open discussions among the various departments, especially on the critical issues, helped IIT Kanpur to come up with new educational programmes. Indian Institute of Technology Kanpur believed in students' responsibility by allowing open access to expensive computing facilities. Computer Centre was operated 24×7 and IIT Kanpur had an open-door policy for academics, engineers, and scientists from other organizations to use its computing facilities. Computer education and awareness were spread to all important research and design (R&D) organizations in India by teaching a large number of intensive courses on computing. All students of engineering, regardless of their disciplines, were taught the basics of computing. Several low-cost good quality books on computing were written which spread computer education. Indian Institute of Technology Kanpur was the first to start academic programmes in computer science of high quality which produced a large number of leaders in the profession. Indian Institute of Technology Kanpur faculty, besides consulting for industry also took part in formulating policies on IT development, which led to initiatives in software export and human resource development appropriate for the growth of our IT industry.

REFERENCES

Banerjee, Utpal K. (ed.) (1996), *Computer Education in India: Past, Present and Future*, New Delhi: Concept Publishing Co.

Parthasarathy, Balaji, http://www/cbi.umn.edu/iterations/parthasarathy.htm (last accessed 23 December 2009).

Rajaraman, V. (1969), *Principles of Computer Programming*, New Delhi: Prentice-Hall.

_____ (1971a), *Principles of Computer Programming*, New Delhi: Prentice-Hall.

_____ (1971b), *Analog Computation & Simulation*, New Delhi: Prentice-Hall.

Subba Rao, E.C. (2008), *An Eye for Excellence*, New Delhi: HarperCollins India.

part II
self-reliance in electronics and telecommunication

Jawaharlal Nehru names the first TIFR computer TIFRAC (Tata Institute of Fundamental Research Automatic Calculator) as Homi Bhabha and D.Y. Phadke look on, 1962. *Photograph courtesy TIFR*

M.G.K. MENON

6 Homi Bhabha and Self-Reliance in Electronics and Information Technology

As part of the celebration of Homi Bhabha's birth centenary, the Indian Physics Association had brought out a special issue of *Physics News* in which I had written an article entitled 'Memorable Moments with Homi'. In that I had discussed many qualities that defined his personality strongly. The first of these was the intensity with which he pursued anything he took in hand. Second, being a true internationalist along with diverse interests in different disciplines, he had a strong sense of nationalism. Third, he was a visionary, and had the enormous ability to actualize every plan he envisioned. In addition, there are many other traits that Homi had, which I know about, but have not been able to write about earlier. This essay is an attempt to open a window to Bhabha's life and work.

Bhabha had a strong sense of friendship and affection for those whom he held in deep respect and also a commitment to achieve self-reliance in every sphere. This was largely due to his sense of strong nationalism and his belief in India's potential to achieve outstanding success in the field of science and technology.

Bhabha had great affection and admiration for two individuals who had greatly influenced him in his life and work—Jawaharlal Nehru (whom Homi always addressed in his letters as 'Dear Bhai'), the first prime minister of India, and J.R.D. Tata. Both of them were staunch nationalists with an exceptionally international outlook.

During the early 1950s, Bhabha would frequently meet Nehru over tea or dinner, once in almost every two weeks (My personal contacts with Nehru were close and frequent in the period of the second half of the 1950s. This was largely for discussions relating to the Pugwash Movement in which Bhabha also had a strong interest). Bhabha, Nehru, and J.R.D. Tata were great visionaries. All of them wanted India to stand on its own feet, but their approaches were different. Interestingly, all of them, as also P.C. Mahalanobis (1867–1954)* and S.S. Bhatnagar were connoisseurs of art and culture.

The Sino-Indian border hostilities in late 1962 dealt a devastating blow to Nehru; Bhabha would often tell me how upset he was with these developments and their impact on Nehru's image. He was always at Nehru's side to cheer him up and encourage him. He decided to do more, and started to think more about issues of national defence. Bhabha realized that he had to do something about matters where science could play an important role in strengthening India's defence. Both Bhabha and Nehru were great friends of Patrick Blackett, the British Nobel Prize winner, who had a seminal role in the British war effort through the use of science. Blackett was a member of the Tizard Committee that was instrumental in the development of the Radar Screen for Britain that was Britain's saviour in the World War II. He was also one of those who had used operational research successfully in various areas of the war effort.

Bhabha had done outstanding work at Cambridge University, UK, during the 1930s. His work in theoretical physics had been greatly influenced by his role model P.A.M. Dirac. Bhabha was also keenly interested in practical matters relating to a wide area including art, architecture, landscapes, and sculptures. It may be remembered that he had taken

* Many will not be aware that Mahalanobis, who established the Indian Statistical Institute (ISI), also included statistics as one of the new sciences, thereby enabling the strong foundation of science and technology in India. He was particularly close to Gurudev Tagore. Gurudev had strong faith in the judgement of Mahalanobis, not only in his knowledge of science but also in his understanding of literature. In many cases Mahalanobis worked as Tagore's literary agent. Mahalanobis was also one of the visionary scientists, and played a significant role in the development of computer systems in India.

a Tripos in Mechanical Engineering at Cambridge before going on to science. Whilst in Cambridge, he had developed great friendships with experimental scientists like John Cockcroft, who won Nobel Prize in 1951 for his invention of the first accelerator, which led to the splitting the atomic nucleus, and with Patrick Blackett, who won Nobel Prize in 1948 for his investigation of cosmic rays using his invention of the counter-controlled cloud chamber.

Because of the outbreak of the World War II, Bhabha could not continue his research in Europe. He joined the Indian Institute of Science (IISc) in Bangalore, at the invitation of C.V. Raman. Though he continued his work on highly mathematical aspects of particle physics, he also got involved in cosmic ray research using experimental arrays sent up on high flying balloons. This was largely because of the impact that Millikan[†] had made, by his trip to India for this. Bhabha had to build his own experimental equipment, which consisted of cosmic ray detector systems such as counters and related electronics. When he moved to Bombay (now Mumbai) to set up Tata Institute of Fundamental Research (TIFR) in Kenilworth, he pioneered the further development of such items.[‡] Soon, with his other preoccupations, he found out that he had needed an experienced person to look after this area. He found the ideal person in D.Y. Phadke (of St Xavier's College) who joined the TIFR as an associate professor.

Phadke was was deeply interested in a range of technical matters. He would always keep himself abreast with the latest developments in science and technology. He was not interested in publication of papers or taking out patents. He was a visionary who understood the significance of innovation. He was a person with whom I have had several discussions on matters concerning vacuum technologies, microwave engineering, accelerator technologies, and mechanical engineering among others.

One person, whom Bhabha had influenced and persuaded to join TIFR, was R. Narasimhan. He was appointed to work under D.Y. Phadke. Narasimhan had done his BE in electrical engineering from the College of Engineering, Guindy, in Madras, and went to Caltech

[†] Robert A. Millikan (1868–1953).
[‡] Daniel, Gokhale, Pereira, Sitaram, and many others were associated with this effort.

where he did his MS in electrical engineering on a scholarship provided through the J.N. Tata Endowment for Higher Education of Indians. He did his PhD in mathematics from Indiana University. He was assigned by Homi to lead the project to develop the first Indian digital computer—Tata Institute of Fundamental Research Automatic Calculator (TIFRAC).

Tata Institute of Fundamental Research Automatic Calculator had 2700 vacuum tubes, mostly double triodes. It used 1700 crystal diodes and punched paper tape for input/output and teletype printing. It had a ferrite core working memory that was state-of-the-art in those days. The power consumption was 18 kilowatts. With a working memory of 1024 locations of 40 bits (or 5 kilo bytes), the design of the pilot machine was completed in October 1956. Albeit, work on the full-scale machine was started in 1957, and completed in 1959. It needed air-conditioned space for operating, and had to await its location in the new buildings of TIFR. Tata Institute of Fundamental Research Automatic Calculator had its own machine language. I had to learn its language to make use of the system. R. Narasimhan thus successfully led a high technology group in an institution for fundamental research. But he also did pioneering research himself in the borderline area of syntactic pattern recognition and the interdisciplinary area of cognition, education, linguistics, and software.

The full-scale machine was formally inaugurated by Nehru in January 1962. When he came to dedicate the new buildings of TIFR, the machine was referred to as TIFRAC. It was made available to the universities and research bodies free of cost.

Apart from Phadke and Narasimhan, Bhabha also recruited another key person working in the field of electronics. A.S. Rao, who was working at Banaras Hindu University, had done electrical engineering from Stanford University. That was the time when Stanford University and Silicon Valley had entered into a remarkable partnership that changed the face of electronics in the world. Rao had gone to Stanford on a scholarship from the J.N. Tata Endowment for Higher Education of Indians. When Rao had returned, he met Bhabha and worked on a summer assignment on one of Bhabha's balloon experiments. Later, Rao joined TIFR as a Reader. The DPU had also, in it, a nascent group dealing with vacuum, material technology, accelerator technologies, and the like. This had, therefore, in it, more than electronics. It had in it areas of Phadke's interests, such as electron linear accelerator and cyclotron systems, and the like. This developed into what became the Technical Physics Division at AEET and was headed by a remarkable scientist in these areas, C. Ambasankaran. From there, he moved all electronics production, including computers, to Hyderabad, where he had set up the Electronics Corporation of India Ltd. (ECIL) of which he was managing director. Electronics Corporation of India Ltd. produces practically all of the requirements of electronics for the nuclear programme.

During the inaugural address of the second Conference on Nuclear Electronics, organized by the International Atomic Energy Agency (IAEA) in 1965, Bhabha remarked:

It is now well recognized that without a full-fledged programme for the design and development of nuclear electronic equipment, no country can embark on any meaningful atomic energy programme. Thus, in any developing country, which does not already have an organized electronics industry, a self-reliant atomic energy programme will necessitate not only the indigenous development of nuclear electronic instruments, but also organized work on other aspects of electronics such as computers, process instruments, and control systems.

He went on to point out that

the electronics industry is still in its infancy today, and except for radio receiver industry, which has taken root, and a couple of plants producing some electronic equipment for communication and defence, there is hardly any production of professional equipment in the country. The Atomic Energy Commission therefore recognized at the very beginning, as far back as in the late [19]40s, that it would either have to depend wholly on imported electronic equipment for its activity, or to take steps to establish powerful research and development groups in electronics to make the electronic equipment it needed. The work first started in a modest way, by developing Geiger counters needed for the geological survey of minerals. From there... In 1964 the Electronics Production Division (at Atomic Energy Establishment) produced nearly 2,000 different instruments of 30 different types valued at Rs 4 million. The range of instruments included radiation survey meters, scalars and power supplies, amplifiers of various types, single and multi-channel analyzers, and complete nuclear spectrometer systems. All the designs for the various instruments were developed in the laboratories of the Trombay Establishment and every achievement in the field of electronics has been accomplished without obtaining any know-how whatsoever through foreign collaboration.

His confidence in what India could achieve, particularly by commitment to self-reliance, is manifest not only in his efforts relating to the atomic energy programme of India, but also in his vision relating to electronics.

At the IISc, Bangalore, he was particularly interested in the energy needs of India, and the role that nuclear power could play in this. He was also convinced of the importance of fundamental research, particularly in mathematics, nuclear energy, and high energy particle physics. As he began to deal with practical aspects of these programmes, he started to appreciate the importance of experimental work, particularly at the frontiers. This was not only to be in nuclear electronics and related aspects of information technology (IT), but also in relation to areas of technical physics: vacuum devices, accelerators, material science, and IT on a general basis, and microwave engineering. Bhabha encouraged the growth of technology in TIFR in a great way. This was apart from the growth of fundamental research in TIFR which had gone on to new areas of radio astrophysics and molecular biology. The cosmic ray programme was also taking momentum. With an expansion of its horizons to cover all the windows through which one could look out at the universe—not only the optical window that one was familiar with, and the radio window that had come up and was being pursued at TIFR but also the new cosmic windows through which one could learn a great deal about the universe. One could know more about the new developments relating to X-rays, infrared neutrinos space technology, and so on.

Like Bhabha, Mahalanobis also had a wide circle of friends abroad. This was one way he kept abreast with latest developments relating to digital computers. These friends included Norbert Weiner of MIT and Bernal of Birkbeck College, London. In addition, Mahalanobis had very close contacts with the Soviet Union, as a result of which a large Soviet computer, URAL, was installed at ISI in 1958. There was also an effort to design and build, as a collaboration between ISI and the Jadavpur University, a second generation transistor-based computer called ISIJU, which was commissioned in 1966 at the Jadavpur University. This was, however, not a very successful venture.

Both Bhabha and Mahalanobis had a penchant for inviting distinguished scientists from abroad to visit their institutes, TIFR and ISI, where the subject matter experts would give lectures and spend extended time periods. It was, thus, that Maurice Wilkes (of the Cambridge University, UK) came to TIFR, and Norbert Wiener visited ISI. These visits had a great impact not only on the younger scientists in these institutions but also led to the start of many new activities. Thus, today, ISI has one of the finest laboratories for soft computing in the country. In addition, the institute does a great deal of work in areas of pattern recognition, fuzzy logic, and neural networks. This has involved the leadership of people like Dwijesh Dutta Majumder and Sankar Pal, and visitors such as Weiner and Zadeh. Dutta Majumder also played a major role in the development of memory systems.

In addition to the efforts in Kolkata, there were the large mathematical problems that needed to be solved for designing control systems for nuclear reactors. A.S. Rao dealt with those by building analogue computers.[§] Thus there were a number of efforts, including one at the IISc Bangalore, to build analogue computers for specific purposes.

From mid-1950s, Homi Bhabha was very familiar with the work done by John von Neumann and had discussions with him on several occasions abroad. John von Neumann had conceptualized the design of a general purpose computer with stored programs and was the one to have built the first computer with this architecture, in 1952 at Princeton. Bhabha was a frequent visitor of Princeton, and was also deeply interested in von Neumann's abilities in applied mathematics. I am aware, on a personal basis, that Bhabha spent considerable time during the 1960s, almost until his passing away, reading many books relating to computers. Through discussions with individuals such as Emanuel R. Piore, IBM's Director of Research, and Dick Garwin, a professor of physics at Columbia University (who was also a consultant to IBM, and was sent to look at TIFRAC), Bhabha wanted to understand the possibility of further developments based on indigenous efforts, and how this progress would meet future computing requirements of TIFR and India.

It was becoming clear to all of us (Bhabha, Phadke, Narasimhan, and myself) that TIFR would need to acquire one of the commercially available large machines. After detailed discussions and the appointment of a four-member committee of TIFR staff members (with expertise in computer systems in the US), it was decided to purchase one of the machines made by Control Data Corporation, the CDC 3600. This system was finally acquired in May 1964. There was also a 160A computer

[§] These were developed by end of 1959.

and a large training programme for software engineers and computer maintenance professionals associated with this purchase. Since its installation in TIFR, over 150 institutions from all over India have used the CDC system.

The purchase of the CDC 3600 computer by TIFR was important for another reason. It established a friendship between Bhabha and Jim Miles, a senior vice president of CDC, whom Bhabha had visited in Minneapolis. In discussions with Jim Miles, it turned out that memory systems for the CDC computers were being made in Singapore using low-cost labour for stringing the ferrite core memories. Bhabha thought that this could also be done in India, which would initiate the start of sub-systems for large computers. He visited the chief designer of CDC, Seymour Cray, who later became famous as the designer of the Cray Super Computer System. Bhabha told me afterwards that he felt that India should be able to design and build a super-computer on its own, which would have innumerable uses. His mind was always working ahead and fast.

Soon after the Sino-Indian border hostilities of 1962, the Atomic Energy Commission recommended to the government that an Electronics Committee be set up 'to survey the needs of the country in electronic components and equipment and to recommend measures for planned development of electronics, so that the country as a whole may become self-sufficient in this field in the shortest possible time and in the most economical manner'.[¶]

Bhabha became the chairman of this committee. Other members were S. Bhagavantam and Vikram Sarabhai, with A.S. Rao as member secretary. In our discussions Bhabha had told me about how he regarded electronics as an all-pervasive empowering technology. He worked very hard on the report of the Electronics Committee. It would have been one of the areas he would have concentrated on, had he taken on his new responsibilities in Delhi. That was not to be! It was because of this that I took over the responsibility for the field of electronics, when Prime Minister Indira Gandhi persuaded me to do so in 1970 and, in fact, left TIFR in 1975 to move to Delhi.

The message at the beginning of the report of the Electronics Committee by the then prime minister, Indira Gandhi, brings out Bhabha's

---

[¶] From TIFR archives.

commitment to self-reliance, and the importance he attached to electronics as an enabling technology for national development.

It is indeed a tragedy that Dr Bhabha, the prime architect of this Report, did not live to present it. With characteristic vision and foresight, to which achievements in Trombay bear testimony, he recognized the importance of the electronics industry and the need to make India self-reliant in this field in the shortest possible time. The very fact of his agreeing to be Chairman of the Electronics Committee in spite of his preoccupations with the atomic energy programme, is a measure of the importance which he attached to the development of electronics in India. Every page of the Report bears the imprint of his genius, skill and thoroughness and attention to detail. The fruition of the many significant ideas that have found expression in this Report will be a fitting tribute to his memory.**

The Bhabha Committee on 'Electronics in India' was set up in August 1963. It submitted a series of interim reports, almost twenty-one in number, from February 1964 to September 1965. These were all put together and consolidated in the final report. It was not meant to be a document to be strictly followed in terms of production or costs of various items. It recognized the fact that civilian and military production would have to be dovetailed, as also public sector and private sector production. It was looking at the field from the viewpoints of materials, components, and equipment, with standardization and self-reliance as key elements. The report was completed well before the integration process in the semi-conductor industry had made possible the solid state electronics that characterizes the field today. It clearly recognized the fact that this was a rapidly developing area, of both science and technology. The rate of change, that was technology-led, was so great that report did not think it necessary to go into market surveys.

In June 1975, under the auspices of the Electronics Commission, the developments that had taken place since the original Bhabha Committee Report, were put together as a new perspective report on 'Electronics in India'. Even this can well be regarded as highly outdated today, considering the nature and the prospect of the electronics and the almost daily transformation taking place in the field. Bhabha's personal belief concerning the importance of research and his confidence that it will enable new technologies, were all vindicated by all that we see in the

** This message was given by Indira Gandhi when the Bhabha Committee report was submitted after the tragic death of Homi Bhabha in 1966.

field of electronics today. India's development strategy in this field has to be based on the philosophy of self-reliance and on self-confidence.

Nehru was to inaugurate the International Conference on Cosmic Rays held in Jaipur in December 1963. Though he could not come for the inaugural function, he attended the last day when he could meet the scientists, and spoke at the valedictory banquet. I recall his arrival that morning in Jaipur and the long discussions that Bhabha, Vikram Sarabhai, and I had with him, particularly on all these new developments and opportunities.

Bhabha and I had several discussions during the conference. We discussed issues relating not only to the future of the cosmic ray research programme but also about what TIFR could do for India's defence system, and the use of advanced science in various areas for technological development.

Tata Institute of Fundamental Research's first contributions to national defence came in the form of supply of specialized components. This started soon after the 1962 hostilities with China, when it was discovered that Transmit-Receive (TR) switches were in short supply. Transmit-Receive switches were required for the operation of the radar systems. Bhabha asked that these be supplied to defence through efforts in the microwave engineering group under Phadke. R.V.S. Sitaram took specific charge and the task was accomplished.

After Bhabha's death, two major defence projects were taken on. One was referred to as the Air Defence Ground Environment System (ADGES) project for the Indian Air Force, and the other the Army Radio Engineer Network (AREN) project for the Indian Army.

The ADGES project involved computer handling of data received from radar systems through various types of telecommunication devices (LOS, troposcatter links, and cable) to guide intercepting air defence vehicles and deal with incoming aerial attacks. This was successfully accomplished and handed over to the Indian Air Force. This work was led by P.V.S. Rao whose earlier work was as a member of the team that built TIFRAC. Later, Rao worked on speech recognition.

The AREN plan involved mobile communication links from forward army positions through various levels up to Army Headquarters. This called for an automatic electronic switch. This was successfully accomplished by a group led by M.V. Pitke and Phadke, and in parallel, by a group under R.P. Shenoy at the Electronics and Radar Development

Laboratory (LRDE) in Bangalore. This became the heart of later developments relating to electronic exchanges in the country, particularly those built on an indigenous self-reliant basis by Centre for Development of Telematics (C-DOT) under the leadership of Sam Pitroda, in which M.V. Pitke and G.B. Meemamsi (of Department of Telecommunications) were important members. The latter had worked on electronic exchange in the Telecommunication Research Centre.

I would also like to mention certain aspects relating to the setting up of the Tata Consultancy Services (TCS) and its foray into large-scale software business.

Usually, on the occasion of council meetings of TIFR, the council as a whole or some members of it, particularly Jeh and Rustom Choksi, would visit laboratories in the institute, and also would have lunch with the faculty members. Sometimes the occasion for the visit was when some dignitary would visit the institute. During one such visit, which was after the first computer, named TIFRAC, had been designed and built in India, Jeh wanted to know more about the field. When Jeh talked to Bhabha about this, he suggested that Jeh should ask me to see him on this at Bombay House, which I did. Jeh started by referring to the enormous size of TIFRAC, and wanted to know what technology developments are taking place which could change the picture completely. I told him about the rapid developments in the field of microelectronics—first with the transistor and then with integrated circuits that had just been invented. This discussion was in early 1960s. Jeh rapidly concluded by saying that this would not be the right time for an industry or foundation to invest.

Many years later, after I had succeeded Bhabha as Director, TIFR, I was invited by Jeh for lunch in the Board Room. Quite surprisingly, he asked me to come a little earlier for a discussion. He had not given up the idea of the Tatas moving into the field of computers (he kept ideas in his mind for a long time). I explained to him what I knew about global developments, and more particularly, that there would be significant opportunities in hardware relating to various subsystems and software. He referred to this topic in the Board Room lunch discussion when the director in-charge of TCS (P.N. Agarwala) was present. To cut a long story short, the Tatas embarked on a plan for TCS in 1968 under the dynamic leadership of F.C. Kohli, who had been transferred to TCS from his position as deputy general manager in Tata Electric Companies.

This plan involved software programming for various categories of users, particularly from abroad. Kohli initially reported to P.N. Agarwala.

There was also the joint venture with Burroughs Corporation in the US. In this connection I visited Burroughs and others in the US around that time. Today, TCS is a jewel in the crown of the Tatas, and there are also several efforts relating to hardware in various Tata companies. Notable was the acquisition of Computer Maintenance Corporation (CMC) by TCS.

The early days of work at TIFR were characterized by three types of activity: (a) design and development of experimental capabilities (including counters of various types, amplifiers, discriminators, power supplies, etc.), (b) bringing the most distinguished scientists in the world, particularly in pure mathematics and areas of fundamental physics, to spend time at the institute and give courses and lectures, and (c) research relating to theoretical physics, pure mathematics, cosmic rays, nuclear physics, etc. It was through the first of these lines of activity that the capabilities for self-reliance in experimental work grew at TIFR.

REFERENCES

Sharma, Dinesh C. (2009), *The Long Revolution: The Birth and Growth of India's IT Industry*, Noida: HarperCollins.

Udgaonkar, B.M. (1985), 'Homi Bhabha on Growing Science' in Sreekantan, B.V., Virendra Singh, and B.M. Udgaonkar (eds), *Homi Jehangir Bhabha: Collected Scientific Papers*, Bombay: Tata Institute of Fundamental Research.

SAM PITRODA

7 Telecom Revolution and Beyond

Information and Communication Technology (ICT) has revolutionized the development paradigm of India. With 700 million mobile phones in 2010, and increasing at the rate of 10 to 15 million every month, month after month, India is on the move towards becoming a nation of 1.15 billion connected people. It is also well recognized and respected the world over for its ICT talent and potential—it is exporting over USD 70 billion worth in software services. Indian multinationals are fast emerging as leading players on the global map, and the country boasts of a large talent pool of young ICT-savvy engineers and entrepreneurs. Along with this growth, India has also pioneered in innovating new products, services, and business models in the telecom space to improve access, reduce cost and create opportunities for many, even at a very low average revenue per user (ARPU) compared to any other part of the world.

The Information and Communication Technology revolution in India has its roots in the invention of the transistor in 1947, stored programme, controlled digital switching, wireless technologies, and optical fibre-based cable infrastructure. It also has roots in Homi Bhabha's vision for electronics and his ability to collect and inspire young talent in the late 1950s and early 1960s to work on electronics at the Tata Institute of Fundamental Research (TIFR). Since the invention of the transistor in 1947, it has created multitrillion dollar application opportunities for new products and services related to radio, television, control, instrumentation, military hardware, computers, phones, servers, set-top boxes, games, consoles, and thousands of other gadgets. Essentially, electronics, transistors and ICT have become pervasive, with implications for all human activities whether at home, work, schools, colleges, or in businesses, hospitals, factories, governments, etc. In the present day scenario it is impossible to think of any human endeavour of any substance without electronics and ICT playing a key role in facilitating features and functionalities.

Bhabha understood the importance of electronics, and this vision translated into the formative plans for India's research in science and technology (S&T) activities. He systematically focused on building young talent and gave them the freedom to explore new frontiers in electronics. He gave them the initial vision, institutional framework, and tools to explore simple, perhaps unrelated, experiments in designing and developing new techniques and systems to create building blocks of today's telecom revolution.

Bhabha recognized the importance of advanced electronics in the instrumentation required for physics research, and set up a separate group for this purpose at TIFR. Digital technology was the basis for all types of instrumentation required for experimental particle physics research, and sophisticated equipment was built for cosmic ray studies at the institute and its field stations. Experimental investigations of extensive air shower experiments needed complex electronics circuitry that was the forerunner to the emerging digital techniques. The complex calculations could only be handled by a digital computer. His strong links with a number of universities in the UK and Europe that were building computers for physics research must also have influenced Bhabha to decide on building India's own computer in 1956. The instrumentation group first built a pilot machine and then the full-scale computer TIFRAC—Tata Institute of Fundamental Research Automatic Computer—with a state-of-the-art-architecture. The team associated with this pioneering project acquired the confidence to build large complex electronics systems even with simple, basic components. This experience, somewhat unique in the country, turned out to be very crucial when TIFR was called upon to build large systems required for national defence. Also important was the excellent professional environment and the outstanding infrastructure.

I entered into the Indian telecom sector during early 1980s. Having spent fifteen years working on digital switching systems in the United States, I was visiting India to give a presentation at an IEEE meeting in Mumbai. There I had a chance to meet a few young scientists from the TIFR like Madhu Pitke, P.V.S. Rao, and others. Also, I had an opportunity to connect with M.G.K. Menon through my work with the Electronics Commission in Delhi. My initial interactions with him convinced me that like in the US, there was a small but very capable talent pool at TIFR which was engaged in exploring technologies related to digital communications. Similarly, I also met with G.B. Meemamsi in the Department of Telecom (DoT) in Delhi who was leading a small team of engineers working on digital communications at the Telecom Research Centre (TRC). In those days it used to take ten to fifteen years to get a telephone connection, and India had around 2 million connections for 750 million people. The telephone was indeed a precious commodity, and at times seen as a luxury meant only for the urban elite. In fact, having been born and raised in Orissa, I had never used a telephone before coming to the US.

However, based on my experiences in the US, I was convinced that telecom could become a major tool for nation building. Further, it was my strong belief that ICT could bring about openness, accessibility, connectivity, networking, democratization, and decentralization, and as a result, social transformation. Fortunately, I had an opportunity to make a presentation to the then Prime Minister, Indira Gandhi, on a plan to modernize telecom institutions and infrastructures. At this meeting, where she had summoned her entire cabinet to her house for an one-hour presentation, I put forward a proposal to build indigenous digital switching technology using young Indian talent from TIFR and TRC, with a focus on accessibility, rural telecom, indigenous development, local production, and digitization of the Indian telephone network. This plan required strong political will at the highest level in the government, and commitment from a core team of young talent from TIFR and TRC.

Indira Gandhi's government gave a concrete shape to my proposal, and with help from the DoT, Department of Electronics (DoE), and TIFR, a team led by Pitke, the Centre for Development of Telematics (C-DOT) was launched in August 1984 to develop a family of digital switching systems in a time period of thirty-six months for USD 36 million. Centre for Development of Telematics was set up with the specific intention of indigenizing digital switching technology to meet India's unique requirements. It planted the right seeds for the ICT revolution in the country a quarter century ago. It was the start of a big idea with an opportunity for generational change. It was an idea which could affect people in urban and rural areas, in all walks of life, and connect the nation in a very modern way to bring about transformation at many levels. It was crucial that this big idea was articulated in a manner that would convince the political leadership and compel everyone to commit to realizing the dream. One of the key elements in operationalizing this idea was the political will provided by Prime Minister Rajiv Gandhi with national visibility, unconditional support, and egalitarian management. For implementation, this idea also required young talent with new energy, a different work culture, new work ethics, and norms and values.

The overall strategy was to design, develop, and manufacture products suited to Indian climatic conditions, especially for rural exchanges without air-conditioning, at substantially lower costs. The key was to couple this with training young talent in ICT to manage, maintain, and develop technology for the future. C-DOT focused on public-private partnerships with a clear understanding that the products developed by it will be manufactured by public and private companies. This required support from the government with new policies and regulations, as well from the unions, to start the process of privatization in telecom.

The first product was a small rural exchange to connect villages. Thereafter, a small PBX was delivered for the business community. Then came a medium sized 2000-line digital exchange, a 16,000-line urban exchange, and eventually a 40,000-line mega exchange for the metropolitan areas. All of this was achieved with young talent whose average age was twenty-three years without any experience or background in digital communications technologies. Today, over 20 million lines of C-DOT exchanges are in service. Further, the rural exchanges were used to provide STD-PCO facilities to improve access to telephones nationwide. Due to the perceived benefits of the STD-PCOs to the masses, the privatization of telecom started in the mid-1980s with almost no resistance in India.

Centre for Development of Telematics was essentially a bypass to the legacy system which was saturated with bureaucratic tardiness, vested interests, large unions, confused priorities, and political interference. It was clear then that to plant any new ideas or initiatives in the Indian system, a bypass was essential as a catalyst to encourage out-of-the-box thinking. If the same new experiment had been initiated as a project under DoT, it would have been killed instantly. Rajiv Gandhi as prime minister understood and appreciated the bypass mechanism to expedite the process of development. In many ways C-DOT became the signature project of India's quest for modernization and infused in a technologically diffident nation a new vigour. It was also an experiment in problem solving to usher in generational change with scalable and sustainable systems to improve the lives of the masses in India. It provided digital switching network infrastructure nationwide and STD-PCOs all over the country to improve access to telephones. It also created a large pool of young talent to design, develop, and manufacture digital technology in the country.

In this process the contribution of young talent from TIFR guided by Pitke was very critical. Immediately after the initial success of C-DOT, the Telecom Commission was established to give more autonomy and flexibility to develop the telecom industry. The idea was to model the commission after the Atomic Energy and Space Commissions to have powers required to expedite the process of modernization. As we planned to increase the number of telephone lines from 2 million to 20 million, the support of telecom union leaders was critical. We spent eighteen months with the labour unions to work out an agreement to stop hiring more people as per the old norms, and to bring manpower requirements closer to international standards.

With the Telecom Commission, agreement with labour unions, availability of indigenous product designs, local production base, and private entrepreneurs, the process was in place to digitize India's telecom network to expand from 2 million to 20 million lines. The next big challenge was the mobile revolution on the horizon in the early 1990s. Analogue mobile phones were being introduced in the US at the Global System for Mobile Communications (GSM) standards for global mobile systems and were in the formative stages in Europe. Against the pressure from analogue mobile phone lobbies, the Telecom Commission decided to wait for the GSM standards to emerge. As an early experiment, Mahanagar Telephone Nigam Ltd. (MTNL) for Delhi and Bombay was set up as a separate company with potential for listing on the public stock exchanges. Similarly, Videsh Sanchaar Nigam Ltd. (VSNL) was also set up as a company for international operations. This gave an opportunity to bring in private parties for mobile telephony and initial licenses were issued for metropolitan areas. Simultaneously, the Telecom Regulatory Authority of India was created as an independent body to regulate the telecom sector.

All of these initiatives, coupled with the Indian entrepreneurial expertise, led to a substantial investment and growth in mobile telephony. Indian operators, after spending almost a decade meeting the needs of the metropolitan and major urban areas, decided to move into second- and third-tier cities and rural areas to find exponential growth in mobile subscribers. In the process, they also invented new business models to suit Indian conditions with prepaid services and the ability to make profits at substantially lower ARPU than their global counterparts. However, in this frenzy of adding subscribers at an unprecedented rate, Indian operators imported all of the needed technology, products, and devices, and at times, services, from well-known international companies. As a result the indigenous Indian telecom manufacturing industry got killed. Today, unfortunately, almost all of the telecom equipment is imported and the numbers are huge. All the efforts of the C-DOT era to build local ancillary industry and manufacturing capabilities basically vanished in a short span of one decade.

India today imports substantial electronics hardware which is expected to increase four-fold in the next decade or so. The next big national challenge for the electronics industry is to build Indian hardware manufacturing base to produce television sets, laptops, computers, servers, mobile phones, wireless equipment, set-top boxes, and other hardware which are required in very large quantities to meet the growing needs in education, health, industries, government, defense, and other markets.

While seeds for the telecom revolution were being planted in the mid-1980s, quiet software service activities were beginning to strike roots and gain a foothold in the global software market. With young talent, Tata Consultancy Services (TCS), a Tata industry enterprise then headed by F.C. Kohli, had built a strong team of software engineers to address a growing demand for such engineers in the US market. Early models were based on labour arbitrage, where software engineers in India for the same level of talent and output used to cost perhaps five to ten times less than their counterparts in the US. With a massive demand for addressing the 'Y2K' challenge for the year 2000, a large number of Indian entrepreneurs started building software companies for the export market in the US. As a result, several other large companies were born along with TCS such as Wipro, Infosys, HCL, and many others. With proper incentives from the government, in a short span of a couple of decades, software export industry became a major earner of precious foreign exchange for the country. In the process, India and Indians gained global respect and recognition for the technical talent and built Indian multinationals with global brands to address markets not only in the US but also in many parts of Europe, Latin America, and the Asia-Pacific.

Initial efforts focused on software conversion led to new opportunities in financial services, manufacturing, legal, and other software services. The labour arbitrage model slowly moved to the back office related services for insurance, credit cards, travel, transport, and many other industries, leading to creating a large number of jobs in several major metropolitan areas in India. In this process, Bangalore became the IT hub for the Indian software and outsourcing industry.

While the telecom and software revolution was underway in 1991, economic reform led by Manmohan Singh started dismantling the licence raj with a focus on privatization, liberalization, and globalization. This initiative fueled a frenzy of entrepreneurial activities in electronics to expand coverage for television, telecom, entertainment, news, media, and many other new opportunities.

As we entered the twenty-first century it was clear that coupled with the growth in telecom and economic liberalization, India would continue to grow at a substantially higher rate based on local demands. Recognizing the need for human capacity to fuel this growth, Manmohan Singh as prime minister set up a National Knowledge Commission (NKC) to look at knowledge institutions and infrastructure required for the twenty-first century to meet future growth and opportunities. The commission looked at five aspects of knowledge—access, concepts, creation, applications, and services. For access, the commission looked at literacy, libraries, broadband, networks, portals, translations, and affirmative action programmes. For concepts, it focused on schools, vocational education, higher education, distance learning, open courseware, teachers' training, and other related challenges. To focus on knowledge creation, the commission looked at innovation, entrepreneurship, patents, copyrights, and other related issues. It also focused on applications related to agriculture, health, small- and medium-scale industries, and traditional knowledge. Finally, the commission also looked at the use of knowledge in improving governance. The sum total was that twenty-seven subjects were examined and 300 recommendations were submitted to the prime minister for speedy implementation. One of the major recommendations was to create a National Knowledge Network (NKN) to connect 1,500 nodes with ultimately 40 gigabit bandwidth to connect all universities, research laboratories, and major libraries to improve collaboration and data sharing. Knowing that all modern research requires a multidisciplinary approach, much more collaboration, and will happen at a much faster pace than ever before, the NKN will be critical for India's effort in education, innovations, and global competitiveness. This network has been authorized by the cabinet and is being built at present. In fact, over 100 nodes are already functioning connecting several major education and research institutions all over India.

This was possible mainly because India has close to a million kilometres of optical fibre built as the backbone network for the mobile operators. This huge national asset remains underutilized and can fuel the next revolution in connectivity. With this massive fibre network, we are now focused on building a Public Information Infrastructure to connect not only our universities and laboratories but also our 2,000 municipalities and 2,50,000 panchayats.* The key to these efforts relate to a commitment to democratize information and plant seeds for open government which will enable transparency, accountability, and empowerment of the citizenry. This will also be critical for strengthening ongoing government initiatives in this regard such as the Right to Information (RTI) Act, especially at the grassroots. Public Information Infrastructure will not only provide fibre connectivity to all 2,50,000 panchayats but will also focus on building six new open platforms related to broadband, universal identification, geographic information system, security, and applications and payment.

The key to Public Information Infrastructure is e-governance and delivery of public services such as food distribution, national employ-

---

* Local governments.

ment guarantee scheme, pension, land records, birth certificates, police reports, etc. Most of these crucial services which impact citizens lack proper information infrastructure. And hence have no adequate systems of transparency and accountability, resulting in inefficiencies and cost overruns. Through Public Information Infrastructure and connectivity to 2,50,000 panchayats along with proper application software at the panchayat level, it will not only be possible to collect proper information about infant mortality, female literacy, etc., but it will also help deliver appropriate payment to people related to pension, employment guarantee schemes, and other government services. At the panchayat level it will also be possible to improve training, financial management, education, health services, and much more.

It is recognized that the web and internet have far reaching implications on the way we conduct business at work, and live at home. The internet is transforming business models, delivery systems, education, health, governance, and as a result making information and communication technology pervasive. The key challenge in India is to really use ICT to bring about generational change to impact disparity, demography, and development. The disparity between the rich and the poor, urban and rural, and educated and uneducated, can be addressed only with a clear focus on inclusive growth and the needs of people at the bottom of the pyramid. India's unique demography of 550 million below the age of twenty-five further demands focused attention on education, nutrition, and job creation to provide opportunity and prosperity for the young generation.[†] Finally, development initiatives related to infrastructure for energy, transport, education, etc. needs to be expedited with the help of ICT tools and capabilities.

The first phase of the telecom revolution to connect a billion people in India is about to end, while an exciting second phase of the ICT revolution to democratize information to create a vibrant democracy with empowered citizens, and a focus on openness and accountability, is about to begin.

[†] For more details please visit http://blogs.hbr.org/radjou/2009/11/can-india-reap-its-demographic.html (last accessed on 25 December 2010).

SAM PITRODA AND M.V. PITKE

8 Homi Bhabha's Role in Fostering
   Electronics Development
   C-DOT and C-DAC

Homi Bhabha recognized the importance of advanced electronics in the instrumentation required for research in physics and set up a special group for this purpose at the Tata Institute of Fundamental Research (TIFR). Digital technology was the basis for all types of instrumentation that is required for experimental particle-physics-research. Sophisticated equipments were built for cosmic ray studies at the institute and its field stations. Experimental investigations of extensive air-shower experiments needed complex electronic circuitries that were forerunners to the emerging digital techniques. The complex calculations could only be handled by a digital computer. Bhabha's strong network with a number of universities in the UK and Europe that were building computers for physics research must also have influenced him to decide on building India's own computer in 1956. The instrumentation group first built a pilot machine and then the full-scale computer—Tata Institute of Fundamental Research Automatic Computer (TIFRAC)—with a state-of-the-art architecture. The team associated with this pioneering project acquired the confidence to build large, complex electronic systems even with simple, basic components. This experience, somewhat unique in the country, turned out to be very crucial when TIFR was called upon to build large systems required for national defence. All this was made possible by the excellent professional environment and the outstanding infrastructure at TIFR. It was among the very few research institutions in India where research in advanced experimental physics led to the development of indigenous electronics technology. This, as one can see, was done at the European Organization for Nuclear Research (CERN) on a much larger scale where data transmission and processing techniques had stretched to the limit, and led to several path-breaking developments like the world wide web (www), grid computing, and super-high-speed broadband intercontinental communication.

In mid-1970s a team at TIFR designed, built, and delivered the most advanced mobile switching system for military applications. This experience helped the team to acquire basic knowledge and confidence required for developing a larger switching system like public telephony. An opportunity came when in early 1980s the government decided to set up a plant for manufacturing the latest switching equipment for public telephony. The timing was very opportune for a number of reasons. Switching technology was undergoing a major transformation due to advancements in solid state electronics; the availability of microprocessors and development tools, etc. brought a significant change in the state of affairs. At that time Sam Pitroda had pioneered the development of an innovative digital switching architecture with multi-microprocessor control. A group of competent scientists at the Telecom Research Centre (TRC) in Delhi had also developed the first computer-controlled analogue switch under very formidable conditions. Based on the expertise and experience of the three teams, the Centre for Development of Telematics (C-DOT) was set up in 1984. The objective was to develop technology for a family of telecom switching systems to meet the urgent needs of the country. With the delivery of more than 60 million lines of switching equipment of various types, C-DOT has been one of the most successful technology development efforts. In addition, it had a seminal role in the foundation of the Centre for Development of Advanced Computing (C-DAC). In late 1980s, when India faced serious challenges in importing advanced computers, C-DAC played a decisive role. It successfully took on the challenge of developing advanced computer systems that would be more powerful than the imported supercomputers. The success of C-DAC's lies in the creation of an environment that was very conducive for young engineers and scientists to produce world-class products.

C-DOT

The Telecom Challenge

Public telephony in India, until recently, belonged to an older generation of technology which did not exploit fully the potential of computer and digital techniques. An exceptionally reliable and rugged infrastructure was completely owned and operated by a very conservative service provider. Only a few basic facilities were available to the subscribers. The network was 'switch-centric', that is, the telephone exchanges were central to the telephone network. Transformation began in the late-1970s with rapid advances in computer and component technology and the expanding needs of data communication. In the changing network architecture, functions of the telephone exchanges changed a lot. It also signalled the entry of smaller players in a field that was almost completely dominated and controlled by large multinational companies. The new technology, however, could be managed by smaller groups of entrepreneurs with relatively modest investments. As a result, several small companies emerged in the US and Europe that began development and manufacture of telecommunication products like private branch exchange (PBX), messaging systems, and voice mail for value-added services.

During this period, the Department of Telecommunication (DoT) in India was trying its best to meet the ever-increasing demand for more telephones and to deal with the aggressive marketing pressures of multinational companies for sale of new switching equipment. Being aware of the technology trends, in 1980, the Government of India appointed a committee under the chairmanship of H.C. Sarin (former secretary, Ministry of Defence, Government of India) to explore the possibilities of setting up a factory for manufacturing Electronics Switching System (ESS) with a production capacity of half a million lines per year. This decision attracted the attention not only of the well-established manufacturers, but also the young digital switch designers around the world. The early 1980s saw a major transformation of communications technology caused by rapid developments in semiconductor components and computers, which clearly showed that digital switching was going to be the key technology in the immediate future. There was a more dominant role for computers and digital technology now. This gave great hope to those who were engaged in developing new communication systems. G.B. Meemamsi's team had built an electronic exchange at the telecommunication research centre in Delhi; Sam Pitroda had pioneered a very innovative digital switch with multi-microprocessor control; and M.V. Pitke's team at TIFR had built a digital mobile switching system for tactical communication. This project was funded by the then Department of Electronics (DoE) of the Government of India which was also actively promoting the development of electronics technology in the country. Its secretary, P.P. Gupta, also became a key supporter in this initiative. Setting up of the Sarin Committee influenced Pitroda to visit India frequently to mobilize support for local development of switching technology, meet team leaders, and to prepare a plan of execution. One of the important actions was to successfully convince the government to select digital switching technology for the new factory.

A Word about the Technology

The telephone switch was one of the most complex and most reliable systems ever developed. A down time of only 1/2 hour was allowed in twenty-five years! Once it was installed, it could not be shut off. All repairs, modifications, and upgradations needed be done in hot condition! Intelligent use of duplication/redundancy in design ensured this. This was one of the reasons for which it remained a monopoly of only a few companies. In the late 1970s, a few large telecom companies from the US, Europe, and Japan monopolized the supply of telecom switching equipment all over the world. This equipment, though based on a solid reliable basic component, was designed for operation in the urban environment of the West because that is where most of the market was. Analogue electromechanical switches based on the cross-bar technology were optimized to match the telephone traffic prevailing in those countries. They required clean, well-controlled, air-conditioned environment. The design catered to the requirement of a large number of telephones with well-dispersed traffic and relatively fewer calls per line. However, India required just the opposite. Here, a large number of subscribers attempted simultaneously to make calls through a telephone exchange that was capable of handling only a few subscribers simultaneously. The control circuitry was hard-wired with very limited call processing capacity. It used to get bogged down as soon as the number of call attempts reached beyond its capability, creating a chaotic condition. Modifying this design to meet our requirements was not only difficult but also very expensive. Also, there was the experience of failure in one of the previous projects. What was required for the emerging telecom market in India was a cost-effective, reliable, and rugged system that was easy to operate, maintain, and possibly manufacture in India. Special requirements of the rural areas were also important.

However, favourable situation was also developing on several fronts. The construction of low-power-consuming complementary metal oxide semiconductor (CMOS) circuits was very important, especially for the rural automatic exchange (RAX). The availability of the IBM PC helped in low-cost testing and manufacturing as the task reduced to a series of assembling and testing printed circuit boards. In addition, the availability of high performance microprocessors, high level language (HLL) software, and development tools were great aids for software development. We also managed to get licence for UNIX from AT&T—the key environment for switch development in those days. Digital signal processing (DSP) devices, essential for handling functions like signalling, were emerging very fast. The computer was entering the telecom field in a big way, which implied a bigger role for computer hardware and software. These developments had a strong influence on the US telecom industry. Development of small switches came within the realm of entrepreneurs, who were tired of working with old technology and wished to develop something on their own. Some of them set up their own organizations which could provide important consultation services. However, in India the well-established component industries manufacturing professional components under licence from the top US and European companies were struggling to survive due to the very small size of the market. The availability of manpower situation was very good. Several young engineers and scientists were looking for new challenging opportunities. The Indian Institutes of Technology and several engineering colleges with excellent infrastructural facilities and competent faculties were keen to work with us. Also to be noted in the setting up of C-DOT is the very unique and highly complementary nature of the talent coming from three sources: the US's innovative telecom industry, TRC's telecom service operations, and TIFR's computer and digital technology group. Added to this was the support of the DoE which was keen to provide the administrative and financial support. All these beneficial conditions helped in the design, development, and execution of the project at C-DOT.

Notwithstanding this helpful situation, it was not easy to convince the government, especially the DoT, to support such a project. There was little confidence in indigenous technology development. Even large industrial corporations were reluctant to take any risk with any new technology development. There was hardly any success story worth mentioning in this field. Almost everyone seemed to be happy and comfortable with imports, even though they were expensive and not well-suited for application in India. Considerable groundwork had to be done. After outstanding achievements in the US, Sam Pitroda was looking for a challenging opportunity in India. He had developed and commercialized a digital switch (DSS580) with innovative multi-microprocessor control, and was ready to move to India for a challenging opportunity. He provided inspiring leadership and a strong motivating force required for the large talented project team. Parallel efforts were launched in several directions to garner support for the project. These included meeting with influential friends, politicians, and journalists, meeting top scientists and technologists, sending articles to the press, dealing with the strong opposition of some bureaucrats, and finally making a presentation outlining his plan and ideas to the then prime minister, Indira Gandhi, who gave a favourable indication. Rajiv Gandhi, who was also present at this meeting, was quite impressed by Pitroda's proposal. This was followed by visits and meetings in the US and India for finalizing a detailed plan of implementation. This turned out to be far wider than just the initial plan of setting up a factory with a production capacity of half a million lines annually. The state of technology in the country was such that a total solution was required to meet our requirements—a solid, rugged, cost-effective product, finely tuned to meet our needs. No import solution was available. It would encompass vendor development centred around the local component industry, development of prototypes for different applications, devising a low cost process of manufacture, packages for training, and technology transfer, etc. The 'marketing effort' was stupendous even though we had to deal with one big customer, the telecom department. Work started

FIGURE 8.1   Telephone guru Sam Pitroda

with the support of the DoE and TIFR even before it was formally approved by the cabinet on 7 July 1984.

The plan envisaged this to be a joint project of the DoE and the DoT under the administrative control of the DoE, setting up a factory with annual production capacity of 5,00,000 lines of exchanges each with average switching capacity of 4,000 lines, known as ESS3. This was to be accomplished in thirty-six months with a budget of Rs 36 crores. As per the cabinet note the organization would be a registered scientific society 'vested with the total authority and flexibility outside Government norms to ensure dynamic operation'. The cabinet note that was approved had clearly spelt out the special facilities that were provided for rapid project implementation. Vigorous action started on many fronts. A three-tier organization was set up, consisting of the governing council, the steering committee, and the project board. It may be noted that this was slightly different from other research and development (R&D) institutions as the focus was on rapid development and delivery in a fast project mode. Role of the well-empowered steering committee became very crucial here. Budget control and timely delivery of the project was most important. The first task was to get the core team consisting of members from TRC and TIFR on board and to finalize a system architecture after examining and evaluating various possibilities, and come up with tentative specifications taking into account the telecom department's requirements and the specifications as laid down in the 'tender document'. After several rounds of discussions and arguments, a simple time-space-time architecture was finalized. The design took into account the environmental specifications and the problems relevant to India. This was followed by a tentative design of various subsystems which gave a broad idea of hardware and software requirements and an estimate of quantities of various component types. This was important for vendor development. The focus was on making the best use of existing infrastructure as far as possible, and to open up new avenues to the local industry. There were no problems in getting reliable passive components like capacitors, resistors, relays, switches, cables, and connectors. The famous microprocessor 6502 was selected for control operation as this was in the manufacturing line of Semiconductor Corporation Ltd. The experience of TIFR was valuable in several respects. The defence switching project experience provided a simple, low-cost, and highly rugged packaging solution advantageous for the rural systems. It also had a unique signalling handling subsystem that vastly improved the real-time call processing power. It also had a simple but effective duplicated control for uninterrupted service.

A nationwide campaign was launched in many directions. Meetings were organized in important cities with manufacturers, entrepreneurs, and small-scale industrialists to make presentations on our plans. In addition, specifications of various types of components and quantities were also requested. For the first time there was a market for professional components in quantities of millions. Seminars were conducted at IITs and universities, presenting the project plan and giving them specifications of the exciting and challenging work ahead. Articles were also written in leading newspapers explaining our plan and its benefits. Considering the extremely stringent time schedules, it was not possible to go through the normal route for projects. Work had to be moved closer to people. Delhi was convenient for the TRC team and Bangalore was suitable for the TIFR team (as it was located in Bangalore) for technology transfer of the earlier project to ITI. Moreover, the presence of several vendors, academic institutions, and R&D organizations was an additional factor. There was a very favourable environment for hardware development and manufacture. It was also easy to get good quality office space in Delhi. Offices and facilities in Delhi were set up at the (former) Akbar Hotel where well-furnished space was available on attractive terms. Similarly, one full floor in a large commercial building (Sneha Towers) was acquired for operations in Bangalore. Tata Institute of Fundamental Research was reputed for its environment and administration that nurtured high technology development. Largely due to this reason, TIFR was adopted as a model for C-DOT and an outstanding professional environment was created with help of experts from TIFR. Several institutions from all over India, including the IITs and IISc Bangalore, provided very enthusiastic support and collaboration. The Bangalore office of C-DOT was temporarily located at TIFR Bangalore (inside IISc campus) where the first vendor development conference was held.

The Centre for Development of Telematics system was built from a basic switching module of 128 ports. This module could operate as an independent switch like a PBX or a rural switch with appropriate software and hardware add-ons. As the project plan was getting finalized we had to do much more than setting up the ESS3 factory. We needed cost effective PBXs and rural areas required an inexpensive rugged and reliable switch. These circumstances gave us an excellent opportunity to prove the functionality of most of the hardware much before the large switch was ready for manufacture. It gave us time for stabilizing the hardware and achieving the desired reliability. The Private Branch Exchange was ready, and its technology was transferred to a number of manufactures from the public, private, and joint sectors. The first PBX unit manufactured by Meltron was installed at the *Indian Express* offices at Nariman Point in Mumbai. Field trial of the first RAX installed at Kittur near Belgaum turned out to be an exciting event. It was a full-fledged pulse code modulation (PCM) digital switch through which one could make calls anywhere in the world. It provided facilities that were not available in most urban areas. It brought good quality telephony to the village for the first time. Villagers from the neighbouring areas used to visit Kittur to talk to their children in the US! There was a great demand for this switch, and 'RAX-a-Day' plan was launched. This was ideal for serving public villages in the remotest parts of India. Its impact was enhanced by the cost-effective pay phones developed for public call offices all over the country. The impact of RAX was studied by the National Institute of Bank Management (NIBM), Pune. The study summarized the benefits to the people as 'saving in time and money, better prices for agricultural products, increased sales and returns to the traders, quicker medical attention and health services, increased social interaction, better law and order control and faster flow of information/ news'. The unique experience in developing military products helped in designing RAX with a simple, rugged, and highly reliable system well matched to the situation in rural India and very soon became an outstanding success. N.R. Narayana Murthy, the Founder-Chairman of Infosys, says about his RAX experience:

My memory goes to a wintry morning when I was driving with a friend of mine from France to Nagarhole forest near Mysore city. Throughout the journey, I was waxing eloquent about Sam and his work. My friend, a perfect gentleman, after listening to this monologue for a long time, probably got tired. He gently said that he would believe all I said if he could call his wife in Paris from Nagarhole and the communication was clear. We stopped at the first ISD booth at Nagarhole and my friend dialed Paris. His wife's voice came through loud and clear. He smiled. And extended his hand and congratulated me as if I had wrought this revolution. I was proud of Sam, C-DOT, and India.

There were difficulties even in getting fairly simple components like cabinets and frames made as per our specifications. Almost all products were produced in collaboration with some foreign companies. Even the most highly reputed indigenous business houses were focused on foreign collaboration and were not keen to help us. We finally decided to motivate a couple of intelligent mechanical engineers who successfully designed elegant, rugged, and cost-effective cabinet frames and other mechanical parts with help from a very talented computer-aided design (CAD) savvy entrepreneur who had his small shop in an industrial slum in a remote suburb of Mumbai.

The large switch for urban application (MAX) was a bigger challenge. It was designed for a capacity ranging from 400 lines to 40,000 lines. Its hardware was quite complex and the software even more so. Packaging was also a challenge and it took a considerable time to solve many of the tricky problems. A 10,000-line MAX system was ready for trials in the laboratory in August 1987, and a similar model was installed for public service at Ulsoor in Bangalore in August 1989. The switch came with different capacities ranging from 400 lines to 40,000 lines. The Centre for Development of Telematics thus had core telecom switching technology to meet the vast requirements in India: PBX for business applications, RAX for rural areas, and MAX for towns and cities. This demand for telephone service could not be met by one public sector company, the Indian Telephone Industries Ltd. It was important to get active support of all—the public, the private, and the joint sectors. Many companies showed interest in manufacturing C-DOT switches. These included houses engaged in manufacturing electronics products, the state electronics corporations, and the large public sector companies like ITI, Bharat Electronics, and Bharat Heavy Electricals. A cost-effective process of production and packaging was developed by C-DOT by selecting and developing equipment like PC-based testers well matched to the needs of relatively small-scale manufacturers with modest investments. The Department of Electronics helped manufacturers by importing this equipment in the form of kits. For the first time the private sector was playing a significant role in an area that was reserved exclusively for the public sector. The process of technology transfer which started with the PBX technology was transferred to thirty-nine companies. The rural exchange technology was transferred to thirty-six companies, and the MAX technology to twenty-one companies. It is estimated that by 2004 more than 60 million lines were delivered. At about Rs 5,000 per line, this has been recognized as one of the most successful technologies developed in India.

The success of any technology that is developed for large-scale application is proven only by the 'value' it creates—in this case the number of lines produced, supplied, and deployed, the vendors and ancillary industries created, and, above all, the number of people that were trained in various areas. The Centre for Development of Telematics has been very successful on all these counts. It may be interesting to know that projects for developing telecom switching technology were launched in Brazil and Korea in the late-1970s. Centro de Pesquisa e Desenvolvimento em Telecomunicações (CPQD) in Brazil very successfully developed the system TROPICO, which was widely deployed in the country. A total of 7.8 million lines were installed. Its success was rather limited probably due to lack of support and the strong marketing drive of foreign companies. The Korean switching technology was developed by the Electronics and Telecommunications Research Institute (ETRI) at Daejon. It is one of the leading research institutes in the world with many significant achievements to its credit Switching system family TDX* was a great success with deployment

---

* Telecom switching system from Daewoo Telecom of South Korea.

of more than 15 million lines in Korea and some countries in the region. Factors that contributed to the success of TDX include close collaboration with a number of manufacturers during the development phase and the expertise in computers and semiconductor technologies. Members of C-DOT had opportunities of interacting with both these groups on several occasions. Importantly, it is worth mentioning that C-DOT has delivered far more lines than the ETRI technology.

The Centre for Development of Telematics undertook a number of activities associated with the mission of providing telecom facilities in a variety of ways. Payphone was a very critical requirement. All public call offices (PCOs) were run by the telecom department, and it was not very easy to make long distance calls. Automatic public payphones did not exist. Coin-operated public phones served only local calls. The Centre for Development of Telematics was instrumental (with help from the telecom department) in getting developed locally low cost, rugged, and automatic payphones for privately operated PCOs that have reached the remotest corner of the country. One could reach any part of the world at a very modest cost and this vastly improved the telephone accessibility. It provided opportunities for a large number of small entrepreneurs, especially those in the rural areas, and the model was later widely followed in other countries as well.

The other project was the development of a large parallel processor for two key applications—weather modelling and radio astronomy image processing. In 1987, India was facing problems in importing supercomputers like the CRAY for the weather research programme of the Department of Science and Technology (DST). Large parallel processing systems require high performance and high speed interconnection systems for inter-processor communication. The Centre for Development of Telematics had considerable experience in designing high speed interconnection networks which were the basis of its products. It had created an infrastructure for rapid design and implementation. After several rounds of discussions and deliberations, architecture was finalized to meet the specific requirements of the user, DST, which supported this work. By a happy coincidence the Radio Astronomy group of TIFR was also interested in parallel processing for image processing applications, and the architecture planned was very suitable for this purpose. Therefore, strong support also came from this group. The main objective of the project was to deliver a machine with capabilities equal to or exceeding those of CRAY XMP14 machine for the weather model T63. Weather modelling work was entrusted to the Centre for Atmospheric Sciences at IIT Delhi. The processor system was called CHIPPS—C-DOT High Performance Parallel Processing System.

Single Algorithm Multiple Data (SAMD), a variation of the Single Instruction Multiple Data (SIMD) architecture, was designed for this purpose. Knowing the complexity involved in designing a supercomputer in terms of component technology, packaging, thermal design, and software effort, it was decided to match the application and algorithm to the parallel architecture. It supported features like (a) intensive computation at the algorithm level, catering to plausible parallel execution with different data without significant inter-processor communication and (b) an efficient mechanism for transposing the data for further computation. Thus, the SAMD architecture emerged. This was similar to SIMD architecture but it was for elevating the atomic unit of computation from instruction level to algorithm level. The system was designed to support up to 256 processing elements with 256 banks of the main memory called Multidimensional Access Memory (MDM). The Processing Elements (PEs) and the main memory were interconnected through a fully non-blocking interconnection network (ICN) which is logically a cross-bar switch. A master controller orchestrates these computing blocks and also provides the I/O system and the programming environment.

The processing elements for the first models were based on Inmos T800 Transputer—a 32-bit processor with peak performance of 32 MFlops at 25 MHz. It is used essentially as floating point engine which can be upgraded by more powerful processors. The interconnection network is a fully non-blocking virtual cross-bar switch (512×512) which interconnects PEs and MDMs at 8 Mbps per link. For a 256-node system, the communication bandwidth is 2.048 Gbps. A page flip mechanism with 256 predetermined and stored connectivity (patterns) provide faster reconfigurability of the switch in only a few microseconds. This results in a highly simplified interface with very low overheads. Sparse packaging and use of CMOS components simplify cooling requirements.

Machines of various sizes up to 192 nodes were built for testing various applications. Test results of the performance for the main application of weather modelling were as follows. A T63 model with nine vertical levels for ten days has been implemented on the number of nodes best suited for this application, 48 nodes on CHIPPS 64. Codes for T16 and T63 were run on CRAY and CHIPPS. It was found that CHIPPS 16 was 3.5 times slower than CRAY, while CHIPPS 64 was only about 1.5 times slower than CRAY. Another model, the T80 model of the National Meteorological Center (USA), was successfully ported on 64 and 192 node CHIPPS. It was observed that only 128 nodes were required for matching the algorithm.

Several applications for radio astronomy research were successfully developed by the National Radio Astronomy Centre (Pune) on CHIPPS 16 and 64. These include image formation and enhancement—Parallel 2D FFT for large data, Pulse Search Data Analysis, and Modelling of Interplanetary Shocks. In a typical application, CHIPPS 64 was found to be eight times faster than the Super Sparc-2.

At the Indian Institute of Science (IISc), CHIPPS 64 was used for analysis of molecular dynamics trajectories and for simulation of adsorption in zeolite.

There was some exploratory work on possible upgradaton of CHIPPS to teraflop levels. Digital Equipment Corporation (DEC) Alpha and powerful Reduced Instruction Set Computers (RISC) were to be the new processing elements. A 64×64 gallium arsenide switch was developed for the interconnection network at the Microprocessor Laboratory of the International Centre for Theoretical Physics in Trieste, Italy.

The morale-boosting experience resulted in several initiatives, including the Centre for Development of Advanced Computing (C-DAC). In late 1980s India faced several problems in the import of advanced computers, and C-DAC successfully took on the challenge of developing advanced computer systems—more powerful than the imported supercomputers. Its success lies in the creation of an environment that was very conducive for young engineers and scientists to make significant technical contributions, and to develop globally competitive products.

C-DAC

The Supercomputer Challenge

The arrival of fully functional and inexpensive microcomputers generated keen interest around the world in building large and powerful systems using large number of microcomputers. Parallel processing was one of the obvious choices for achieving supercomputer performance (in specific applications) at very low costs. Parallel processing became a key area not only for the university and R&D labs, but also for computer manufacturers. Around mid-1980s, India faced problems of acquiring high performance computers, especially supercomputers, owing to the restrictions placed on export of high technology items by certain countries. Work at C-DOT was a morale booster for the scientists who came up with several innovative ideas of building supercomputers based on parallel processing approach. This led to founding of the C-DAC in April 1988 as a mission. The objectives were set as follows:

- To build up high quality R&D manpower;
- To collaborate with the growing hardware and software industry.

The immediate goal was to develop and commercialize a parallel supercomputer with a peak computing power of 1,000 MFLOPS.

As to be expected, there were several problems in setting up C-DAC. These were overcome by a very supportive DoE (now Ministry of Information Technology) as in the case of C-DOT, which was set up on the lines of TIFR. During the early days, C-DAC was supported well by the association of two key administrators who had a long experience of working at TIFR. Initially, with a core team of highly competent and motivated engineers, the centre was started in the Pune University campus. This was further expanded by getting the best talent that was available in the country. For the first time a dynamic environment was created that would promote, design, develop, and implement advanced computers and computer-based systems for large-scale applications. It would also help provide young engineers and scientists a 'hassle free' environment for creativity and innovations. As a result, apart from meeting the main objective of building supercomputers, there were significant contributions in fluid dynamics, engineering design, computational physics and chemistry, image and signal processing, climate modelling, biotechnology, etc. The Centre for Development of Advanced Computing continues to be a vibrant organization providing arguably the best environment for the engendering and incubation of new ideas.

Among the first tasks was the choice of technology and the architecture. In 1988, the available choices were vector-pipelined processors like the CRAY, multi-machines based on standard microprocessors, or pursuing emerging architectures like the dataflow or the VLIW (Very Large Instruction Words). Vector-pipelined processors required very high speed nanosecond devices and special fabrication technology, and hence had to be dropped. The choice left was that of parallel processing architectures which were then on the horizon. Considering the potential for commercialization, the options were shared—memory multiprocessor machines or distributed memory message passing multiprocessor machines. The first type had limitations of the number of processors and hence it failed to provide supercomputer-class performance. There were hardware and software problems too. Hence the choice fell on distributed memory message passing machine with theoretically unlimited scalability. The choice of the processor needed careful consideration—the choice was between the off-the-shelf microprocessors then available, like 80386, 68020, 88100, and the InmosT800 transputer. T800 had an on-chip floating point unit, good computing power, and built-in support for interprocessor communication, micro- coded context switching, and a sound theoretical basis for parallel processing. A cross-bar switch was available as a peripheral and Occam was a concise and effective language for expressing parallelism. Transputer thus became a logical choice.

The architecture was finalized by mid-1989, and the first 64-node prototype was ready by mid-1990.

A system was designed grouping the T800s in a cluster of 64 nodes. Each node consists of a T805 transputer and 4 or 16 MB memory. The cluster contained four 96×96 cross point switch planes. Of the ninety-six links, most were used for the compute nodes, but some were for input/output to disks, host interfaces, spares, and sixteen for interconnecting between clusters. A 256-node system (four clusters) was running by mid-1991. By chaining the systems it was possible to build 1024 or larger node machines. It was found that up to eighteen hosts could be connected to a 256-node PARAM (the name is both an acronym for Parallel Machine and also Sanskrit for Supreme) which is designed to sit as a back end to a Sun or similar system. Simplified architecture is shown in Figure 8.2.

A PARAM board containing four nodes and memory can be replaced with one that also has an i860 with 8 MB memory and a 60 MB/sec data transfer mechanism between the i860 and the transputers. The i860s could be viewed either as vector accelerators attached to the transputers (via remote procedure calls), or the transputer's communication links could be used to develop parallel code for the i860s.

The Centre for Development of Advanced Computing has also built a large and impressive collection of software. This includes compilers (C and Fortran), system software, utilities, and tools. Just about everything was done ab initio. While economics was a factor, it was also done to get expertise in building software.

In addition to the basic utilities for ordinary and parallel programming, C-DAC has visualization tools and a substantial collection of specific applications, including image processing, finite element analysis, DSP, synthetic aperture radar analysis, computational fluid dynamics, auditory spectrograms, logic simulation, protein sequencing, and electron structure. There was also significant work in parallel libraries and parallel numerical algorithms. PARAM was built essentially to eliminate the need to buy commercial systems and also to develop in-country expertise.

The centre decided to develop a series of machines with progressively higher processing power. The next models of PARAM were based on T9000 transputer. In principle, such a system would have teraflop performance capability. Also, faster peripherals were developed for

FIGURE 8.2   PARAM Padma

improvement in networking access as well. The plan was to build a 4–8 Central Processing Unit (CPU) shared memory system with performance of about 100 MFlops.

PARAM Padma is C-DAC's next in the series of high performance scalable computing cluster, with a peak computing power of 1 TFlop. The hardware environment is powered by the compute nodes based on the state-of-the-art Power 4 RISC processors, using Copper and SOI technology, in Symmetric Multiprocessor (SMP) configurations. These nodes are connected through a primary high performance System Area Network, PARAMNet-II, designed and developed by C-DAC, and a Gigabit Ethernet as a backup network.

The PARAM Padma is powered by C-DAC's flexible and scalable HPCC software environment. The storage system of PARAM Padma has been designed to provide a primary storage of 5 TB scalable to 22 TB. The network-centric storage architecture, based on state-of-the-art Storage Area Network (SAN) technologies, ensures high-performance, scalable, and reliable storage.

The Tera-Scale Supercomputing Facility (CTSF) of C-DAC is located at the C-DAC Knowledge Park in Bangalore and houses the PARAM Padma—the most powerful supercomputer in India—and C-DAC's next generation high performance scalable computing cluster with a peak computing power of 1 TFlop.

PARAM 10000 is a 6.4 GHz parallel computer, which is scalable up to teraflop range. It has three compute nodes and one server node. The file server is e250a and the compute nodes are e250b, 250c, and 250d. Each node is dual quad processor SMP (Shared memory, Symmetric multiprocessor) system having 2 MB of level 2 per CPU cache. The processor is based on Sun Microsystems's Ultra Sparc architecture, each operating at 400 MHz UltraSparc 64-bit RISC CPU. Each computer node has 512 MB of main memory, extendable up to 2 GB, while each server node has 2 GB of main memory. PARAM 10000 computer node configuration has 2 MB external cache per CPU, 100 fast ethernet card in each node, and Solaris 7 (Solaris is being used), besides additional components for the file server: 512 MB memory, 9.1 GB Ultra SCSI HDD, and 4mm 12/24 GB tape drive.

As part of its activities, C-DAC has also set up a National PARAM Supercomputing Facility (NPSF) in Pune, where C-DAC is headquartered, to allow researchers access to HPC systems to address their computer-intensive problems. The efforts of C-DAC in this strategically and economically important area have thus put India on the supercomputing map of the world along with select developed nations of the world. As of 2008, fifty-two PARAM systems have been deployed in the country and abroad, eight of them at locations in Russia, Singapore, Germany, and Canada. Unfortunately, C-DAC did not focus enough to demonstrate common applications like the T80 weather model for a direct comparison of performance with a CRAY machine which was being used by the Indian Meteorological Department. The Centre for Development of Advanced Computing did not take into account the evaluation-feedback provided by the users and take necessary action.

The latest in the series of processors is called PARAM Yuva, which was developed recently, and was claimed to have been ranked sixty-eight in the list of Top 500 in November 2008 at the Supercomputing Conference in Austin, Texas, United States. 'The system,' according to C-DAC scientists, 'is an intermediate milestone of C-DAC's HPC road map towards achieving petaflops (million billion flops) computing speed by 2012.'

A novel feature of PARAM Yuva is its Reconfigurable Computing (RC) capability, which is an innovative way of speeding up HPC applications by dynamically configuring hardware to a suite of algorithms or

FIGURE 8.3   PARAM Yuva

applications run on PARAM Yuva for the first time. The reconfigurable computing hardware essentially uses acceleration cards as external add-ons to boost speed significantly while saving on power and space. The Centre for Development of Advanced Computing is one of the first organizations to bring the concept of reconfigurable hardware resources to the country. It has not only implemented the latest RC hardware, but also developed system software and hardware libraries to achieve appropriate accelerations in performance.

GARUDA is a collaboration of scientific and technological researchers on a nationwide grid comprising of computational nodes, mass storage, and scientific instruments. It aims to provide the technological advances required for enabling data- and computing-intensive science and engineering applications for the twenty-first century. One of GARUDA's most important challenges is to strike the right balance between research and deployment of the innovation into complex scientific and engineering endeavours being taken undertaken today.

Graphics and Intelligence based Script Technology (GIST) Group of C-DAC facilitates use of Indian languages in IT. In its endeavour to stay abreast with technologies worldwide, GIST has been adopting the latest concepts to be able to stay tuned with the internet-enabled world.

As part of the mandate given to C-DAC to address the growing demand for trained manpower in the extremely fast-moving sector of IT, C-DAC established its Advanced Computing Training School (ACTS). The centre currently offers a variety of course options in software technologies, Enterprise System Management (ESM), geomatics, VLSI designs, digital multimedia, and the Program for Advancing Computer Education (PACE). The Programme for Advancing Computer Education seeks to impart training in the language of the respective state.

How do C-DOT and C-DAC fare? The former had to operate in a rather hostile environment with a demanding and uncompromising customer—the DoT. This, however, made C-DOT a great success story with the purchase of more than 50 million lines of switches at a cost of about Rs 5,000 per line. This became by far one of the most successful technologies developed in the country. It also helped India to usher in the telecom revolution. The Centre for Development of Advanced Computing demonstrated and delivered successfully a few state-of-the-art products in a surprisingly short time. However, commercialization of these products was not easy. It was a bit unfortunate in not having any demanding customers. Nor did it have any strong peer pressure. The Centre for Development of Telematics was working in a rigid project mode, and after completing the assignment (mission), it did not have any challenging project in the new industrial environment of 1995. This was most unfortunate because with all the talent and experience it could have transformed itself into a global telecom R&D centre. On the other hand, C-DAC was working in an R&D centre mode and continued with new activities of its own choice. If only it had taken interest in networking technology/products, India would have become a world leader in this area.

part III
innovation and prospects in the indian IT industry

A young Homi Bhabha at his drawing board. *Photograph courtesy TIFR*

N.R. NARAYANA MURTHY

9 The Indian Software Industry
Past, Present, and Future*

It has been nineteen years since the reforms of 1991 brought sweeping changes to the Indian business environment, unleashing the forces of globalization that have profoundly changed India. Though many industries benefitted from the reforms, the Information Technology (IT) industry, in particular, flourished in the open business environment. It led the way in the new, flat world of globalized business and its success has made India a major player in the international software market.

Over the last two decades, the IT industry has contributed enormously to both India's economy and its society. The industry was languishing in the business-unfriendly climate between 1975 and 1991 with extremely slow growth rates. In 1991, it achieved revenues of less than USD 100 million. Compare that to the 2008 report by NASSCOM, India's premier trade body, which states that the IT-BPO (Information Technology-Business Process Outsourcing) sector had generated 2 million direct jobs and 8 to 9 million indirect jobs in the secondary and tertiary sectors of our economy. Software exports have boomed in the past five years, rising from Rs 58,240 crore in 2003–4 to a projected figure of 2,16,300 crore in 2008–9. Between 1998 and 2008, the Indian

* This essay has been compiled from several speeches and articles of the author.

IT industry's exports offset nearly 65 per cent of the cost of India's cumulative net oil imports.

The information technology business, in general, involves studying a corporation's business functions, and then building software applications that fully and faithfully mimic these business functions. Often, the charter is to upgrade an existing software application to handle new technologies or enhanced business functions. There is also the periodic need to take care of bugs in the application or to make minor improvements for effectively handling the evolution of the business. Sometimes, the opportunity may come in the form of selecting a well-known software package based on its suitability among other options, and then help implement the package for the customer. Until five years ago, these four activities contributed almost 90 per cent of the revenue of software companies. Today, they contribute about 70 per cent of the revenue, with the rest coming from new activities like BPO, Infrastructure Management Services (IMS), Independent Validation Services (IVS), and Systems Integration (SI).

Indian software talent is in great demand in developed nations. Most Fortune 500 corporations leverage the services of Indian IT companies for these activities. India, which is often referred to as the software factory of the world, has seen an IT boom that has contributed to growth in a number of economic sectors, including hospitality, airlines, automobiles, housing, construction, and healthcare.

Socially, the IT industry has had a powerful impact in many parts of the country. The seven states that lead in India's IT exports (Andhra Pradesh, Delhi, Haryana, Karnataka, Maharashtra, and Uttar Pradesh, mentioned in alphabetical order and not export revenues) have seen a rapid expansion of their tertiary education systems. The number of new colleges founded in these states in the last decade is six to seven times the number of colleges founded in other states. Over 70 per cent of the industry's workforce is between twenty-six and thirty-five years of age. This demography of young workers has benefitted significantly from the extensive and continuous training and development programmes initiated by IT companies. In addition, the IT industry has spearheaded diversity in the workplace where women make up over 30 per cent of the workforce, and over 60 per cent of IT companies employ differently abled individuals. Finally, employee stock options have led to democratization of wealth amongst its workers, moving more people into the Indian middle class than any other sector of the Indian economy.

However, there are significant domestic and international challenges to the future success of the Indian IT industry. Government policies have not kept pace with the growth of the IT industry. Roads, railways, airports, and ports are in desperate need of being upgraded. Traffic snarls are a fact of life. Electricity supply remain patchy at best. Around 95 per cent of India's software exports originate from nine Tier-I cities whose infrastructure is barely able to handle this burden. Tier-II and Tier-III cities are unable to fully participate in the economy due to poor access, infrastructure, and talent shortage. Corruption continues to be a major concern. Secondary reforms are needed to improve the velocity of business. Millions of Indians still live in poverty, completely shut out from the benefits of the IT age. The internet access in India is primarily available in the twenty-two largest cities and about 52 million Indians connected to the internet, but the number is an extremely small percentage of the total population.

India's higher education system remains mediocre and continues to be hampered by politics and bureaucracy. Private educational institutions remain highly regulated. A recent report by NASSCOM states that the industry could face a shortage of up to 3.5 million workers by 2020. This shortage could seriously threaten India's continued success in the global IT sector.

India operates in an increasingly competitive international market. Our global competitors stand to capture as much as 10 per cent of India's market share if suitable efforts are not made to remedy our poor infrastructure, slow bureaucracy, and the shortage of quality talent. Indian IT companies must work harder and be more innovative than ever to earn the trust of their clients and convince them to sign new contracts in the midst of a global economic downturn caused in part by several major corporate scandals. Public sentiment against the perceived threat of outsourcing and loss of jobs to India has been exacerbated because of high unemployment rates. There are very real concerns that laws may be passed in some of our major export markets to restrict or penalize domestic companies creating software and BPO jobs overseas.

Despite these challenges, there is still cause for optimism for the future of the Indian IT industry as it continues to adapt and leverage technology in innovative ways. To understand where the IT industry is headed, it is important to understand where it has come from. A brief history of the industry is provided here, followed by an assessment of its current state. This essay also looks at emerging trends that are likely to shape the industry over the coming decade.

THE EVOLUTION OF IT AND THE GENESIS OF THE INDIAN SOFTWARE INDUSTRY

The rise of a global IT sector depended on a number of historical developments in the area of computer technology. It was during the 1940s and 1950s that the US government institutions, universities, and corporate research laboratories worked to harness and invent computer technologies. These developments led to the mainframe computer and the industry was dominated by IBM, Burroughs, UNIVAC, NCR, Control Data Corporation (CDC), and Honeywell. However, these computers were not only physically large, but also cumbersome to use and quite expensive. A key development came with the emergence of mini computers and supermini computers which were smaller and cheaper. This was complemented by the development of new software systems that made it easier for humans to interact with computers and made it possible to solve more complex technical problems and large-scale commercial applications requiring real-time updates of databases.

The advent of the personal computer made technology more accessible to the individual user. These computers could solve problems beyond the typical technical and commercial applications. They were able to handle office automation applications, multimedia applications, and could be used as clients in client–server computing. Personal computers provided a user-friendly interface while supermini computers and mainframes took care of the heavy computing and database chores. These developments made computing more democratic and accessible to a larger number of people; it was no longer restricted to a few professionals.

The emergence of the internet only pushed the boundaries of democratizing computing access. The internet enabled people around the world to be connected as virtual communities. Such communities became invaluable to businesses and also changed the ways in which corporations did business. For instance, the internet helped consumers interact with corporations in buying and selling of products and services from the comfort of their homes on a 24×7 basis, thus significantly bringing down the costs of services like banking, hospitality, and travel.

The genesis of the software industry in India started around the late 1970s and early 1980s when four factor conditions for the explosion of software services were realized. First was the unbundling of software from hardware. This was largely due to a court decision in the US in the early 1970s, which opened up opportunities for technology entrepreneurs to introduce better-value-for-money software products than were available on the then predominant IBM and BUNCH computer systems—IBM, Burroughs, UNIVAC, NCR, CDC, and Honeywell. Second was the introduction of sophisticated yet value-for-money mini and supermini computers like DEC, Data General, PRIME, and APOLLO. These machines debunked the myth that computers had to be huge, as well as expensive to buy, maintain, and use. Thus, more and more corporations in the US started buying these machines and building systems on them. Third was the introduction of inexpensive, powerful, and easy-to-use Relational Database Management System-based Online Transaction Processing (OLTP) systems. Such systems allowed corporations to build the much-needed management systems to handle customers, products, raw materials and sub-assemblies, inventories, finance, payroll, and other hygiene systems. Since most of these supermini computer manufacturers did not have the manpower to do in-house development of such application software systems, a number of high-tech entrepreneurs came forward to provide services.

While the first three factor conditions were on the demand side, the fourth factor was on the supply side. Largely due to Nehru's post-Independence focus on higher education, India had developed abundant talent over the years in new hardware technologies, which were becoming very popular in India. In 1977, India saw a great opportunity when certain restrictive foreign direct investment policies led to the exit of IBM from India. The immediate impact was that many multinational corporations (MNCs) such as Honeywell and DEC were forced to form alliances with Indian firms. Similarly, Burroughs Corporation established a relationship with Tata Consulatancy Service (TCS), thus providing significant learning opportunities for Indian firms and its workforce.

GOVERNMENT POLICIES: PRE- AND POST-1991

Developments in computer hardware and software helped lay the technical foundations for the IT industry's growth. It is important to note that the phenomenal rise of India's IT sector would not have been possible without a series of government reforms, particularly those initiated in 1991.

The potential of IT was recognized by the Indian government as early as the 1960s, but it took little action to foster development in this area. Indeed, some of its policies outright hindered the industry's growth. During the late 1950s and early 1960s, a limited number of computers were imported, but were available for use only at select academic and research institutions. The government forbade the import of the latest IBM models to protect the Electronics Corporation of India Ltd. (ECIL), a government enterprise. Harsh fiscal measures also stymied computer imports, with ruinous duties of 150–300 per cent levied on all imports. Import licences were extremely difficult to acquire and regrettably India fell behind in taking advantage of advanced technologies as they occurred at record pace in the West.

However, not every government policy was destructive to the economy; a number of far-thinking initiatives actually aided the development of the fledgling industry. The Computer Policy of 1984, drafted by N. Seshagiri, facilitated the import of computers—for both end-users and software exporters. In 1986, the Mantosh Sondhi Committee allowed companies to import hardware against a promise to export software, an early example of sound government policy helping an industry to grow. Finally, the leadership of N. Vittal, the then secretary of the Department of Electronics (DoE), saw a number of reforms that helped to speed up and decentralize decision making.

The result was that Wipro and Hindustan Computers Ltd. (HCL) emerged as leaders in the hardware business, assembling central processing units based on Intel and Motorola chips. In the software area, TCS, Infosys, Patni Computer Systems, and Tata Unisys specialized in application and office productivity software. These companies took up customized application development, re-engineering existing applications from an old technology to a contemporary one or from one level of functionality to a higher level and performing maintenance to remedy bugs and organically evolve the software to keep pace with changing business practices.

It was also during the pre-1991 era that the country's top educational institutions, including the IITs and the RECs, introduced computer science as a subject of specialization at the undergraduate level of study.

It was around the same time that firms such as Aptech and NIIT were founded to train laypersons in the use of computers, further increasing the talent pool of educated, computer-literate individuals.

These early steps proved crucial for the industry to benefit from the economic reforms initiated in the budget proposals of 1991, when a severe economic crisis forced India to rethink its unviable, debilitating, and protectionist policies. The reforms, spearheaded by the then Prime Minister P.V. Narasimha Rao and his Finance Minister, Manmohan Singh (present Prime Minister of India), initiated a slew of reforms to liberalize India's economy.

The economic reforms solved four major bottlenecks to the growth of Indian IT companies. First was the introduction of current account convertibility, which helped remove hassles for Indian IT companies in obtaining foreign exchange for activities such as opening offices, hiring employees abroad, and hiring consultants from abroad in branding, marketing, and quality. Second was the abolition of the office of the Controller of Capital Issues (which neither understood capital markets nor business and, therefore, rarely allowed any premium at Initial Public Offers [IPOs], thus making equity not a viable financing option for entrepreneurs) that freed companies to hire investment bankers to decide on market-driven IPO pricing. This policy helped both the entrepreneurs and the investors benefit from the prospects of growth in the earnings of the company. This was god-send for the debt-shy IT entrepreneurs.

Third was to allow foreign companies in hi-tech areas 100 per cent ownership of their Indian subsidiaries. With 100 per cent equity ownership assured, major international corporations including IBM, Oracle, SAP, Microsoft, and Sun Microsystems opened offices in India. This policy decision did not impact Indian software companies on the customer front in India since their customers were primarily abroad. However, the presence of these companies enhanced competition for talent and forced Indian companies to bring many new competitive employee-oriented policies. Several of these MNCs established captive development centres in India. Indian IT companies were pushed to benchmark against global standards in quality, customer service, sales, marketing, and other areas of operational excellence.

The fourth policy was the reduction and rationalization of tariffs and duties on components, sub-assemblies, and products. The duty on software imports came down to zero. A zero duty on software, low duties on hardware, and zero tax on export profits were the ideal incentives for the software industry to aim for accelerated growth. Free markets incentivize companies to innovate and make it cheaper, faster, and better for customers to buy and use products and services designed by market players.

India is an excellent example of how innovation was used to leverage the power of globalization to produce high quality software, on time and within budgeted cost for global clients, particularly those in G8 countries. For instance, in the 1980s, the idea of going to the US prospects to sell our expertise in large-scale software development made people sceptical as to whether US companies and Indian companies could work together, particularly due to the huge time zone gap of 9.5 hours to 12.5 hours. That literally meant India and the US were as different as night and day! So, we started discussions on how to overcome this huge problem and convert this disadvantage into an advantage. The result was the unleashing of two major innovations—the 24-hour workday and the Global Delivery Model (GDM), both of which have become immensely successful models for remote, large-scale software development. In fact, GDM and the 24-hour workday have brought about a revolutionary change in productivity and quality of software development in the world. Perhaps, these two ideas are the most seminal contributions from India to the world in recent times, ranking on par with the lean manufacturing concepts introduced by Japan in the 1950s.

The 24-hour workday concept combines the prime time (8 a.m. to 6 p.m. of a working day) of the staff of a company A with the prime time of another company B located in a time zone 10 to 12 hours away to create a 24-hour workday. In other words, the workers of company B will be busy delivering productivity even when the workers of company A are sleeping! This reduces the time-to-market for innovations of company A and improves its competitiveness. This concept is extremely useful in near-real-time removal of bugs in a software system. Such productivity relay systems require complex technology-based systems and protocols that have been designed and implemented by Indian IT companies.

The Global Delivery Model leverages the power of software factory approach for remote, customized software development. In a typical project, about 20–30 per cent of the total effort that is customer-interaction-intensive is delivered at customer site, while 70–80 per cent of the total effort that is process-intensive is delivered from remote, scalable, process-driven, talent-rich, and cost-competitive development centres in countries like India. Therefore, using the GDM model, the customer gets better-value-for-money software on time and within budgets 95 per cent of the time compared with 45 per cent success rate using the traditional models during the 1980s.

Around the same time, N. Vittal, Secretary of the DoE, Government of India, took additional steps to accelerate the development of the IT industry through the Software Technology Parks of India (STPI) initiative. Designed as a scheme for 100 per cent export-oriented software companies, the STPI scheme allowed businesses to import duty-free software and hardware, and install their own earth stations or use the STPI earth stations for satellite-based data communications. They could also obtain tax-free status for exporting software from their own software centres at any location in the country. The data communications facility provided by STPI was in direct competition with Videsh Sanchar Nigam Ltd. (VSNL), the government-run telecommunications institution. The competition between these two entities led to an ever-increasing quality and bandwidth for data communications facility.

OTHER FACTORS FOR SUCCESS AND GROWTH

The Indian IT industry also benefitted from another important historical factor—familiarity with the English language. One of the most commonly cited advantages India held over other low-cost IT providers was its large pool of talented, educated, and English-speaking professionals. English being the de facto international language of business, the English-speaking Indian IT professionals could effectively communicate with their foreign clients, especially with the American firms such as General Electric (GE), Nortel, and American Express which made up the early wave of foreign customers working with the Indian IT industry. The willingness of Indian managers to adopt the best global practices in key areas like corporate governance and a well-established common legal framework made clients feel more comfortable and confident of doing business in India, compared with many other competitor-nations.

Indian IT companies realized pretty early that quality was a differentiating factor to win in the marketplace. These companies committed themselves to demonstrate that they were capable of delivering predictable and repeatable results that met international benchmarks for quality and productivity for their products and services. Therefore, these companies embraced quality standards like ISO 9001, Six Sigma, Malcolm Baldridge, and Level 5 (the highest level) of Capability Maturity Model (CMM) (of the Software Engineering Institute at Carnegie Mellon University in the US) to enhance the probability of success of large software projects from the then prevailing 45 per cent to an acceptable 95 per cent. Indian IT firms did so well in this certification race that they soon made up 65 per cent of the total companies worldwide holding the CMM Level 5 certification.

The cumulative effect of these factors—some technological, some resulting from government initiatives, a few innovations, and adherence to global practices by individual companies—accelerated the industry growth rates to 60–70 per cent. The reputation of the Indian software industry was tested and acknowledged when the Indian companies successfully managed to complete the time-bound upgradation of millions of software applications to handle the transition to the post-2000 era. Y2K triggered a massive boom in demand for the services of Indian software companies and confirmed India's reputation as the software development centre of the world.

SHIFTS IN THE INDUSTRY

The onset of the current millennium saw the IT industry undergo major shifts in the types of products and services it offered, and how it delivered these offerings. Some of these changes are described in this section.

From Application Development and Maintenance to Product Development

Much of the early work of the Indian IT industry revolved around Application Development and Maintenance (ADM). It involves studying the requirements of a business function for a corporation and building a software application that mimics such a business function conscientiously; upgrading an existing software application to handle new technologies or enhanced business functions; and taking care of bugs in the application or making minor improvements in the application to handle the evolution of business. Around the late 1980s, Infosys recognized that there was a market for a product aimed at a vertical industry like banking (in this case, a centralized banking solution) instead of providing a customized solution for the same problem for each new client in banking. Generally, it is known that such products provided higher per capita revenue productivity and are more profitable than services. Infosys recognized early on that scalability was much more difficult in service revenues and that Indian companies had to move towards products to handle accelerated revenue and profit growth. Thus, exclusive focus on service revenues began to change in the Indian software industry when Infosys introduced *Bancs2000*, a product platform for handling the core banking requirements of a large bank in India.

In July 2000, *Bancs2000* was re-launched as *Finacle*, a highly scalable, secure, and versatile version leveraging the power of the internet and addressing the real-time banking needs of global banks for their multi-country and multiple-currency operations. Infosys was successful in selling *Finacle* to a variety of clients—large Indian banks in the private and public sectors, multinational banks in India, building societies, and large banks in Asia, Europe, Australia, South America, Africa, and the US.

The following case study illustrates the versatility and power of *Finacle*. ICICI Bank was started by the Indian government as a development financing institution in the early 1950s and was transformed by visionary leadership into a universal bank in the post-deregulation and liberalization era to cater to the needs of India's growing masses and corporate sector. The value proposition of this bank was to leverage the power of technology to offer best-in-class customer service, efficiency, and cost that would place it on par with foreign banks but on a larger scale and at a lower cost. Today, ICICI Bank is the largest private sector bank in India and the second largest bank in India, next only to the venerable State Bank of India. *Finacle* helped ICICI Bank to manage its huge customer base and multiple subsidiaries by seamlessly integrating multiple applications including core banking, trade finance, credit cards, mutual funds, and data warehousing systems. ICICI Bank became the first Indian bank to offer internet banking in 1997, based on *Finacle's* banking solution. Today, it is the leader in e-banking services, an important area of growth. Internet banking and large number of ATMs at ICICI Bank increased transaction volumes and, due to *Finacle*, the bank scaled up seamlessly from 4,00,000 transactions a day in 2000 to nearly 2.1 million in 2005.

There are lessons for the Indian industry in the success of *Finacle*. *Finacle* succeeded because it offered a robust, scalable, secure, and contemporary product. It brought in enormous experience and domain expertise available in banking at Infosys. *Finacle* demonstrated that Indian IT companies can succeed in products if they can combine the technology knowledge of Indian software professionals with the domain expertise of banking professionals. *Finacle*'s success also demonstrated to the rest of the world that Indian IT had come of age and had the management and technology expertise to create enterprise-level products that have become the best-in-class products in a specific industry on a global basis. *Finacle*'s success brought a worthy Indian competitor like *I-Flex* which is now part of Oracle Corporation. *Finacle, I-Flex,* and other Indian software products have demonstrated that it is possible to produce large, world-class software products from India.

Business Process Outsourcing

As the Indian IT industry was approaching the new millennium, it was time for new thinking and new ideas of adding value to global corporations. The confidence that the Indian IT companies had acquired from delivering world-class software solutions came significantly from strict adherence to process orientation, technology expertise, and excellent work ethic. It was realized that these qualities could lead to another huge opportunity to create jobs for a large number of unemployed science, commerce, and arts graduates. This idea led to the creation of specialist companies that focused on BPO to provide process-oriented, back-office functions for their international clients.

The initial area of focus of BPOs was customer service for hi-tech companies like GE and Dell. The Indian staff of the BPO operations of these companies would manage the help-desks and answer calls from the customers of GE and Dell in the United States. The typical problems ranged from trouble-shooting to installation of proper software or hardware components for their remote customers. By 2000, several Indian companies had entered the BPO market and the industry expanded to financial and accounting services. The onset of 2002 saw companies specializing in BPO operations in the area of human resources. By 2004, the industry had entered the BPO operations in the purchase function of large US and European corporations.

The industry grew because it offered foreign companies an opportunity to reduce their sales, general and administrative (SG&A) expenses. Outsourcing work to the Indian BPO sector provided a number of key advantages to foreign companies—cost reduction was the most obvious. It is possible to hire an Indian graduate at a fraction of the cost of hiring a similar skilled graduate in the developed world. However, there are more important reasons for the success of our BPO industry. Indian software and consulting companies worked with BPO companies to reengineer and fine-tune processes to improve costs, productivity, and response times of operations for a business function. This industry leveraged the power of 24-hour workday described earlier and the Indian professional demonstrated good work ethic and learning abilities. With the help of Indian BPO companies, several well-known corporations have reduced their time-to-market for new product launches. Leveraging the power of Indian BPO companies, these global corporations have been able to swiftly react to changing customer preferences and provide 24-hour customer services without escalating their costs. They have been able to seamlessly handle the problems of integration of heterogeneous systems arising from mergers and acquisitions.

Today, the industry continues to be innovative and adaptive to enter new areas of BPO. Trade promotion, mortgage services, and healthcare are some of the sectors that offer significant future growth—companies like Infosys BPO and Genpact have invested heavily in training and innovation. A significant innovation is the concept of near-shore BPO centres where the BPO work is undertaken in a low-cost country near the client's base. Healthcare BPO work for American companies has to be handled within the borders of the country rather than in Bangalore for legal and logistical reasons. This requirement has led to Indian BPO companies expanding their expertise to on-shore process management. Another important innovation that Indian BPO companies have introduced is platform-based BPO. In a platform-based BPO application, a BPO company develops an entire business function process as a platform and takes up end-to-end responsibility for handling the relevant business function for a customer on a per-transaction fee basis rather than per-person-month basis. Such platforms provide easier scalability of revenues for BPO companies since the revenue is not linked to person-month effort.

Most estimates predict a bright future for the BPO industry since there is ample scope for reengineering and efficiency in business processes in a large number of corporations throughout the world. A recent report by McKinsey estimates that by 2020, the BPO market will be twice as large as the market for software services, with its market size increasing from USD 220 billion in 2008 to at least USD 900 billion in 2020. This growth will likely be driven both by the natural growth of the industry and by an increase in business processes that can be performed offshore.

Business processes in areas of finance, accounting, human resources, and procurement will continue to be significant drivers of growth, constituting an estimated 70 per cent of the market opportunity. According to estimates, by 2020, banking and financial services will be the largest segment of the market opportunity with an estimated market size between USD 125 billion and USD 135 billion. Green supply chain and smart grid implementation will be other areas of growth.

Independent Validation Services

In 2001, Infosys engineers realized that a considerable part of its market opportunities was enhancing the capabilities of existing applications. Such enhancements required an extensive testing regime to ensure that the enhanced application complied with all the requirements of existing functionalities as well as enhanced functionalities. Our engineers also observed that their customer staff was spending a significant part of their time in testing applications delivered by vendors since there was generally no formal robust methodology adopted by vendors for testing. Often, customers found that even a thoroughly tested and certified application did not perform up to expectations either in response time for an online application or throughout for a batch application. Thus, it became clear that there might be an independent business opportunity focusing exclusively on independent testing services. However, the challenge lay in convincing the customers that such testing could be outsourced to a company with professionals specially trained in the use of advanced testing and performance measurement tools.

The success of Infosys in Independent Validation Services (IVS) led to many other companies establishing such IVS units focused on providing testing services to customers; since then IVS has expanded rapidly. Today, this service is recognized as extremely valuable by global customers. The testing service has brought in several new ideas including testing of e-commerce applications, highly-scalable applications, peak-load testing, middleware, usability, and real-time, embedded applications.

The benefits of IVS are clear as the following case studies demonstrate. A large, international healthcare services provider hired an Indian testing services company to create a validation strategy and implement it for a new, online customer ordering system. The Indian company developed an advanced automatic tool for this project, reduced the testing effort by almost 50 per cent, and ensured an error-free system for deployment on time and within budget. It resulted in savings of nearly USD 1.5 million, reduced maintenance effort, and an increased confidence in the abilities of their IT team.

As businesses become ever more competitive and seek to cut costs wherever possible, reliable and efficient testing services based on methodologies, tools, and practices will become critical to reduce the time-to-market deployment of robust batch and internet-based systems. According to *Datamonitor*, the global market opportunity for testing services is likely to increase from USD 18 billion in 2008 to USD 30 billion in 2012.

Infrastructure Management Services and Remote Infrastructure Management

The Infrastructure Management Services (IMS) is perhaps one of the broadest services offered by IT companies. It involves managing the operations of data centres and core IT systems of an enterprise, including infrastructure like hardware, software, connectivity, and people. It includes management of software application, support services for hardware platforms and desktop computing services, security, and management of information. It has the potential to reduce cost of operations, eliminate huge backlogs of service requests, and improve security, efficiency, response times, and coverage of the data centre.

While traditional IMS remains important, Remote Infrastructure Management (RIM) has been growing rapidly. Remote Infrastructure Management is a prime example of the power of the GDM to reduce costs of operation, improve productivity, and leverage the power of the 24-hour workday concept in infrastructure management. Labour costs generally account for over 40 per cent of IT infrastructure budgets but RIM has the potential to reduce it by 45 per cent. Over the last seven years, RIM has become the fastest growing segment, growing at a rate of over 60 per cent annually. According to NASSCOM, by 2020, the core addressable market for RIM is expected to be between USD 120 billion and USD 130 billion. Traditional IMS services such as networks, servers, desktop, and helpdesk services will be performed remotely in the future, and the RIM market will offer the highest growth opportunity, accounting for 20–25 per cent of the incremental growth in this market. Although current penetration of RIM is only around 10 per cent, this figure is expected to grow to 55 per cent by 2020.

EMERGING TRENDS THAT WILL SHAPE THE INDUSTRY

A recent study by McKinsey argues that three global megatrends will reshape the Indian IT industry landscape over the next decade. They are macroeconomic and demographic trends, environmental trends, and business and technology trends.

Macroeconomic and Demographic Trends

The annual birth rate in the developed nations has been decreasing over the last two decades, resulting in the reduction of the working age population and an increase in the population of retired people. It is estimated that Japan's working age population will decline from 81.6 million today to 75 million in 2020, and the number of employees retiring from the services sector is likely to exceed 3 million in the next ten years. To put this in perspective, the number of such retiring people in Japan is 50 per cent higher than the entire workforce employed by the Indian technology and business services industry today. The number of people aged 60 and above in the US will expand from 38 million today to an estimated 54 million by 2020 as the baby boomer generation starts entering the retirement age.

The implications of these demographic trends on the IT industry are serious. There are two major implications of such a demographic trend. First, the number of people capable of providing important services like healthcare, banking, hospitality, legal, accounting, and travel reduces while the number of people requiring such services remains the same. Second, the segment of population that has retired has lower disposable income and requires cost-effective services; therefore, these nations will have to depend upon nations like India and China to provide cost-effective, essential services remotely for the aged people in developed nations. New productivity enhancing solutions based on redesigned processes will be needed to handle this huge likely demand.

Environmental Trends

Global warming is a source of increasing concern for all of us on this planet. However, IT can play a significant role in reducing global warming. There are two key areas with immense potential for the software industry to contribute to reduction of carbon: smart grids and the green supply chain.

The way of reducing overall carbon intensity is to improve utilization of the generated power on a global or at least a regional basis. Smart grids help reduce regional imbalances in power availability by managing demand and supply of power in real time, a huge opportunity for software developers. The IT expenditure for smart grid technology is expected to grow at a compounded rate of over 6 per cent in North America during 2009–14, a growth rate higher than that of the financial, manufacturing, or healthcare sectors. Analysts estimate that the total market potential for smart grid-related IT services may be as high as USD 10 billion over the next five years.

Over the last several years, rising energy costs, concern about CO_2 emissions, and government regulations have led companies around the world to focus on managing greener supply chains. As a result, the market for software and services in energy management is projected to grow to USD 20 billion to USD 22 billion. The major opportunities for growth will be in better energy management of production processes in energy-intensive manufacturing industries, optimization of supply chains to improve energy efficiency, and energy trading schemes.

Business and Technology Trends

Business models have undergone significant changes in recent times in response to new technologies and changing consumer preferences. This has led to disaggregation of the value chain. Competition is no more restricted to intra-industry competitors, but also to companies from other sectors that use innovations to insert themselves in inter-industry value chains. For instance, today, the distinction between a mobile operator and an online portal is fast decreasing as mobile operators have moved to content dissemination on their own platforms.

Similarly, newspapers compete for readership not just with online portals, but also with mobile operators. These are huge opportunities for Indian IT companies.

One of the most significant trends amongst traditional product companies is the decline of revenues from product sales or licence fees and an increase in revenues from services. This has caused supplier networks and ecosystems to emerge. Forrester, an industry analyst firm, has predicted the emergence of Software Innovation Networks built around open standards, middleware platforms, and software-as-a-service (SaaS) paradigm. While firms like SAP and Oracle have built supply-side ecosystems around middleware, SaaS vendors like Salesforce.com have built ecosystems around their hosted platforms.

Public Sector Opportunities

Public sector units and governments in developed countries have been slow to adopt new technologies. Governments and public sector units in developing nations have yet to leverage the power of IT on a large scale. However, countries like India, China, and Brazil have moved rapidly to install large-scale application systems in IT for tax management, e-governance, management of power generation and distribution, healthcare, food distribution, security, defence, and other vital functions of the government. Post 9/11, most governments in the developed world have focused on improving many of their security systems. These are huge opportunities.

New Technologies and Paradigms

Cloud computing is an internet-based development, harnessing the use of computing power. Users access cloud services through web browsers while their data is stored on servers. Typical cloud applications include SaaS, utility computing, Web services, and platform-as-a-service (PaaS). Cloud computing represents a number of powerful advantages for enterprises. It allows them to tap into talent both internally and externally. Companies such as Apple and Facebook have leveraged this advantage by allowing developers to contribute applications that are run on the company's platforms. Cloud computing provides a big opportunity for Indian IT companies in areas like security, cost-effective development, and deployment of SaaS for their customers.

Effect of these Megatrends

The effect of these megatrends will most likely be a three-fold expansion of the addressable market (total revenue potential) for technology and business services from USD 500 billion today to approximately USD 1.5–1.6 trillion by 2020. According to the McKinsey estimates, these currently untapped segments will drive up to 80 per cent of this incremental growth. This growth includes USD 190–220 billion from new verticals in developed countries, USD 230–250 billion growth from new segments such as small and medium businesses, and USD 380–420 billion growth from new geographies, especially the BRIC nations (Brazil, Russia, India, and China).

WHAT SHOULD WE DO TO CONTINUE OUR SUCCESS IN IT?

For the first time in the recent history of India, we have received global acclaim. And this has been in just one field, software exports. While what we have achieved is creditable, we are still at the very early stages of our marathon. If we have to make good of our potential, then there are certain urgent initiatives that the country—the political leadership, the bureaucracy, the academia, and the corporate leadership—will have to take up. Here are a few ideas.

Become Visa-independent

The biggest risk to this industry is the huge dependence of Indian companies on work visas issued by host countries for our professionals to stay there and complete the assignments. Given that unemployment is increasing in developed countries, there is a high risk of some of these countries abolishing work visas like the H1B. Such a situation will impact the industry heavily since almost half of the revenue of the software segment of the industry comes from on-site services which require these visas. There are several remedies for mitigating this risk. A few of them are as follows:

• Recruit local talent in the host countries to perform all customer-site activities. This requires extra expenditure and the ability of the senior management of Indian companies to work with a multicultural workforce, particularly from developed countries.

- The industry should drive non-linear revenues by creating and monetizing intellectual property. While it has built a growing brand in technology and business services, the industry has to achieve a similar recognition for its software products. This requires building a strong investment ecosystem with collective participation of product companies, industry bodies, academia, and the government.

- The industry players must build specific solutions in selected domains like logistics, embedded systems, and port management.

Evolve a Consensus on the Usefulness of IT

Quick decision-making and focused implementation of policies is essential to bring the benefits of IT to the vast masses of our country. This requires a consensus amongst all hues of political thinking that IT will indeed help the lot of the common man. We cannot afford prolonged discussions on whether or not IT is good. In fact, our political leaders have to become evangelists for technology, in general, and IT, in particular. They have to lead by using IT themselves and demonstrate how productive they have become by using IT. This is particularly important if BPO companies have to create jobs for the rural folks.

Embrace Competition

As my friend, Rahul Bajaj, has often said, the greatest management guru is competition. Unless Indian companies realize the importance of competition and customer focus, the use of IT will not become all-pervasive in the corporate world. This is even truer of government departments and the public sector. For these institutions to deliver faster, better, and cheaper services to the citizens by way of e-governance and e-commerce, they have to invest heavily in IT and reap the benefits on an urgent basis.

Reduce Friction to Business

Today's competitive and dynamic business environment demands that quick decisions be made right in the boardrooms rather than waiting for approvals from New Delhi. In a developing country like India, the government plays an important role in the destiny of a corporation. Further, as Indian companies move towards increased globalization, the governments at the centre and the states will have to push the envelope on reducing the rule set. This requires quick and decentralized approvals from state capitals and proximate government offices, if at all, rather than from New Delhi. The government has to become a catalyst rather than a controlling authority. While the government has, by and large, become responsive to the needs of the corporate world, it is a question of fine-tuning in a few more areas.

Enhance Availability of Talent

Barring the last two years, the software and the BPO industries have had a robust growth in the previous five years. The domestic IT industry has grown equally fast during the same period. The demand for IT is likely to continue over the next ten to twenty years. Thus, the need of the day is to improve the supply-side situation. The IT industry is absorbing a large number of engineering and science graduates and is, in fact, attracting a large number of professionals from other areas of engineering such as power, construction, automobiles, steel, etc. Several countries have launched initiatives to attract Indian software professionals. Thus, unless we take urgent steps to start new colleges to produce IT professionals, increase focus on IT education in our existing curricula, and enhance the intake at various existing institutions of learning, the industry will not be able to grow at the required pace to reach the USD 300 billion target by 2020. Further, the quality of education provided has to be improved significantly. This requires that we allow private universities to come up and also invite well-known educational institutions from abroad to establish a presence in India and thereby create a competitive scenario. There is also a great need for increased interaction between Indian industry and academia to push the envelope in applications and software engineering practices. This is particularly true if we want to become better at product development.

Improve Infrastructure

It is unrealistic to expect the IT and the software industry to grow indefinitely unless we improve basic infrastructure like airports, roads, hotels, housing, schools, and power. Generally, development of a nation has to be organic and all-round. It is improbable to see how we can reach the USD 300 billion target for software exports with our existing physical and technological infrastructure. If we want the internet to be ubiquitous and benefit the common man, then affordable broadband facility has to reach every village. In a developing country like India, the pricing of these services has to be a small fraction of the disposable incomes for various segments rather than being linked with costs of similar services abroad. Improvement of infrastructure in rural areas is very critical to create BPO job opportunities in rural India.

Embrace e-Governance to Realize Transparency

It is necessary that there be transparency in governance and policy formulation. This is mandatory if we want world-class companies to participate in our nation-building process and in making our IT industry strong enough to be globally competitive. E-governance will improve transparency, reduce corruption, and improve consumer comfort. Projects like the Unique Identification number (UID) are a good start.

Create Suitable Conditions for Increased Entrepreneurial Activity

India has done a good job in creating a suitable rule set for attracting venture capital to the country. The results are already perceptible. Indian rules on Employee Stock Option Plans are probably among the best in the world. However, in certain areas like labour laws, we have to reduce the hassle of dealing with the complex rule sets of myriad state and central government institutions, if we wish to fully reap the benefits from the above progressive measures.

Liberalize Rules for Internet, Data, and Voice Communication

The internet will be a key vehicle of growth for the Indian economy. Restrictions in India on voice-over-IP and on connectivity between the PSTN and private networks for voice and data should go. Given that world-class communication infrastructure is a key factor condition for software exports, such barriers may hamper the long-term growth prospects for this sector.

Rationalize the Duty Structure for Manufacturing

Unless our hardware industry grows in a big way, we will not be able to leverage the power of IT for the common man. Hardware costs will have to come down, which can happen only by increasing volumes. This requires a rationalized duty structure that supports value-addition through manufacturing. We have to improve the supply-chain efficiency by improving our customs operations, port-handling, banking, government-factory interfaces, and a host of factors that reduce speed and increase corruption in the government services.

Create a Regulatory Framework that Enables Indian Companies to become World-class

Attracting global customers and investors requires that we enhance their comfort levels by instituting global standards in corporate governance. Similarly, bureaucratic procedures in setting up trading offices, branches, and subsidiaries have to be minimized. We have to change our mindset from one of thinking that we are doing the international investors a favour to one of making them feel welcome.

Companies to Focus on Operations to Move Up the Value Chain

By and large, Indian hardware companies have had some focus in their operations. However, this can hardly be said of Indian software companies. In fact, the most common complaint of clients abroad is that most Indian software companies claim every area under the sun as their area of expertise! While there may be many reasons for this, including low volumes in specific areas, such unfocused operations lead to erosion of credibility and low quality of service to clients. A stronger focus will also help software companies obtain domain knowledge and thereby move up the value chain.

Develop Better Appreciation for IT

It is universally agreed that a key reason for the failure of IT projects is the inability of the end-users to appreciate the value that IT can bring to the table. An offshoot of this is the unwillingness of the end-users to pay a fair price for software.

Often, users do not show adequate interest in allocating quality time to project personnel from their IT vendors. Usually, this results in inordinate delays and cost overruns. Coupled with the fact that the opportunity cost of taking up an Indian project is very high for an Indian software company, this explains why most Indian software companies are loath to taking up domestic projects. However, this mindset is changing in recent years since there are huge opportunities in IT in the government sector and in the public sector in India.

Create Better Brand Equity Abroad

High growth, high per capita revenue productivity, and high margins require attracting the best customers in the marketplace and the best employees from the local talent pool. This can only be done by establishing strong brand equity on a global scale. India has not been able to create a single global brand so far. The software industry offers an opportunity to break this jinx but this initiative requires visionary thinking, considerable spending, and excellent execution.

Better Collaboration between Industry and Academia

Our desire to move up the value chain and to become innovators in IT and BPO requires that we leverage the enormous capabilities of our academic institutions. Our brethren in academia have to enhance their focus on problem-solving orientation rather than the traditional Indian mindset of research for research's sake.

As we ponder the developments over the last twenty-five years, there is great satisfaction in the progress this industry has made in competing in international markets, in accepting globalization, in benchmarking with global best practices, and in accepting competition from outside. But, these are just the first few steps of the marathon. Jawaharlal Nehru laid the foundation for knowledge-based industries in India, and presented the country with an opportunity to move into the next orbit. We are confident that the political leadership, the bureaucracy, the corporate leaders, and the academia will move forward with even greater enthusiasm and fulfil the dream of our first prime minister.

S. RAMADORAI

10   IT and Global Footprint

To trace the footprint of 'computerization' (as the IT industry was yet to be born) in India, one needs to travel back in time. Among the visionary leaders of post-Independence India, one man, Homi J. Bhabha stood tall. He advocated the case for atomic energy way back in 1948 when there were no nuclear power reactors in the world. USA itself set up the first commercial nuclear power reactor nearly nine years later. So convincing were his ways that Prime Minister Nehru did little to disagree. Bhabha recognized the importance of science and technology, not just for India's economic progress, but also as a means to improve the quality of lives.

With the help of a grant of Rs 45,000 from Sir Dorab Tata Trust and the support of J.R.D. Tata, Bhabha established the Tata Institute of Fundamental Research (TIFR) in Bangalore in 1945. Six months later, he shifted the institute to Bombay. The institute became the cradle of India's atomic energy programme and was involved with the early growth of IT in India.

In the 1960s the Government of India felt the need of a strong indigenous electronics base for both security and national development. An Electronics Committee was set up, not surprisingly, under the Chairmanship of Bhabha. In its report in 1966, the Committee focused on computers as tools 'to the development of a new outlook and a new scientific culture'. In 1970 the Department of Electronics (DoE) came into being as a 'scientific ministry' directly under the prime minister.

At the Centre was a socialist government struggling to deal with poverty and natural disasters that affected millions of Indians. It was a highly regulatory environment then, a challenging time for free enterprise. Importing of computers was a complex process. Some of us experienced this first hand. Imagine bright, young, and enthusiastic US trained computer experts raring to go but trapped in the myriad regulatory haze of a government in the licence raj. With a domestic market not ready and a government not willing, what other option was there but to look westwards. The spectacular growth of the IT industry as we know it today, took place because of the government and also in spite of it.

When the Indian software industry started in the late 1960s, we started with several handicaps and needed to learn everything from scratch. The globalization of the IT industry in India is punctuated with IT-enabled services (ITES) that were able to create a value transition for our clients. It is these value transitions that created the business opportunity for the industry at every stage of its evolution.

In the beginning we had to bootstrap our understanding of IT and the domains it is applied to. Not only did we have to learn programming languages, we also had to learn the many idiosyncrasies of the computer, operating systems, utilities, etc. We needed to understand the processes of software development. This was the first step in value transition—we started as team members, module leaders, and project leaders in small assignments where we were essentially sub-contract staff. Since we had to depute our programmers to client locations overseas, we also had to grapple with complicated administrative, visa, legal, and tax issues of various countries and prepare our technologists to work in foreign environments in terms of developing social skills.

The evolution to turnkey projects and executing projects off-shore was the second step in the value transition. We developed competencies in project management, quality and delivery processes, and infrastructure management. We started building our own fledgling products. We were moving from pure cost arbitration to a cost plus quality value-add.

The next step in value transition came from systems integration and outsourcing assignments, with responsibility for managing large, multi-vendor engagements. We built a small number of world-class products which signalled the onset of the wave of innovation. Our credential established in the West, positioned us well, to sell cost plus value plus innovation value-add.

Today Indian software companies are globally positioned with intellectual competencies to serve an array of offerings in several domains, technologies, with processes to deliver complex solutions, and to sell and support these in all parts of the world. As we say to our customers in Tata Consultancy Services (TCS), we have the capabilities to not just run the business but also help you transform it. There is a realization that to leverage investments in IT, it must become a more integral part of the overall business strategy.

For greatest impact, IT systems should not be viewed as an 'add on' but must be embedded in the process of planning the business strategy. Management processes, departmental workflows, and decision-making data systems—all of these must adapt to a new and efficient way of functioning. We must note that the innovation in technology we speak of is both disruptive and sustainable, to use the language made so popular by Clayton Christensen. Every disruptive innovation creates a series of sustainable innovations that help consolidate the new path opened by it. The IT industry is a classic example of this simple but powerful truth.

GLOBAL FOOTPRINT—DEFINITION, ORIGIN, AND DEVELOPMENT

When you build a new business, as we were doing back then, acquiring the first customer is always the greatest challenge—it is that crack in the door that one looks for, that with further perseverance makes further inroads easier. In the IT industry, at least from an Indian perspective, 'opening up' may be traced to two defining events. The first was TCS being asked by Burroughs Corporation (now part of Unisys) to install its application systems for US-based clients. Burroughs was attracted by the combination of software engineering talent and the English language that it had found in TCS's workforce. This was the beginning of the 'body-shopping' business, which entailed the dispatch of Indian programmers to the sites of overseas clients. But before TCS could do that, it had to acquaint itself with Burroughs systems software and hence had to import the systems by giving software export guarantees to the Government of India. This was a bold and innovative step. Tata Consultancy Services won the mandate against stiff competition. With the rise of the internet and communication technologies there was soon a realization that much of the work could be managed at far lower costs from India itself and the off-shoring model took form. In a paper titled 'Moving Tata Consultancy Services into the "Global Top 10"', Dossani and Kenney (2004) argue that 'these changes set the stage for undertaking work in India rather than overseas at the customer's site' Texas Instruments (TI) in 1985, in response to the New Computer Policy of the Government of India. Taxes Instruments, whose wholly-owned foreign subsidiary was the first to enter the Indian software industry since IBM's departure in 1978, persuaded the government to supply it with scarce satellite bandwidth and used programmers working out of its offices in Bangalore. Soon, several multinational firms imitated TI's delivery model and began to do product development work in India'.

We understand 'IT and Global Footprint' in a nuanced sense. On the one hand, it refers to the IT industry spreading its wings across the globe. The pioneering work by Indian IT companies is being followed by countries both big and small, like China to Singapore, striving to get a share of this global business.

On the other hand, it refers also to enabling customers to extend their footprint. To take an example, the idea of an extended enterprise became a practical reality when customers and suppliers could access a company's IT system from their locations, thus becoming part of an extended enterprise. As Dossani and Kenney point out, firms used to work on the client's site because they could not afford to buy or rent computers locally but, in the process, needed to offer different programming skills from those needed to work on machines from IBM, Burroughs, VAX, etc. 'It was not until tariffs were reduced and Unix became an accepted programming standard in the mid-1980s that offshore work for clients became feasible' (Dossani and Kenney 2004). In a fundamental sense, the final piece in this deep shift came with the origin and development of 'remote project management' which subsequently became the 'Global Delivery Model' and ended with the current 'Global Networked Delivery Model'—breakthroughs for which TCS can take credit.

Yet another perspective could well argue that the IT industry as we know today began with the separation of software from hardware. A crucial factor as Michael Cusumano (2004) observes is that software was bundled with hardware and sold together; moreover, it was not 'open'.

This separation of the software from the hardware, together with the new platform of personal computers (PCs) that emerged in the 1970s and IBM's decision to outsource the operating system to a start-up company called Microsoft Corporation was decisive in a deep, generational sense. Once made independent of hardware, software has made strides that would have been unthinkable otherwise.

The next platform—the World Wide Web—did something that was astonishing: liberating users from a particular machine. Today, we take it for granted that we can access the WWW from anywhere and any machine, but when it started, it was a celebration of freedom. To this background, if we add the Y2K problem, which does have a very Indian ring to it, and attempts to find a solution to it, we can gauge the vital factors that explain the global footprint of IT.

THE Y2K 'PROBLEM'

In a case study 'Tata Consultancy Services: Globalisation of IT Services', John D. Roberts and Gary Mekikian (2009a), while discussing the Y2K problem, observe that

As the twentieth century came to a close, the Y2K problem threatened to bring multi-trillion dollar Western economies to a halt, shut down computerized defense systems in North America and Europe, leave nuclear power plants without control systems, and imperil key public health and transport systems. At this time, the provision of IT services was the exclusive domain of large Western technology companies and accounting firms with consulting arms, but Indian companies were being invited to help governments and large multinationals alike to resolve the Y2K problem in their software, before time ran out. Chief Information Officers (CIOs) who would talk only to trusted suppliers like IBM, Andersen Consulting (also known as Accenture) and the like, found themselves shipping millions of lines of proprietary software code to India to have the time bombs diffused in Indian Y2K factories. Even prestigious companies like Accenture were subcontracting Y2K work to Indian companies.

As the race against time gathered steam, Indian IT consulting firms were there with the right tools, resources, and market position to take advantage of the opportunities. It is now common knowledge that Indian firms played a large part in facilitating humankind's technological transition from the second to the third millennium without major disruptions.

In another study the duo co-authored, they note that, 'By the time the world breathed a sigh of relief at the end of the day on 1 January, an estimated USD 300 billon had been spent on IT services' (2009b).

Quite possibly, the IT industry as we know today could well have emerged even in the absence of the Y2K problem, but it is doubtful if the scale of the business would have been the same. To be sure, Indian IT companies were already exporting software, principally to the USA and some parts of Europe. What the Y2K problem did was to demonstrate that Indian IT companies, who did bulk of the work, were capable of much more than they were thought capable of—giving them an enormous global exposure in a compressed time span.

As CEO of TCS during those eventful times, I can testify to this. Y2K was a seriously disruptive element and turned out to be a game-changing factor; we seized the initiative. Once we accomplished this feat, what the Y2K work did was give us scale, which then began to attract scale. We need not look for evidence of this in industry figures but in one simple incontrovertible fact. Indian IT firms that shunned the Y2K work, for whatever reason, have just not able to rise to the level of those that did. The IT industry is full of legendary misses but this would surely rank very high.

THE INTERNET

The impact of the Internet on growth within the IT industry and, through that, on industry has been phenomenal and extremely well-documented. However, we need to note that the internet transformed the IT industry from one focused only on businesses to one that extended also to customers. As Roberts and Mekikian note, 'But with the advent of the Internet and inexpensive Web technologies, thousands of companies began to sprout up to provide Web-based consumer services, which created a whole new market for IT services companies—catering to Web-based companies such as Amazon.com and eBay' (ibid.).

The emergence of internet is indeed an amazing phenomenon. In the late 1990s, an Indian infrastructure finance company discovered a 'novel' financing structure for a project through the internet. While the cliché is that the world has become smaller (ironically, it has not), the more appropriate way to understand this is to see how technology stands as a magnifier of ideas. If Newton saw more because, as he modestly said, he was standing on the shoulders of giants, in today's context we can say that we can also stand on many shoulders. It is largely due to the advent of the search engines like Google, Yahoo!, and Bing that the internet helps people access work done in the remotest corners of the world and expands everyone's horizon and footprint.

Although it could not have been part of its conscious agenda, the internet, by bifurcating the IT industry into business and consumers, introduced far-reaching changes. While the enterprise side of the business led the innovation since the inception of the industry, in the last decade or so, it is the set of innovations catering to consumers which is driving the industry while also influencing innovation for enterprises. If we add to this the deep changes still happening within the telecom business, shifting from a network-based business to one driven by software, the potential for further changes is enormous.

Much has been made of the so-called Web 2.0 and so on. Tim Berners-Lee scoffed at the term and all that has gone with it because, to him, this is what the internet is all about and was meant to be since its birth. It makes collaboration easier and simpler, if there is a will, and can really strive towards a different model of software development than hitherto considered feasible. Arguably, the greatest benefit of the current generation of internet technologies is that they have spread innovation wider, letting a larger number of people participate and contribute meaningfully towards some concrete benefit. The innovation ecosystem has become more extended than before.

As mentioned earlier, innovation and the IT industry go together, in a mutually reinforcing and beneficial relationship. Of course, there are many ways to approach innovation, but one which has caught the imagination of many companies is the idea of open innovation models. There is no argument over the absolute importance of R&D but only that its trajectory is undergoing a fundamental change; it is now widely accepted that the size of R&D budget per se cannot guarantee positive results. It is the quality of work and path-breaking innovation that will take firms forward. I take pride in saying that TCS, then a division in Tata Sons, was the first IT company in India and among the earliest in the world, to set up the Tata Research and Development and Design Centre (TRDDC) in 1980, before any Indian IT company even considered the idea. And we have continued in that mode ever since, continuously introducing innovative changes and also adapting to the environmental changes. Success comes to those who can do both, for instance, imbibing the principle of co-creating value, we have patented a methodology we call COIN, which stands for co-innovation, where we work with both customers and technology partners in creating innovative products and services.

EXTENDING THE GEOGRAPHY

While India has begun the globalization of IT services, many countries are now developing their competitiveness to attract more of this business or certain specific parts to them. Randeep Sudan et al. (2010) describe how several countries are already involved and how they are sharpening their strengths to attract more business in IT and ITES. Quoting McKinsey & Co., they estimate the IT market to have been worth USD 500 billion in 2008. The ITES market estimates vary significantly between USD 171 billion in 2008 and projected to be USD 239 in 2011 (Gartner) and USD 700–800 billion by 2012 according to NASSCOM. It is generally accepted that opportunities (and compulsions) to outsource more and more of these will only grow. The footprint will become more global than before.

Among the most interesting revelations is that Canada follows India in market share, claiming 29 per cent to India's 54 per cent in the global off-shore IT services market and 27 per cent to India's 37 per cent in the ITES market. The Philippines follows Canada in the ITES market with 15 per cent, with the rest scattered over Ireland, Mexico, Central and Eastern Europe, China, and others. One dimension becomes clear—country size per se is not relevant but what is relevant is the talent pool. Countries with smaller population can be expected to have a specialized focus (Canada and Ireland) while countries like India and China can target both the general and the specialized. There have been many engaging debates in the global media and in academic circles on how these footprints will shape the two industries.

GROWING, DIVERSE FOOTPRINT

Being in business, we naturally tend to think from commercial perspectives, but the potential of IT extends beyond. Its ability to influence development, its role in national defence, and its role in governance is quite simply as important as its role in business. E-governance initiatives are becoming more of a necessity than a fanciful way of conducting operations. Importantly, its potential to enhance the quality of governance has also equally been recognized. The very term 'digital divide' tells us that we still have a long way to go, notwithstanding all the spectacular achievements that the IT industry has made. Internet has a seminal role in functioning democracies. It works as a powerful medium of communication, and facilitates common people to address their day-to-day issues in a more effective way.

Whatever the divergent views on this topic, there is a consensus that any lowering of entry barriers could potentially enlarge the footprint. We have seen this in a spectacular manner in cell phones. There is so much that people can do with cell phones that certain businesses (cameras) are under serious threat. However, their capacity to help people with less resources and to reach the far corners of the world is truly astounding. The role being played by cell phones in social amelioration is very well documented. The battle is not over because all the elements that were there in the early stages of IT can now be seen in the mobile phone industry. Interestingly, some software bundled with and working with specific hardware (handsets), some working with any handset, proprietary software, and at times even in absence of interoperability, handsets working in select countries. As any intuitive reader would have gathered by now, overcoming some of these obstacles is critical to further extending IT's global footprint.

Another factor that could increase the footprint is the growth of what has come to be called 'cloud computing', if it fulfils the potential that many have come to associate with it. This is not the occasion to enter into a detailed discussion on cloud computing but the fact is that even governments of advanced economies have begun to embrace it. In the US, the federal government and even some states have already gone ahead. In the UK, the government has recently finalized plans for cloud computing. Many large companies and also small- and medium-sized companies are also strong advocates.

THE FUTURE

In an industry where there are several layers of both technology and firms, it is difficult to visualize the shape of the future. Boundaries are getting blurred, as technology is facilitating competition from anywhere and anyone. Technology opens up a world of possibilities. Those who seize hold of it will make big strides. We simply have to look at some of the 'new' businesses that some technology firms have entered within the last five years to realize how profound the changes are and what they hold further for the future. Of one thing, I am sure: Leadership consists in being able to influence change rather than merely respond to it. The footprints will belong to the new leaders.

REFERENCES

Dossani, Rafiq and Martin Kenney (2004), 'Moving Tata Consultancy Services into the "Global Top 10"', *JSME*, Vol. 1(2).

Cusumano, Michael A. (2004), *The Business of Software: What Every Manager, Programmer, and Entrepreneur Must Know to Thrive and Survive in Good Times and Bad*, New York: Free Press.

Roberts, John D. and Gary Mekikian (2009a), *Tata Consultancy Services: Globalization of IT Services*. Stanford Graduate School of Business.

_____ (2009b), 'Note on the Services Industry', Stanford Graduate School of Business, 24 April.

Sudan, Randeep, Seth Ayres, Philippe Dongier, Siou Chew Kuek, Arturo Muente Kunigami, Christine Zhen-Wei Qiang, and Sandra Sargent (2010) [2008], *The Global Opportunity in IT-Based services*, Washington DC: World Bank.

F.C. KOHLI

11 Evolution of Information Technology in India
A Personal Perspective

As an outstanding physicist with an engineering background, Homi Bhabha had a very clear vision in all areas of science and technology ranging from particle physics to digital electronics. He could see very clearly what the electronic revolution could do for India. With the support of M.G.K. Menon and R. Narasimhan, he launched into frontier areas of science of those times. One such area was building India's first digital computer in 1960. There is universal agreement now that the computerization of the country and growth of Information Technology (IT) started from that point. As indicated by others in the book, dissemination of computers in India initiated through this effort was quickly followed by the arrival of IBM 1620 at IIT Kanpur and thereafter by the CDC 3600 at the Tata Institute of Fundamental Research (TIFR) as a National Computational Facility. As part of the Tata group of companies, my journey into computers and IT began with my association with this national facility. In the rest of the essay, I shall delve into our vision of enlarging the usage of computers in India, ranging from process control to business, possible impediments due to the socio-political climate in India, successes and failures, and also what we should be doing to get an edge on IT supremacy.

THE COMPUTER ERA—THE BEGINNINGS

My association with CDC 3600 happened through the Tata Electric Companies (TEC) who made extensive use of the computer in various ways such as computerizing of operations, maintenance, and design of the Tata electric grid and power system applications such as Load Flow Analysis and Transient Stability studies. The Tata Electric Company moved from using the analogue Network Analyser at the Indian Institute of Science, Bangalore, to the digital computer at TIFR. The next step for TEC was the installation of a digital computer to control the grid that included hydro-stations and the thermal station at Trombay. These were the Koyna hydro-power station of Maharashtra State Electricity Board, the Tarapore atomic power plant, and the thermal plant of Railways at Kalyan near Mumbai. However, the Government of India was very reluctant to sanction TEC an import licence for importing the digital computer from Westinghouse Corporation, USA, as it was of the view that India was not ready to move from analogue to digital system. Its reasoning was based on the fact that at that time the UK, France, Germany, and Japan were still on analogue computers and there were only three or four digital installations in the US. The point I want to make is that the move from analogue to digital technology in the country was envisaged quite early. Of course, in spite of the above hurdles, computerization in TEC did take place—largely due to the National Computation facility and the computer people at TIFR. In short, the move from analogue to digital technology for several applications in the country would not have taken place without the leadership that TIFR provided.

In 1969, when I assumed charge of Tata Consultancy Services (TCS), we saw tremendous potential in the areas of automation, precision control in manufacturing systems, studies in utilities, and processing of large volumes of data, particularly for the finance industry and the government. In a sense, this could be called the launching of IT in India.

Early Years of Computer Applications

Tata Consultancy Services faced immense challenges in the initial years since the technology was new and moving very rapidly. This required that all those working with new technology needed continuing education and to work closely with the US and the West. We recognized that the country had outstanding capability and quality of minds which can be tapped into. In January 1975, in the presidential address to the Computer Society of India's annual convention in Ahmedabad, I said,

Lastly, I want to say that many years ago there was an industrial revolution, and now is the time for revolution in Information Technology, which requires neither mechanical bias nor mechanical temperament. Primarily, it requires the capability to think clearly. This we have in abundance. We have an opportunity even to assume the leadership. If we miss this opportunity, those who will follow us will not forgive us for our tardiness and negligence.

At that time there was a lack of availability of hardware in India and restrictions on imports of computers and related equipment. The attitude of the government was not favourable in those days towards import of computers and TCS had to wait for three years to get the import licence to get a Burroughs B6800 computer. Tata Consultancy Services was willing to undertake exports much in excess of the cost of the computer. This action delayed building capability in north India with regard to software industry in the early stage of development.

Some of us saw the future of IT for India and its consequent benefit to the country. Tata Consultancy Services had designed the Permanent Account Number (PAN) system for the department of Income Tax in 1976. Following that project, the Department of Revenue gave TCS the assignment to computerize the entire Income Tax system. We had progressed with the project significantly, and after we had completed the first half of the project, the government at that time strongly argued against any computerization for India and this resulted in cancellation of the project. Had this project been completed, India would have been perhaps the first country to computerize the entire working of the Income Tax department.

We, however, kept on updating our technology knowledge base, and also reviewing current trends so that we may go for more complex, comprehensive assignments in the future. The very first assignment that TCS got and the first for India from abroad was towards the end of 1974. The assignment was done entirely out of the country. It was a healthcare system for Burroughs in the US. Burroughs then was the second largest computer company after IBM. Over the years, TCS achieved recognition for its services. After 1984, there was a proliferation of software companies in India to handle the Y2K problem in which TCS took a leading role. The success of those efforts gave a big boost and confidence to the Indian IT industry.

India and the World IT Market

India's revenue from software services in 2009–10 was about USD 73.1 billion. The total worldwide software market is worth USD 2,000 billion, out of which outsourcing services are about USD 300 billion. India's domestic software market is about USD 12 billion, the outsourcing is about USD 54 billion, and the hardware industry is about USD 11.7 billion, while exports stand at USD 0.3 billion. Much of computer hardware and components are imported. Overall, the country's exports are substantial. We are providing services at the upper end of the spectrum in engineering design, embedded systems, financial systems, and decision support systems, apart from building software tools. The country is accepted as a source of reliable and quality service providers. There is also work done at the lower end like Business Process Outsourcing services, which provides employment for a large number of people. The industry has created over 2.5 million jobs for professionals and many more at the support level.

GROWTH FACTORS FOR IT APPLICATIONS

Every country that has deployed IT extensively has seen increased employment growth. Large and small enterprises, retail services, and individuals have become highly efficient and productive. This is true not only in the West and Japan, but also in the South Asian countries and China.

Coming to India, the level of computerization is extremely low. India has hardly any hardware industry. Its software industry is mainly export-oriented and the software is written largely in English. There is a need to use computers extensively in all spheres like government, defence, manufacturing, financial industry, agriculture, transportation, education, and retail services. There are 900 million people who do not speak English; they need software in Indian languages and hardware at affordable prices. The hardware and software output is less than 2 per cent of the world IT output. As of November 2010 India had 40 million PCs compared to 1 billion worldwide. In most of the advanced countries, the government sector constitutes 50 per cent of total computerization, that is, of federal, state, transport, defence, and other sectors, but in India, it is about 10 per cent. There is some computerization in the industrial and manufacturing units, but they are exceptions. We are, however, going to be forced to computerize because of globalization and the convergence of computers and communications, which offer great opportunities. In business and industry, we are already seeing enterprise resource planning, inventory management, processing, and automation.

Hardware Manufacturing

As mentioned earlier, there is hardly any hardware industry in the country. At the government level there is not sufficient recognition that IT is both software and hardware, and not software alone. To achieve the desired level of computerization, India would need to add 20 million PCs per year. In addition, it would need digital components for digital television sets, communications including mobile phones, industrial controls, video and sound equipment, automobiles, and other industries including defence. The three stages in the manufacture of digital components are:

• *Design Engineering*: This is carried out using special advanced software on computers, requiring microelectronics engineering skills.

• *Embedded Software*: As part of increasing functionality, more and more software is being embedded into the hardware as 'below OS level' software. Microelectronics engineers and software engineers can be trained to provide such services.

• *Fabrication Outsourcing*: Fabrication requires silicon foundries. Fabrication facilities are available outside the country (Taiwan, Singapore, Korea, Thailand, and Malaysia), and it can be outsourced.

Fortunately, the first two stages constitute 80 per cent of the cost of the digital components, for which India can build necessary skills and experience. About five years ago, there was an effort to assemble fully configured PCs for less than Rs 10,000. Last year HCL placed in the market fully configured computers with monitors for less than Rs 10,000 per set.

Software Design and Development for Domestic Use

For countrywide application of computers, India needs software (operating system, middleware, and application software) in Indian languages. Considerable work on software in Indian languages is being done at C-DAC, IITs, NCST, and many other institutions. Today we have Open Source Operating System (Linux), Middleware like Foxpro and MY SQL, and a few applications available in all twenty-two Indian languages, but more application packages need to be translated. This needs greater and sustained support on the part of software companies for release of early versions of their packages to be translated into Indian languages.

Software for Small Engineering Units

In Coimbatore there are more than 5,000 small engineering workshops, and each workshop has ten to twenty highly skilled and innovative workers. They engineer and supply automotive components, pumps, motors, and castings. Each piece is designed on the shop floor requiring considerable time and repeated attempts. However, they have limited access to CAD/CAM, materials science, and advanced processes. Tata Consultancy Services has set up a centre for engineering where CAD/CAM software and other related software will be available on dial-up or internet lines. They will train these units in the use of relevant software. The company has worked out an arrangement with UniGraphic Systems for the design of software and with ATKearney for procurement solutions. These units can be made highly productive and cost effective as they have no overheads.

Use of IT in Retail Small Shops

Shopping malls, where the middle class essentially shops, would continue to grow. However, the presence and proliferation of shopping malls invariably affects the small shops and stores. India has 10 to 12 million small shops—each is run by the owner and two to three assistants, including their families, and supports about ten people on an average. This adds to over 100 million people. The small shopkeepers can play supplementary and complementary roles to the shopping malls. They can use IT to become convenience and personalized stores.

At the Indian Institute of Technology Bombay, the Management Science and Computer Science disciplines have initiated a study leading to a development that will provide

• Inventory management applications using artificial intelligence, algorithms, and innovative techniques to lower inventory and supply chain management costs;
• System for cash management to reduce financial layouts and allow for quicker recoveries;
• Client relationship management, building on their existing client relationships and providing for personalized services.

There are hundreds of other applications that need to be explored to make IT relevant to the Indian situation.

ROLE OF IT IN EMPLOYING THE EDUCATED FORCE

India produces about 3 million graduates with about 4,00,000 in engineering including 50,000 diploma holders, 1.2 million in sciences, and the rest in other disciplines. Out of these 3 million graduates, 25 per cent are employable with some training but without any supplementary education, and another 25 per cent at the lower end, who can handle routine jobs. About 50 per cent are good and with some additional training they can be very useful to the society. A two-semester supplementary education (six months) programme that includes courses and tutorial on (a) system engineering and system modelling; (b) logic and operation research; (c) programming skills, programming style, proof of correctness, and extensive coding; and (d) rapid reading to achieve speed of 300–50 wpm, writing essays, and speaking, is recommended.

We need to experiment with 10–15 prototypes on a pilot scale first before expanding the programme.

Employment of Trained Graduates

Currently a situation exists where trained students in areas other than computer science opt for a career in software services rather than their own area of specialization such as mechanical or power engineering.

The manufacturing industry has to appreciate that unless they have input of higher knowledge, they will not be able to meet the future requirements. Electricity Boards have not recruited a single MTech during the last ten years and one can see the results. There is no reason why the industry cannot match salary levels for these highly educated knowledge builders. It is an opportunity lost and the price one will have to pay will be obsolescence.

The Indian Institutes of Technology and others producing MTechs need to market their graduates to the industry so that they are employed in their specific disciplines of graduation.

EDUCATION FOR THE FUTURE

India contributes too few students with Masters and PhD degrees in engineering. Innovation, creativity, and development of new technology in engineering are related to the number of Masters and Doctorate-level professionals that a country produces. To increase this number, the country needs more world-class undergraduates comparable to the standards of the IITs. However, there are 50–60 colleges that get students at entry-level, with a score of 85 per cent and above at the 10+2 level. The background and calibre of these students is similar to those at the IITs. The quality of undergraduate education at these colleges can be upgraded to IIT standards.

A study has been made about the gaps between these colleges and IITs, and a detailed report has been submitted to the government. The deficiencies pertain to autonomy, governance, finance, faculty, curriculum, libraries, and labs. We should have these colleges as prototypes by next year and then this can be implemented at 50–60 more colleges all over the country. The output then will be 30,000–40,000 world-class graduates instead of 3,000 at present.

FUTURE OF SOFTWARE, EDUCATION, AND TRAINING FOR THE FUTURE

Software systems have become large and complex. All systems in operation have not met all the requirements, and not all software system projects are completed within the cost and time schedules (overshooting cost by 50 per cent and time by 90 per cent). Systems are difficult to modify, maintain, and repair; this crisis situation needs to be addressed. We need to design and build software systems that are reliable, cost effective, modifiable, and extensible. This will require use of service-oriented architecture, tools like Wiki, Blogging, and many other tools.

Systems in the future will have to address uncertainty, complexity, distributed operations, and operation with no latency, and provide solutions to business issues and business strategy, and use technology to support the solution and the process.

Therefore, people who develop systems for the future will require good knowledge in three core disciplines:

- *Systems Engineering*: Systems Engineering will enable recognizing and handling complexity, perceiving systems as a network of inter-related subsystems, understanding the needs and constraints of all stake-holders and building both quantitative and qualitative models. It will provide tools for stakeholder analysis framework; cybernetic influence diagrams, viable system model, interpretive structural modelling, and system dynamics.

- *Software Engineering*: Software Engineers will require scientific knowledge in design and construction of computer programs. Software techniques will become increasingly structured, disciplined, and built on a mathematical basis as required of any engineering discipline. Software engineers will need education and learning in design of algorithms, artificial intelligence, decision support systems, fuzzy logic, formal methods, chaos theory, set theory, and predicate calculus and many other areas of mathematics. Software as an engineering discipline will require engineering attributes like reusability, extensibility, maintainability, reliability, testability, interoperability, and quality.

- *Concurrent Engineering*: Concurrent Engineering, in contrast with sequential development, provides for overlapping of different stages of the development process, concurrently rather than sequentially. It encourages interaction and sharing of information within diverse groups of individuals, who may be in different places. Essentially, it encourages cross-functional teams who simultaneously focus on different phases of the development cycle.

In this essay, I have mentioned how several contemporary applications took-off but some of them could not be realized due to the socio-political climate existing at that time. Nevertheless, the efforts led India to lead global Y2K efforts, which in turn made India the IT superpower and the world gained confidence in India's capability in software design, implementation, and maintenance. I have further mentioned the steps to be taken in terms of quality human resources to help India maintain its leadership in IT.

To conclude, the vision of my presidential address to the Computer Society of India in 1975 is still there. We have come a long way and now are on equal footing with developed nations. We still have miles to go to make an IT revolution that erases the digital divide in society. I strongly believe that we shall reach the peak soon.

NANDAN NILEKANI

12 The Potential of the Unique Identity Number in India

Since the Unique Identification (UID) project was announced last year, it has attracted a lot of attention and discussion from the public. In meetings with government bodies and civil society organizations, the opinions we have encountered on the role of the Unique Identification Authority of India (UIDAI) have been strongly held. The Unique Identification project, as one newspaper noted, is an 'ambitious ... game changing scheme', and the wide interest in the project is consequently expected.*

Unique Identification Authority of India on its own has a restricted mission: issue a unique identity number for every resident in the country, which can be easily used by the resident to establish their identity. The real impact of the number, however, will come from how governments and service providers utilize the UID number in welfare schemes, service delivery, and in interactions with residents.

IDENTITY AND BENEFITS

The Unique Identification project is part of an approach to growth that Indian governments have embraced since the early decade—growth with an emphasis on inclusion. This is a different track from the focus of governments in the 1990s, where the overarching emphasis post-

* 'A game changing scheme', *The Hindu*, 13 November 2009.

reform, after decades of subdued, disappointing growth rates, was on accelerating India's GDP growth.

Governments and residents alike are recognizing that the changes India needs to embrace cannot be limited to our markets alone. Unless we make changes to our social and welfare schemes so that the poor can participate in India's growth, we risk widening inequalities and limiting opportunities for the poor, leaving a large proportion of the country behind as we move up the development arc. India's interventions cannot be selective—our poverty, our slums, our weakened agriculture sector, and our low access to health and education are presently an indelible part of the Indian landscape, as real as our growing cities and expanding industry.

The urgent need to make our social programmes more effective and ensure inclusive growth has been a big impetus behind the UID project. The lack of a reliable identity number for residents has played a significant part in weakening our welfare programmes, however well-funded and well-intentioned they have been. Across our public programmes, one problem that has turned out to be ubiquitous and persistent over the years has been the issue of 'leakage'—the problem of funds across our public schemes not reaching the beneficiaries they are intended for. The fundamental challenge here for governments is the absence of reliable identity verification. Without this, the government has difficulty confirming whether funds and benefits targeted for the poor have successfully reached them, or have been diverted.

This lack of visibility for governments and unreliable identity verification has enabled large-scale diversion of funds, weakening welfare schemes across India. The Public Distribution System (PDS) of indirect transfers to the poor of food, fertilizer, and fuel, for example, has faced leakages that impact the efficacy of the scheme. The Mahatma Gandhi National Rural Employment Guarantee Scheme (MGNREGS), a direct benefit programme which has become one of the landmark, best-funded social projects over the last few years, is facing the same challenges that have affected India's previous social programmes, in the diversion of funds.

Till date, however, there has been no universally accepted, easily verifiable identity number that both residents and agencies can use. Identity verification in India has long been inexact and dependent on an assortment of documents, which have varying levels of acceptance with different arms of the government and with private service providers. Residents are also required by different agencies to produce different documents for proof of identity and proof of address prior to accessing benefits and services. The lack of such documents—most common among the poorest residents—and the cost of multiple verification procedures exacerbate the lack of access for the poor to public programmes, benefits, and services. For much of the poor in India, the challenge thus lies in their lack of visibility to the state, untouched by welfare, benefits, and services.

Banking and insurance services, for example, are inaccessible to the poorest residents because they face difficulties in meeting the 'Know Your Customer' (KYC) requirements of banks. Less than 60 per cent of India's population, as a result, can access bank accounts, and insurance and pension coverage are at even lower rates. This lack of financial access, in turn, constrains economic participation for the poor—it limits their capacity to save and invest, limiting their opportunities and their potential income growth, even within a vibrant economy.

There are clearly immense benefits from a mechanism that uniquely identifies a person, which, by giving the resident a number that s/he can use for life, ensures instant identity verification. The ease of proving identity only once, and the ability to verify the number conveniently to a host of state and non-state agencies with diverse interests–PDS, MGNREGS, banking, NGOs, private sector firms—will bring down transaction costs for both the resident and the agency; it can also make the delivery of our welfare programmes more inclusive, and enable the government to implement and tailor effective direct benefit programmes that are targeted to the individual.

WHY NOW? THE TIMING OF THE UIDAI

UIDAI was established in February 2009, as a body attached to the Planning Commission. This is not the first effort at implementing an identity infrastructure—previous attempts to implement an identity number took place in the 1990s, but this time, the government has taken up the effort on a national, well-funded scale.

The information that the UIDAI intends to collect while issuing the UID number will be the resident's basic demographic and biometric information. The database containing the UID numbers and linked information will be stored on a central server. Enrolment of the resident will be computerized, and information exchanged between registrars enrolling residents for the UID number, and the central database will be over a network. Verification of the resident's identity will be online.

India's effort to implement the UID number places it among a host of developing countries that are now attempting to build a coherent identity infrastructure. In South Asia itself, India's neighbours Bangladesh and Pakistan have recently implemented national, biometric-linked identity systems.

In doing so, developing countries are now joining the raft of developed nations that implemented identity infrastructure many decades earlier. Identity number infrastructure has long been a broad, complex task, requiring significant public investment, vast information collection and data compilation mechanisms, a reliable de-duplication system, and an effective means to communicate the number and associated benefits to a country's residents. Developed nations had implemented these mechanisms successfully by the mid-twentieth century—the effort was made easier in these nations due to lower population density, the availability of funds, and more systemic, widespread service delivery and government infrastructure.

In developing countries, such de-duplication has become possible only recently, due to the surge in effective biometric technologies, and low-cost end-user systems to collect demographic and biometric information. However, a workable identity solution has emerged for these countries, including India, as the focus in the West has shifted towards identity systems in the context of security. The US, for example, has long had a social security number, but the Bush government in 2005 made an effort to introduce the 'Rearing and Empowering America for Longevity against Acts of International Destruction' (RealID), an identity number linked to biometrics, in the interests of homeland security and to track terror suspects in the country more effectively. In the UK as well, security concerns paved the way for policies such as closed-circuit television (CCTV) cameras in public places as well as efforts to introduce a new identity system that tracked non-citizens in the country.

In India, the UID effort is closer in spirit to the social security number systems implemented in the 1940s and 1950s than these recent efforts. The Indian government's focus is to implement an identity number that enables better delivery of services, and addresses the identity verification challenges poor residents face across the country.

The Unique Identification number has significant implications in India for the means to tackle poverty. Poverty, after all, is never just about shortages in food, clothing, or the lack of a house. Rather for the poor, poverty is a condition of their lives, caused by a lack of access to the various resources and economic systems that are available to the rest of the country. The poor lack access to skills that would earn them a higher wage, to markets that would bring them better prices for their goods, to good schools and healthcare that would give their children a chance for a better life. And they are often surrounded by the social norms of caste and class within their community that further limit their opportunities.

Consequently, the poor lack the tools to participate effectively in our formal markets and institutions—many of the poor exist in the informal economy, and depend on non-organized systems for resources, such as moneylenders for finance, the informal sector for employment, and slums for housing. As a result, they lose out significantly in terms of their personal gains from India's economic growth, the gains of which are weighted towards the middle class.

The Unique Identification number, by tackling our challenges in access, would help address the shift in aspirations that have accompanied India's development over the last two decades. In the 1970s and 1980s, people's aspirations focused on basic essentials—*roti, kapda, aur makaan* (food, clothes, and a house). Since reforms in the 1990s, the emphasis moved to community infrastructure, in the form of *bijli, sadak, aur paani* (electricity, roads, and water). In recent years, as growth has accelerated and access to basic infrastructure has improved further, aspirations among the poor have shifted again. The focus today is on 'soft' infrastructure that empowers the individual, and the demand is for a 'bank account, mobile phone, and identity'. Each of these is something a poor resident aspires to have in order to improve her access to resources and markets.

The Unique Identification number would also enable governments to respond to people's needs faster and more effectively. With the UID, access to services could be tailored to the individual's age, their socioeconomic group, and their particular needs. For example, the child of a below poverty line (BPL) family could be eligible for healthcare vouchers linked to the child's UID number, which would enable the child to receive free immunizations from any hospital. The BPL family could also be eligible for UID-linked direct cash transfers, which would allow them to purchase basic necessities such as food and clothing for the child and family.

Once the child enters school, UID-linked education vouchers would allow him/her to attend the school of choice. As an adult worker, UID-linked access to finance and insurance would encourage savings, investment, and the implementation of entrepreneurial ideas. A mobile identity, with mobile rights and entitlements, would also enable the resident as an adult, to migrate with greater security and safety, in order to get the best possible incomes and contribute most effectively to the economy. And during periods of unemployment, reliable, UID-linked access to welfare would ensure a subsistence wage, and access to pension in old age would ensure a level of security.

Linking the UID across the lifecycle of services for the resident would make governments far more accountable to individuals in the benefits they receive and their entitlements. The visibility of the resident to the state would make it easier to deliver benefits and services, and ensure that these reach the beneficiary.

FROM INVISIBLE TO VISIBLE— IMPLICATIONS FOR THE RESIDENT

The increased 'visibility' for the resident through the UID number will be a source of increased economic and political power for the resident. The biometric aspect of the UID infrastructure will, in particular, play a critical role in increasing accountability for governments and broadening access.

As biometric technology becomes more reliable and effective, governments across the world have turned to it due to concerns around rising fraud in delivery of services. Across India, for example, biometric technology has become a means for improving delivery systems in states such as Andhra Pradesh, which have implemented iris-based verification in the state's PDS delivery infrastructure. It is difficult to verify identity on demographic information alone—particularly to verify without doubt that the service or benefit was delivered to the person it was intended for. Biometrics technology presents a way for governments to verify identity effectively, and ensure lower rates of fraud and duplicates in the delivery of services.

Biometric-linked authentication to access benefits, for example, would make it very difficult for service providers to deliver resources and benefits to those who are not entitled to it, and to deny them to those who are. A UID-linked system at a MGNREGS worksite, for example, would require workers to verify their presence through biometrics in order to work. The wages that are due to them could then be transferred directly to a UID-linked bank account, from where money can be withdrawn only through UID authentication.

Such an approach, while it increases the visibility of the resident to the government, also increases the accountability of the government to the resident, since the resident's relationship with the state is far more direct, and the government knows at once whether the money has reached the resident or not.

Biometric authentication also makes it easier to deliver public resources and services through a variety of agencies—public, private, and non-profit. Once identity verification is mobile and easily done, benefits can be delivered in direct form, in the form of vouchers and cash for the resident, which can be redeemed at any agency.

Certainly, for governments and individuals alike, strong identity for residents has real economic value. While weak identity systems cause the individual to miss out on benefits and services, it also makes it difficult for the government to account for money and resource flows across a country. In addition, it complicates government efforts to account for residents during emergencies and security threats.

In fact, the effect of technology in disseminating information and economic power to individuals from poor and rural communities has been seen before across our institutions, markets, and governance systems. For example, a poor resident faces multiple constraints when accessing markets—the distance and cost of travel, the gatekeepers with whom he must negotiate, and even the treatment he faces in his interactions. Technology solutions, including online trading systems and mobile phones, have empowered individuals, allowing them to negotiate directly, at lower costs, and with lower risks of exclusion.

Even as the UIDAI implements a broad online identity infrastructure and confirms identity to authenticating agencies, it will take steps to protect the privacy and security of resident information. For example, identity verification of residents is done through live authentication, where the resident presses his finger on a biometric machine to verify his record, and the confirmation comes back from the central database in a few seconds. A stored biometric record cannot be used to access services—it can only be used by the database for de-duplication.

Additionally, the information stored in the central database will be accessible to no one outside the UIDAI, including the enrolling agencies, and the authority will have clear audit mechanisms in place to track access of the information. During identity verification, the authority will not divulge any UID-linked information—answers to verification queries would only be in the form of a 'yes' or a 'no'. The UIDAI will also ensure that information to the UID database is sent over a secure network, and the registrars and enrollers have secure systems implemented to ensure the safety of the data.

THE UID NUMBER AND THE STATE-RESIDENT RELATIONSHIP

The way governments across the world approach identity infrastructure has an undeniably significant impact on not just how residents can access services and benefits, but on a broad spectrum of other issues, including that of security, privacy, and the evolution of public identity in the country.

Identities are inevitably in part social constructions, which respond to how public programmes are shaped, and how governments conduct the enumerations of their people. Projects that help identify and account for the residents in a country, after all, help fundamentally define state policy, and a move from the groupings of the census to the individual enumeration of the National Population Register and the UID number is likely to affect how the government interacts with the residents in India.

The impact that the UID number would have on public policy and, more broadly, identity politics is not really clear at this early period in the project, but I believe there are reasons to be optimistic. The UID project implies a shift in how we view identity, since the census began enumerating populations and groups. Identity in India has long been defined strongly on the basis of group allegiance, including class, region, religion, and caste. Welfare programmes in India have accordingly defined their boundaries and identified their beneficiaries based on these groupings. Governments have similarly used such enumeration to decide which communities ought to receive specific welfare programmes and services. These enumeration approaches have long shaped how Indian residents viewed their political identity, and the collectives they viewed themselves as a part of, while negotiating for resources with the state—the entitlements defined for backward castes, for example, have led to groups across the country agitating to be re-defined as backward caste in government lists and the census.

However, recent efforts in India such as the MGNREGS have begun to focus on defining individual identity more clearly, in order to deliver benefits better. This follows in the tradition of successful welfare programmes around the world. For instance, social security programmes in the US and Europe focused on delivering direct benefits and entitlements to individuals, on the basis of identity numbers issued to the poor.

The key difference between the group approach that has dominated in India so far and the UID approach would be in how the government targets benefits and resources towards its residents. The UID number is the first programme that focuses on the individual as the primary identifier, rather than the family, the community, or the class group the individual belongs to. This change in orientation gives us the opportunity to bring about vast changes in how public and private services are delivered, giving residents across the country greater flexibility in accessing resources. Government programmes can potentially be tailored to individual residents based on a variety of indicators including their age, their income, their location, and their health and level of education, with the confidence that such programmes can be delivered with low leakages. Such a shift may require welfare programmes to change their focus from directing food or fuel en masse to an identified group of beneficiaries, and instead target individual beneficiaries more effectively with cash transfers or vouchers.

More broadly, as the visibility of the resident in social schemes and programmes changes from the group to the individual, such an approach may also encourage residents to view themselves less through the collective lens that has prevailed so far—where benefits have been associated with regions, castes, and communities—and focus more on their individual needs. It creates the potential for India to implement a wide-ranging transformation in our developmental approach, and in access, over the next decade.

THE INFRASTRUCTURE OF
THE UID NUMBER

The goal of the UIDAI—issuing 600 million UID numbers over the next five years—is undeniably an ambitious one. Unique Identification Authority of India will have to do fresh enrolments to ensure clean information in its database, since existing databases average 20 per cent or more in duplicate and fraudulent entries. An initiative of this scale is certainly unprecedented, and all the more of a challenge considering the size and diversity of India's geography, and the difficulties in reaching the marginal communities in the country.

A key advantage of the UID implementation approach, however, is that it will leverage the existing public and private infrastructure across the country to enroll residents into the UID. Under this approach, the UIDAI will be the regulatory authority managing a Central ID Data Repository (CIDR), which will issue UID numbers, update resident information, and authenticate the identity of residents as required. Any organization in any part of the country can, if it fulfils certain infrastructure requirements, be a 'registrar'—an agency that enrolls residents for the UID number. Registrars will process UID applications, and connect to the UIDAI's central database to de-duplicate resident information and receive UID numbers. These registrars can either be enrollers, or will appoint agencies as enrollers, who will interface with people seeking UID numbers. The authority will also partner with service providers for authentication, and a UID issued by any registrar would be accepted by all other registrars, thus eliminating the need for repeated identity verification.

The model as the UIDAI expects to implement is thus an open, participatory one, and can include government agencies, educational institutions, hospitals, banks, private companies, civil society agencies, and NGOs. Such an approach, combined with planned outreach efforts for groups such as tribals and the disabled, also helps us ensure that we reach individuals across the country.

Unique Identification Authority of India envisions that through this infrastructure it will issue a unique identification number (UID) to all Indian residents that is reliable and robust enough to eliminate duplicate and fraudulent identities, and is biometrically linked, enabling it to be verified effectively, and at low cost.

Unique Identification Authority of India has designed the enrolment process to be as streamlined as possible. The enrolment process for the UID number will begin with a resident submitting his/her information to a UID enrolling agency with supporting documents. Once the enroller verifies the resident's information, it will submit the resident's application request through the registrar to the UIDAI's central database. The central system will then run a de-duplication check, comparing the resident's biometric and demographic information to the records in the database to ensure that the resident does not already have a UID number.

Unique Identification Authority of India will have processes in place to prevent repeated fraudulent efforts to enroll for a UID number, to ensure the security of the system. Since the de-duplication also compares biometric records, it would catch individuals enrolling with a different set of demographic details.

Once the UID number is assigned, the authority will forward the resident a letter which contains his/her registered demographic and biometric details. This letter may have a detachable portion which has the UID number, name, photograph, and the biometric details of the resident. This will ensure that the resident knows if there are mistakes in her UID information, and she can accordingly contact the relevant registrar or agency.

The implementation processes of the UIDAI will be based on the most effective approaches in service delivery systems in India, aided by the best technology available. All data entry that the enrolling agencies take up for the UID number will be done in English. It can then be converted into the local language using standard transliteration software, and verified for accuracy by the registrar. The letter UIDAI sends to the resident will consequently contain all demographic details in English as well as the relevant local language. The enrolment stations will have systems in place to ensure that enrolment is as resident-friendly as possible, and does not marginalize residents because of their illiteracy or lack of information on the UID number.

There are some defining features of the proposed UID infrastructure, in order to ensure a system that is flexible for registrars, and reliable and accessible for residents.

The Unique Identification number will not guarantee rights, benefits, or entitlements; it is primarily an enabler, which would allow governments to tailor services, benefits, and entitlements for residents far more effectively. Unique Identification Authority of India, on its own, will limit its role to the issue of unique identification numbers that are linked to a person's demographic and biometric information, and its guarantee is solely for the identity linked to the number. Since the number does not imply or guarantee any kind of right, including citizenship, it will be issued to all residents in the country.

Nevertheless, the UID number would be an important first step in enabling the government to target and deliver services to poor residents more effectively. The biometric-linked authentication for the UID number, in particular, would significantly improve the poor's access to resources they are entitled to, with minimum leakage and fraud. The emphasis of the UIDAI in enrolment is, consequently, explicitly pro-poor, and the registrars that the UIDAI plans to partner with in its first phase of enrolment will include the MGNREGS and the PDS, which will help bring large numbers of the poor and underprivileged into the UID system.

The Introducer System

As mentioned earlier, the UIDAI will enroll residents into the database afresh, rather than from existing identity databases, in order to limit existing problems of duplicates and inaccurate information from seeping into the database. The authority will consequently verify the demographic and biometric information of each resident before enrolling them into the database.

A challenge that the UIDAI faces with enrolment, however, is that most of the poor and underserved population in India lack identity documents, and the UID may be the first form of identification they have access to. Since the focus of the UIDAI is inclusion, the authority must ensure that the UIDAI's Know Your Resident (KYR) standards don't become a barrier for enrolling the poor. One approach the UIDAI plans in order to tackle this challenge is the introducer system, where residents can use a network of approved 'introducers' who can confirm that the information that the resident provides the registrar is valid.

This is an idea that is borrowed from the banking system, when customers without identification who wish to open a bank account get introduced to the bank by an existing customer. In the UID registration process, registration may be done through registrars like banks, insurance firms, as well as central and state government departments. In each of these institutions, introducers would be approved individuals who already have a UID number, and who help residents without documents get registered for a UID. The availability of multiple introducers would also protect poor residents from harassment by a single introducer when they attempt to get a UID number through this system. Such introducers for the UID may come from the government, the registrars, and NGO agencies.

Flexibility for Registrars

It is apparent that within the UIDAI system, the registrar agencies will play an important role. They will link up with the UIDAI for identity enrolment, and may tailor some of their processes accordingly—the UID authority will provide standards to enable registrars collect demographic and biometric information in a uniform, transferable way. Nevertheless, they will retain significant flexibility in their processes, including issuing cards, pricing, expanding KYR verification, collecting demographic data on residents for their specific requirements, and in authentication.

Enrolment into the UID Number will be Demand-driven

The Unique Identification number will be voluntary and demand-driven, and the momentum for enrolment will come from residents enrolling for the UID in order to avail of the services and benefits that are linked to it.

However, it is entirely possible that the number, like the social security numbers in the US and Europe, will eventually become mandatory as registrars require residents to cite the number to avail of critical government and private sector services such as banking, insurance, and payment of taxes. Since the UID would be the most reliable identity proof available, government and private agencies in India are, in time, likely to shift to this for identity verification.

Online Identity Verification

The authority will offer residents with a strong way to establish their identity through an online system. Here, agencies attempting to verify UID information can compare the resident's demographic and biometric information with the record stored in the central database.

ENABLING A TRANSFORMATION FOR
SERVICE DELIVERY IN INDIA

The impact of the UID number will clearly be a wide-ranging one for residents, public and private agencies, and governments. The digitization that the UID number enables in proving identity will replace a vast paper-based system that had established itself across India's service delivery infrastructure for decades. For residents the UID will become the single source of identity verification, and they will be spared the challenge of repeatedly providing supporting identity documents each time they wish to access services such as obtaining a bank account, passport, driving licence, and so on. The Unique Identification number will give residents mobility of identity, and pave the way for high levels of inclusion for poor and underprivileged residents. The number will also, in time, improve access for residents to a variety of services, and ensure high interoperability and mobility of such services.

Registrars and service agencies across India will gain greatly from the de-duplication that the UID makes possible. Enabling registrars to clean out duplicates from their databases will bring about significant efficiencies and cost savings. For registrars focused on cost, the UIDAI's verification processes will ensure lower KYR, and for registrars focused on inclusion, such as banks, a reliable identification number will enable them to broaden their reach into groups that till now have been difficult to authenticate.

For governments, the elimination of duplication and fraud under various schemes can save the government exchequer upwards of Rs 20,000 crore a year. It will also provide governments with accurate data on residents, enable direct benefit programmes, and allow government departments to coordinate investments and share information.

In time, the impact of the UID number is likely to grow more significant. The ability of individuals to verify themselves anywhere in the country becomes valuable as migration and urbanization intensify with growth. The Unique Identification number, with its 'anytime, anywhere, anyhow' biometric verification process, also addresses the problem of trust within a transaction for agencies carrying out both face-to-face and remote service delivery. The online verification of UID can make geographical distances irrelevant to the delivery of a multitude of services, allowing agencies across a variety of sectors such as banking and finance to provide remote services.

Removing the need for multiple verification processes also reduces costs for service providers. Additionally, replacing brick and mortar infrastructure in these industries with low-cost technology applications will lower transaction costs even further. By facilitating such remote, easy verification of identity, the UID number thus becomes the glue for service providers to bring together existing technologies and create end-to-end, low-cost, electronified models, where individuals can transact with micro-amounts as small as ten rupees, equipped with little more than a mobile phone.

Such a low-cost, accessible model would help bring in millions more people into India's burgeoning economy. And as the UID-linked network becomes ubiquitous, the applications on top of it will explode in number, potentially expanding into a variety of different services.

The Unique Identification project thus opens up a vast array of new possibilities for our future, and offers a foundation on which a host of applications can be built. For example, the UID number of each resident can be linked to a bank account, through which the government can provide a variety of direct services and benefits—health and education services through vouchers, and cash benefits. Such service delivery also enables governments to establish rights-and-benefits relationships directly with individuals. The increased negotiating power this enables for individuals will mean both fairer, more transparent public delivery systems and stronger, more enforceable rights.

CHALLENGES FOR THE UIDAI

The implementation of the UID number is not a simple task in a country with one billion residents, where residents avail of a variety of services and agencies, and come with different needs and demands. The multiplicity of services residents depend on, for example, comes with adoption challenges with the UID number—the number will have to target residents through a variety of registrars to ensure that a critical mass of residents across demographic groups is reached in a short period of time. Unless this is done, the UID number will not be successful.

The Unique Identification number will also have to keep its pro-poor focus in mind during enrolment, and this means that its strategy will have to include reaching out to large parts of the rural country, and enabling large numbers of touch points for enrolment across rural India. It will also have to make substantial outreach efforts in order to ensure that marginal and minority communities are not left out of enrolment, and thus later shut out from services. The focus on the poor will require the UID authority to innovatively address the difficulties in address verification, name standards, lack of information on date of birth, and hard-to-record biometrics.

The infrastructure demands for the project will also be significant. The Unique Identification database, for example, will have to handle records that approach one billion in number. This creates significant challenges in biometric de-duplication as well as in administration, storage, and continued expansion of infrastructure.

Technology, in particular, is a key part of the UID programme, and this is the first time in the world that storage, authentication, and de-duplication of biometrics is being attempted on this scale. The authority will have to address the risks carefully—by choosing the right technology in the UID architecture, biometrics, and data management tools; managing obsolescence and data quality; designing the transaction services model, and innovating towards the best possible result. Despite the challenges in the implementation of this project, I believe that it can be done effectively, and it will be well worth the effort.

The Unique Identification project can help India fulfil its renewed vision for development—to leverage our social investments to broaden access to the economy and our markets. It has the potential for us to leapfrog an entire generation in terms of access and in the delivery of services. For the poor, it can become a bridge to greater opportunity. It would enable us to offer residents across India the security of our social systems as well as the opportunities of our markets. The effective implementation of the UID will mean a fundamental transformation—in our development, our potential for growth, and in the lives of Indians across the country.

U.R. RAO

13 India in Space

Recognizing the role of space activities in stimulating the growth of technology and industry, in advanced fields such as electronics, communication, cybernetics, and materials engineering, Homi Bhabha and Vikram Sarabhai constituted the Indian National Committee for Space Research (INCOSPAR) in 1962, under the umbrella of the Department of Atomic Energy (DAE). The committee under the chairmanship of Vikram Sarabhai started space activities in India by establishing an Equatorial Sounding Rocket Station over the geomagnetic equator at Thumba, Thiruvananthapuram, for carrying out scientific investigations in atmospheric sciences, meteorology, and astronomy.

With the untimely demise of Bhabha in 1966, Sarabhai took charge as the chairman of the DAE and consolidated all the space activities under the Indian Space Research Organisation (ISRO). Realizing the vast potential of space technology for addressing a variety of socio-economic problems of the nation, particularly in the areas of communication, education, disaster management, weather forecasting, and management of natural resources, ISRO soon focused its attention on developing a vibrant, application-oriented Space Programme on a totally self-reliant basis. The essay provides a brief summary of the spectacular growth of ISRO from the humble beginning in 1962, which has made India a leading global space power.

Vikram Sarabhai's speech delivered on 2 February 1968 at the dedication ceremony of The Equatorial Rocket Launching Station (TERLS) at

Thumba vividly describes Homi J. Bhabha's contribution to the establishment and development of space technology in India as follows:

I feel keenly the absence today of Homi Bhabha, with whom I visited this spot four years ago (Figure 13.1). With characteristic vision, he recognized the great importance of advanced technologies involved in atomic energy, in the exploration of space, and in electronics. In 1961, the subject of exploration of outer space for peaceful purposes was allocated to the Department of Atomic

FIGURE 13.1   Homi J. Bhabha and Vikram Sarabhai at Veli Hill,
Thiruvananthapuram, where the Space Science and Technology Centre
(now renamed as Vikram Sarabhai Space Centre) was established

Energy. Soon thereafter the Indian National Committee for Space Research was constituted. Quite early, the committee decided to establish a sounding rocket range on the geomagnetic equator at Thumba. It consciously laid emphasis on creating facilities, which would permit a study of problems in aeronomy in the region, since the programme could be conducted with small sounding rockets involving a modest budget. Moreover, the scientific results would have a direct bearing on a better understanding of meteorology, of great practical significance to the Indian economy.

The major responsibility for setting up the new activity naturally fell on the scientific personnel of the Physical Research Laboratory, and in October 1963 the administrative charge of TERLS was formally entrusted to the Physical Research Laboratory under the direction of Sarabhai. Through this, Bhabha was following a precedent, which had worked very successfully in the early stages of the Atomic Energy Programme when the Tara Institute of Fundamental Research played a major role.

DEVELOPMENT OF SPACE TECHNOLOGY

In order to achieve total self-reliance in the development of space technology, ISRO, initiated the development of a family of indigenous sounding rockets in 1965, capable of launching 10 to 100 kg payloads to an altitude of 60–550 km, for carrying out scientific experiments in atmospheric sciences, meteorology, aeronomy, and astronomy. Realizing the immense potential of satellites for the development of the nation in a variety of disciplines such as education, communication, broadcasting, management of natural resources, meteorological forecasting, and disaster management, ISRO took the major step of designing and building its first satellite Aryabhata in 1972 and accordingly signed an agreement with the USSR Academy of Sciences for launching the satellite using the Intercoms Rocket.

Following the successful orbiting of Aryabhata in 1975, ISRO under-took the design, operation, and launching of two experimental remote sensing satellites, Bhaskara 1 and 2, and an experimental communication satellite APPLE. Thereafter, ISRO quickly embarked upon the design, fabrication, and launching of operational INSAT series of communica-tion satellites and IRS series of remote sensing satellites. The INSAT series of satellites, beginning with INSAT-1B in 1983, which have undergone four generations of development over the last three decades, initiated a total communication revolution in the country, in addition to providing round the clock meteorological information for weather forecasting and disaster management. Likewise, ISRO fabricated and launched the state-of-the-art IRS series of multi-spectral remote sensing satellites, beginning with IRS-1A in 1988, with progressively improved spatial resolution from 36 m to 0.8 m, for optimal management of natural resources.

Parallely ISRO started developing state-of-the-art satellite launching rocket technology, beginning with a modest SLV-3 launching vehicle in 1983, capable of launching 40 kg satellite into a near-earth orbit. This was followed by the successful development of powerful, state-of-the-art rockets such as Polar Satellite Launch Vehicle (PSLV), capable of launching over 1,800 kg satellite into a polar sun-synchronous orbit, and Geosynchronous Satellite Launch Vehicle (GSLV), capable of launching 2,000 kg satellite into a geostationary orbit. An up rated PSLV was, in fact, used for successful launching of India's first moon mission, Chandrayaan-1, in 2008. Geosynchronous Satellite Launch Vehicle, with the indigenously developed powerful cryogenic upper stage, capable of launching over 3 tonnes satellite into GTO is now being readied for launch. Indian Space Research Organisation has also started preparing for its first manned mission by 2014, using the upgraded GSLV. During the last four decades, ISRO has developed total capability in space technology, to become a very significant space power in the world. So far ISRO has launched about fifty-two satellites for providing communication, meteorological, and remote sensing services, about half of which were launched from the Indian Space Port at Sriharikota using its own rockets.

USE OF SPACE TECHNOLOGY FOR NATIONAL DEVELOPMENT

Largely due to the INSAT series of multipurpose geostationary satellites, ISRO can now boast of having one of the world's largest domestic communication satellite system with over 170 communication transponders operating on eight geostationary INSAT satellites. In addition to providing long distance communication, with about 6,000 two-way speech circuits covering 150 routes, INSATs are extensively used for radio networking, administrative, business, and computer communication, and VSAT networking. INSATs are providing regular half-hourly meteorological pictures for continuous weather forecasting and cyclone monitoring. With over 100 channels of national broadcasting, INSATs have brought news and entertainment programmes in various languages to the living rooms of over 90 per cent of the Indian population. INSATs are extensively used for spreading education across the country and for providing tele-medicine services to remote rural areas by connecting them with super-speciality hospitals in major cities.

The IRS series of remote sensing satellites of ISRO have become the backbone of India's natural resource management system by continuously providing valuable inputs on forestry, agriculture, water resources, mineral deposits, waste-land identification, urban growth, and a variety of valuable information needed for national development. Remote sensing inputs have become vital for monitoring and management of agricultural crops, particularly for initiating a sustainable 'ever-green' revolution required to ensure food security for the entire country in the coming years. Space images are being regularly used to provide valuable advance information on the location of major potential fishing zones based on the measurement of ocean temperature and phyto-plankton distribution. A unique application of remote sensing is in the Integrated Mission for Sustainable Development (IMSD), aimed at generating locale-specific prescription for development of land resources at micro-level to achieve enhanced agricultural productivity on a sustainable basis. Encouraged by the success of the project, ISRO has now established a large number of Village Resource Centres (VRCs) for delivering benefits of space technology directly to grassroot rural communities through single-window delivery system. Remote sensing imageries have become vital for monitoring and management of natural disasters such as floods, cyclones, tsunamis, earthquakes, landslides, and drought conditions.

SPACE SCIENCE ACTIVITIES

A number of satellite-borne payloads to study celestial X-ray and gamma-rays have provided valuable astronomical observations. Space satellites and associated ground-based observations are extensively used to study meteorological phenomena, aerosol distribution, atmospheric dynamics, and global warming phenomena. Chandrayaan-1, the first moon mission of India, has not only mapped over 60 per cent of the moon's surface for minerals, but has also detected the presence of water for the first time.

The next decade is expected to see many more scientific instruments for intensive planetary exploration, studying solar phenomena, undertaking global warming studies, and carrying out astrophysical investigations.

SPACE INDUSTRY

Bhabha had stressed the importance of involving Indian industries in scientific development, stating that India cannot be satisfied by merely building a few islands of excellence, but needs to build a nation of competence by involving Indian industries in scientific and technological development. ISRO recognized the importance of this statement at least three decades ago by involving a large number of industries in the development of space technology, which has yielded highly satisfying results. It also established its own commercial wing under the name Antrix in the mid-1980s, with the responsibility for nurturing Indian industries, and marketing ISRO products and services worldwide. It is very heartening to note that in just over two decades Antrix has become a significant world player in space, reaching a revenue figure of over Rs 10 billion a year.

The Indian Space Programme, which started with a modest beginning in 1963, has, in the last four decades, built up an impressive capability and a high degree of self-reliance in the development and application of space technology. India's efforts in the exploitation and extensive use of space technology inputs, particularly in the areas of communication, TV broadcast, education, meteorology, management of natural resources, environmental monitoring, disaster management, and sustainable integrated development, are truly creditable. Indian Space Research Organisation has also built very strong academic and industrial linkages to strengthen the space technology base in India. With the establishment of Antrix, ISRO has entered the global commercial space market.

Since its inception, ISRO has developed total self-reliance in satellite and rocket technology, developed operational launch vehicles for launching satellites from the Indian spaceport at SHAR, and established an elaborate infrastructure, including satellite and rocket fabrication facilities, test facilities, tracking network, and launch pads. The cumulative expenditure for all the activities of the Indian Space Programme during the forty-four years since 1962 is a modest sum of about Rs 300 billion, which makes the programme a very cost-effective one.

The spectacular development of space technology and its extensive applications to tackle basic socio-economic problems of India have been possible due to the foresight of Bhabha and Sarabhai, who laid ISRO's foundation, and the extraordinary leadership provided by the successive leaders in nurturing and guiding the national space programme.

part IV
future perspectives

Homi Bhabha. *Photograph courtesy TIFR*

H. PETER HOFSTEE

14 Computer Architecture from 1970–2030

Computer Architecture is the art of mediating between what technology provides and what software can effectively use. A computer architect must, therefore, have a firm understanding of technology fundamentals, and must be able to anticipate how technology will evolve and how this is likely to impact computer design. Similarly, a computer architect must have a firm understanding of what software can (and cannot) enable and must understand how software technology could evolve in the future.

This essay makes an attempt at a high-level analysis of the evolution of processors from the early 1970s to the early 2030s, a period defined by the use of integrated circuit technology. Until five to ten years ago the field of computer architecture enjoyed relative stability. On the one hand integrated circuit technology improved in a systematic and predicted fashion, and, on the other hand, sequential programming remained stable as the dominant user-level programming model. Thus computer architects operated within a well-defined set of constraints.

Albeit, this scenario has changed a lot. Scaling of conventional integrated circuits is slowing down and device scaling can be expected to come to its end within the next quarter century. While cost per transistor is expected to continue to improve, the frequency at which we operate transistors is now nearly constant. The energy per transistor switch is now improving at a rate similar to the rate at which transistors are added, and this rate is expected to degrade further. Computer architects have not been able to continue to sufficiently grow the performance of single-thread (sequential) applications under these new constraints and have had to resort to more hardware-efficient multi-core and multi-thread architectures for performance growth at historical levels. Automatic compiler-based parallelization has been unable to sustain the expected performance improvements without changes to the sequential programming model, and the industry is working feverishly to parallelize applications to preserve end-customer value growth.

In this essay we argue that as technology slows down even more, we have to look beyond concurrency as an enabler of efficiency, and more seriously consider adding locality as a fundamental enabler of efficiency and performance. Just as transitioning from sequential to parallel programming poses a significant challenge to our industry, so does expressing locality in our algorithms and programming languages.

Today we regard processors that exploit locality such as Cell, GPUs, and FPGAs as specialized, but this is no different from how we viewed multiprocessors before technology fundamentals forced the industry to adopt them pervasively to ensure continued performance growth.

Obviously, making predictions more than twenty years into the future is a hazardous enterprise. Breakthroughs can and do occur especially when old ways of doing business are under threat. The aim of this essay is to provide a directional framework based on fundamentals that can be adjusted if the future turns out differently than predicted here.

THE ORIGINS OF THE VON NEUMANN MODEL— BEFORE 1970

While it is not the objective of this essay to provide an overview of the history of computing pre-1970, it is instructive to briefly review the history of the stored-program computer.

While today the word 'computer' is almost synonymous with a programmable device, early computers were designed and built to perform a single function like a cash register, calculator, or tabulator. One might argue that today's equivalent of these early computers is the Application-Specific Integrated Circuit (ASIC). The analogy is imperfect as many ASICs now contain programmable elements.

Over time the reach of computers was improved by architecting computers to be reconfigurable. Thus the work to design a computer for a specific function was split between the engineers who built the computer

components, and the engineers who configured them for a specific purpose. While, of course, there is a trade-off here as reconfiguration takes
time during which the computer cannot be used and further efficiency is
lost if the number of types of reconfigurable modules is limited, the gains
in flexibility made the reconfigurable computer an enduring concept.
Today its most common incarnation in silicon is the Field Programmable Gate Array (FPGA), which contains a collection of configurable
universal logic elements and configurable memories. 'Programming' an
FPGA is equivalent to configuring the logic elements and their interconnections. Today's FPGAs store their configurations on the chip, typically in the form of trapped charges on floating gates. The 'P' in FPGA
perhaps points out that originally there was no distinction between a
(stored) program and a configuration. Today a 'program' commonly
refers to a sequence of instructions and most people would not want to
call an FPGA a stored-program computer, though they would probably
be happy to refer to an FPGA as a 'stored configuration' computer.

The notion of configuring a computer to perform a specific function
by performing sequential steps, where each step is specified (configured)
by an instruction stored in a program memory, was contemplated by
Alan Turing (1936) (and also by Konrad Zuse). The term 'von Neumann
architecture' in which von Neumann (1945) described one of the early
computer designs (EDVAC) whereas 'Harvard Architecture' refers to
computers with a separated instruction and data store. The abstraction
provided by the stored-program computer has allowed computers to
evolve as universal information processors, programmable by a wide
public. The abstraction is not without cost; separation between the
instruction/data store and the processing elements, and ignoring locality
in our instructions, cause a performance and efficiency challenge (called
the 'von Neumann bottleneck' or 'memory wall') because memory is
neither infinitely close nor does it provide infinite bandwidth.

THE FIRST THIRTY YEARS OF INTEGRATED
CIRCUIT PROCESSORS—1971–2000

While it would take another decade for the personal computer to emerge,
the first single-chip microprocessor, the Intel 4004, appeared in 1971.
Sequential programs, most commonly expressed in the C programming
language (developed by Kernighan and Ritchie in 1972), became the
dominant means of programming microprocessors.

Microprocessor benchmarks measured the performance of sequential programs. While performance was first typically expressed in instructions per second, appropriate when much of the code was still written in assembly, the Spec benchmarks that measure performance on a set of programs written in (sequential) C and were introduced in 1992 have become the most often referenced measure of processor performance.

Technology scaling of integrated circuits provided the fundamental ingredient that enabled the remarkable growth of processor performance growth over this period. As predicted by Gordon Moore (1965), the number of transistors on an integrated circuit has grown exponentially, initially doubling each year, and currently doubling about once every two years.

Ideal CMOS scaling, as defined by Robert Dennard et al. (1974), predicts that as we reduce all the physical dimensions on an integrated circuit and its operating voltage by the same factor, frequency of a scaled design would increase linearly, and chip power density should remain constant. Table 14.1 compares two processors three decades apart.

Table 14.1   1971 Microprocessor vs. 2000 Microprocessor

	1971 (Intel 4004)	2000 (Intel Pentium III Xeon)
Technology	10 micron (PMOS)	180 nm (CMOS)
Voltage	15V	1.7V
#Transistors	2,312	28M
Frequency	740KHz	600MHz–1GHz
Cycles per Inst.	8	~1
Chip size	11mm^2	106mm^2
Power	0.45W	20.4 W (600MHz @ 1.7V)
Power density	0.04W/mm^2	0.18W/mm

Source: Intel Microprocessor Quick Reference Guide, http://www.intel.com/pressroom/kits/quickreffam.htm

Of course, the comparisons here are crude as the 4004 was different in functionality than the Pentium III. None the less, the comparison is instructive and we make some simple observations:

•   The number of devices on a chip has grown very nearly at the rate predicted by the reduction in feature size and growth in chip size (69 M vs. actual 28 M);

- The supply voltage has come down at a significantly lower rate than predicted by ideal scaling laws (1.7 V vs. 0.27 V) and power densities have increased;
- Frequency has increased at a much faster pace than predicted by only considering technology improvement (600 MHz vs. 41 MHz);
- Performance has improved significantly faster (about 10,000 times) and more if one accounts for differences such as increases in word length;
- Efficiency, as defined by the performance divided by the product of the number of transistors and their operating frequencies, has declined by about a factor of 1,000.

We now look at each of these in a bit more detail.

The growth of the number of devices per mm^2 closely corresponds to what one might have predicted, though the fact that the 4004 contained little storage might have led one to suggest that densities should have improved more.

Supply voltages have not come down as fast as scaling theory requires. Increased field strengths in the transistor are used to deliver increases in transistor performance beyond what scaling theory would predict. The penalty in terms of power density is much smaller than a first-order calculation would suggest. We speculate that this is because a majority of power in the 4004 was associated with input/output (I/O).

Frequencies increased about fifteen times faster than predicted by ideal scaling. A factor of about six times could be attributed to the (relative) increase in supply voltage, no doubt enabled by a significant amount of engineering in the gate oxide and transistors to prevent breakdown. The remaining factor can be attributed to improvements in circuit design and deeper pipelining, though the 4004 already took eight cycles to complete an instruction.

One might say that the increase in performance is nearly proportional to the increase in frequency, once we account for the effects of pipelining which allows an instruction to be completed every cycle.

The reduction in efficiency should not surprise us. Significant micro-architectural enhancements were required to maintain an effective instruction completion rate of about one instruction per cycle once instruction pipelining was introduced. Most significant of these enhancements is the introduction of ever larger on-chip caches to compensate for the fact that main memory latencies have not improved much (the memory wall). Caches now dominate the transistor count of microprocessors. A rule of thumb is that quadrupling the size of a cache doubles its performance, thus efficiency degrades at about the same rate performance improves. Other micro-architectural improvements; superscalar and out-of-order processing, branch prediction structures, deeper pipelines, etc., similarly do not result in a performance improvement directly proportional to the number of transistors invested to realize them. AT^2 notions of complexity also point at an increase in area (and number of transistors) proportional to the square of latency improvements.

Our conclusion is, therefore, that while the period from 1971 to 2000 delivered about four orders of magnitude in performance improvements within a single programming paradigm, this period also resulted in close to three orders of magnitude in reduced efficiency in order to maintain the sequential programming model.

MULTI-CORE PROCESSORS: 2001–10

In 2001, IBM introduced the Power 4 dual-core processor. While the processor still provided substantial single-thread performance gains over its predecessors, IBM had come to the conclusion that the best way to leverage the available transistors, and more importantly the available power, was to instantiate a second core. Because server systems typically contain multiple processors, and server workloads such as transaction processing have long been multi-threaded, the disruption to server applications was limited to having to deliver application and operating system SMP-scaling at a somewhat faster rate than if a traditional path had been followed. Within five years, multi-core became pervasive.

The 2001 international technology* roadmap for semiconductors still predicted microprocessors operating at frequencies in excess of 10 GHz by 2010 and approaching 30 GHz by 2016, even though there was a growing recognition that this would require unacceptable levels of power and unprecedented processor power densities. The most popular system form factors, desktop, portable personal computers, tablets, and smart phones place a strict upper bound on the amount of power that

---

* International Technology Roadmap for Semiconductors, 2001 Edition, http://www.itrs.net/Links/2001ITRS/Home.htm

can be dissipated without discomfort in the form of environmental heating and noise. Thus per-socket power budgets have stagnated at between 100 W and 130 W for a typical high-end PC.

To make matters worse, transistor oxide thickness is now limited by tunneling current through the gate, and without reductions in oxide thickness, it becomes increasingly difficult to reduce the supply voltage. Because a reduction in supply voltage is required to increase operating frequencies within a constant power budget, chip operating frequencies have stagnated at about 4 GHz. Without increases in frequency, the main driver for single-thread performance disappeared, and by 2005 all major vendors of microprocessors for computer systems had introduced or announced multi-core products.

Even without reductions in the transistor gate oxide thickness, chip capacitance increases as feature sizes are reduced. High-K dielectrics and new transistor topologies such as dual-gate and fin-fet allow control over the transistor channel to be maintained at reduced supply voltage, but it seems that these types of changes are required merely to allow us to continue to grow the number of transistors on a chip and maintain operating frequency, thus allowing us to use the additional transistors to instantiate more cores without having to degrade the performance of an individual core. In 2010 multiple 8-core microprocessors have been introduced.

Unlike most server applications, most applications for personal computers have been single-threaded and major programming effort is required to ensure that the performance potential of the multi-core processors translates into an improved user experience.

The dominant architecture for multi-core processors is the symmetric multi-processor, where main memory is shared coherently between identical processor cores. There are multiple reasons this configuration is dominant:

- The shared memory model allows memory to be flexibly allocated across different processors or processes;
- The shared-memory model allows sequential programs to be incrementally parallelized using programming languages such as Open MP;
- The shared-memory architecture allows applications that do not use all cores to benefit from improvements in memory capacity and bandwidth to deliver a performance improvement;

- Symmetric designs where a single core is replicated multiple times enable reduced chip design costs.

As long as (a) the number of transistors doubles every couple of years, (b) as long as the energy per switched transistor comes down at a rate similar to that with which the number of transistors grows, and (c) with modest improvements in architecture and efficiency of the cores themselves, historical performance growth rates can be maintained, albeit that we have to consider throughput (for example, SpecIntRate) rather than single-thread (that is, SpecInt) performance metrics.

The multi-core path to performance improvements does put significant additional pressure on memory bandwidth. In the past on-chip caches typically doubled with each technology generation, which meant that even if performance doubled every couple of years, main memory bandwidths had to grow at a slower rate, roughly proportional to the frequency increase of the processor. From 65nm (dual-core) to 45nm (quad-core) and to 32 nm (8-core) the number of cores has indeed doubled with each generation. When additional transistors are used to grow the number of cores rather than to grow cache per core, off-chip bandwidth requirements grow at a much faster rate. This is now causing significant increases in the power associated with main memory. The bandwidth challenge can be met with new technologies, such as on-module or embedded DRAM and high-bandwidth 3D memory.

BEYOND MULTI-CORE—2011–20

While it is expected that transistor densities will continue to improve, it is also expected that starting with the 22 nm node power densities, at constant frequency and switching factor (the percentage of transistors that switch per cycle), will start to increase or, more likely, frequencies will have to start to come down. While this does not signal the end of the multi-core era, it does imply that there is yet another gap that must be filled if the industry is to deliver performance growth at historical rates. Further adding to the concerns is that it seems likely that the delay of scaled wires will start to increase at about the same time, which implies that additional engineering will be required to make a core run at even the same frequency when migrated from one technology to the next.

Of the three main reasons for migrating from one technology node to the next, cost, power, and performance, performance in the form of chip operating frequencies has stagnated, power is showing diminishing returns, and cost is under pressure as an increasing number of wire levels is required to maintain performance. An increasing number of levels requires more than one mask to successfully image, due to the fact that the wavelength of the light source is far larger than the feature sizes that are created.

Thus at some point the question might arise if shrinking feature sizes is still the most effective means of reducing cost per transistor. It is not likely that we can systematically and exponentially reduce costs without shrinking feature sizes, but it is likely that costs will continue to decrease for a substantial period of time even when the 'last' technology node has been introduced, just by virtue of the fact that the capital and development expense associated with the manufacturing equipment will be amortized and eventually only the operating and materials costs remain. Techniques like 3D integration (stacking of multiple layers of silicon) allow system areal densities to continue to improve.

It is, therefore, likely that transistor budgets available to architects will continue to grow exponentially through the next decade, but it is also likely that we must find means other than replicating conventionally architected cores to deliver the exponential increases in performance the market expects.

As long as transistors budgets improve, the market will favour designs that are general-purpose enough to attract a market large enough to allow designs to be realized in every technology node. Designs that are too specialized and cannot attract a large enough market will not sustain the investment levels required to stay ahead of more general-purpose designs that are improved with every new technology node.

We must, therefore, seek methods of further improving efficiency to deliver growing performance at a constant power budget, with only modest improvements in power from technology with architectures that can be broadly applied. Fortunately, the opportunity to deliver on this exists though it will come at the expense of requiring modifications to the algorithms and applications beyond the introduction of concurrency.

Besides concurrency, locality is a key enabler of efficient execution. Dally et al. (2004) have estimated that the majority of the power required to execute a typical program is associated with moving the data around, and yet our programming languages ignore locality and treat memory as an infinite and infinitely close resource.

In the Cell Broadband Engine (Kahle et al. 2005), a nine-core processor used in the Playstation3 game console introduced in 2006 and in a wide variety of other products since then, programs execute on eight of the nine cores out of core-specific 256 kb 'local store' memories and software is responsible for scheduling transfers of code and data between these memories and system memory. These transfers are asynchronous, allowing many of them to be in flight at the same time and thus provide a non-speculative mechanism for hiding the latency associated with accessing main memory. A conventional ninth core runs the operating system and can be used to provide coordination. By explicitly controlling locality, the eight 'synergistic processor element' cores often deliver performance comparable to that of a conventional core with 1-2 MB of cache. This efficiency enabled the Cell processor to implement nine cores in 90nm technology with a transistor budget comparable to that of a conventional dual-core processor.

Graphics processors provide further evidence that substantial gains in efficiency are possible. While graphics processors were traditionally applied just to render images with specialized hardware pipelines, more recently graphics processors have significantly increased the level of programmability and flexibility, with programmable shaders, and the most recent GPGPUs[†] (or General-Purpose GPUs) present themselves as highly threaded data-parallel programmable processors. Applications of modern GPUs include physics, image analysis, and computer vision as well as image rendering, image compression, and decompression.

While of course the date is somewhat arbitrary, we have chosen 2011 as the start of this period because it combines the introduction of mainstream integrated heterogeneous multi-core processors with the availability of a portable programming language (OpenCL) that allows applications to exploit this hardware beyond graphics. AMDs roadmap includes a 2011 heterogeneous processor (Fusion) for portable and desktop computers. OpenCL, introduced by Apple to enable the broad use of computational accelerators in a portable framework, allows programmers to express locality and enables the efficient use of data-parallel hardware with a programming standard for vectors in a C-like language.

Just as not every application can be productively parallelized, not every application will benefit from the performance improvements that

[†] See gpgpu.org

can be achieved when application locality and predictability (vectors are one example) are enhanced and expressed. However, the large number of applications that have been successfully ported to the Cell processor and GPGPUs, indicate that we can anticipate substantial performance growth on a broad variety of workloads.

INCREASING SPECIALIZATION—2021–30

When the energy per transistor switch stops improving and eventually the per-transistor cost stabilizes a much greater degree of hardware differentiation becomes economically feasible. This will give reduced-function and appliance-type devices an increased advantage over systems built from general-purpose programmable hardware.

The opportunity to improve efficiency through specialization is large. While multi-core designs no longer increase the efficiency gap compared to algorithms realized in hardware, and locality and predictability-aware programming and architectures may even reduce the gap somewhat, often there are three orders of magnitude (or more) of difference between a program executing a task and that same task realized directly in hardware.

Field Programmable Gate Arrays provide a middle ground. While they are typically at least an order of magnitude less efficient than a corresponding solution with non-gate-programmable hardware examples abound where FPGAs provide a performance advantage, usually coupled with a very significant power efficiency advantage. Field Programmable Gate Arrays provide the biggest advantage compared to conventional processors on computationally intensive problems that can be highly localized, for example, by laying out a computationally intensive loop as a hardware pipeline without non-local memory references. Thus far the main limiter to broader use of FPGAs has been the work required to program them, but programming of FPGAs in higher-level languages is beginning to take hold, and it seems likely that as higher-level languages and algorithms become more locality-aware, the ability to map them efficiently and automatically to FPGAs will improve.

The step from FPGAs to more custom hardware is perhaps more tractable once applications are expressed with a sufficient degree of locality to enable an effective mapping to hardware gates. The key remaining issue is a trade-off between programmability and efficiency. Note that if a piece of hardware needs to perform ten different tasks of similar complexity and if we assume FPGAs are ten times less efficient in their use of transistors, a direct solution in hardware is still likely to deliver a power-efficiency advantage.

By using 2030 as an end date of this period is perhaps rather pessimistic. It is meant to indicate that past this date substantial improvements are more likely to result from a consideration of new applications or new functionality, or from fundamentally new technologies to build processors than from continued performance improvements based on semiconductor technology and computer architecture. Also, in an industry as dynamic as ours, twenty years has proven to be a long time and predictions that extend further into the future are likely to be of rather limited value.

The main objective of this essay has been to encourage computer architects to take locality (and predictability) seriously as key enablers of efficiency. Expressing locality to a sufficient degree so that a tool chain can partition the data with the computation enables us to effectively map to ever more power-efficient hardware. Doing so also increases our ability to efficiently parallelize on today's multi-core processors and extends the multi-core roadmap. Just like concurrency, locality and predictability are fundamental enablers of computational efficiency and just like concurrency; locality will become a concern for general-purpose programming as technology considerations will force us to simultaneously improve efficiency and performance.

REFERENCES

Dally, W.J., U.J. Kapasi, B. Khailany, J.H. Ahn, and A. Das (2004), 'Stream Processors: Programmability with Efficiency', *ACM Queue*, Vol. 2, No. 1, pp. 52–62.

Dennard, R.H., F.H. Gaensslen, H-N. Yu, V.L. Rideout, E. Bassous, and A.R. LeBlanc (1974), 'Design of Ion-Implanted MOSFET'S with Very Small Physical Dimensions', *IEEE Journal of Solid-State Circuits*, Vol. 9, No. 5, pp. 256–68.

Kahle, J.A., M.N. Day, H.P. Hofstee, C.R. Johns, T.R. Maeurer, D. Shippy (2005), 'Introduction to the cell multiprocessor', *IBM Journal of Research and Development*, Vol. 49, No. 4/5, pp. 589–604.

Moore, G.E. (1965), 'Cramming more components onto integrated circuits', *Electronics* Vol. 38, No. 8, pp. 114–17.

Neumann, J. von (1993) [1945], 'First draft report on the EDVAC', *IEEE Annals of the History of Computing*, Vol. 15, No. 4, pp. 27–75.

Poznanovic, D.S. (2006), 'The Emergence of Non-von Neumann Processors', K. Bertels, J.M.P. Cardoso, and S. Vassiliadis (Eds.) (2006), *LNCS*, 3985, pp. 243–54.

Turing, A.M. (1936), 'On Computable Numbers, with an Application to the Entscheidungsproblem', *Proceedings of the London Mathematical Society*, 2(42): 230–65.

R.K. SHYAMASUNDAR

15 Software Engineering
*Craft-to-Discipline-to-Science**

To put it quite bluntly: as long as there were no machines, programming was no problem at all; when we had a few weak computers, programming became a mild problem, and now we have gigantic computers, programming has become an equally gigantic problem.

—Edsger Dijkstra, 1972, Turing Award Lecture

In this essay, we take a historical view of the development of the programming discipline. Starting from the early days of programming for the computers to machine-independent programming, we trace the key evolutions, challenges, and dreams of the field. While discussing early efforts towards building of digital computers, we shall briefly take a look at the effort of the Tata Institute of Fundamental Research (TIFR) in the mid-1950s. During the course of development, we touch upon aspects that have lifted programming from a craft (or art) to an independent, matured discipline. We shall also highlight the computing challenges needed to cope up with the demands of the grand challenges of science and the need of large-scale information

* The article is based on the works of a large number of researchers. The author is greatly indebted to leading computer scientists Edsger W. Dijkstra, N. Wirth, and C.A.R. Hoare, whose works have played a key role in taking computer science through such a transition in only a few decades and whose writings have influenced the article.

*systems for infrastructure, cyber-physical systems, biology, etc. We argue how
these demands, combined with evolutions in hardware architecture, have
led to new demands for robust, performance-driven, productivity-oriented
programming. With the discipline playing a vital role in the study of natural
and artificial processes, we discuss as to how computing is making an impact
on the discoveries of science, and the way the practice of science and scientific
collaboration is evolving.*

EARLY ERA OF SOFTWARE ENGINEERING

The commissioning of the Electronic Numerical Integrator and Computer (ENIAC) in 1943 at the Moore School of Engineering, University
of Pennsylvania, heralded the digital computing era. Programs were
represented by plugged interconnecting wires and had full conditional
branching facilities. Subsequently, they were represented by settings
of function tables without the need for changing the interconnecting
cables. This allowed the programmer to think of the machine as a
sequential machine and ignore the problems of coordinating parallel
activities. Memory extensions were carried out and ENIAC remained in
use till October 1955. While ENIAC was faster than any other existing
computer, the time required for setting up the problem dissuaded its
usage for problems that did not require extensive computation. The
team had embarked on a new computer, the Electronic Discrete Variable Automatic Computer (EDVAC), recognizing such pitfalls. The
main drawback of setting up the problem was overcome in EDVAC
through the notion of a stored program concept envisaged in a report
by John von Neumann. The design took great advantage of the fact that
a program can read and modify itself. However, the lasting contribution of the stored program concept was that it made it a practical and
attractive proposition to use a computer to assist with the preparation
of its own program, thus leading to the development of programming
tools/aids such as assemblers, compilers, operating systems, etc. The
Electronic Discrete Variable Automatic Computer was commissioned
at the Ballistic Research Laboratory in 1947 and continued its operation till 1962. Also worthy of recollection is the effort towards a stored
program compute called Electronic Delay Storage Automatic Calculator
(EDSAC) at the Cambridge University, UK. It started in 1947 under
the leadership of Maurice V. Wilkes and became operational in 1949.
One of the most significant contributions of the effort was the set of

'initial orders', a wired-in program that provided what would now be called a rudimentary assembler and loader. Within the next few years, several stored program electronic computers were successfully built in the US and other places, and the computer industry started to emerge. New technologies developed and computers increased enormously in speed and capacity, and were used for an ever-growing variety of applications.

Box 15.1 lists some of the early programming languages.

Box 15.1   Early Programming Languages

Computers were initially used for computation rather than for data storage and communication. The early computer languages, therefore, catered mainly to numerical mathematics. The first widely known language, Fortran, was developed by IBM in 1957. This was followed by the first Algol version in 1958 (developed by a committee) and its official successor in 1960. COmmon Business-Oriented Language was created by the US DoD in 1962 specifically for business applications.

Box 15.2 depicts the early efforts on multiprocessor systems. The impact of languages like Fortran and Cobol is immeasurable. It is interesting to note that the drive towards early multiprocessor systems continues to have an impact on the contemporary systems (Denning and Dennis 2010).

Box 16.3 shows the early efforts in India and reflects the position we had at that time. While the rapid strides in semi-conductor technology

---

Box 15.2   Early Multiprocessor Systems

1.   Burroughs B5000 was the first multiprocessor architecture designed in early 1961 by a team led by Robert Barton. The instruction set was attuned to the Algol language and was very simple and efficient even by today's RISC standards. Its working storage was organized as a stack machine and its code was 're-entrant', enabling multiple processors to execute the same code simultaneously while computing on separate stacks. Peter Denning and Jack B. Dennis (2010) lament that the Burroughs innovations on the nested multitask computations could resolve many of the current research challenges. The B5000 was followed by B5500, B6700, and the defence variant D850.

2.   The first time-sharing (TS) system appeared in 1963 designed by John McCarthy at MIT and implemented on an extended DEC PDP-1. It provided the interactivity that batch processing systems lacked.

Box 15.3   Reflection of the Indian Scene around 1959: TIFRAC

a.   Tata Institute of Fundamental Research Automatic Calculator (TIFRAC) was designed and developed by a team lead by R. Narasimhan. It was started in 1955 and was operational by 1956. The full-scale version was started in early 1957 and completed by 1959. It was commissioned in February 1960. It was named TIFRAC in 1962 when the new TIFR buildings were inaugurated by Prime Minister Jawaharlal Nehru.

b.   R. Narasimhan and K.S. Kane developed the first assembler for TIFRAC. These were written in a series of commands of 1s and 0s in comparison to an Operating System of today which has a host of applications with graphic interfaces, enabling almost anybody to use a PC with ease. It was almost certainly the first item of system software to be implemented in India.

in the West was a definite factor as to why the drive could not be carried forward with the same zeal factors like comprehension of the effort needed; application ranges and the political climate also played their role in not being making a stride forward in the computer hardware and system manufacturing sector.

The rapid growth of computing power and its availability led to the deployment of computers in a variety of critical and non-critical sectors. As software was extendable and flexible, 'processes' were continuously replaced by software (often referred to as process control concept). Such a trend dramatically increased the demands on software engineers. Programs and systems became increasingly complex and almost impossible for a single individual to fully understand. The abundance of computing resources coupled with a significant drop in their cost inevitably reduced the attention given to good design. At the expense of quality, the pursuit of profit became paramount; this naturally resulted in the deterioration of programming quality. As pointed by N. Wirth, our limitations in designing complex systems are no longer determined by slow hardware, but by our own intellectual capability. From experience, we know that most programs could be significantly improved, made more reliable, more economical, and easier to use.

To address the challenges faced in engineering software, the NATO Science Committee in early 1967 organized a conference of scientists representing various member nations, on possible international actions in the field of computer science (possible actions included the setting up of an International Institute of Computer Science at a later date). The conference was to shed further light on the many current problems in software engineering, and also to discuss possible techniques, methods, and developments which might lead to their solution. It was hoped that the conference would be able to identify present necessities, shortcomings, and trends, and that the findings could serve as a signpost to manufacturers of computers as well as their users. The degree of the crisis could be gauged by the declaration[†] of the Algol 68 committee to the International Federation for Information Processing (IFIP) council: '...as a tool for the reliable creation of sophisticated programs, the language was a failure....' The honesty and the courage with which the committee of experts evaluated the outcome is something very unusual.

The term 'software engineering' was coined in the NATO-sponsored conference in 1968 (Naur and Randell 1969). It refers to the highly disciplined, systematic approach to software development and maintenance. In the conference, difficulties and pitfalls of designing complex systems were explored in depth, and a search for solutions began that concentrated on better methodologies and tools. The problems of migrating software based on the needs, constructing systems with large teams, determining software quality, etc. were some of the important problems identified for serious research in the 1968 NATO conference on software engineering. Since 1968, the development of software engineering has been intimately tied to (a) efforts for automating (or systematizing) program documentation and (b) emergence of these tools and their improvement.

The expectation was that, ultimately, analytic verification and correctness proofs would replace testing. Salvation was sought in 'better' programming languages, in more 'tools', and in automation. The most prominent of such tools were languages reflecting procedural, modular, and object-oriented styles of programming. To be considered 'better', a language should be useful in a wider area of application; it should be more like a 'natural' language and also offer more facilities. For example, PL/1 developed by IBM in the early 1960s (in use by 1964), was designed to unify the scientific and commercial worlds. It was advertised under the slogan 'Everybody can program thanks to PL/1'.

[†] C.A.R. Hoare (who was member of the committee) in his Turing Award lecture notes that the report was suppressed by IFIP.

Programming languages and their compilers became a principal corner-stone of computing science, but they neither fitted into mathematics nor electronics, the two traditional sectors where computers were used. A new discipline soon emerged, which was called computer science in the US and informatics in Europe.

Computer manufacturers seized on the idea of time-sharing systems and soon announced time-sharing systems for their large mainframes, for example, IBM360/67, General Electric GE-645, etc. It turned out that the transition[‡] from batch processing to time-sharing systems was vastly more difficult than anyone had anticipated. Among other difficulties, the operational problems were too complex; research had to be conducted 'on the job'. The topics of multiprocessing and concurrent programming—central ingredients of time-sharing systems—had not been encountered before and were insufficiently mastered. Consequently, systems were promised but could not be completed and delivered on time. The difficulties brought big companies to the brink of collapse.

The important developments by Dijkstra, Hoare, and others did not—or rather could not—change the software situation or dispel all difficulties overnight. Industry could change neither its policies nor its tools rapidly enough to be of use to programmers, who were restricted to working with available tools and languages, none of which incorporated these new ideas in the 1968 timeframe. Nevertheless, intensive training courses on structured programming began to be organized, notably by Harlan D. Mills at IBM. Even the US Department of Defense (DoD) realized that software problems were urgent and becoming more so. For its part, the DoD initiated a project that ultimately led to the programming language Ada, a highly structured language suitable for a wide variety of applications.

While the concepts of structured programming slowly gained acceptance, notably in academia, another movement started to invade the programmers' world. It was spawned by the spread of the Unix operating system, which Ken Thompson had developed at Bell Labs, and in its simplicity contrasted markedly with the complexity of MIT's Multics. Unix was specifically designed for, and was small enough to fit, the rapidly emerging minicomputers. It was a welcome relief from the

---

[‡] It is of interest to note the remarks of Edsger Dijkstra (2010) wherein he says the IBM 360 had serious flaws in its I/O organization.

large operating systems established on mainframe computers. In its wake came the language C, which had been explicitly designed by Dennis Richie, also at Bell Labs, to support the development of Unix. It was, therefore, at least attractive, if not mandatory, to use C for developing applications that ran under Unix, which thus acted like a Trojan horse for C. But C did not carry the spirit of structured programming. It was rather like an assembler code in the disguise of a remotely Algol-like syntax. Neither did it allow for strict checking of data types. From the point of view of software engineering, the rapid spread of C, therefore, represented a great leap, albeit backwards.

EMERGENCE OF PROGRAMMING AS A DISCIPLINE

It was mainly Edsger W. Dijkstra and C.A.R. Hoare who recognized the problems endemic to programming and offered new ideas. In 1965, Dijkstra wrote one of his seminal papers 'Notes on Structured Programming' and declared programming to be a discipline rather than a craft. Also, in 1965, Hoare had published an important paper about structuring data. These ideas had a profound influence on new programming languages. New languages were the vehicles in which these new ideas were to be expressed. Structured programming became supported by structured programming languages. Methodologies for programming referred to as top-down programming started to emerge. In 1967, Robert W. Floyd had suggested the idea of assertions of states that had to be always valid at given points in a program. It led to Hoare's seminal paper titled 'An Axiomatic Basis of Computer Programming', postulating the so-called Hoare logic. A few years later, in 1975, Dijkstra deduced from it the calculus of predicate transformers and provided a mathematical basis. Programs were no longer just codes for controlling computers, but static texts that could be subjected to mathematical reasoning. Although these developments were recognized at some universities, they virtually went unnoticed in industry. Indeed, Hoare's logic and Dijkstra's predicate transformers were used to formally establish the correctness of small programs. Significant amount of work was carried out to axiomatize programming language constructs of languages like Algol and use proof systems to establish the correctness of programs assisted by theorem provers. Cooks' seminal result of coming up with the notion of relative completeness in 1974 in the context of Godel's incompleteness result led to a vast amount of work on establishing the correctness of programs through proof systems. Naturally, there was a need for automation to support these endeavours. A huge amount of effort has gone in to provide tool support for establishing the correctness of programs like theorem provers, proof assistants, model checkers, etc.

Correctness of Programs

There are two approaches to establish the correctness of programs. In the first, referred to as a two-language approach, assertions are provided in a formal logical language. Then, the correctness of the final assertion is established using the proof system for the underlying programming language relative to the given assertions. Notions like partial correctness (a program is said to be correct with respect to given assertions provided it terminates in a state satisfying the final assertion starting from the state satisfying the initial assertion) and complete correctness (the program is guaranteed to terminate in a state satisfying the final assertion starting from a state satisfying the initial assertion) emerged. One of the first attempts was the development of a program verifier for the language Pascal; this had a far-reaching effect on using verifiers for proving correctness of small programs. However, for industrial-scale programs, efforts are focused on using formal systems interactively or in a semi-automatic manner in order to establish correctness. The fallout from all such efforts was a clear semantics and confidence towards building robust and reliable compilers or translators. While reflecting on his 1969 Axiomatic Basis paper, Tony Hoare (Hoare 2009) strongly supports the role of testing as being mutually supportive to correctness: '... success of tests is that they test the programmer, not the program ... The experience, judgment, and intuition of programmers who have survived the rigors of testing are what make programs of the present day useful, efficient, and (nearly) correct. Formal methods for achieving correctness must support the intuitive judgment of programmers, not replace it.'

Model Checking

The technique was originally developed by Ed Clarke and Allen Emerson in 1981 and consists of building a finite model of a system and checking that a desired property holds in the model. Two general approaches to model checking are used in practice (Clarke et al. 1999). The first approach is based on specification in temporal logic proposed by Amir

Pnueli in 1981. The method consists of modelling systems as finite state transition systems and efficient search procedure is used to check if the given transition system satisfies the model of the specification given in temporal logic. In the second approach, both the specification and the system are modelled as automata and are compared for conformance; various notions of conformance such as observational equivalence, refinement orderings, language inclusion, etc. are used. Further, the approach could be recast in terms of automata, thus relating the approaches.

Model checkers have distinct advantages over proof checkers and theorem provers for the verification of circuits (hardware) and protocols. One distinct advantage is that it is quite automatic. Typically, the model checker either terminates asserting the correctness of the assertion/specification or arrives at a counterexample that shows why the specification is not satisfied. The main disadvantage of model checking has been the state-explosion problem. McMillan used Ordered Binary Decision Diagrams to represent state transition systems efficiently, thus scaling up the size of the systems that can be model checked. The latter is the reason for wide acceptance of hardware model checking by the industry.

Model checking is also widely applied for software (referred to as software model checking). The approach requires the creation of a mathematical model of the application, and specifying the system properties using temporal logic and running the model checker looking for compliance. The automation and the comprehensive nature of the approach are distinct advantages. While it has made impressive strides, large-scale industrial use of model checking is still elusive (Long et al. 2008). One of the success stories has been the Slam project (Ball et al. 2004) that has been used in the Windows device driver development; the tool is available as Static Drive Verifier (SDV) for the device driver developers. The lack of studies of third party evaluation of model checking for industrial applications has been one of the main factors impeding widespread acceptance by industry.

Theorem Proving

Theorem proving is the process of finding a proof of a property from axioms and inference rules. In the approach of applying theorem proving for correctness of programs (or systems), both the system and its desired properties are expressed as formulae in some formal mathematical logic defined by a set of axioms and a set of inference rules. While the classical correctness of programs is concerned with proof construction by hand, here we consider machine-assisted theorem proving. These are widely used for the mechanical verification of safety-critical systems. The theorem provers range from completely automated to interactive assistants. Automatic theorem provers based on the resolution principle, such as SPASS and Vampire, are quite sophisticated and are capable of finding long proofs even for problems having thousands of axioms. However, they are limited to first-order logic. Higher-order logic (HOL) extends first-order logic with lambda notation for functions and with function and predicate variables. It supports reasoning in set theory, using the obvious representation of sets by predicates. Higher-order logic is a natural language for expressing mathematics, and it is also ideal for formal verification. Moving from first-order to higher-order logic requires a more complicated proof calculus, but it often allows much simpler problem statements. The built-in support for functions and sets in HOL often leads to shorter proofs. Conversely, elementary identities (such as the distributive law for union and intersection) turn into difficult problems when expressed in first-order form. There are fully automatic HOL theorem provers such as TPS and Leo and user-guided assistants like HOL4, Isabelle/HOL, Coq, PVS, etc. While systems like HOL4, Isabelle/HOL, and Coq are based on Logic of Computable Functions (LCF) of Robin Milner, PVS does not expand everything down to primitive inferences.

One distinct advantage of theorem proving is that it can deal directly with infinite state spaces as it relies on techniques like structural induction for proofs involving infinite domains. Some of the notable applications for establishing the correctness of computer systems are proving the capability of simultaneous processing by AAMP7G microprocessor, integrity of the Greenhills-178 operating system (Long et al. 2008).

SMT Solvers

Propositional satisfiability (SAT) procedures dates back to Emil L Post (1921) and Bernays (1920). Recent advances have rendered them useful for an impressive spectrum of applications ranging from debugging to verification of systems. They have found wide applications in bounded model checking and for generating proofs of unsatisfiability. Propositional satisfiability procedures can also be extended beyond the propositional realm to decide the satisfiability of quantifier-free formulas in a theory such as equality or arithmetic, or even a combination of such theories. The resulting procedure decides satisfiability modulo theories (SMT) and can be applied to range of applications for system checking (Shankar 2007).

There has been marked use of theorem provers for proving the correctness of systems and, further, application to mechanization of mathematics has shown a great progress (four colour theorem, Jordan curve theorem, large developments in measure theory and multivariate real analysis) (Gordon 2008).

EVOLUTION OF PROGRAMMING LANGUAGES

Structured programming had a significant impact in the industry as well as academia in the development of programming languages. Pascal invented by N. Wirth was one of the first programming languages founded on structured programming principles and widely used in academia. The arrival of Unix operating system had a huge impact in the programming world. It was a welcome relief in the world of computer systems as it was small enough to be fitted on the emerging minicomputers. Dennis Richie had developed a programming language called C to support the development of Unix. While C did not carry the rationale of structured programming, it served to build efficient systems. From the scientific perspective, it was a step backwards; however, it remains the preferred language for realizing high-performance systems even today.

In 1966, Dijkstra wrote a seminal paper about harmoniously cooperating processes, postulating a discipline based on semaphores for the synchronization of concurrent processes. This demonstrated how mutual exclusion of actions by processes can be realized in a multiprogramming environment. This laid the foundations for architectural evolution of synchronization, reasoning about concurrent programs, and development of multiprogramming systems. Around the same time, there were efforts to develop languages for discrete event simulation by Olen-Johan Dahl and Kristen Nyggard. The result was the language Simula, whose fundamental concepts were somewhat hidden till the emergence of object-oriented languages/methodologies.

Industry was plagued by large, complex systems. The question was whether mathematical theories would ever solve real problems when the analysis of simple algorithms was demanding enough. An eventual solution to the dilemma of mathematical rigour for small programs against the intractability of large programs as they existed in industry emerged in the form of a disciplined manner of programming, rather than from rigorous scientific theory.

Information hiding concept put forward by David Parnas in 1972 provided a basis for modularity and solutions for some issues of software engineering. Information hiding embodies the notion of breaking up large systems into sub-parts called modules, and defines clearly their interfaces. If module A wants to use module B, the designer of A need not know the details of the functioning of B, but only the properties as stated by its interface. Around the same time, the proposal of abstract data types by Barbara Liskov captured information hiding in a succinct manner and provided a breakthrough for building large software systems. The principle referred to as modularization is one the most important contributions to software engineering, which enabled the construction of systems by large groups of people. The concept of modularization is greatly enhanced by the technique of separate compilation with automatic checking of interface compatibility. The P and V semaphores proposed by Dijkstra were like the 'goto statements' and was leading to problems in synchronization. Hoare came up with the concept of monitors that provided the capability of mutual exclusion at a method level. The first implementation of monitors was incorporated in the language Concurrent Pascal designed by Per Brinch Hansen. Just as structured programming had been the guiding spirit behind Pascal, modularization was the principal idea behind the language Modula-2, Pascal's successor, again designed by N. Wirth in 1979. In fact, the motivation for Modula-2 actually came from the language Mesa, an internal development of the Xerox Palo Alto Research Center (PARC), and itself a descendant of Pascal.

It is of interest to note that at TIFR under the National Centre for Software Development and Computing Techniques (NCSDCT), described separately in a chapter by S. Ramani, there was an early effort on developing a compiler on Basic Combined Programming Language (BCPL) through cooperation with University of Cambridge; the author, while visiting University of Cambridge in September 2010 as a Distinguished Visiting Fellow under the Royal Academy of Engineering, UK, noted that there is still interest on BCPL while discussing with

M. Richards. During this period several distinguished visitors like M.V. Wilkes, FRS (University of Cambridge), W. Wulf (CMU), Per Brinch Hansen (USC/CalTech), C.A.R. Hoare, FRS (University of Belfast, Oxford University), Robin Milner, FRS (University of Edinburgh), and Rod Burstall (University of Edinburgh) visited NCSDCT during late 1970s. This led to a lot of theoretical and experimental work on communication and concurrency and, in fact, a language called CCN Pascal on the lines of Concurrent Pascal was designed and developed on the home-grown TDC series of computers (discussed in Chapter 3). This was a complete top-down experiment involving both hardware and software (OS and compilers). Perhaps this initiative should have been seriously taken to the next level.

C.A.R. Hoare had fully envisioned that in the future programmers would have to cope with the difficulties posed by concurrent processes. He proposed Communicating Sequential Processes (CSP) in 1978, based on the concept of channels and message passing, laid the foundations for distributed programming languages, and brought out succinctly the need of non-deterministic environment. The rendezvous communication mechanism along with concepts of modularization and separate compilation was adopted by the language Ada, which was largely based on Pascal. This language was sponsored by the DoD of USA and has a significant presence. A host of languages came into existence both in academia and industry, with variations of the basic message passing primitives and variations of shared/distributed memory models. Embedded systems have given rise to the family of event-driven languages referred to as reactive languages, such as Statecharts, Esterel, Lustre, etc. (Shyamasundar and Ramesh 2010). These languages are in wide use for hardware and software design, and hardware-software co-design.

A variety of distributed programming languages have been in use that can be broadly categorized into: (a) concurrent languages based on shared variables, and (b) concurrent languages based on message passing.

Inspired by CSP, the message passing paradigm has been used widely on a variety of parallel machines with distributed memory. The high-performance community needed a language that would enable the use of distributed machines, which would permit the use of the widely used Fortran or C libraries—the hallmark of scientific computing. This lead to the widely used package called Message Passing Interface (MPI).

Since its use in 1993, MPI has been standardized and is used widely; it has given rise to packages such as OpenMP.

In the beginning of 2000, it was noticed that sequential programming was falling below Moore's law. In spite of pipelining, complex out-of-order execution, hierarchical caching mechanisms, etc., the sequential throughput was falling below expectations due to the three walls: power efficiency, instruction-level parallelism limitations, and memory latency. Computer architects were unable to continue to sufficiently grow the performance of single-thread (sequential) applications under these new constraints. Automatic compiler-based parallelization was unable to sustain the expected performance improvements without changes to the sequential programming model, and the industry worked hard to parallelize applications to preserve end-customer value growth. To quote Peter Hofstee, 'while the period from 1971 to 2000 delivered about four orders of magnitude in performance improvements within a single programming paradigm, this period also resulted in close to three orders of magnitude in reduced efficiency in order to maintain the sequential programming model' (see Chapter 14). For these reasons, the industry along with academia aggressively pushed for newer architectures, referred to nowadays as Multi-Core Architectures. Aggressive research and development have lead to highly significant hardware-efficient multi-core and multi-threaded architectures with a significantly improved performance. Currently, there has been widespread deployment of multi-core architecture alongside the advent of heterogeneous accelerators such as Graphics Processing Units (GPU), Cell Processors, and FPGA-based custom accelerators. Programming multi-core machines has been a challenge and many new languages such CUDA for GPUs and another family referred to as PGAS (partially global address space) languages have arisen. The latter family includes languages such as X10 (IBM), Chapel (Cray), and Fortress (Sun) that have been under development for the past few years. The PGAS model essentially has a fixed number of places with one or more threads of control, with globally partitioned arrays that can be accessed from all processes, distinction between global arrays and local variables lies with and limited global synchronization. The real performance and productivity is still to be assessed. Some of the important points research has shown are as follows:

- Concurrency is no longer the only enabler of performance,

- Locality and predictability shall play a vital role for enhancing the performance for multi-core architectures and beyond,
- Algorithms need to be looked afresh for keeping performance, productivity, energy efficiency, etc. within appropriate ranges, and
- Programming language design and analysis need to follow hardware evolution, particularly for pets-scale and exascale computing requirements.

PROGRAMMING-IN-THE-SMALL VS. PROGRAMMING-IN-THE-LARGE

In the mid-1970s, a shift in the scale of applications led from the discipline of programming to the discipline of software system management. This arose from the understanding that constructing large, complex systems is not at all the same as the task of writing small individual programs even if the individual program is huge. The fact is that the development of large systems requires coordination of many people, maintenance and control of several versions, and the possibility to reconstruct the old version after the evolution of the system. While large individual program construction was addressed by concepts such as information hiding and abstract data types, systematic construction of large systems came somewhat later.

In the second NATO Conference on Software Engineering, the existence of a large gap between communities of software development practice and software research was noted by Strachey and others. The theme has resonated quite well in these two groups and has led to good practices based on sound theory, and building up of tools for software construction and management.

For the first time, Deremer and Kron (1975) made an explicit distinction of construction of individual programs and construction of large system that needed a coordination among several people through the coining of phrases 'programming-in-the small' and 'programming-in-the-large' respectively. Their main aim was to get the attention of researchers for the arriving at methodologies, tools, etc. for the latter. The nature of the change is summarized in Table 15.1. Software management required enormous focus from software requirements to realization and, at the same, timely managed migration of systems to new technology or new requirements. That is, it needed to look at the whole software cycle. Formal models and tools arose in an ad hoc

Table 15.1   Programming-in-the-Small vs. Programming-in-the-Large

Basis	Programming-in-the-Small	Programming-in-the Large
Characteristics	Emphasis on specific algorithms	Emphasis on system structures, interfaces, and coordination among people
Data Issues	Data structures/data types	Databases
Control Issues	Programs execute once and terminate	An assembly of modules continuously executes and interacts among various modules
Specification	A Mathematical function	Relationship between sequence of states and states
State Space	Reasonable	Large state space with complex structure
Management	Individual effort	Team effort
Tools and Methods	Data-structures, compilers, debuggers, linkers, loaders	Programming environments with version control, configuration management, document production, and report generation

manner for purposes of organized recompilation, with tools for configuration management and version control. Now, some of these tools have matured and are quite sophisticated that would allow bug tracking, bug mining, etc. Mary Shah (1986) has nicely articulated the next challenges in software engineering in Table 15.1.

With widespread use of software particularly for its flexibility and adaptability, time to deliver has become one of the prime movers, particularly for business applications. This has lead to processes for rapid software development where time to deliver is the key concern (not even the cost), which looks for reuse of generic systems like ERP and COTS. Here, configuration plays a vital role to meet specific organizational requirements. One of the serious challenges has been models and tools for software construction by configuration as it will have a serious impact on the economics.

In the absence of concrete behavioural models, the industry has relied upon a process-oriented view, focusing more on the development process for the software. As discussed earlier, programming-in-the-large is concerned with the whole lifecycle of the software development effort: conceptualization, requirements, architecture, system realization, testing, maintenance, etc. The software development efforts have been conceptualized via various software development process models to arrive at good practices for software development. One of the early models was the waterfall lifecycle model and is still by far the most common way of scheduling and managing projects. Nevertheless, the most fundamental issue with the waterfall lifecycle is that defects introduced early in the process are not identified or fixed until late in the process. Certain kinds of strategic defects—specifically requirements and architectural defects—are three or four orders of magnitude more expensive to repair in the waterfall lifecycle because they have broad sweeping implications. This is inherent in the waterfall lifecycle because testing comes at the end. In short, the problem with the waterfall lifecycle is that it fundamentally assumes each step in the process can be completed more or less without serious defects, but in fact that is demonstrably untrue. When the defects are finally identified and repaired, the cost is very high.

The spiral (also known as the iterative) lifecycle has become popular in addressing the concerns associated with the waterfall lifecycle. The basic advantage of the spiral lifecycle is that the system is tested far earlier and far more often. This results in the identification and repair of defects much earlier and at a significantly reduced cost. The spiral lifecycle essentially breaks up the development project into a set of smaller projects, and incrementally adds capabilities to the system, but not before validating the ones already present. Each addition of a set of capabilities is called a 'spiral' or 'increment'. Each of these sub-projects is more limited in scope, produced with much greater ease, and has a much more targeted focus than the entire system.

Taking clues from experts who could create wonderful programs by just rolling up their sleeves and working hard until the system worked, a further step was taken into agile development methods such as Extreme Programming (XP). These methods stress the communication between the team members and customers, the simplicity of the code, the feedback from testing, courage, and pride. In XP, each step should last only a few weeks, and after each period the developed code should be functioning perfectly. In a sense, XP has rediscovered what Frederik P. Brooks, father of IBM System/360, wrote: 'Grow, don't build software.'

Carnegie Mellon University developed a tool for objectively assessing the ability of the US government contractors' processes to perform a contracted software project. The underlying model referred to as Capability Maturity Model (CMM) is based on the process maturity framework first described in Watts Humphrey's 1989 book *Managing the Software Process*. Even though CMM was developed from the field of software project development, it is used as a general model to aid in improving organizational business processes in diverse areas such as software engineering, system engineering, project management, software maintenance, risk management, system acquisition, information technology, services, business processes, and human capital management. It may be noted that CMM has been used extensively worldwide in government, commerce, industry, and software development organizations.

It may be noted that while several processes have been developed, no one process is suitable for all. One of the somewhat automatable process has been the approach of model driven development that has found wide usage in industry.

Model Driven Development and Unified Modelling Language

Software is an ever-increasing part of the computing problem. A growing percentage of computer-related costs is attributable to software. There is a dire need to arrive at processes that would assure high productivity, reliability, support, flexibility, and cater to adoption of different technologies. In short, the community demanded vision necessary to support interoperability with specifications that address integration through the entire systems lifecycle: from business modelling to system design, to component construction, to assembly, integration, deployment, management, and evolution. Such a vision was embodied in the OMG's Model Driven Architecture™ (MDA™). It describes how the MDA defines the relationships among OMG standards and how they can be used today in a coordinated fashion, and how the approach helps in the creation, maintenance, and evolution of standards. It is important to realize that the rationale of MDA is to provide a roadmap and vision that will include and integrate all of the work done to date, and to point the way to future integration standards. It provided such a specification using the Unified Modelling Language (UML). A UML-based specification is a model whose properties can be expressed graphically via diagrams, or textually via an XML document. Unified Modelling Language allows one to specify, visualize, and document models of software systems, including their structure and design, in a way that meets all of these requirements; it can be used for business modelling as well as other non-software systems. Using any one of the large number of UML-based tools, one can analyse one's future application's requirements and design a solution that meets them, representing the results using UML 2.0's thirteen standard diagram types. UML 2.0$ defines thirteen types of diagrams, divided into three categories: six diagram types represent static application structure; three represent general types of behaviour; and four represent different aspects of interactions:

- *Structure Diagrams* include the Class Diagram, Object Diagram, Component Diagram, Composite Structure Diagram, Package Diagram, and Deployment Diagram
- *Behaviour Diagrams* include the Use Case Diagram (used by some methodologies during requirements gathering), Activity Diagram, and State Machine Diagram
- *Interaction Diagrams*, derived from the more general Behaviour Diagram, include the Sequence Diagram, Communication Diagram, Timing Diagram, and Interaction Overview Diagram
- Using such model specifications, several formal tools are also available for establishing formal correctness and analysis at various abstraction levels. (See Shah 1986)

LARGE-SCALE INFORMATION SYSTEMS

Organizational information systems have become a necessity and serve a variety of purposes within an organization. They have revolutionized business practices and approaches. Such organizational information systems can be treated as systems of systems obtained by integration of systems, components, and services. All these things have become possible due to achievements of software engineering. Typical examples of achievements are revolution in business practices effected by Google, essentially due to new algorithms that have enabled a scalable architecture for information searches; cloud computing infrastructure supported by Amazon, Google, IBM, Microsoft, etc. is yet another example of revolution due to a new software architecture.

From the perspective of the underlying science and engineering knowledge base, software is the least understood and the most

---

$ Unified Modelling Language, UML 2.0, Object Management Group, 2010.

problematic element of large-scale systems. Software and software project failures are among the dominant causes of system cost, schedule overruns, and failures of systems to satisfy the requirements of those who procure and use them. Despite the careful application of modern software engineering techniques, software failure is far more prevalent than hardware failure as a cause of major system outages. While some problems are caused by poor practice, the root cause of most system problems is our inadequate software knowledge base.

There is yet another level of grand challenge for software engineering. Information dominance has become a key stake for companies and nations from a variety of perspectives. Realization of such a goal needs complex systems that are characterized by an integration of platforms,[¶] sensors, decision nodes and possibly tactical systems connected via heterogeneous wired and wireless networks. Such systems have been referred as Ultra Large Scale Systems (ULS) (Clarke et al. 1999). These are essentially socio-technical ecosystems. These are systems wherein the classical reductionist[**] approach is not applicable. Some of the reasons lie with the characteristics of socio-economical systems such as incomplete specification, not having full control over the organization, and not necessarily rational decisions.

Although systems comprise far more than software, it is the software part that fundamentally makes it possible to achieve the envisioned goals Note that software for ULS may also present the greatest impediment to realize goals. Thus, software for ULS is a grand challenge that has to be attacked through an interdisciplinary approach.

TOWARDS SOFTWARE SCIENCE

It is reasonable to hope that the relationship between computation and mathematical logic will be as fruitful in the next century as that between analysis and physics in the past. The development of this relationship demands a concern for both applications and for mathematical elegance.

— John McCarthy, Turing Award Winner

[¶] The combination of hardware and software that provides a virtual machine that executes software and applications. Software platforms include operating systems, libraries, and frameworks.

[**] An approach to understand the nature of the complex systems in terms of interaction of its components or fundamental entities.

The concept of computation existed long before the invention of computers. The notion of computing emerged through the pioneering formalization of the notion of algorithm (or automatic computation) in a variety of ways by A. Church, Alan Turing, Emil Post, and A.A. Markov. In 1968, Herbert A. Simon argued that certain phenomena are artificial in the sense 'they are as they are only because of a system's molded by goals or purposes, to the environment in which it lives. If natural phenomena have an air of *necessity* about them in their subservience to natural law, artificial phenomena have an air of *contingency* in their malleability by environment.' The contingency of artificial phenomena created doubts as to whether they fall properly within the compass of science. Consistent with this viewpoint, Richard Feynman in 1983 said, 'Computer science differs from physics in that it is not actually a science. It does not study natural objects. Neither it is mathematics. It's like engineering-about getting to do something, rather than dealing with *abstractions*.' Using similar viewpoints, Juris Hartmanis, treating computing as sciences of the artificial, argues how the mathematical structures cannot be challenged by theory of experiments. He further argues that the role of experiments in computer science is to demonstrate the constructible universes in contrast to the role of experiments in natural sciences like physics.

The crux of computing lies in programming. Early works of Edsgar Dijkstra and Tony Hoare demonstrated that 'abstraction' is the key feature for good programming and it is this that distinguishes it from classical engineering. The role of abstraction is succinctly captured by Niklaus Wirth (2008) who says, 'Computer system involves machines of great complexity. This complexity can be mastered intellectually by one tool only: *abstraction*. A language represents an abstract computer whose objects and constructs lie closer to, and reflect more directly, the problem to be represented than the concrete machine.'

Programming consists of two parts: the what part (a formal description of the problem) and the how part (how do we solve problem). Perhaps, loosely speaking software engineering could be treated as a way to realize the total solution to the problem combining the solutions of sub-problems. Looking at classical engineering systems, the physical systems are underpinned by well-understood mathematical foundations and can be used to predict the behaviour and attributes of a physical system. Further, measurement can be used to compare them and validate the mathematical models. Thus, measurements can be understood in terms of universal physical concepts. Lord Kelvin said: 'When you can measure what you are speaking about and express it in numbers you know something about it. If you cannot measure it, you cannot improve it.' Thus, the question is: Does Kelvin's statement apply in respect of software engineering? Software systems are abstract systems designed to support a variety of processes that may include interaction with the world/environment including humans. They are not constrained by the physical world (as highlighted already; they come under the Sciences of the Artificial). Thus, capturing software complexity does not seem reasonable. Then, can we call it a science? Let us look from a general perspective to gain insights into these aspects.

With the extensive use of computers, computation had become in-dispensable by the 1980s and the status had been upgraded from a tool to exploit existing knowledge to a means to discover new knowledge. In fact, it was this phenomenon that led the Nobel Laureate Ken Wilson to say that computation had become the third leg of science joining the traditions of theory and experiments. This led to the birth of 'computa-tional science' referring to the search for new discoveries using computa-tion as the main method. Scientists from different fields started saying that they have discovered information processes in their field. To quote the biologist David Baltimore (Nobel Laureate): 'Biology today is an information science. The output of the system, and the mechanics of life are encoded in a digital medium and read out by a series of reading heads. Biology is no longer solely the province of a small laboratory. Contributions come from many directions.' Even in physics, it is seen in the work of Richard Feynman who showed that quantum electro-dynamics (QED) was nature's computational method for combining quantum particle interactions. The long standing claim of Galileo that nature is written in mathematics was challenged by Stephen Wolfram in his book *A New Kind of Science* where he claims that nature is written in the language of computation. Even though the role of information can be seen in the works of Norbert Weiner, it is only recently that computing as science has been accepted by scientists.

As argued earlier, in order to keep performance, productivity and power efficiency, it is very important for keeping up performance and productivity with power-efficient hardware. This calls for new ways to program. As Peter Hofstee has speculated, performance and productivity with the power-efficient hardware beyond multicore can come only at the expense of requiring modifications to algorithms and applications beyond the introduction of concurrency. This automatically calls for new paradigms of computation and programming. This only means a new driving force will be needed to serve the demands. In other words, the hardware/programming has to closely emulate information processes.

On an entirely different plane, new ways of collaborations, interactions, social behaviours have emerged while the entire web is treated laboratory. The recent collaborating way of doing science in the context of the announcement by Vinay Deolalikar that 'P=NP'. Moshe Vardi, editor-in-chief of *The Communications of the Association for Computing Machinery*, highlights the breakthrough collaborations that emerged in the way science is practised:

What was highly significant, however, was the pace of discussion and analysis, carried out in real time on blogs and a wiki that had been quickly set up for the purpose of collectively analyzing the paper. This kind of collaboration has emerged only in recent years in the math and computer science communities. In the past, intense discussions like the one that surrounded the proof of the Poincaré conjecture were carried about via private e-mail and distribution lists as well as in the pages of traditional paper-based science journals. Several of the researchers said that until now such proofs had been hashed out in colloquiums that required participants to be physically present at an appointed time. Now, with the emergence of Web-connected software programs it is possible for such collaborative undertakings to harness the brainpower of the world's best thinkers on a continuous basis.

Clay Shirky (2010) argues that the emergence of these new collaborative tools is paving the way for a second scientific revolution in the same way the printing press created a demarcation between the age of alchemy and the age of chemistry: 'The difference between the alchemists and the chemists was that the printing press was used to coordinate peer review. The printing press didn't cause the scientific revolution, but it wouldn't have been possible without it.'

Another recent paradigm referred to as 'crowd-sourcing' is being widely treated as information process. Jeff Howe coined the word 'crowd-sourcing' to reflect how the power of the crowd is driving the future of business. From a software technology perspective, a collaborative intelligence of the crowd can be seen in an open source development, where it attracts users and liberate the crowd to study, change, distribute, and enhance by adding new features into existing open source projects. Crowd-sourcing has begun to be used widely in network security.

Looking at the way science being discovered or practised, we can say that there are signs of the emergence of a social computer. According to this European Union proposal in which the author is a participant, the social computer is another future computational system that harnesses the innate problem-solving, action, and information-gathering powers of humans and the environments in which they live, in order to tackle large-scale social problems that are beyond our current capabilities. The hardware of a social computer is supplied by people's brains and bodies, and the environment where they live, including artefacts, while the software is the people's minds, laws, organizational and social rules, social conventions, and computer software. Similar to what happens within a conventional computer and more interestingly within naturally occurring reasoning and control systems like the human body, a social computer exhibits an algorithmic behaviour and problem-solving capabilities which are the result of very large numbers of local computations, decisions, interactions, data, and control information exchange.

To quote Peter Denning, '[the] future of computing is nothing but the study of natural and artificial information processes.' The direction of doing science and impact the way science is practised shall be fascinating where stakeholders include physical processes, artificial processes, and humans. From an economics perspective, it is worth noting the impact of globalization and offshoring of software. Its impact and directions of impact on this globalized world remains to be seen. Vardi (2010) envisages the possible impacts of this. However, the mantras would remain: innovate, develop, produce, educate, compete, and invest.

From the above discussions, one can see that several initiatives in terms of computer science and technology were taken almost on a contemporary level in India. It was on Homi Bhabha's initiative that the digital computer was built in the mid-1950s. The impact would have been felt at all stages by the society if computer science and technology had been promoted the way Bhabha championed programmes like energy and space. With new initiatives by the government and private sector with reference to IT, I believe the impact of IT will be passed to society and will bridge the digital divide as far as possible.

REFERENCES

Ball, T., B. Cook, V. Levin, and S. Rajamani (2004), 'SLAM and Static Driver: Technology Transfer of Formal Methods inside Microsoft', *TR, MSR-TR-2004–8*, Microsoft Research, January.

Clarke, Edmond, Orna Grumberg, and Doron A. Peled (1999), *Model Checking*, MIT Press.

Denning, P.J. and J.B. Dennis (2010), 'The Profession of IT, The Resurgence of Parallelism', *CACM*, 53, 6, June, pp. 30–2.

Deremer, F. and H. Kron (1975), 'Programming-in-the-large vs Programming-in-the-small', *Proceedings of the International Conference on Reliable Software*, Los Angeles, California, pp. 114–22.

Dijkstra, Edsger W. (2010), 'Interview', *CACM*, 53:8, August, pp. 41–7.

Giunchiglia, Fausto, et al. (2010), 'The Social Computer', Under submission to European Union, September.

Gordon, Mike (2008), 'Twenty Years of Theorem Proving for HOLs: Past, Present and Future', *LNCS*, 5170, pp. 1–5.

Hoare, C.A.R. (2009), 'Retrospective: An Axiomatic Basis for Computer Programming', *CACM*, 52: 10, October, pp. 30–2.

Long, Barry, Juergen Dingel, and T.C. Nicholas Graham (2008), 'Experience Applying the SPIN Model Checker to an Industrial Telecommunications System', *ACM ICSE*, pp. 693–702.

Naur, Peter and B. Randell (eds) (1969), 'Software Engineering, Report on the SE Conference 1968', Brussels: NATO Scientific Affairs Division, January.

SE Institute (2006), 'Ultra-large Scale Systems: Software Challenge of the Future', Pittsburgh: Carnegie Mellon University.

Shah, Mary (1986), 'Beyond Programming-in-the-large: The Next Challenges of Software Engineering', *LNCS*, 244, pp. 519–35.

Shankar, N. (2007), 'Beyond Satisfiability: Extensions and Applications', in S. Ramesh and P. Sampath (eds), *Next Generation Design and Verification Methodologies for Distributed Embedded Systems*, Springer, pp. 213–25.

Shirky, Clay (2010), *Cognitive Surplus: Creativity and Generosity in a Connected Age*, London: Allen Lane.

Shyamasundar, R.K. and S. Ramesh (2010), *Real-Time Programming: Languages, Specification and Verification*, World Scientific Publishing.

Tou, J. and P. Wegner (eds) (1971), Data Structures in Programming Languages, SIGPLAN Notices, February, pp. 171–90.

Vardi, Moshe (2010), 'Globalization and Offshoring of Software Revisited', *CACM*, 53, 5, Editors' Letter, May.

Wirth, N. (2008), 'A Brief History of Software Engineering', *IEEE Annals of the History of Computing*, July–September, pp. 32–9.

A. PAULRAJ

16 Wireless Technology and Services in India*

Wireless services in India started with a single wireless telegraph link in Calcutta a little over a hundred years ago and, after many years of slow growth, has expanded dramatically in recent years to reach over 560 million mobile wireless phones (March 2010). This makes India the second largest in the world in wireless subscribers, the largest being China. A large population, low wire line telephony penetration, falling tariff, and rising income levels have made India the fastest-growing wireless nation. Despite the success of its wireless services sector, India, however, largely relies on imported technology for its networks.

This essay has four sections. In the first, we outline the evolution of global wireless technology and networks and discuss emerging trends. Next, we trace the history of wireless networks in India, policy evolution, and current trends in services. In the third section we survey wireless R&D and manufacturing in India. We conclude in section four with suggestions for reviving the telecom equipment industry.

* I would like to thank Sandeep Chennakeshu for many useful comments and discussions on this subject. Comments received from Rajat Gupta are also appreciated.

EVOLUTION OF WIRELESS TECHNOLOGY

G. Marconi, the name most associated with mass-market wireless services, demonstrated the feasibility of wireless telegraphy, progressing
from small home experiments in 1895 to an experimental transatlantic
wireless link in 1901. Though Marconi has received much credit for
commercialization of the wireless technology, the underlying scientific
discoveries go back to at least fifty years earlier. Most prominent of
these were J.C. Bose in India, O. Lodge in the UK, E. Branly in Paris, and
N. Tesla in the US. In 1894, J.C. Bose demonstrated the first milli-
metre wave radio transmission using gunpowder to create a burst of
radio energy, which rang a bell a few feet away. Following Marconi's
commercial success, technology improvements came rapidly in the early
part of the twentieth century. However, the roots of today's pervasive
mobile wireless technology go back to D.H. Ring and W.R. Young, both
at Bell Labs, who proposed the fundamentals of the cellular concept and
frequency reuse in 1947. Another key concept of handover, a technique
for transferring calls between cells, was proposed by A. Joel in 1970, also
at Bell Labs, and work began on a full-fledged mobile telephony system
involving the key principles of cellular frequency reuse, handover, and
multiple access. In the eleven decades since those early beginnings in
the nineteenth century, wireless technology has transformed our world,
from satellite radio and HDTV broadcasting, to mobile telephony and
the now emerging mobile broadband. We have over 3.5 billion wireless
mobile phone users in a total world population of 6.5 billion, and it
is in mobile services that wireless has made the greatest impact on our
society. Mobile broadband is still in its early stages and will usher in
a big new era of wireless services that deliver rich multimedia internet-
services to a variety of devices including handheld products.

A number of core technologies have underpinned the success of
mobile wireless. Some examples are multiple access, MIMO, adaptive
modulation, and coding and relays. We discuss these briefly.

The origins of multiple access date back to Marconi's proposal
for 'tuned circuits' or, equivalently, Frequency Division Multiplexing (FDM). This allows multiple links to be established from a single
transmitter base to a receiver, with each link using a distinct frequency
channel. Frequency Division Multiplexing strictly refers to each link
terminating at different geographically dispersed users. The connection
from the transmitter base to the dispersed receivers is referred to as the

downlink. When these dispersed users transmit back to the base, again with distinct frequency channels, it is called the uplink and this access mode is referred to as Frequency Division Multiple Access (FDMA). The dispersed users must carefully control their carrier frequencies to arrive in their own allotted channel at the receiving base. In a cell with a base station and its multiple dispersed users, the FDM downlink and FDMA uplink is referred to as FDM/FDMA. Both digital and analogue modulation schemes can use FDM/FDMA. For digital modulation, two other multiple access technologies have evolved: Time Division (TDM/TDMA) and Code Division (CDM/CDMA). Time Division uses time slots instead of frequencies to distinguish users. In Code CDM/CDMA, users are separated by unique spreading codes. Ideally, these codes must be time-synchronized and orthogonal. Each user's transmitted bandwidth is greatly enlarged by the spreading code, hence the term 'Spread Spectrum'. For the CDMA uplink, time synchronization is generally not practical and users' codes are generally chosen to be non-repetitive over a long period, which does not guarantee the codes to be orthogonal. Henceforth we use CDMA to refer to CDM/CDMA and likewise for TDMA.

There was a vigorous debate of CDMA versus TDMA in the mid-1990s about the relative spectral efficiency, roughly amounting to throughput per cell for a fixed amount of spectrum in the network. The key to such efficiency lay in clever ways to deal with the challenges of fading, interference, and handover. While both TDMA and CDMA found equally effective ways to deal with these challenges, there were practical reasons favouring CDMA as the more convenient approach. Consider fading, since time diversity (realized via coding and interleaving) was not effective for slow moving or static users, and space (that is, antenna diversity) in transmit was not easily feasible; fading was best tackled by frequency diversity. In Code Division, the bandwidth spreading offered an easy way to capture such diversity with a Rake receiver (though 1.25 MHz CDMA used in IS-95, a CDMA bases interface, often offered little diversity). In Time Division, wider bandwidths can also be achieved by a higher degree of time multiplexing leading to higher burst date rate to each user. This, however, required high peak power during the transmission of the burst and a more complex equalizer. Time Division resorted to Frequency Hopping (FH) to capture diversity. Frequency hopping has some undesirable side effects such as delay, but offered reliable frequency diversity. In another key area of interference mitigation, CDMA's bandwidth spreading and power control offered a natural way for interference averaging, while TDMA's tools of power control and structured frequency hopping were less effective. On the other hand, CDMA needed fast power control to manage near–far interference, while TDMA was more robust to this problem. Code Division can also use full frequency reuse in every sector and cell, easing radio planning. Time Division needs different channels in each sector, but allows reuse across cells with sufficient FH support. The arguments for and against CDMA and TDMA were finely balanced, and both technologies became well established with TDMA-based Global System for Mobile Communications (GSM) remaining the dominant technology.

The 3G standard adopted a 5 MHz channel (wideband) WCDMA, reducing the problems of insufficient bandwidth of the IS-95 standard, and this firmly established CDMA's dominance in 3G networks. In the late 1990s, as the demand broadband data increased, the weaknesses with CDMA in wideband channels became apparent. First, as channel bandwidth increased beyond 5 MHz, more and more multi-path arrivals became resolvable, and the self-interference caused by multi-path degraded CDMA's performance, particularly on the uplink. Additionally, CDMA used the same modulation and code rate across the entire channel bandwidth, despite the strong variation in signal-to-noise ratio (SNR) across a wide channel, thus reducing its efficiency.

A new approach called Orthogonal Frequency-division Multiple Access (OFDMA) with its approach of using a large number of narrow, mutually orthogonal, sub-channels emerged as preferred access technique for broadband systems needed in 4G. Orthogonal Frequency Multiple Access has significant advantages over CDMA in channel widths beyond 5 MHz and also scales to much higher bandwidths. Practical OFDMA (and even CDMA) systems also incorporate some TDMA. Likewise, some CDMA-like spreading is often incorporated in OFDMA to mitigate strong interference. In summary, 1G used FDMA, 2G used both TDMA and CDMA, 3G used wideband CDMA, and 4G adopted OFDMA.

Multiple Input Multiple Output (MIMO), another key technology, goes back to the work of Stanford University researchers who proposed use of multiple antennas to transmit and receive, and to implement a new concept called spatial multiplexing. Spatial multiplexing works when the spatial signatures at the receive antenna array induced by the different transmit antenna streams are quasi-orthogonal and hence separable. Multiple Input Multiple Output spatial multiplexing multiplies the effective channel bandwidth by the number of antenna pairs and has stirred enormous interest. Multiple transmit and receive antennas used in MIMO can also be used for link diversity. The first commercial system to adopt MIMO and OFDMA was developed by Iospan Communication Inc. in the US during the late 1990s, and this work eventually became the basis of 4G wireless standards. WiMAX and 3GPP Long Term Evolution (LTE) have both adopted MIMO-OFDMA, as also WiFi IEEE 802.11n standard. Multiple Input Multiple Output spatial multiplexing has been extended to a multi-user format, wherein a base station transmits dedicated streams to different users. On the downlink, multi-user MIMO requires channel state knowledge to orthogonalize transmissions to different users. Yet another enhancement is called network MIMO, wherein the multiple transmit antennas are dispersed across different cell sites. Network MIMO is useful to support cell edge users. Multi-user MIMO is incorporated in IEEE 802.16e and LTE, and Network MIMO in IEEE 802.16m. Multiple Input Multiple Output has been primarily adopted in 4G standards.

Other key technologies that have contributed to wireless performance improvements include the following:

• Turbo and LDPC channel coding that have enabled links to operate close to Shannon capacity. 3G and 4G standards use turbo and LDPC coding that delivers performance with less than 0.5 dB gap from the Shannon limit.

• Hybrid-Automatic Request for Re-transmission (H-ARQ) is a physical layer ARQ, which outperforms regular ARQ. The Chase H-ARQ allows the receiver to retain information from the earlier transmitted packets and combine this information with the most recent packet before attempting a channel decode. Hybrid-Automatic Request for Re-transmission offers about 1 dB improvement in SINR (Signal to Interference and Noise Ratio) when averaged over an entire network. Another version of H-ARQ is Incremental H-ARQ, where the transmitter sends additional parity bits which are used by the receiver to help decode the burst. Hybrid-Automatic Request for Re-transmission has been used 2G, 3G, and 4G networks.

• Adaptive modulation and coding (AMC) allows use of modulation and coding rate to be chosen to suit the channel SNR. When used along with repetition coding, AMC allows wireless links to operate from SNRs ranging for −8 dB to +25 dB. Again, AMC can be found in 3G and 4G standards.

• Opportunistic Scheduling (OS) refers to assigning the most favourable (highest SNR) frequency or time slot to a user, as against a random channel assignment. Opportunistic Scheduling can improve spectral efficiency by about 20 per cent in practical networks. Opportunistic Scheduling is again primarily used in 4G networks.

Emerging Technologies

A number of wireless techniques are being developed for possible incorporation into future standards. Some of these are as follows:

• Network Coding (NC) refers to techniques when, for example, two bit streams are XOR'd to form a single stream before transmission. If the recipient already knows one of the component streams, the unknown stream can be easily extracted. In certain network topologies, such techniques can offer 20 per cent to 30 per cent improvement in spectrum efficiency. Network Coding is incorporated in IEEE 802.16m.

• Relays and Cooperation help when a direct link from a source to destination node is infeasible due to excessive path loss or interference. In such cases, a relay can be used to break the link into shorter hops. In cooperative networks, multiple nodes in vicinity cooperate (that is, act as a single connected system) to establish radio links, thus outperforming nodes acting alone. Cooperation can be used to from virtual MIMO configuration and thereby benefit from array, diversity, and multiplexing gains of MIMO.

• Cognitive radio refers to the dynamic use of spectrum resources. Unlike traditional networks where links are assigned to permanent frequency channels, in a cognitive network, the nodes monitor the network and pick a frequency channel with the least interference. Cognitive radio thus makes more efficient use of frequency spectrum resources. The lack of guaranteed resources, however, can upset QoS (Quality of Srvice) guarantees. Both cooperation and cognitive concepts have not yet entered mobile standards.

EVOLUTION OF WIRELESS NETWORKS AND SERVICES

Though Marconi is credited with commercializing wireless services, a number of others also soon offered commercial services, such as R. Fessenden in the US and A.S. Popov in the former USSR. Marconi Company launched the first commercial wireless telegraphy in 1901. This Marconi network rapidly expanded across the English channel in 1899, and across the Atlantic by 1905. By 1908, wireless voice telephony became available. Wireless remained the key to ship to shore communications where undersea cable telephony could not compete. The start of mobile wireless communications on land probably originated with the development of automobile phones by Motorola for the Detroit police in 1941.

The advent of the modern cellular networks began in 1983, with the launch of the Advanced Mobile Phone Service (AMPS). This became the first standardized cellular service in the world and is often referred to as 1G. It used analogue FM modulation and was based on FDMA with 30 kHz channels. While AMPS was launched in the US, many parallel analogue wireless networks were started in Europe: C450 in Germany, Radiocom in France, TACS in the UK, NMT in Scandinavia, and JTAC in Japan. The initial growth of cellular telephony was slow due to high cost of equipment and the steep subscription rates. Also, mobile phones needed bulky hardware that was installed in car trunks, making it a 'business executive' technology. A breakthrough in convenience was the development of handset phone called Dynatac in 1983 by Motorola.

The industry moved to digital modulation and TDMA with 2G technologies to take advantage of voice compression, advanced modulation, and coding techniques and security. Second generation 2G technologies—IS 54 in the US, PDC in Japan, and GSM in Europe—in the early 1990s used some versions of QPSK (Quadrature Phase Shift Keying) or Gaussian Minimum Shift (GMSK) digital modulation. Both GSM and IS-54 (and its evolution IS-136) saw rapid deployment in the mid-1990s. Soon, the advantages of GSM became apparent and GSM began to replace IS-54 in the US. Around this period, Qualcomm introduced a CDMA based IS-95. The success of Qualcomm's CDMA was helped considerably by South Korea, who developed a commercial system with a patent licence from Qualcomm. After many years of refinement,

IS-95 and its variants began to win worldwide deployments in late 1990s. With advances in semiconductor technology and rising subscriber base, handset sizes and prices began to drop significantly in the late 1990s and, globally, the number of subscribers reached 300 million by 2000. This period also saw the introduction of short messaging service (SMS), which proved attractive in emerging countries.

The advent of 3G came with Wideband CDMA standard developed by 3GPP standards body and later ratified by ITU as an IMT-2000 standard. The growth of WCDMA network was initially slow due lack of handset equipment, but by 2006 these bottle necks were overcome and its growth accelerated. In parallel, 3GPP2 track was offered with CDMA 2000, an improved version of IS-95. Qualcomm also offered a wireless packet technology EVDO Rev 0 and later Rev A. Meanwhile, more advanced version of WCDMA called HSDPA (High Speed Downlink Packet Access) was standardized and deployed worldwide. A more advanced version with high speed uplink known as HSPA (High Speed Packet Access) was standardized and saw commercial roll outs in 2009. There is another enhancement known as HSPA+, which adds higher level QAM modulation and 2×2 MIMO to HSPA, but has as yet to see significant uptake. Though 3G has remained primarily a voice service, the introduction of HSDPA and HSPA has given 3G significant data capability. Unfortunately, the 3G operators still have limited spectrum, which while adequate for voice has fallen significantly below the needs of data intensive services such as used by smart phones and notebook/netbook computers and tablets/pads. The AT&T network in the US, for example, is unable to handle the demands of the Apple iPhone (a smart phone) data traffic. In the past two years, data traffic has been increasing dramatically, exceeding a 100 per cent compounding rate annually, greatly stressing the data capability of 3G networks. While HSPA is being deployed to meet some of this need, a transition to a 4G data technology is clearly needed. However, this still does not address the problem of backhaul (communication of data from the radio network to the core network), which will get even more stressed as data rates increase with 4G.

The early beginnings of 4G began towards the end of 1990s when Iospan Inc. developed a MIMO-OFDMA system, which demonstrated an unprecedented 10 Bps/Hz peak spectral efficiency links. The robust operation of MIMO-OFDMA, combined with increasing problems of making MIMO work in CDMA, resulted in a strong shift to MIMO-OFDMA as the new technology for 4G. The first global standards to embrace MIMO-OFDMA were IEEE 802.16d and 802.16e, which were ratified in 2004 and 2005 respectively. Worldwide Interoperability for Microwave Access (WiMAX) is an industry forum that supported equipment development and certification based on IEEE 802.16 standards. This victory of MIMO-OFDMA in WiMAX was rapidly followed a clean sweep across other broadband technologies WLANs (IEEE 802.11n), UMB (a Qualcomm proprietary system which has since been abandoned), and 3GPP LTE.

Worldwide Interoperability for Microwave Access is 4G technology, which delivers high speed and reliable broadband wireless access. The technology can be deployed in cell sizes ranging from 15–20 km radius in rural, 1–2 km cell radius in urban, 0.2–0.5 km radius in dense urban to 100 feet cell radius indoors. Worldwide Interoperability for Microwave Access can serve mobile/nomadic and fixed users. Its use of OFDMA and MIMO enables it to offer high data rates (large bandwidth channels) and higher spectrum efficiency compared to CDMA-based 3G technologies. It can be used in channel bandwidths ranging from 3.5 to 20 MHz (later 40 MHz). It is available primarily in TDD (time division duplex), though a FDD (frequency division duplex) mode is defined but has not been supported by vendors. Time Division Duplex has some advantages for data networks and with MIMO. Worldwide Interoperability for Microwave Access is currently available in 2.3–2.4GHz, 2.5–2.7GHz, 3.4–3.6GHz, and 3.6–3.8GHz bands. It uses an end to end all IP network and all popular IP applications including Voice over IP work well on WiMAX networks. The high spectral efficiency of WiMAX makes it cost effective for operators, especially in India where spectrum costs are very high. Finally, the simpler all IP standard allows WiMAX infrastructure and devices to be cheaper than 3G HSPA devices.

Next generation Long Term Evolution (LTE) is a 3G-evolution technology very similar to WiMAX. The LTE standard was completed in 2008 and is at least 2–3 years from being a commercially mature technology. Though LTE is dubbed to be an evolution of 3G, it has no real backward compatibility with 3G, except that, but very importantly, LTE has spectrum profiles that are compatible with 3G bands. The deployment of LTE will need new equipment for infrastructure and terminals while WiMAX is a well-standardized technology with wide terminal availability and is already in global deployment.

The market segments of WiMAX and LTE technologies will be different. Worldwide Interoperability for Microwave Access has been deployed by mostly green field operators who acquired large spectrum assets in the 2.3–2.4 GHz and 2.5–2.68 GHz bands. There are some limited deployments in 3.5 GHz bands, but it is usually a fixed service. Worldwide Interoperability for Microwave Access operators support fixed and mobile services and are focused on data access services than on voice. These operators also acquired spectrum at much lower cost than 3G incumbents, because broadband data is a new (and as yet unproven business case) service, but growing rapidly. Worldwide Interoperability for Microwave Access is also well positioned to meet the growing demand for internet access from non-phone devices. Its operators will offer internet access to homes and small business via fixed CPE (Consumer Premises Equipment), and to portable and mobile laptop, netbooks, cameras, and Mobile Internet Devices (MIDs) users via external data cards (USB dongles) or embedded modems. A new demand for WiMAX has come from mobile routers that bridge WiMAX to WiFi, allowing WiFi devices to connect to WiMAX mobile network. Other emerging applications for WiMAX are vertical markets for broadband data such as smart grid, machine-to-machine communications, and even certain enterprise applications.

While LTE can compete in WiMAX markets, its big advantage is that current 3G voice operators will naturally migrate to LTE in view of similar band profiles and thus LTE will eventually inherit the large base of 2G/3G subscribers. It will take another 2–3 years for LTE to reach WiMAX's degree of maturity and it is expected to overtake WiMAX by 2015. India has allocated TDD broadband spectrum in the 2.5 GHz band to BSNL, who are deploying WiMAX, albeit slowly. The government also announced that blocks in the 700 MHz and 3.3–3.6GHz bands will be auctioned as they become available to offer fixed WiMAX and rural wireless broadband segments to consumers. The government now appears to be on track to auction broadband spectrum to private operators shortly and rapid roll out of WiMAX by the end of 2010 is anticipated. Long Term Evolution will also be a contender of broadband services in India.

TELECOM SERVICES IN INDIA

The telecom service in India started in 1851 with an electric telegraph line between Calcutta and Diamond Harbour and was operated by the Public Works Department of the British East India Company (BEIC). Its inventor, William O'Shaugnessy, came to India as a surgeon for the BEIC in 1823 and invented the electric telegraph in 1839, just a few months behind and independently of Samuel F.B. Morse in the US. With the support of then Governor General, Shaugnessy began building a 4,000-mile nationwide telegraph network in 1853 connecting Calcutta, Delhi, Peshawar, Bombay, and Madras. The network was completed in 1856 and Shaugnessy become India's first Director General of Telegraphs. In 1881, the Government of India licensed The Oriental Telephone Company Ltd. for opening telephone exchanges at Calcutta, Bombay, Madras, and Ahmedabad. The first commercial telephone call was made in January 1882, in Calcutta. The first experimental wireless telegraphy links in India were demonstrated as early as 1902 and a Department of Wireless Telegraph was set up. Wireless telegraphy came into routine use in Calcutta at Diamond Harbour in 1908. By 1920, a Madras–Port Blair wireless telegraph link was established. In 1921, CW (continuous wave) radio transmitters began to replace spark gap systems in India. In 1927, the UK–India wireless telegraph links were established and upgraded to wireless telephony in 1933. In 1923, the Indian Radio Telegraph Company was formed and merged with the Indian Cable Company in 1932. In 1947, after independence, all telephone and telegraph companies were nationalized, and was run by the Department of Post, Telephone and Telegraph under the Ministry of Communications. In 1985, the postal services were separated and the new Department of Telecommunication (DoT) was formed, becoming India's local and long-distance operator. In 1986, DoT was reorganized, with the services in the four metros carved out into a new public sector unit (PSU), Mahanagar Telephone Nigam Ltd. (MTNL), and international telephone services handled through another PSU, Videsh Sanchar Nigam Ltd. (VSNL). In 2000, the remaining nationwide telephone services inside DoT were incorporated into a third PSU, Bharat Sanchar Nigam Ltd. (BSNL). In 2002, the Tata Group of Companies acquired 45 per cent stake in VSNL.

The growth of the wired Indian telephone network was very slow. Moreover, except for the armed forces and a few private corporate networks, wireless telephony was unknown till the mid-1990s. At the time of India's independence in 1947, there were 80,000 telephone subscribers in India. The growth of telephone connections remained painfully slow, reaching 9,80,000 lines in 1971, 2.15 million lines in 1981, and 5.07 million lines in 1991, all in a country that was approaching a billion people.

The first mobile phone service in India was launched in 1985 on a non-commercial basis. Mobile services were commercially launched only in August 1995. In the initial five years the annual subscriber additions were modest and reached 10.5 million by 2002. Although mobile services followed the New Telecom Policy 1994, market growth was hampered by high spectrum and equipment costs. The Telecom Regulatory Authority of Indian (TRAI) was established in 1997 and helped create a strong focus on telecom policy (like the FCC in the US).

The New Telecom Policy in 1999, in part, enabled the growth of mobile telephony, primarily by moving away from high fixed spectrum fee to a lower fixed fee and revenue sharing model. The current revenue share is 15 per cent. Further, the concept of Unified Access Licence (UASL) rationalized the licensing policy and allowed UASL operators to provide fixed and wireless services. Initiatives such as Calling Party Pays (CPP) and interconnect charges helped vitalize the industry. Other accelerating factors were the rapid price erosion in cost of infrastructure equipment and phones (handsets), and the sheer market volume allowing operators to amortize fixed costs more efficiently. The number of mobile phones grew to 16 million in 2003, 32 million in 2005, 200 million in 2007, and 560 million in 2009. The Average Revenue per Subscriber (ARPU) in India is less than USD 5 per month, making it the lowest in the world.

The next mass-market wireless service in India is broadband. India currently has only 8 million broadband (all wired) lines serviced through Digital Subscriber Line (DSL) technology. There are another 6 million low-speed dial-up lines, but they offer very limited internet experience. The total number of internet users stands at 81 million, largely due to heavy resource sharing through internet shops. The majority of new internet connections use low-speed dial-up connections. Digital

Subscriber Line based connections have limited appeal because of the high cost, limited copper loop availability (only 35 million lines nation-wide), and poor quality of the copper local loop. Moreover, DSL is only possible in urban areas, where a local loop exists. Wireless broadband offers significantly better economics and superior convenience (mobility) compared to wired DSL technology.

India seriously lags behind other emerging and developed economies in broadband access. Given the increasingly rich media internet content, only a dedicated broadband connection—at least one per household and better still, one per person—can offer a full-spectrum internet experience. The US has recently set a goal of 100 million broadband connections at 100 Mbps each by 2020. Simply put, broadband internet penetration with 8 million lines is abysmally low, translating to 0.7 per cent penetration and growing at only 0.1 per cent per year. In India, given our weak physical infrastructure, pervasive internet access can act as our virtual infrastructure and be a powerful enabler of many core segments of Indian society: industry, education, commerce, governance, and social connectivity. There is a tremendous unmet demand for internet access in India, perhaps in excess of 100 million subscribers based on currently projected price points for wireless broadband service. This demand will only grow rapidly in the coming years. The Indian government's own goal for broadband connections for 2010 is 20 million lines and rising to 100 million by 2015.

Wireless broadband internet can serve both mobile and fixed users. Apart from 24×7 personal access to high-speed web browsing, email, rail/air booking, banking, and social networking, enterprises can expand online customer support, online ordering, and e-commerce, and local/city governments can expand e-governance and public information services. Many new applications such as video security enabled by machine-to-machine connections will increasingly dominate broadband internet use after 2012.

While WiMAX is the best option for offering wireless broadband in India, LTE can also participate in this market after 2013, when it gains maturity. WiMAX has a worldwide footprint; it has a huge vendor ecosystem with low equipment prices (lower than 3G) due to the architecture of the standard, vendor competition, and no monopolistic trends present in CDMA and 3G technologies with consequently large Intellectual Property Rights (IPR) tax.

Indian Telecom Industry

India imports about USD 12–14 billion of wireless equipment. Only about USD 1.5 billion of this can be considered to be local value addition, mainly through assembly of phones, and is carried out by major original equipment manufacturers (OEMs) like Nokia, Samsung, and Motorola. The participation of Indian companies in wireless technology has been shrinking for the past two decades. A discussion of the major segments of this industry follows.

Indian Companies

Public sector

Telecom industry started taking shape in India with the setting up of Indian Telephone Industries Ltd. (ITI) in 1948 in Bangalore. It was the first PSU in independent India and is indicative of the importance that Jawaharlal Nehru, the then Indian prime minister, gave to the development of an indigenous telecom equipment capability. Till the 1990s, ITI manufactured large Strowger and Crossbar exchanges, small local exchanges, and telephone equipment under licence agreements with western companies. A notable exception was switches based on C-DOT technology. Later, ITI entered into a number of joint ventures with US, European, and Chinese companies for diverse range of transmission products. Since the late 1990s, ITI has been running at a loss and was declared a sick unit in 2003. The Indian government has tried to revive ITI with large cash grants. Attempts to sell or merge ITI have so far not succeeded and its future remains uncertain. Many other central and state PSUs also built telecom equipment such as VSAT terminals and digital STM radios, again, mostly based on licenced technology from abroad. The also have faced severe difficulties in recent years and have suffered declines.

C-DOT

This was a GoI-funded R&D unit formed in 1984 under the Chairmanship of Sam Pitroda, a visionary telecom leader who returned to India after a successful career in the US. It successfully developed and transferred technology for Rural Exchange (RAX) and Private Automatic Branch Exchange (PABX) switches to a number of small/medium manufacturers from 1988 onwards. The MAX switch (up to 50,000 line capacity) was successfully developed by 1995 and the technology transferred to ITI. Over 1000 MAX switches based on C-DOT technology have been installed and have been the mainstay of the DOT voice network. The success of C-DOT in switch design remains a singular achievement in indigenous telecom technology. However, in recent years C-DOT has not been able to sustain the success of RAX and MAX developments during the early 1990s. Its inability to develop a Mobile Switch removed a major opportunity to participate in the exploding mobile wireless market.

Private Sector

From the 1950s to about 1989, efforts by the private sector to design and manufacture telecom equipment was severely limited due to the restrictive licensing policy of the Indian government, which was focused on protecting the public sector. Early companies in this segment included ARM (now ICOMM Tele), Himachal Futuristic Communications, and BPL (Telecom). Due to licensing restrictions, these companies never developed the market scale to build a credible R&D capability to compete against the giant Telecom Multinational Companies (T-MNCs). A particularly promising company is Midas Communications Ltd., which developed an innovative wireless local loop product, known as CorDECT, based on a Digital Enhanced Cordless Technology (DECT) technology. Midas successfully marketed CorDECT to over six countries and has so far sold over 2 million lines. The share of CorDECT in the Indian market remains limited and the company is trying to reenter the market with a GSM technology. VNL has also built low-power off-grid solar GSM base stations that show great promise in emerging countries. Shyam Telecom, Terracom, Coral, Pointred, and Matrix are other examples in the private sector with some local capability but are no match for the T-MNCs.

Engineering Service Companies

India has built a vibrant engineering services industry which carriers out mostly software and some hardware development for MNC clients. Wipro, Sasken, Infosys, Mindtree, and others all have a sizable business in telecom services. Their revenue from telecom-related engineering services is estimated to be USD 6 billion in 2009. However, none of these companies have emerged as a significant telecom equipment provider for the Indian market, which continues to be dominated by T-MNCs.

A number of factors played a role in the eclipse of the local telecom equipment industry. First, the barriers to entry, including import duty, of foreign manufactured equipment were rapidly reduced after National Telecom Policy (NTP)-1999. This allowed T-MNCs to successfully outbid ITI with long-term vendor financing which proved to be irresistible to DoT. Next, the private sector began to take an increasing share of the telecom services (current share about 65 per cent), and opted for the most advanced global technology to remain competitive in quality of services and network economics. Finally, there was no determined effort by the government to help the local industry, which has been forced out of product development or manufacturing. Some of these companies have moved to a trading model, wherein the telecom equipment is imported in a fully or partially assembled form, and only final assembly is undertaken before supply to end customers. There is usually only minor, if any, value addition. Clearly, revival of an indigenous telecom sector has to receive a high priority.

Foreign Companies

T-MNCs

With the growth of the Indian mobile market, Nokia, Motorola, LG, and Samsung have set up cell phone assembly plants to take advantage of tax incentives. The value addition in these plants is estimated to be less than 7 per cent of the end product price. Ericsson and Alcatel–Lucent also do some assembly and test of wireless infrastructure equipment in India. Alcatel–Lucent entered into a joint venture with C-DOT for development of WiMAX products for the Indian market. The net local value addition still remains focused in final assembly and test areas, and hence remains small. No value addition in the core technologies such as semiconductor design or manufacturing is undertaken by T-MNCs in India. The government has not mandated value addition in core technologies, as is happening in China.

Venture Funded Small Companies

In recent years, venture funded companies in the US have built significant engineering backends in India. Two notable companies are Beceem Communications and Tejas Networks. Beceem commands 65 per cent of the WiMAX semiconductor market worldwide and has 100 per cent market share in US 4G semiconductor. It has 80 per cent of its 200-person design team in India. Tejas is an optical switch company that is almost 100 per cent India-based and has done very well in the mid and lower segments of SDH switches both in the Indian and emerging markets.

Wireless services in India have seen dramatic growths in recent years through the expansion of mobile voice networks. With over 560 million users, cellphone has become the symbol of India's growth and dynamism, and has proven to be a truly transformative technology. The cellphone has put in the hands of even the weakest sections of Indian society, a technology marvel, which would allow him or her to connect with anyone anywhere in the country or indeed the world. Clearly, the next revolution of broadband wireless is now close at hand, and may prove to have even more impact on the India's economic growth and productivity.

The dark cloud in all this good news is the inability of Indian technology companies, with very few exceptions, to participate in the huge opportunities in equipment design and manufacturing offered by India's massive telecom expansion. Telecom technology is very R&D intensive and takes large and higher risk investments to build each of the different pieces of this great industry. This will need concerted policy support from the Indian government to help create a globally competitive Indian telecom equipment industry. I am sure that if Homi Bhabha was alive today, he would be at the forefront to persuade the nation of this worthy cause.

REFERENCES

Banerjee, P. (2008), 'India S&T 2008 Report', New Delhi: National Institute of Science, Technology and Development Studies.

Mani, Sunil (2008), 'The Growth Performance of India's Telecommunications Service Industry, 1991–2006; Can it Lead to the Growth of a Domestic Manufacturing Hub', Working paper 390, Trivandrum: Centre for Development Studies.

Paulraj, A. (1997), 'The Evolution of Mobile Communications', in A. Paulraj, C. Schaper, and V. Roychoudry (eds), *Communication, Control, Signal Processing and Computing*, New York: Kluwer, pp. 141–54.

Saha, B. (2004), 'State Support for Industrial R&D in Developing Economies: Telecom Equipment Industry in India and China', *Economic and Political Weekly*, Vol. 39, No. 35 (28 August–3 September), pp. 3915–25.

RAHUL JAIN, JAIKUMAR
RADHAKRISHNAN, AND PRANAB SEN

17 Quantum Computation
Its Promise and Challenges

Quantum computation is an exciting development in computing. It is based on perhaps the most profound scientific discovery of the twentieth century, quantum mechanics. A robust theoretical framework of quantum computing has been established. In this essay, we discuss the quantum circuit model and describe its power. Then, we discuss the developments in quantum computing, the limitations of this model of computing, and the current view of the feasibility of implementations.

Computation today has reached a level of sophistication that could not have been imagined some fifty years ago. Mundane problems of book keeping and esoteric simulations of complex physical systems are all performed using a computer. Computers are physical devices. They trick nature into performing computations for us. Their design and effectiveness depend on the laws of physics. Ironically, when simulating physical processes on a computer, we are, actually, coaxing nature to reflect on itself using its own laws.

Yet, Richard Feynman observed that despite their enormous power, computers seem to have limited power in simulating quantum systems of moderate size. He wondered if this difficulty could be turned on its head, and one could exploit the quantum nature of physics at small sizes to design even more powerful computers. In the past two decades, quantum computing has been an area of intense study. Several abstract and idealized models of computing based on quantum principles have been studied, and many questions from classical computing have been re-examined. Simultaneously, vigorous experimental attempts have been made to realize quantum devices where the quantum algorithms developed on idealized models could be implemented.

Quantum computation today is a fertile area of research. Amazing quantum algorithms have been developed. Techniques have been devised to understand the limitations of the power of quantum computing. In many cases, this has resulted in a better understanding of the entire process of computation, including well-established notions of classical computation. Indeed, these developments afford exciting opportunities and challenges for researchers.

In this short note, we touch upon some of the developments in quantum computing, with the hope that they provide the reader with a useful context to study the detailed descriptions in the references listed at the end of the essay, and also many excellent accounts widely available on the internet.

THE MODEL OF COMPUTATION

In this section, we will set up a model for studying quantum computation in order to understand how it resembles and differs from the corresponding models of classical computation. One main promise of quantum computation is that it has the potential to be more efficient than classical computation. In this essay, we use the circuit model for computing Boolean functions. In this model, efficiency of computation is measured using the number of basic operations (or gates) required to realize the function in question. This quantity will, of course, depend on the basic gates the circuit is allowed to use and on what we mean by computing a function. We will, therefore, describe the familiar models for classical and probabilistic computation in a way that makes them resemble the model for quantum circuits we will use (Sipser 1996; Arora and Barak 2009; Nielsen and Chuang 2000; Yao 1993).

Classical Deterministic Computation

Consider the process of computing the sum of two bits. We imagine that the input is stored in registers and in each step some operation is applied to these registers, for instance, the following circuit performs this task.

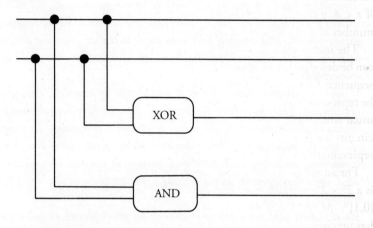

It has four registers, the first two contain the input bits, and the remaining two are initialized to zero. In each step, a logical operation (a simple gate) is applied to the contents of some of the registers and the result is stored in a new register. As stated, this computation is reversible, because we never overwrite the input registers. As we will see, when considering quantum computation, it is important for us to allow gates that overwrite the registers whose inputs they use. A NOT-gate that flips the content of some register is reversible, but an AND-gate that computes the AND of two registers and stores the result in the first (say) is not. If we want our computations to be reversible, we cannot use many of the familiar gates in our computation. However, classical computation can be carried out using reversible gates with only moderate loss in efficiency. For example, the AND operation can be simulated using the following reversible Toffoli gate, that acts on three registers by taking the AND of the first two and XORing it with the third (the result is stored in the third register). It is easy to see that the Toffoli gate can simulate all basic two-bit gates efficiently. Circuits on n registers made of these gates compute invertible Boolean functions with n-bit inputs and n-bit outputs.

Given an arbitrary Boolean function, $g : \{0, 1\}^n \to \{0, 1\}^r$, we say that a circuit $f : \{0, 1\}^n \to \{0, 1\}^m$, $(m \geq n)$ realizes g, if for all $x \in \{0, 1\}^n$ $f(x0^{m-n})[1, r] = g(x)$,, that is, if the last $m-n$ registers are initialized to 0, and all but the first r registers are omitted at the end, then the resulting function with n-bit input and r-bit output is g. Note that even if f is reversible, a function g realized by it need not be reversible (for example if $r < n$, g cannot be reversible). The complexity of g is the minimum number of Toffoli gates required to construct a circuit that realizes g.

The matrix associated with a circuit: A function $g : \{0, 1\}^n \to \{0, 1\}^n$, can be described by a vector of 2^n n-bit strings, one for each possible input sequence. Our circuits compute such functions and their behaviour can be represented using such vectors (which are just a disguised form of the usual truth table representation). To make the analogy with quantum circuits more easily, we will need the following somewhat different representation.

For an n-bit reversible operation, $g : \{0, 1\}^n \to \{0, 1\}^n$, its matrix M_f is a $2^n \times 2^n$ matrix whose rows and columns are indexed by elements of $\{0,1\}^n$: $M_f(\sigma, \tau) = 1$ iff $f(\tau) = \sigma$. Note that each row and each column has precisely one 1: M_f is a permutation matrix.

Classical Probabilistic Computation

Probabilistic computation differs from deterministic computation in two respects. First, the set of allowable operations, in addition to the Toffoli gates, includes the random coin toss gate, which we represent as follows.

No matter what the initial content of a register to which this gate is applied, the result is 0 or 1, each with probability ½. In other words, the 2×2 matrix corresponding to this gate is.

$$\begin{pmatrix} 0.5 & 0.5 \\ 0.5 & 0.5 \end{pmatrix}$$

When random coin toss gates are mixed up with other gates, the computation is not deterministic, and can no longer be represented by a permutation matrix. In fact, for any fixed input $\tau \in \{0, 1\}^n$, the output of such a circuit $f(\tau)$ is a random variable taking values in the set $\{0, 1\}^n$. It is, therefore, natural to define the matrix M_f associated with such circuits by $M_f(\sigma\ \tau) = \Pr[f(\tau) = \sigma]$.

Given that the output of probabilistic computation is not completely determined by its input, we need to define when a circuit with coin toss gates can be said to realize a function. Fix a function $g : \{0, 1\}^n$ $\rightarrow \{0, 1\}^k$, we say that a probabilistic f computes g, if for all $x \in \{0, 1\}^n$, $\Pr[f(x0^{m-n})[1, k] = g(x)] \geq \frac{3}{4}$, that is, if we initialize the last $m\text{-}n$ input registers to 0 and omit all but the first k registers from the output, then on all inputs, the output of the resulting circuit agrees with the value specified by g with high probability (the threshold $\frac{3}{4}$ is usually not significant). The probabilistic complexity of g is the minimum number of gates required to construct a circuit that realizes g.

Note that the matrices defined above (consisting of rational entries) are stochastic matrices: the sum of the entries in each column is 1. It is important to recognize that each basic gate is itself a stochastic matrix (deterministic gates are permutation matrices, which are special stochastic matrices). The result of applying gates $f_1, f_2, ..., f_t$ in succession corresponds to a computation represented by the matrix $M = M_{f_t} \cdot M_{f_{t-1}}$ $...M_{f_2} \cdot M_{f_1}$. Our choice of representing computation as matrices instead of truth tables allows us to view the composition of operations as a multiplication of matrices. This will play an even more fundamental role when we consider quantum computation.

Quantum Computation

We just saw that at any point in the computation of the probabilistic circuit on n registers, the state of the registers is described by a probability distribution over 2^n possible states. In a quantum circuit, the state of the registers at any point is a *superposition* supported on 2^n states. A superposition is a vector of real entries* whose squares sum up to 1. The component of this vector corresponding to state τ gives (upon squaring) the probability that when the measurement is performed, the content of the registers is observed to be τ.

In this essay, we will only be able to give superficial description of the quantum formalism. It will be helpful to illustrate its amazing power through an example. A gate frequently employed in quantum circuits is the Hadamard gate

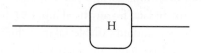

---

* In general, one is allowed complex entries, the sum of the squares of whose absolute values is 1, but we will not need complex values in our discussion.

which may be viewed as a reversible version of the irreversible coin toss gate. It acts on one register and is described by the following matrix:

$$\frac{1}{\sqrt{2}}\begin{pmatrix} 1 & 1 \\ 1 & -1 \end{pmatrix}.$$

This gate already exemplifies the strange effects of quantum interference that quantum computation exploits. Suppose a register has been initialized to 0. A Hadamard gate if applied to such a register leaves it in the

state $\dfrac{1}{\sqrt{2}}\begin{pmatrix} 1 \\ 1 \end{pmatrix}$;

that is, if we observe its contents now (that is, measure it), we will see 0 and 1 with equal probability. If the register is initialized to 1 and the same operations are repeated, again we observe 0 and 1 with equal probability. Thus, the behaviour of this gate is similar to the coin toss gate we introduced in our study of probabilistic computation.

The difference, however, is the following. If we initialize the register in an equal superposition of 0 and 1, say the initial state vector is

$$\frac{1}{\sqrt{2}}\begin{pmatrix} 1 \\ 1 \end{pmatrix},$$

and apply the same sequence of quantum operations, then the resulting state vector will be, that is, we will observe 0 with probability one: the destructive interference has reduced the probability of observing a 1 to zero. There is no destructive interference in classical computation: *If an initial state of 0 and 1 can both result in a 1 with non-zero probability, then any probabilistic combination of these states will lead to a 1 with non-zero probability.*

We will now see how such destructive interference helps in computation. Suppose we have a function $f: \{0, 1\}^n \to \{0, 1\}$; let $F: \{0, 1\}^2 \to \{0, 1\}^2$, be its reversible implementation using two registers, that is, $F (a, b) = (a, a, \oplus b)$ for all $a, b, \varepsilon \{0, 1\}$. Suppose we are given access to an implementation of F and we wish to determine if f is a constant function, that is, whether $f(0) = f(1)$. The following classical circuit does the job:

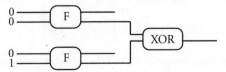

This circuit uses two copies of F; no classical circuit with just one F can determine if f is a constant function with probability better than ½. We will now see a quantum circuit that exploits quantum interference to solve this problem with just one copy of F!

Deutsch-Joza (1992) algorithm: Consider the following circuit[†]:

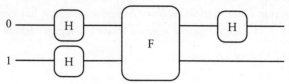

The registers start in the joint state

$$\Psi_0 = \begin{pmatrix} 0 \\ 1 \\ 0 \\ 0 \end{pmatrix}.$$

After the Hadamard gates are applied to the two register, they are left in the state

$$\Psi_1 = \frac{1}{2} \begin{pmatrix} 1 \\ -1 \\ 1 \\ -1 \end{pmatrix}.$$

Now, consider the case $f(0) = f(1) = 0$. Then, the sequence of states is:

$$\Psi_2 = \frac{1}{2} \begin{pmatrix} 1 \\ -1 \\ -1 \\ 1 \end{pmatrix}; \; \Psi_3 = \frac{1}{2} \begin{pmatrix} 0 \\ 0 \\ 1 \\ 1 \end{pmatrix}.$$

On the other hand, if $f(0) = 0$ and $f(1) = 1$, then

$$\Psi_2 = \frac{1}{2} \begin{pmatrix} 1 \\ -1 \\ -1 \\ 1 \end{pmatrix}; \; \Psi_3 = \frac{1}{2} \begin{pmatrix} 0 \\ 0 \\ 1 \\ 1 \end{pmatrix}.$$

[†] We are presenting here a version of Deutsch's algorithm; this was generalized by Jozsa to multiple input functions.

Notice that if the two registers are measured at the end, the first register will be in the state 0 in the first case. Although we did not present the detailed calculation, the same conclusion holds when $f(0) = f(1)$. In the second case, the state of the first register in the end will be 1 (again the same conclusion holds even when $f(0) = 1$ and $f(1) = 0$). We have thus achieved with one copy of F something no classical probabilistic circuit can do with probability of error less than ½.

The key notation: The computation of amplitude vectors above can be carried out more effectively using some special notation. For example, the amplitude vector $\begin{pmatrix} \alpha \\ \beta \end{pmatrix}$,

is represented in this notation as a $\alpha |0\rangle + \beta |1\rangle$, where $|0\rangle$ and $|1\rangle$ indicate explicitly the index of the component of the vector. Similarly, we write

$$\begin{pmatrix} \alpha \\ \beta \\ \gamma \\ \delta \end{pmatrix} = \alpha |00\rangle + \beta |01\rangle + \gamma |10\rangle + \delta |11\rangle$$

The basic unit in quantum computation, analogous to the bit of classical computation is referred to as a qubit.

Let us analyse the quantum circuit using this notation.

Starting state: $|\psi_0\rangle = |01\rangle = |0\rangle |1\rangle$.

After the Hadamard gates: The Hadamard gate acts on one register and takes $|0\rangle$ to $\frac{1}{\sqrt{2}}(|0\rangle + |1\rangle)$ and $|1\rangle$ to $\frac{1}{\sqrt{2}}(|0\rangle - |1\rangle)$. Applying this transformation to each component above, we obtain

$$|\psi_1\rangle = \frac{1}{2}(|0\rangle + |1\rangle)(|0\rangle - |1\rangle).$$

After F: The state becomes

$$\begin{aligned} |\psi_2\rangle &= |0\rangle(|f(0)\rangle - |\overline{f(0)}\rangle) + |1\rangle(|f(1)\rangle - |\overline{f(1)}\rangle) \\ &= (|0\rangle + (-1)^a |1\rangle)(|f(0)\rangle - |\overline{f(0)}\rangle), \end{aligned}$$

where $a = 0$ if $f(0) = f(1)$ and 1 otherwise.

After the last H: The final state is

$$|\psi_3\rangle = |a\rangle(|f(0)\rangle - |\overline{f(0)}\rangle).$$

Clearly, the first register has value a, which is the answer we want. *Quantum operations*: If a permutation matrix is applied to an amplitude vector the result is still an amplitude vector (that is, the sum of the squares of its components is 1). Other matrices also have this property—the unitary matrices. For example, if we view the state vector of a single register geometrically, then rotating it by an angle θ, will not disturb its length; this operation corresponds to the unitary matrix

$$\begin{pmatrix} \cos\theta & -\sin\theta \\ \sin\theta & \cos\theta \end{pmatrix}.$$

The (normalized) Hadamard matrix is also a unitary matrix. In quantum computation, we allow in addition to the Toffoli gate, all single-register unitary gates (2×2 unitary matrices) and the two-register Hadamard the gate.[‡]

QUANTUM ALGORITHMS

Earlier, we have seen a toy quantum algorithm viz. the algorithm of Deutsch that, given a reversible implementation $F: \{0, 1\}^2 \to \{0, 1\}^2$, for a function $f: \{0, 1\} \to \{0, 1\}$, defined by $F(a, b) = (a, a, \oplus b)$ tells whether $f(0) = f(1)$ or not, with only one call to F. In this section we will learn about more non-trivial quantum algorithms.

The first non-trivial quantum algorithm that we discuss is the famous algorithm of Peter Shor (1997) for factoring integers into prime factors efficiently, that is, in time polynomial in the number of bits required to describe n, or in other words, in time polynomial in the logarithm of n. Classically, the best known algorithm for this problem is a randomized algorithm that takes time about $2^{(\log n)^{1/3}}$. Shor's result was a breakthrough in quantum algorithms, and directly led to immense interest and excitement about quantum computation. Integer factorization is an important problem both theoretically and practically. Many widely used public-key cryptosystems like Rivest Shamir Adleman algorithm (RSA) base their security on the assumption that no efficient classical

---

[‡] In fact, it turns out that we may restrict attention to only single register gates and two register gates, but this is not important for us now.

algorithms for integer factorization exist. The seminal work of Shor shows that the advent of practical quantum computers will render RSA and many similar cryptosystems insecure. Given an integer n, Shor's algorithm first uses a standard efficient classical randomized procedure to reduce factoring n to computing the order of integers modulo n. That is, in order to factor n it suffices to solve the following problem called order finding: given any integer a such that a and n have no common factors, find the smallest positive integer x, called the order of a modulo n, such that a^x has remainder 1 when divided by n. Shor solves the order finding problem by a quantum algorithm based on a procedure called the quantum Fourier transform. This procedure is nothing but the well-known discrete Fourier transform of signal processing adapted to operating on quantum superpositions instead of classically described vectors, and is efficient to implement. Given integer a, the algorithm first creates an equal superposition over the sequence of the remainders of a^i when divided by n, for integers i ranging from 0 to n^2. The sequence of these values is periodic with period equal to x, the order of a modulo n. Applying the quantum Fourier transform over n to this superposition gives an equal superposition over a sequence consisting roughly of multiples of n/x. Measuring this superposition gives us an integer which is close to a multiple of n/x. Dividing this integer by n followed by some efficient classical post-processing, gives us a fraction of the form k_1/x where k_1 is unknown. By repeating this procedure, we get another fraction of the form k_2/x. Unfortunately, both k_1 and k_2 can have common factors with x, and so, we cannot recover x by looking at the denominators of the individual fractions k_1/x and k_2/x. However, the least common multiple of the denominators of the two fractions will be x with high probability. The overall algorithm is efficient since the quantum Fourier transform as well as the classical pre and post processing are efficient. Thus we get an efficient quantum algorithm that factors n with high probability.

Next, we discuss a quantum algorithm by Grover (1996) that can search for a desired element in an unsorted database containing n elements in time roughly $\sqrt{n}$. Any classical algorithm, even randomized, will require roughly n time to search an unsorted database with high probability. The algorithm starts by creating an equal superposition over all the elements of the database. Let us call the vector that gives amplitude of 1 to the desired element and 0 to every other element as the target vector. The initial amplitude vector of the algorithm is the equal superposition vector which makes an angle of approximately $\pi/2$ with the target vector. The algorithm then applies two transformations alternately: flipping the sign of the amplitude of the desired element, and flipping the amplitudes of all the elements around the average amplitude. Both these operations can be implemented in time polynomial in the logarithm of n. A pair of these transformations rotates the amplitude vector of the algorithm by an angle of about $2/\sqrt{n}$ towards the target vector. Thus, applying the pair about $\frac{\pi}{4}\sqrt{n}$ times brings the amplitude vector of the algorithm very close to the target vector. Hence, measuring the amplitude vector of the algorithm at this point will yield the desired element with high probability. This is how Grover's algorithm manages to find the desired element in an unsorted database of n elements in about $\sqrt{n}$ steps with high probability. It is also known that a quantum algorithm cannot take significantly less than $\sqrt{n}$ steps for this problem (Bennett et al. 1997; Ambainis 2002), and hence, Grover's algorithm is essentially optimal. Grover's method has been generalized to a quantum algorithmic technique called amplitude amplification (Brassard et al. 2000), wherein it is possible to amplify the success probability of a subroutine from p to a constant by making only about $1/\sqrt{p}$ iterations of the subroutine. Classically, about $1/p$ iterations are necessary, and also sufficient, for this amplification.

Grover's algorithm has been used as a subroutine in quantum algorithms for many problems leading to polynomial speedups over the best possible classical algorithms for these problems. There has also been a non-trivial extension of Grover's algorithm by Ambainis (2007) using quantum walks, which are a generalization of random walks to the quantum world. Ambainis used quantum walks to solve the element distinctness problem, where given a set containing n elements, we want to know if all the elements are distinct or not. Classically, this problem requires about n steps even if the algorithm is randomized. Quantumly, by a two-level application of Grover's search, it was known how to solve it using about $n^{3/4}$ steps. However, the best quantum lower bound known for this problem was about $n^{2/3}$ (Aaronson and Shi 2004; Ambainis 2005; Kutin 2005). It was hence an open problem whether there was a better quantum algorithm for this problem. Approaches based on Grover's search seemed not to yield anything better than $n^{3/4}$

steps. It was thus a breakthrough when Ambainis came up with his quantum walks based algorithm, that solved the problem in about $n^{2/3}$ steps, showing that the lower bound was indeed tight. Subsequently, Ambainis's quantum walks based framework has been greatly refined (Szegedy 2004; Krovi et al. 2010), leading to new quantum algorithms for many search problem that offer non-trivial polynomial speedups over their best possible classical counterparts.

The order finding idea behind Shor's algorithm has been extended to a general problem of finding periods of functions defined over groups, called the hidden subgroup problem. The case where the group is abelian can be solved efficiently by a quantum algorithm using the same quantum Fourier transform based approach as in Shor's algorithm (Kitaev 1995; Mosca and Ekert 1998). No efficient classical algorithm is possible for this problem in its full generality. Efficient quantum algorithms for some other number theoretic problems, for example solving a number theoretic equation called Pell's equation and finding the so-called class group of a number field, have been discovered (Hallgren 2007, 2005; Schmidt and Vollmer 2005). These algorithms use non-trivial variants of the abelian hidden subgroup problem. No efficient classical algorithms are known for these problems, and in fact, the presumed difficulty of solving Pell's equation classically lies at the heart of a cryptosystem by Buchmann and Williams. The hidden subgroup problem has been studied for non-abelian groups too, and efficient algorithms have been obtained for some special cases (Ivanyos et al. 2003; Friedl et al. 2003; Bacon et al. 2005; Ivanyos et al. 2008). The non-abelian hidden subgroup problem is interesting because an efficient solution to the general problem would give an efficient quantum algorithm for the so-called graph isomorphism problem, a combinatorial problem for which no efficient classical algorithms are known. However, some limitations of the quantum Fourier transform approach to solving the non-abelian hidden subgroup problem have also been recently discovered (Hallgren et al. 2010).

A new quantum algorithm for evaluating Boolean formulae was recently discovered by Farhi, Goldstone, and Gutmann (2007). Classically, there is a randomized algorithm that can evaluate a Boolean formula with n variables in about $n^{0.753}$ steps. There is also a matching lower bound for randomized algorithms. The best known quantum lower bound for this problem was $\sqrt{n}$. However, no faster algorithm than the optimal classical randomized one was known in the quantum setting. Farhi et al.'s result was therefore a breakthrough. Their algorithm is based on a non-trivial quantum walk. Following Farhi et al.'s work, a non-trivial connection between a large class of quantum algorithms and an abstract linear algebraic model of computation called span programs was recently discovered by Reichhardt (2010), leading to deep insights into the nature of these quantum algorithms.

A quantum algorithm for efficiently approximating certain properties of the solution to a system of linear equations was recently given by Harrow, Hassidim, and Lloyd (2009). Their algorithm is based on a novel use of a quantum algorithmic technique called phase estimation, first introduced by Kitaev (1995). Harrow et al. also indicate why it may be impossible for classical algorithms to efficiently approximate these properties of solutions of systems of linear equations.

Efficient quantum algorithms have also been discovered for approximately evaluating some types of polynomials, using deep connections between knot theory and quantum computation (Freedman et al. 2002; Aharonov et al. 2009; Aharonov et al. 2007). These polynomials have great importance in knot theory, combinatorics, and statistical mechanics. No efficient classical algorithms are known for these problems.

Recently, an efficient quantum algorithm was discovered for a cryptographic problem called information locking (Fawzi et al. 2010). Information locking is a uniquely quantum phenomenon wherein a classical message of n bits can be locked into a quantum cipher text of n qubits using a very short classical key. A person possessing the key can unlock the quantum cipher text efficiently and recover the original classical message. However, in the absence of the key any measurement on the quantum cipher text, even one that is hard to implement by a quantum algorithm, yields very little information about the original classical message. The non-trivial advantage of quantum computation is that it is possible to lock n bits of clear text into n qubits of cipher text using a key of about $\log n$ bits, whereas any classical procedure locking n bits of clear text into n bits of cipher text requires n bits of key. This quantum algorithm is based on a novel connection between embeddings of l_2-norm into l_1-norm and information locking, and uses an efficient quantization of a classical norm embedding algorithm of Indyk.

QUANTUM COMPLEXITY THEORY

Why are some problems difficult to solve using computers? Which problems are more difficult to solve than others? These are some of the questions that are studied in Complexity Theory. An example of a difficult problem is factoring, which has been discussed in the previous section; this is just the tip of an iceberg. There are a whole lot of much harder problems, then even harder and harder, and the list goes on.

The inherent hardness of a problem is counted in terms of the resources needed to solve it using a standard computer called the Turing Machine. One key resource that is considered is time. The class of problems that are thought to be easy or tractable are the ones that take time that grows only as a polynomial function of input size. This class is referred to as PTIME (for Polynomial Time). Often we allow the algorithms to use randomness and permit some small probability of error in the solution. The class of problems that can be solved in such a manner in polynomial time is referred to as BPP (for bounded error probabilistic polynomial time). The class of problems that can be solved in polynomial time, with small error, using a Quantum Turing Machine is called BQP (for bounded error quantum polynomial time). Since a classical computer is just a special case of a quantum computer, it is easily seen that BPP is contained in BQP. One big question that confronts complexity theorists is whether BPP = BQP. This is a precise mathematical formulation of the question, are there problems that a quantum computer can solve efficiently, but a classical randomized computer cannot.

Another key resource that is counted is space, that is, memory. The class of problems that can be solved using polynomial amount of space is referred to as PSPACE (for polynomial space). Since a classical Turing machine cannot use more than a unit memory in a unit time, it is clear that PTIME is contained in PSPACE. This leads to another big mystery for complexity theorists: Is PTIME = PSPACE? It can also be shown that BPP is contained in PSPACE, but again the reverse containment is not known. Let us now provide a different power to a PTIME machine that of non-determinism or in other words the power to makes guesses. The class of problems that can be solved in polynomial time with this extra power is referred to as NPTIME (for non-deterministic PTIME). This leads us to the central problem in complexity theory: Is

NPTIME = PTIME? This is one of the seven 'Millennium problems' and Clay institute has an award of one-million US dollars for its solution! It can be shown that NPTIME is contained in PSPACE and again the reverse containment is not known. Indeed, the zoo of complexity classes has more such mysteries than facts that can be rigorously proved!

Now we could combine the powers of randomness and non-determinism and this leads to a setting in which a polynomial time probabilistic machine, referred to as Verifier, interacts with an all powerful machine, referred to as Prover. The Prover, though all powerful, cannot be trusted, and hence the Verifier should verify the claims made by the Prover. The class of problems using such Interactive Proofs is class called as IP. In a celebrated result proved about two decades ago it was shown that finally IP catches up with PSPACE, indeed IP = PSPACE (Shamir 1992). In other words interactive verification in polynomial time equals deterministic solution in polynomial space.

About a decade ago the quantum analogue of IP referred to as QIP was defined. It was shown that QIP contains a surprising property that is not believed to be contained by IP: it suffices to have just three messages in the interaction between Prover and Verifier in a QIP protocol to solve any problem (Kitaev and Watrous 2000). Now it is clear that QIP contains IP and hence contains PSPACE. From then on it was an open question whether QIP = PSPACE? This has been recently resolved by Jain, Ji, Upadhyay, and Watrous (2010) who have shown that indeed QIP = PSPACE. Hence adding the power of the quantum to interactive proofs does not yield anything new: there is no quantum leap for Interactive Proofs!

Another area that is widely studied in Complexity Theory is that of Communication Complexity. Communication complexity involves studying how much communication is required for performing distributed tasks. Let us say two parties, Alice and Bob want to compute a function $f(x, y)$, when Alice has x and Bob has y. The communication complexity of f is the minimum amount of communication required for computing f. As before one can consider the model in which the parties use randomness; $R(f)$ denotes the communication complexity in this model. One can also consider the model in which the communicating parties are quantum machines; $Q(f)$ denotes the communication complexity in this model. As before, it is easily shown that $R(f) = Q(f)$ for all functions. It is known that there are some partial functions f for which $Q(f)$ can be exponentially smaller than $R(f)$ (Gavinsky et al. 2008), hence there is a lot of saving if we can use quantum communication. A partial function has a set of 'valid inputs' and a set of 'invalid inputs'. Alice and Bob, given an invalid pair of inputs (x,y) may output whatever they want.

However, for total functions, that is, when all inputs are valid, the best separation known between randomized and quantum communication complexity is quadratic. This is known for the Set Disjointness function in which Alice and Bob are given some sets and they are required to determine if they intersect or not. The quadratically better protocol for Set Disjointness is obtained by using the Grover search algorithm as described in the previous section. Now it is widely believed that this quadratic separation is the best one can achieve for total functions. To show if this holds or not is one of the biggest questions open in quantum communication complexity.

Finally, we consider cryptography, which is the art of turning what cannot be done to good use! A lot of current-day cryptography is based on the belief that factoring is hard to do using classical computers. Whenever we transfer money online or use credit cards, we should be thankful that good, fast classical algorithms for factoring are not known to us and also hopefully to any cheating party accessing the data on the internet!

As mentioned in the previous section, quantum computers can factor large integers quite fast and, hence, all the current-day cryptography essentially breaks down if quantum computers become a reality. However, with quantum computers also comes unconditional cryptography, whose security does not depend on any complexity assumption like hardness of factoring. There are schemes in quantum cryptography which are secure just assuming that quantum mechanics is correct (!), for example, the Quantum Key Distribution scheme (Bennett and Brassard 1984).

So, in all, there have been several interesting advances in Quantum Complexity Theory and there are many challenges left for a better and comprehensive understanding.

EXPERIMENTAL IMPLEMENTATIONS OF QUANTUM ALGORITHMS

Experimental implementations of quantum algorithms are still very much in their infancy. Though several physical systems have been proposed to implement quantum bits, quantum gates, and quantum algorithms, all proposals so far have to overcome significant challenges before they can implement interesting quantum algorithms on a sufficiently large number of qubits. Three of the most popular proposals so far are Nuclear Magnetic Resonance (NMR) quantum computation, ion trap quantum computation and solid-state quantum computation.

In a NMR quantum computer, a qubit is modelled by the spin of a nucleus in an organic molecule. In the presence of a strong external magnetic field, the spin either aligns in the direction of the field or opposite to it. This parallel or antiparallel alignment represents the basis states $|0\rangle$ and $|1\rangle$ of the spin. The spin can also exist in a superposition of the parallel and antiparallel alignment states, and thus behaves like a qubit. Several nuclei in the molecule may have the special spin property, enabling them to behave as qubits. Different qubit nuclei should have different so-called resonating frequencies, which means that their spins can be individually manipulated by sending electromagnetic pulses of appropriate frequency perpendicular to the external magnetic field. These resonating frequencies are a property of the molecule. A single qubit gate on a particular qubit is implemented by sending a pulse of the appropriate resonating frequency for a suitable duration. The CNOT gate on two particular qubits is implemented also by a pulse of appropriate frequency, shape, and duration where the conditional flipping occurs because of the mediating properties of the chemical bonds in the molecule. Thus, designing an NMR quantum computer on a certain number of qubits involves synthesizing an appropriate molecule with as many special nuclear spins that can act as qubits, have different resonating frequencies so that each qubit can be individually operated on by single qubit gates, as well as have the suitable chemical bonds that can ensure the implementation of CNOT gates on pairs of qubits. This is a difficult task. Besides this, there are hurdles regarding signal strength and other things with the NMR proposal, making it extremely difficult to go beyond 20 qubits or so. So far, NMR quantum computers with up to 12 qubits have been built. Nevertheless, NMR is still the champion in terms of the number of qubits as well as the complexity of quantum algorithms that have been implemented experimentally so far. The most spectacular quantum algorithm that has been experimentally implemented so far is a simplified version of the quantum order-finding part of Shor's algorithm to factor 15.

In an ion-trap quantum computer, individual ions are trapped in a vacuum container by means of an appropriately oscillating electric field. Each ion has two special energy levels it can be in—the lowest energy or ground state and a particular long-lived excited state. The ion can also be in a superposition of these two states, and thus behaves like a qubit with $|0\rangle$ being the ground state and $|1\rangle$ being the excited state. The ions are well separated in space because of mutual repulsion from like charges, and so can be individually addressed by a laser. Tuning the frequency of the laser to match appropriate energy levels allows one to measure the ion qubits. Tuning the laser to match the frequency of the energy gap between the ground and excited state allows one to perform a single qubit gate on the desired ion qubit. In order to perform a CNOT gate on a given pair of ion qubits, one needs to shine laser pulses on the two qubits with appropriate frequencies and duration, where the conditional flipping is mediated by collective modes of vibration of the ions called phonons. So far, ion trap quantum computers with up to 8 qubits have been designed. Ion trap allows one to implement good quality single qubit gates. However, CNOT gates are difficult to implement. Besides, it is extremely difficult to put more than twenty or so ions in a trap, thus handicapping the scalability of this proposal. Approaches have been suggested to overcome the scalability problem involving an array of ion traps, but it is still very challenging experimentally to implement them.

Two main proposals have been given so far for solid-state quantum computers. The first one involves superconducting circuit elements called Josephson junctions. Here, qubits are modelled either by charge or magnetic flux in these junctions. The second proposal uses circuit elements called quantum dots, where the presence or absence of a particular electron in the dot denotes a qubit. Both these proposals so far have not been able to go beyond two qubits. The hope here is that maybe once the initial teething troubles are overcome, the solid state architecture will allow large scalability allows us in the future to build quantum computers on a chip. Nevertheless, there are many hurdles to both the solid-state proposals, and it is a significant challenge to overcome them.

All the experimental quantum computation proposals so far suffer from significant noise during the course of the computation. This noise destroys the quantumness of the computation very quickly, in a phenomenon known as decoherence. An important theoretical result says that there is a universal noise threshold for quantum computation. By this, there is a small universal constant such that if the noise rate can be brought below this constant, one can do arbitrarily long quantum computation tolerating all the noise and faults that may occur. However, all the experimental implementations now have noise rates far above the fault tolerance threshold. A lot of theoretical and experimental work still needs to be done in order to tolerate more errors in computation as well as bring down the noise rates, before we can see quantum computers solve practical problems.

REFERENCES

Aaronson, S. and Y. Shi (2004), 'Quantum Lower Bounds for the Collision and the Element Distinctness Problems', *Journal of the ACM*, 51(4): 595–605.

Aharonov, D., I. Arad, E. Eban, and Z. Landau (2007), 'Polynomial Quantum Algorithms for Additive Approximations of the Potts Model and Other Points of the Tutte Plane', ArXiv preprint quant-ph/0702008.

Aharonov, D., V. Jones, and Z. Landau (2009), 'A Polynomial Quantum Algorithm for Approximating the Jones Polynomial', *Algorithmica*, 55(3): 395–421.

Ambainis, A. (2002), 'Quantum Lower Bounds by Quantum Arguments', *Journal of Computer and System Sciences*, 64(4): 750–67.

_____ (2005), 'Polynomial Degree and Lower Bounds in Quantum Complexity: Collision and Element Distinctness with Small Range', *Theory of Computing*, 1(1): 37–46.

_____ (2007), 'Quantum Walk Algorithm for Element Distinctness', *SIAM Journal on Computing*, 37(1): 41–53.

Arora, S. and B. Barak (2009), *Computational Complexity: A Modern Approach*. Cambridge: Cambridge University Press.

Bacon, D., A. Childs, and W. van Dam (2005), 'From Optimal Measurement to Efficient Quantum Algorithms for the Hidden Subgroup Problem over Semidirect Product Groups', *Proceedings of the 46th Annual IEEE Symposium on Foundations of Computer Science*.

Bennett, C. and G. Brassard (1984), 'Quantum Cryptography: Public Key Distribution and Coin Tossing', *Proceedings of IEEE International Conference on Computers, Systems and Signal Processing*, pp. 175–9.

Bennett, E., Bernstein, G. Brassard, and U. Vazirani (1997), 'Strengths and Weaknesses of Quantum Computing', *SIAM Journal on Computing*, 26(5): 1510–23.

Brassard, G., P. Hoyer, M. Mosca, and A. Tapp (2000), 'Quantum Amplitude Amplification and Estimation', ArXiv preprint quant-ph/0005055.

Deutsch, D. and Jozsa R. (1992), 'Rapid solutions of problems by quantum computation', *Proceedings of the Royal Society of London*, 439(1907): 553–8.

Farhi, E., J. Goldstone, and S. Gutmann (2007), 'A Quantum Algorithm for the Hamiltonian NAND Tree', ArXiv preprint quant-ph/0702144.

Fawzi, O., P. Hayden, and P. Sen (2010), 'Efficient Quantum Algorithms for Uncertainty Relations and Information Locking', Unpublished manuscript.

Freedman, M., A. Kitaev, and Z. Wang (2002), 'Simulation of Topological Field Theories by Quantum Computers', *Communications in Mathematical Physics*, 227(3): 587–603.

Friedl, K., G. Ivanyos, F. Magniez, M. Santha, and P. Sen (2003), 'Hidden Translation and Orbit Coset in Quantum Computing', *Proceedings of the 35th Annual ACM Symposium on Theory of Computing*, pp. 1–9.

Gavinsky, D., J. Kempe, I. Kerenidis, R. Raz, and R. de Wolf (2008), 'Exponential Separations for One-way Quantum Communication Complexity, with Applications to Cryptography', *SIAM Journal on Computing*, 38(5): 1695–1708.

Grover, L. (1996), 'A Fast Quantum Mechanical Algorithm for Database Search', *Proceedings of the 28th Annual ACM Symposium on Theory of Computing*, pp. 212–19.

Hallgren, R., C. Moore, M. Rötteler, A. Russell, and P. Sen (2010) 'Limitations of Quantum Coset States for Graph Isomorphism', *Journal of the ACM* (forthcoming).

Hallgren, S. (2005), 'Fast Quantum Algorithms for Computing the Unit Group and Class Group of a Number Field', *Proceedings of the 37th Annual ACM Symposium on Theory of Computing*, pp. 468–74.

_____ (2007), 'Polynomial-time Quantum Algorithms for Pell's Equation and the Principal Ideal Problem', *Journal of the ACM*, 54(1).

Harrow, A., A. Hassidim, and S. Lloyd (2009), 'Quantum Algorithm for Linear Systems of Equations', *Physical Review Letters*, 103.

Ivanyos, G., F. Magniez, and M. Santha (2003), 'Efficient Quantum Algorithms for some Instances of the Non-abelian Hidden Subgroup Problem', *International Journal of Foundations of Computer Science*, 14(5): 723–40.

Ivanyos, G., L. Sanselme, and M. Santha (2008), 'An Efficient Quantum Algorithm for the Hidden Subgroup Problem in nil-2 Groups', *Proceedings of the 8th Latin American Theoretical Informatics Symposium*, volume 4957 of Lecture Notes in Computer Science, pp. 759–71.

Jain, R., Z. Ji, S. Upadhyay, and J. Watrous (2010), 'QIP = PSPACE', *Proceedings of the 42nd Annual ACM Symposium on Theory of Computing*.

Kitaev, A. (1995), 'Quantum Measurements and the Abelian Stabilizer Problem', ArXiv preprint quant-ph/9511026.

Kitaev, A. and J. Watrous (2000), 'Parallelization, Amplification, and Exponential Time Simulation of Quantum Interactive Proof Systems', *Proceedings of the 32nd Annual ACM Symposium on Theory of Computing*, pp. 608–17.

Krovi, H., F. Magniez, M. Ozols, and J. Roland (2010), 'Finding is as Easy as Detecting for Quantum Walks', *Proceedings of the 37th International Colloquium on Automata, Languages and Programming* (forthcoming).

Kutin, S. (2005), 'Quantum Lower Bound for the Collision Problem with Small Range', *Theory of Computing*, 1(1): 29–36.

Mosca, M. and A. Ekert (1998), 'The Hidden Subgroup Problem and Eigenvalue Estimation on a Quantum Computer', *Quantum Computing and Quantum Communications* (Lecture Notes in Computer Science), volume 1509, pp. 174–88.

Nielsen, M. and I. Chuang (2000), *Quantum Computation and Quantum Information*. Cambridge: Cambridge University Press.

Reichardt, B. (2010), 'Reflections for Quantum Query Complexity: The General Adversary Bound is tight for Every Boolean Function', Unpublished manuscript.

Schmidt, A. and U. Vollmer (2005), 'Polynomial Time Quantum Algorithm for the Computation of the Unit Group of a Number Field', *Proceedings of the 37th Annual ACM Symposium on Theory of Computing*, pp. 475–80.

Shamir, A. (1992), 'IP = PSPACE', *Journal of the ACM*, 39(4): 869–77.

Shor, P. (1997), 'Polynomial-time Algorithms for Prime Factorization and Discrete Logarithms on a Quantum Computer', *SIAM Journal on Computing*, 26(5): 1484–509.

Sipser, M. (1996), *Introduction to the Theory of Computation*. Boston: PWS Pub. Co.

Szegedy, M. (2004), 'Quantum Speed-up of Markov Chain based Algorithms', *Proceedings of the 45th Annual IEEE Symposium on Foundations of Computer Science*, pp. 32–41.

Yao, A. C-C (1993), 'Quantum Circuit Complexity', *Proceedings of the 34th IEEE Symposium Foundations of Computer Science*, pp. 352–61.

BUD MISHRA

18 Sarve Santu Niramaya
*Computational Biology's Promises
for India**

*The recent biotechnology revolution resembles information technology's early
days of promises, and similar explosive progress and ubiquitous impact. Biotechnology has its own version of Moor's law; it strives to extract pertinent
information from exponentially growing genomic and biomedical (for example, electronic health record) data; it aims to provide cheap and fast access
to health and disease related information; and finally, it is poised to indi-
vidualize medicine by combining statistics from large groups of patients and
their relatives organized in 'G2G (Genome-to-Genome) networks', where
people anonymously share data on their environments and ancestry. It is no
wonder that at the core of the machinery driving biotechnology sits massive
computational networks, and innovative computational biological algorithms. Unlike many other technologies, however, this field thrives on wide-
ranging multi-disciplinary cooperation and collaboration, as can be seen in
the birth and growth of its subfields such as: (i) genomics and other–omics*

* The paper has improved considerably following many insightful suggestions
from several colleagues: most notably, F. Hoppensteadt, S. Kleinberg, G. Narzisi,
K.R. Sreenivasan, M. Subrahmanyam, and A. Witzel of New York University, R.
Parikh of CUNY, A. Nerode of Cornell, P. Soon-Shiong and L. van der Ploeg of
Abraxis, and M. Atwal and M. Wigler of CSHL.

spectra, (ii) bioinformatics and computational biology, (iii) Whole-Genome Association Studies (WGAS), and (iv) computational systems biology. India must prepare now to play a key leading role in this unraveling biomedical revolution with the specific goal of providing universal, ubiquitous, and individualized healthcare to her vast and varied populace. India's rich ethnic diversity provides a unique opportunity to translate her collective genomic information into profound scientific and public health benefits.

'Whither do we go and what shall be our endeavour?' Pandit Jawaharlal Nehru, the first Prime Minister of India, asked a newly independent India on the midnight of 15 August 1947. 'To bring freedom and opportunity to the common man, to the peasants and workers of India; to fight and end poverty and ignorance and disease; to build up a prosperous, democratic and progressive nation, and to create social, economic and political institutions which will ensure justice and fullness of life to every man and woman. We have hard work ahead.'

It may now be argued that India has substantially redeemed Nehru's pledge, as would be apparent from India's recent progress and prosperity, spurred by her leading role in information and communication technology and computer science. India seems to be in a comfortable position to replicate a similar success in the area of emerging computational biology and biotechnology, which could then have an enormous impact on India's agro-science, bio-medicine and healthcare infrastructure, and help it fight poverty, ignorance, and disease. But there are several complications, and India has hard work ahead.

For millennia, India has been a melting pot, which gave rise to the current population of approximately 1.17 billion people (more precisely, according to CIA World Factbook,[†] (an estimated) 1,166,079,217 people on 1 July 2009 with remarkably diverse genealogies and demographics. India's linguistic diversity (with four major language groups: Indo-European, Dravidian, Austro-Asiatic, and Tibeto-Burman; with language isolates like Nihali or great Andamanese), religious multiplicity (with every major religion represented), and racial variety (more than 2,000 ethnic groups) are all a testimony to her ability to merge wave after wave of migratory populations in her great crucible of cultural and genetic assimilation. India's population is made of, quoting

[†] The World Factbook by Central Intelligence Agency (https://www.cia.gov/library/ publications/the-world-factbook/)

Pandit Nehru again, 'separate individual men and women, each differing from the other … a bundle of contradictions held together by strong but invisible threads.'

This rich and dynamic collective history of India can be read from the individual DNAs of each Indian, as encoded in 6 billion base pairs of A, T, C, and Gs, organized in bundles of twenty-three chromosomes of each individual human genome—that 2 m of double-stranded invisible thread. The entire Indian human population can thus be described by about 7.3805818×10^{18} base pairs, if one is to trust CIA[‡] and DoE (Human Genome Project Information[§]) factbook estimates. This entire body of genomic information can be stored in merely 2 Exabytes (EB) of memory, significantly less than the current global monthly internet traffic. But to give it a human perspective, note that this information is equivalent to about 1×10^{12} (1 trillion) copies of Mahabharatas, the great Indian epic, which surpasses in size anything humanly memorized, written, crafted, or understood. While reading and storing India's genomic information may be a surmountable challenge, understanding it with every bit of its nuances, is not!

At a rough glance, this body of genomic information can be described in terms of haplogroups (groups with similar genomic variations) as follows: The Indian male lineage (inferred from Y-chromosomes inherited patrilineally) consists of haplogroups R1a (20%), H (30%), R2 (15%), L (10%), and NOP(10%, excluding R) and the Indian female lineage (inferred from mitochondrial DNA, mtDNA, inherited matrilineally) is primarily made up of haplogroups M (60%), UK (15%), and N (25%, excluding UK). Recently, the Indian sex ratio has been plunging precipitously, with perilous genetic and cultural consequences for the entire population; according to the 2001 census, India's sex ratio is 927 female for 1,000 male (at birth). The situation is worse in states like Punjab, Haryana, and Delhi, but better in few states like Kerala. India's population is rather young with an age-structure comprising: 0–14 years: 30.8 per cent, 15–64 years: 64.3 per cent, 65+ years: 4.9 per cent, and has a population growth rate of 1.548 per cent 2009 (an estimated). As India's population ages, and when the demographic dividends of the current decade are all spent, the healthcare cost of

[‡] Ibid.
[§] http://www.ornl.gov/sci/ techresources/Human_Genome/home.html

the older Indians could become an onerous burden. Preparing for this future, India must step up to innovate and create a unique vision of her own—in biomedicine, biotechnology, and computational biology at all scales ranging from single nucleotides, single molecules, and single cells to individual citizens and her entire population. Concepts from many disciplines must intermingle to fulfil this vision, namely, population genetics, genomics, biotechnology, bioinformatics, genome-wide association studies, and systems biology, as described below.

POPULATION GENOMICS

From the statistical analysis of the haplogroups on the Y-chromosomes and mtDNA, one could attempt to infer a skeletal and rudimentary history of the first human population to inhabit India and its subsequent evolution. To properly interpret these observed haplogroup marker frequencies in an extant population, the population model must include the effects of population sizes, vicariance (population splitting as a consequence of geographical events), ethnic segregation and mixing within the population as well as migration. Most of these processes and their parametric structures, however, remain unknown. Reconstructing this history faces further challenges as it very likely involves a complex population substructure, intricate gene flows constrained by rigid adherence to endogamy (the practice of marrying within a specific ethnic group, as determined by the caste system), and ancestries marked by admixture lineages. India also seems to have experienced many successive population expansions and contractions varying over her vast geography, which exaggerate mutational differences, induced by random sorting of allele frequencies.

From the mtDNA and Y-chromosome data, available prior to 2007, Endicott et al. (2007) have argued that the earliest Indian population arose from a rapid dispersal of modern humans from eastern Africa and subsequent settlement in South Asia, consistent with both 'Out of Africa and Strong Garden of Eden Hypotheses'. The Out of Africa or African Replacement Hypothesis claims that every living human being is descended from a small group in Africa, who then dispersed into the wider world displacing earlier forms; this hypothesis is mainly supported by mtDNA data that point to all humans descending ultimately from one female: the Mitochondrial Eve. The Strong Garden of Eden Hypothesis claims that the out of Africa expansion was followed by a single and relatively fast range expansion and not by a gradual series of expansions outside Africa (the Weak Garden of Eden Scenario). The argument supporting these hypotheses goes as follows: the African human population appears to be the most diverse in terms of polymorphisms (which describe variations in genomes within a species or a population), whereas, in contrast, the non-African populations show somewhat limited diversity. The main non-African mtDNA diversity is limited to haplogroups M, N, and R, and are found in the extant population of South Asia and Australia, while the West Eurasian population mainly exhibits the mtDNA haplogroups: N and R. A similar picture emerges for the Y haplogroups, thus supporting a single migration out of Africa around 65,000 years ago (coalescent time for mtDNA haplogroups M, N, and R). These haplogroup distributions also paint a picture of South Asia as a crossroad of early human migration.

These data also signify other population expansions into the Indian subcontinent just before the Last Glacial Maximum that occurred about 18,000 years ago, when the favourable climatic conditions permitted recent migrations into India. Haplogroups in Pakistan and western-most states of India share a considerable amount of western Eurasian specific haplotypes and hint at a Eurasian migration. Similarly, Austro-Asiatic speaking populations in East Indian states (Orissa, Jharkhand, Bihar, and West Bengal) have mitochondrial and Y-chromosomal haplogroups originating east of India, indicative of an East Asian migration through the northeast corridor of India.

However, the phylogeography described above is simply based on low-resolution uniparental data derived from rather short mtDNA (about 16,596 bps) or a small fragment of Y-chromosome (about 50,000 bps, comprising only about 0.1 per cent of Y), and thus, severely limited by the small number of markers available on them. A recent study by Reich et al. (2009) has attempted to reconstruct Indian population history better by using genotype data of 132 Indian samples from 25 groups, collected with Affymetrix 6.0 SNP array on 560,123 SNPs (Single Nucleotide Polymorphisms, pronounced 'snip'). Single Nucleotide Polymorphisms are DNA sequence variation occurring when a single nucleotide—A, T, C, or G—in the genome differs between members of a species or a population. Single Nucleotide Polymorphisms, making up about 90 per cent of all human genetic variation, occur every 100 to 300 bases along the 3-billion-base-long human genome.

The analysis of Reich et al. (2009) of Indian SNP data revealed further subtle structures in the population and gene flows that were missing from the earlier analyses:

- The structure of the current Indian population could be described in terms of two idealized genetically divergent ancestral populations: ANI (Ancestral North Indians) and ASI (Ancestral South Indians), the former being genetically close to Central Asians, Europeans, and Middle Easterners, and the later being a seemingly distinct human subgroup. ANI-ASI admixtures could be described along an Indian Cline;

- Ancestral North Indian ancestry was estimated to be higher than average in the upper castes (brahmins and kshatriyas) and Indo-Aryan linguistic groups. Ancestral South Indian ancestry was determined to be best represented by the Onge population in Andaman Island;

- Autosomal estimates of ANI ancestries showed a stronger correlation with Y haplogroup frequencies than those of mtDNA, suggesting astrongermale gene flow from groups with high ANI ancestry into ones with less;

- A Principal Component Analysis (PCA) on genotype SNP data revealed an interesting configuration of the Indian population groups, which identified two outlier groups as the Siddi (African ancestry) and the Nyshi and AoNaga (Chinese ancestry), corresponding to the first two principal components;

- Fisher's Fixation Distance (FST) statistics measured the genetic distances, leading to the conclusion that the 19 main Indian population groups showed much more differences than the traditional 23 European groups do. It was suggested that Indian population groups might have been established by a few individuals (founders), followed by limited gene flow;

- It was also proposed that such enduring genetic signatures of founder events support the hypotheses that group distinctions are ancient and preserved in high fidelity because of strong endogamy, a consequence of strict taboos against inter-caste marriages;

- The widespread history of founder events implied a high-rate of recessive diseases, and makes these Indian population groups ideal for extensive studies focusing on genetic diseases and gene mapping.

These studies using SNP arrays to assess the genetic distances have several shortcomings: these arrays are based on known SNPs that were derived using small samples from populations very different from the Indian populations; the probes on the arrays were selected, based on a single reference human genome sequence that may not be sufficiently genetically representative of the Indian groups; and finally, because the technology and the data could not disambiguate haplotypic phasing, the estimates of allele sharing statistics suffer from high uncertainties. Furthermore, SNP array based data remain blind to many other kinds of polymorphisms: for example, CNV (Copy Number Variations) and SV (Structural Variations). To circumvent such concerns, one must develop technologies for sequencing whole-genomes of many individuals, preferably haplotypically. Despite the amazing progresses outlined here, a lot of hard work lays ahead.

GENOMICS AND COMPUTATIONAL BIOLOGY

The preceding discussion leads directly to our next topic, building on a vast body of computational biology literature devoted to mapping, sequencing, and sequence assembly algorithms. The subject has its origin in classical 'stringology' of theoretical computer science (Gusfield 1997), but received a big boost at the start of the Human Genome Project[9] and is again enjoying a revival with the advent of next-generation sequencing technologies (Schuster 2008).

The diploid human genome, containing all our hereditary information, is composed of about 6 billion DNA base pairs in total. The paired bases A (Adenine), T (Thymine), C (Cytosine), and G (Guanine) satisfy a complementarity principle: A pairs with T and C, with G. Thus, as a computational object, a genome could be represented and manipulated as a data structure of a set of strings over an alphabet of size 4.

The bases, Cytosine and Thymine, are smaller (lighter) molecules, called pyrimidines, whereas the other two bases, Guanine and Adenine, are bigger (bulkier) and called purines. Furthermore, Adenine and Thymine allow only for double hydrogen bonding, while Cytosine and Guanine allow for triple hydrogen bonding. As a result, the chemical (through hydrogen bonding) and the mechanical (purine to pyrimidine) constraints on the pairing lead to the complementarity and make the double stranded DNA both chemically inert and mechanically rigid and stable. Thus, despite its uninspiring physics and chemistry, DNA

[9] Ibid.

makes a fascinating information theoretic object through its capabilities for stable storage, high-fidelity template-driven copying mechanism, error-correction, and resilience, and finally, its ability to reorganize through recombination, strand-invasion, mutation, deletion, insertion, translocation, and deletion. Many computational biologists have been drawn to DNA not just for its biological role, but by its simplicity, elegance, and sheer computational power; one could imagine using DNA to construct future computers to solve intractable problems and nanorobots to self-assemble complex materials.

Genomics analysis is deemed fundamental to biology and computational biology, as we have come to envision DNA as defining all of biology almost axiomatically through Crick's central dogma, which states that the information flows unidirectionally from DNA to RNA through transcription and then to proteins through translation. Thus, by understanding how changes to an individual's genome affects transcription (DNA to RNA) and translation (RNA to proteins) of all its genes, we may aim to understand how biology works at a system level, as in the emerging field of systems biology, and the classical subject of '(forward) genetics', an approach to discovering the function of agene by analysing the discernible traits (phenotypes).

If we compare genome sequences of two individuals from a population, we expect that, while most of the sequences will be almost identical, there will be few sporadic differences, giving rise to various polymorphisms (distinctive 'forms' in the population). For instance, an individual's autosomal gene (with two copies, one inherited from the father and the other from the mother) may differ from a copy of the same gene in another individual's genome (or from each other), in various ways: different bases at different positions, a small insertion or deletion, the gene may have different copy numbers, or because the gene is inverted or at a different chromosomal location. If a single nucleotide differs at some position, the polymorphism is called a SNP; if the copy numbers differ, it is a CNV (Copy Number Variations), etc. The effect of polymorphisms on the gene's function can be through many mechanisms and quite complex: it may change the gene's transcribed expression, dosage/amount (due to CNVs) or the final translated protein (due to an SNP) and thus modify the biochemical reactions within a cell, or signalling and communication among various cells. Normally, an individual has two copies of a gene (she is homozygous if two copies are same and heterozygous if they are distinct), thus allowing none, one or both copies of the gene to be distinct from the common form of the gene. In that case, how the genotypic variations determine the phenotypes also depends on the gene's dominance: If the gene's effect is dominant a single mutation can alter the trait, and if the effect is recessive then mutations in both copies would be necessary to alter the trait. Similar polymorphisms, occurring in the regions regulating gene transcription or alternate splicing or in genes for transcriptional factors, alter the phenotypes in an indirect, but more complex manner. A vast amount of polymorphisms occur in synonymous bases of genes, or in introns and intergenic regions with no effect on phenotypes and are thus considered 'neutral'. These mutations drift through the genomes in a population in a random manner, and can be tracked to understand ancestry. Occasionally, a random mutation turns out to present a selective advantage as it gives the carriers an increased fitness. Through selective sweep the mutated variant (allele) increases its population frequency as the result of recent and strong positive natural selection. Since neutral and nearly neutral genetic variation linked to the new mutation will also become more prevalent (as they hitch-hike), the signs of selective sweep can be detected from the haplotypic sequences from a population.

Thus, reverse genetics, ancestry, and population dynamics studies ultimately rely on progress in sequencing technology and algorithmics, raising the following question: How can one read an individual's genome from end-to-end, while making sure that the technology is accurate enough to correctly discern all of the SNPs (and other polymorphisms), and unambiguous enough to determine the haplotypes from the homologous pairs of chromosomes? Because of various inherent technological limitations and computational intractabilities, these goals pose many difficulties, some apparently insurmountable.

The Human Genome Project (HGP) has produced and published a reference sequence of the euchromatic human genome, and determined that the haploid human genome contains approximately 23,000 protein-coding genes (far fewer than the estimate of about 120,000 genes, which had been expected before genome sequencing) and that only about 1.5 per cent of the genome codes for proteins, while the rest consists of non-coding RNA genes, regulatory sequences, introns, and a significant portion with no known function ('junk' DNA).

The Human Genome Project initially produced two unfinished draft sequences by two different methods, one by the International Human Genome Sequencing Consortium (IHGSC) and another by Celera genomics (CG). The published IHGSC assembly was constructed by the program GigAssembler, devised at the University of California at Santa Cruz (UCSC). Unfortunately, these drafts have never been fully validated. In a recent article it was noted:

Of particular interest are the relative rates of misassembly (sequence assembled in the wrong order and/or orientation) and the relative coverage achieved by the three protocols. Unfortunately the UCSC group [was] alone in having published assessments of the rate of misassembly... Using artificial data sets, they found that, on average 10 per cent of assembled fragments were assigned the wrong orientation and 15 per cent of fragments were placed in wrong order by their protocol. Two independent assessments [more recent] of UCSC assemblies have come to the similar conclusions. (Semple 2007)

For various technological reasons, it has only been possible to read short (about 700–1000 bps) and non-contextual (missing location) subsequences of the genome. The problem of inferring the entire genome sequence from many such non-contextual short reads (taken from many identical copies of the genome) has been dubbed 'shotgun sequencing approach', and attracted the attention of many computational biologists. Several of them, with years of experience in developing shotgun assembly pipelines, have argued, 'the sequence reconstruction problem that we take as our formulation of DNA sequence assembly is a variation of the Shortest Common Superstring Problem (SCSP), complicated by the presence of sequencing errors and reverse complements of fragments. Since the simpler superstring problem is NP-hard, any efficient reconstruction procedure must resort to heuristics [giving rise to approximate, incomplete, and less-than-correct solutions] (Kececioglu and Myers 1995).' NP-hard computational problems are assumed not to yield to any computationally feasible approach, unless along-standing conjecture (P ≠ NP) is refuted.

Practically all sequencing pipelines, currently in use, follow search strategies that are strongly influenced by the reasoning above and aim to heuristically compute reasonable approximation of the true genome. Thus, based on heuristic search strategies assembly algorithms can be divided into two major categories: greedy and graph-based. In the greedy category are included algorithms that typically construct the solution incrementally, while choosing the 'locally best' overlapping sequence-fragment pairs to merge at each step. Well known assemblers in this category include: TIGR (Sutton et. al 1995), Phrap (Green 1996), and CAP3 (Huang and Madan 1999).

In the graph-based category, assemblers start by preprocessing the sequence-reads to determine the pair-wise overlap information and represent these binary relationships as (unweighted) edges in a string-graph. Depending upon how the overlap relation is represented in these graphs, two main assembly paradigms have emerged: Overlap-Layout-Consensus (OLC) and Sequencing-By-Hybridization (SBH). Well-known assemblers based on OLC approach include: CELERA (Myers et. al 2000), ARACHNE (Batzoglou 2002), and Minimus (Sommer 2007). Two prominent examples of the other SBH approach include: EULER (Pevzner et. al 2001), and Velvet (Zerbino and Birney 2008). Because of their relation to various graph-theoretic NP-complete problems, Hamiltonian-path problem and Eulerian-superpath problem, respectively, both OLC and SBH approaches face the inherent intractability that lurks in their cores.

A counter-intuitive approach, suggested by a new pipeline, SUTTA (Narzidi and Mishra 2010), is to simply put the computational complexity and intractability question aside temporarily. Instead SUTTA aims to develop an accurate formulation of the problem and solve it exactly. Once it realizes where, in the structure of the formulation of the problem, the computational complexity becomes exacerbating, it tames the algorithm by clever pruning: specifically, SUTTA formulates the assembly problem in terms of a constrained optimization: It relies on a rather simple and easily verifiable definition of feasible solutions as 'consistent layouts'. It potentially generates all possible consistent layouts, organizing them as paths in a 'double-tree' structure, rooted at a randomly selected 'seed' read. Since a path can be progressively and quickly evaluated in terms of an optimality criteria, encoded by a score function of the set of overlaps along a layout corresponding to the path, it can also concomitantly check the validity of the layouts(with respect to various long-range information such as mate-pairs, optical (Samad et. al 1995; Anantharaman et. al 1997; Ashton et. al 1999) or probe (West et. al 2006) maps, dilution, etc.) through well-chosen constraint-related penalty functions, and prune most of the implausible layouts, using a branch-and-bound scheme. Ambiguities, resulting from repeats or haplotypic dissimilarities, may occasionally delay immediate pruning, forcing the algorithm to look ahead, but in practice, do not exact a high price in computational complexity of the algorithm. Additionally, SUTTA is capable, at least in principle, of agnostically adapting to various rapidly evolving technologies. Not surprisingly, an analysis of SUTTA's performance against the existing assemblers demonstrates its unique superiority—it provides the best genome coverage for every allowable error threshold (measured in terms of a feature-response curve).

As the preceding discussion points out, there is now a clearer realization that the sequence assembly problem, with its seminal role in computational biology, needs, and will see, a rebirth: the problem has not been adequately solved and there are many new profitable avenues to explore. We seem to have left many interesting algorithmic 'stones' unturned, which are hoped to attract talented Indian computer scientists to these challenges. Furthermore, a competition, along the line of 'International SAT Competition',** with benchmark real and in silico data and evaluation criteria should be set up for whole-genome sequencing problems.

There is an even more critical issue for Indian genomicists: What reference sequence should be used for population-wide studies in India? How many reference sequences? How representative could Craig Venter or Jim Watson's genomes (the first two to be sequenced) be for the Indian subcontinental population? As we attempt to understand polymorphisms, similar questions arise regarding the HAPMAP project: its coverage and its suitability. If India needs to start a Human Genome project, a HAPMAP project and a Human Population Genome project almost *ab initio* should it not get started as soon as possible? India has hard work ahead.

DISEASE STUDIES

Equipped with tens of thousands of genomes from the extant Indian subcontinental population (or even stretching back to East Africa, Arabian peninsula, Southern Asia and stretching forward to Australasia), we can try to reveal not only her past, but also how evolution has shaped and continues to shape India's collective biology: how her population

---

** The International SAT Competition. http://www.satcompetition.org

lives, mates, reproduces, suffers, and dies. Theodosius Dobzhansky has famously said, 'Nothing in biology makes sense except in the light of evolution.' However, evolution is Darwinian, its unidirectionality induced by the unidirectionality of the biological information flow—as captured in Crick's Central Dogma. Genomes in a population are continuously reorganized by various processes: single point mutations, insertions/deletions (indels), duplications, translocations, and inversions, which via the transcription-translation information-flow alter the regulatory, metabolic, and signalling processes defining the whole organism. More often than not, the effects of these modifications are deleterious, and lead to diseases, deaths and disappearances of species. Occasionally, the new genotype (coded by the genome) leads to an advantageous phenotype (exhibited by a trait), and rapidly diffuses through the population in a selective sweep, while inviting along other hitch-hiking genomic elements (polymorphisms/variants in linkage disequilibria). As one attempts to get a taste of the relation between biology's syntax and semantics by Genome-Wide Association Studies (GWAS), one has to mask out the ancestral hitch-hiking syntactic sugars, salts, and chaffs.

Consequently, determining the etiology of a disease is nontrivial: genomic variants that correlate with a disease trait are not all causal. Additionally, environmental effects modulate the symptoms and severity of a disease. Genetic susceptibility of an individual to a trait depends on type-level causality (the population to which the individual belongs) as well as token-level causality (the gene-environment interactions in the specific patient). Similarly, genetics also plays a significant role in determining if a particular therapeutic intervention is likely to be more effective for a particular population or individual. For instance, in treating lung cancer, one may exploit the known association between response to Gefitinib and Erlotinib and mutations of the EGFR, and thus personalizing a specific treatment for a specific patient. Thus, treating all diseases in a genetic-agnostic manner is neither cost effective nor safe.

Association studies aim to discover genetic variations that differ in frequency between cases (affected) and controls (unaffected) or between individuals exhibiting different phenotypic values. Traditionally, association studies had been built upon low-throughput approaches in which a single putative gene was targeted and genotyped for genetic variants. A classical example is presented by the study that identified a significant association between APOE alleles and Alzheimer disease (Martin et al. 2000). Such analysis may be thought of as hypothesis driven (leading to refutation or validation) and could be conducted by a small laboratory and requiring modest computational and technological resources. As one wishes to scale similar analyses to whole genomes(with all the genetic variants queried simultaneously), not only do the technological and computational burdens grow massively, but the statistical analysis require thoughtful design: one must account for multiple hypothesis testing, suitable null-models reflecting population dynamics (effective size, bottlenecks), Yule-Simpson effects (exacerbated by unknown population stratification and admixtures), and variations in technologies and protocols employed in gathering the underlying data.

Currently, most genome-wide association studies are based on a single phenotype and genotypic information, contained in SNPs. Single Nucleotide Polymorphisms are found to be frequent in the genome; variants in physical proximity tend to correlate in genotype; and the correlations have been mapped substantially by the International Hap-Map Project.[††] Single Nucleotide Polymorphisms-based genome-wide association studies have enjoyed some early successes: Age-related Macular Degeneration (Haines et al. 2005) associated with complement factor H (using 96 cases and 50 controls), Wellcome Trust Case Control Consortium (WTCCC)[‡‡] study for a wide class of diseases, namely, coronary heart disease, type 1 diabetes (T1D), type 2 diabetes (T2D), rheumatoid arthritis, crohn's disease, bipolar disorder and hypertension—showing, for instance, that T1D is associated with six chromosomal regions (using about 12,000 individuals).

Many genome-wide association studies (such as the ones described earlier) have been motivated by and designed to test a specific hypothesis: The common disease/common variant hypothesis. This hypothesis postulates that polymorphic variations in the population of more than 5 per cent frequency might increase susceptibility to common disease (Lander 1999b; Chakravarti 1999). It is argued that such variants have persisted in the population because any one of them is only slightly deleterious or has no effect on an individual until old age. Both recent rapid growth in effective population size of humans (after a population

---

[††] http://hapmap.ncbi.nlm.nih.gov/
[‡‡] http://www.wtccc.org.uk/

bottleneck) and increased lifespan have contributed in sheltering these common variants in an 'evolutionary shadow'. However, there have emerged many counter-examples that do not fit this hypothesis, thus leading to the alternative hypothesis: the rare variant hypothesis. Thus there appears a need for genome-wide association studies, designed to include low-penetrance rare variants (< 1 per cent population frequency), which might impart a moderately large relative risk. Lately, the focus has also shifted to understanding the role of other SV (structural variant) polymorphisms (CNVs, copy number variants, and their analogues) in determining phenotypic variations (Iafrate et al. 2004; Sebat et al. 2004). CNVs are defined as regions of duplications (copy number > 2) and deletions (copy number < 2) greater than 1kb, but no well-developed statistical method for interpreting their contribution to disease exists yet (Ionita et al. 2006; Mitrofanova and Mishra 2009).

The current genome-wide association studies also need to account for systematic 'missingness' (especially for rare alleles). Because of this, a strong haplotypic association may only imply that the truly causal variant lies on the haplotype background and may not have been typed. A population study, using the currently available array or short-sequence-read technologies, relies on estimating likely haplotypes, since the true chromosomal crossover points are unknown (as previous generations are not genotyped). These estimates use the population-wide data to impute the missing haplotype phases, and can be biased by the population structures, effective population size, degree of inbreeding, etc.

A related issue is that of quality control, needed to ensure that cases are well matched to the controls for ancestry. Lack of proper matching can enable hidden variables in association and lead to false-positives or may even mislead the direction of causation/association (Yule-Simpson effect). Usually correction by an inflation factor for 'genomic control' (Devlin and Roeder 1999) or incorporation of population structure by a subset of ancestry informative SNPs have been employed, but since the standard algorithms such as STRUCTURE (Pritchard et al. 2000) or mSTRUCT (Shringarpure and Xing 2009) for population stratification are based on genotyped SNPs, such solutions are not fully satisfactory.

For a population as complex as the Indian subcontinent's, we will need much more accurate data (for example, whole-genome individually haplotyped sequences), capable of revealing SNPs, SVs, and individual haplotype structure. If India holds the result of 'the grandest genetic experiment ever performed on man', as Dobzhansky proclaimed, surely then it needs to be measured, evaluated, and interpreted as best as possible. Aiming to build faster, better, and cheaper biotechnology and GWAS algorithms will involve hard work, but shying away from these tasks is not necessarily an option.

SYSTEMS BIOLOGY

Another issue, though less frequently discussed than deserved, concerns the errors in GWAS owing to incorrect phenotyping. Even for Mendelian diseases, two similar disease phenotypes could be easily confused, thus confounding any GWAS analysis: For instance, a dataset that mislabels FSS (Freeman-Sheldon Syndrome) for SHS (Sheldon-Hall Syndrome) can easily mislead GWAS into an incorrect causative (or associative) interpretation. Similarly, it is conjectured that genetic analysis of chronic fatigue syndrome has been severely frustrated by the heterogeneity of the disease. We could avoid this conundrum if we could extract traits directly and objectively from patient data (Kleinberg and Mishra 2009)—say, the electronic health record (EHR) data; its causal analysis will derive trait (primary and secondary) and sub-trait definitions, and will lead directly to disease etiology and its elucidation in the genetic and environmental contexts.

Causation, its definition and interpretation, have been a topic of interest to philosophers, logicians, statisticians, and AI researchers (Suppes 1970; Cartwright 1994; Kleinberg and Mishra 2010 and 2009). An appealing definition of causation could be based on the concepts of temporal priority and probability raising. In this way, it could be precisely defined in the language of probabilistic computational tree logic (a propositional branching time temporal logic), algorithmically interpreted using the techniques of model checking and statistically scored (to control false discovery rates) using empirical Bayes methods (Kleinberg and Mishra 2010 and 2009). Using this method we may represent relationships such as '(increasing BMI and smoking UNTIL hypertension) causes CHF in 8–10 months', and validate them in a rigorous way that allows us to automatically infer the associated probability of such a relationship from time series data.

Similar notions of causality can be extended to incorporate the effects of genetic variants and environmental covariates. However, such a causal explanation is purely phenomenological and devoid of a mechanistic/molecular basis. One would prefer the underlying models to also explain how biomolecules participating in various biochemical processes are synthesized, transcribed, translated, multi-merized, bound, folded, activated, regulated, metabolized, signalled, degraded, transferred, chaperoned, localized, co-localized, compartmentalized, deactivated, unbound, spliced, post-translationally modified, etc. Such processes can be mathematically represented quite faithfully using various formalisms: Finite State Machines, Ordinary or Partial Differential Equations, or Algebraic Hybrid Models, while enabling for certain of these models to be checked by automated procedures—albeit feasible but slow algorithms. Such algorithms can be made more efficient by incorporating further algorithmic advances, and the challenges they pose will likely attract some of the best algorithmic minds over the next decades. But more practically, they will enable not only an understanding of the disease etiology at molecular and process levels, but also means to therapeutic interventions, be they molecular, genetic, or synthetic-systems-biologic. Hard work, challenges, and opportunities await many young Indian mathematicians and computer scientists, who will be attracted to these emerging disciplines at the interface of computer science and biology.

RECOMMENDATIONS

In summary, the emerging fields of computational systems biology and population genomics analysis could be the next important high technology areas for India to nurture. There are several technological milestones to target: (a) Indian Human Population Genomes Project, sequencing several thousand whole-genomes haplotypically and accurately; (b) High Throughput and Inexpensive Haplotypic Sequencing Technology Project, capable of sequencing genomic DNA from small number of cells and minute amounts of genomic materials; (c) High Accuracy Sequence Assembly Project, aiming to make a quantum leap in the algorithmic technologies underlying accurate haplotypic sequence assembly software (accompanied with better sequence annotation and comparison algorithms); (d) Advanced Genome-Wide Association Studies Project, incorporating improved analysis of ancestry, haplotypes, and causal relations; and (e) Translational Systems Biology Project, focusing on phenotyping, disease etiologies, and systems biology models of diseases (with capabilities for model checking). The possibility of an

Indian Human Population Genome Project is quite tantalizing as a denoument of the 'grandest genetic experiment ever performed'.

Some attention should be drawn to a rather global problem that affects all humans, which could be of immense concern. In humans, per-generation reduction in fitness (ranging between 1 per cent and 5 per cent) appears to be soaring, because of an unusually high rate of recurrent mutations. In a recent essay, Michael Lynch (2010) wrote, '[The] impact of deleterious mutations is accumulating on a time scale that is approximately the same as that for scenarios associated with global warming—perhaps not of great concern over a span of one or two generations, but with very considerable consequences on time scales of tens of generations.' There is, thus, an acute need to invent intelligent approaches of genetic intervention, building upon accurate characterization of the underlying population dynamics (for example, intronic-mutations modifying gene-isoforms).

In the context of just the Indian population, there are several important societal issues to be addressed (and not fully discussed here): (a) increased investment in the so-called third-world diseases (for example, malaria); (b) policies affecting population genetics (for example, sex ratio in Indian population); (c) attention to an aging population and its impact on healthcare; (d) genetically modified organisms and their impact on the Indian agro-industry; and (e) preventive and personalized medicine, its introduction to India, and its inevitable impact on privacy and related issues.

There is one more thing worth touching upon: India has a long tradition and success in statistics, mathematics, and logic. All of these areas will play important roles in the projects, outlined earlier. India must invest in teaching and research in these areas, both in preparation of people developing areas related to bioinformatics and computational biology, and also for mathematicians, engineers, and scientists involved in modeling problems from the life sciences.

This essay is dedicated to the memory of two influential Indian scientists, Padma Bhushan Homi J. Bhabha (1909–1966), the great nuclear physicist and a father of Indian scientific revolution after independence, and Sir J.B.S. Haldane (1892–1964), the great geneticist and evolutionary biologist, who spent his last years in Bhubaneswar as the Director of Orissa State Government Genetics and Biometry Laboratory. Both of them, through their closeness to Pandit Nehru, played key roles in defining India's 'Scientific Temper', which would allow her citizens to think independently, understand, and practise the scientific method in their daily lives.

Finally, one may reflect on the role of technology in India's future. India's ambition should be to continue developing technologies with the goal of establishing herself as a global superpower and a world leader, not necessarily in a military sense or even in an economic sense, but as an idea and example, representing the ambitions of all humanity and having its fount embedded in knowledge, science, and technology—all aiming to end human suffering. The investment in biotechnology, nanotechnology, robotics, etc. would be the necessary steps in moving India in that direction.

The idea of that India would be based on her true intrinsic values, namely her argumentative heterodoxy, her search for a fundamental understanding of truth and nature, technological progress tempered by ethical and environmental concerns, and, most of all, her own perception of the richness of her genetic plurality. The idea of India could resemble the ideal idea of humanity. We must strive never to forget that we are just a temporary clonal eruption of a tiny, fragile, young infantile species that almost went extinct twice. Nor should we belittle the fact that, despite its lowly origin, something bigger holds true for this altruistic, trusting, and tolerant species—more than E. coli or elephants. Perhaps, we already knew that when we decreed that '*Sarve bhadrani pashyantu, ma kaschid dukhah bhag bhabet*'.

REFERENCES

Anantharaman, T.S., B Mishra, and D.C. Schwartz (1997), 'Genomics via Optical Mapping II: Ordered Restriction Maps', *Journal of Computational Biology*, Vol. 4, pp. 91–118.

Ashton, C., B Mishra, and D.C. Schwartz (1999), 'Optical Mapping and its Potential for Large-Scale Sequencing Projects', *Trends in Biotechnology*, Vol. 17, pp. 297–302.

Batzoglou, S., D.B. Jaffe, K. Stanley, J. Butler, S. Gnerre, E. Mauceli, B. Berger, J.P. Mesirov, and E.S. Lander (2002), 'ARACHNE: A Whole-Genome Shotgun Assembler', *Genome Research*, Vol. 12, No. (1), pp. 177–89.

Cartwright, N. (1994), *Nature's Capacities and their Measurement*, Oxford: Oxford University Press.

Chakravarti, A. (1999), 'Population Genetics–making sense Out of Sequence', *Nat Genet*, Vol. 21, pp. 56–60.

Devlin, B. and K. Roeder (1999), 'Genomic Control for Association Studies', *Biometrics*, Vol. 55, pp. 997–1004.

Endicott, P., M. Metspalu, and T. Kivisild (2007), 'Genetic Evidence on Modern Human Dispersals in South Asia: Y Chromosome and Mitochondrial DNA Perspectives', *The Evolution and History of Human Populations in South Asia*, Dordrecht, The Netherlands: Springer, pp. 229–44.

Green, P. (1996), Phrap documentation, http://www.phrap.org/phredphrap/phrap.html.

Gusfield, D. (1997), *Algorithms on Strings, Trees and Sequences: Computer Science and Computational Biology*, Cambridge: Cambridge University Press.

Haines, J.L., M.A. Hauser, S. Schmidt, W.K. Scott, L.M. Olson, P. Gallins, K.L. Spencer, S.Y. Kwan, M. Noureddine, J.R. Gilbert, N. Schnetz-Boutaud, A. Agarwal, E.A. Postel, and M.A. Pericak-Vance (2005), 'Complement Factor H Variant Increases the Risk of Age-related Macular Degeneration', *Science*, Vol. 308, pp. 419–21.

Huang, X., and A. Madan (1999), 'CAP3: A DNA Sequence Assembly Program', *Genome Research*, Vol. 9, No. 9, pp. 868–77.

Iafrate, A.J., L. Feuk, M.N. Rivera, M.L. Listewnik, P.K. Donahoe, Y. Qi, S.W. Scherer, and C. Lee (2004), 'Detection of Large-scale Variation in the Human Genome', *Nat Genet*, Vol. 36, No. 949–52.

Ionita, I., R. Daruwala, and B. Mishra (2006), 'Mapping Tumor Suppressor Genes using Multipoint Statistics from Copy-Number Variation Data', *American Journal of Human Genetics*, Vol. 79, pp. 13–22.

Kececioglu, J., and E. Myers (1995), 'Combinatorial Algorithms for DNA Sequence Assembly', *Algorithmica*, Vol. 13, pp. 7–51.

Kleinberg, S. and B. Mishra (2009), 'Metamorphosis: The Coming Transformation of Translational Systems Biology', *Queue*, Vol. 7, No. 9, pp. 40–52.

———— (2009), 'The Temporal Logic of Causal Structures', in *Proceedings of the 25th Conference on Uncertainty in Artificial Intelligence (UAI)*, Montreal, Quebec, June.

———— (2010), 'The Temporal Logic of Token Causes', in *Proceedings of the 12th International Conference on the Principles of Knowledge Representation and Reasoning (KR)*, Toronto, Ontario, May.

Lander, E.S. (1996), 'The New Genomics: Global Views of Biology', *Science*, Vol. 274, pp. 536–9.

Lynch, M. (2010), 'Rate, Molecular Spectrum, and Consequences of Human Mutation', *Proc Natl Acad Sci. USA*, Vol. 107, pp. 961–78.

Martin, E.R., E.H. Lai, J.R. Gilbert, A.R. Rogala, A.J. Afshari, J. Riley, K.L. Finch, J.F. Stevens, K.J. Livak, B.D. Slotterbeck, S.H. Slifer, L.L. Warren, P.M. Conneally, D.E. Schmechel, I. Purvis, M.A. Pericak-Vance, A.D. Roses, and J.M. Vance (2000), 'SNPing Away at Complex Diseases: Analysis of Single-nucleotide Polymorphisms around APOE in Alzheimer Disease', *Am. J. Hum. Genet.*, Vol. 67, pp. 383–94.

Mitrofanova, A., and B Mishra (2009), 'On a Novel Coalescent Model for Genome-Wide Evolution of Copy Number Variations', *International Journal of Data Mining and Bioinformatics*, Vol. x, No. x.

Myers, E.W., G.G. Sutton, A.L. Delcher, I.M. Dew, D.P. Fasulo, M.J. Flanigan, S.A. Kravitz, C.M. Mobarry, K.H.J. Reinert, K.A. Remington, E.L. Anson,

R.A. Bolanos, H-H Chou, C.M. Jordan, A.L. Halpern, S. Lonardi, E.M. Beasley, R.C. Brandon, L. Chen, P.J. Dunn, Z. Lai, Y. Liang, D.R. Nusskern, M. Zhan, Q. Zhang, X. Zheng, G.M. Rubin, M.D. Adams, and J.C. Venter (2000), 'A Whole-Genome Assembly of Drosophila', *Science*, Vol. 287, No. 5461, pp. 2196–2204.

Narzisi, G., and B, Mishra (2010), 'SUTTA, Scoring-and-Unfolding Trimmed Tree Assembler I: Concepts, Constructs and Comparisons', Unpublished.

Pevzner, P.A., H. Tang, and M.S. Waterman (2001), 'An Eulerian Path Approach to DNA Fragment Assembly', *Proceedings of the National Academy of Sciences of the United States of America*, Vol. 98, No. 17, pp. 9748–53.

Pritchard, J.K., M. Stephens, and P. Donnelly (2000), 'Linkage Disequilibrium in Humans: Models and Data', *Genetics*, Vol. 155, pp. 945–59.

Reich, D., K. Thangaraj, N. Patterson, A.L. Price, and L. Singh (2009), 'Reconstructing Indian Population History', *Nature*, Vol. 461, pp. 489–94.

Samad, A.H., W-W Cai, X. Hu, B. Irvin, J. Jing, J. Reed, X. Meng, J. Huang, E. Huff, B. Porter, A. Shenkar, T.S. Anantharaman, B. Mishra, V. Clarke, E. Dimalanta, J. Edington, C. Hiort, R. Rabbah, J. Skiada, and D.C. Schwartz (1995), 'Mapping the Genome One Molecule at a Time—Optical Mapping', *Nature*, Vol. 378, pp. 516–17.

Schuster, S.C. (2008), 'Next-generation Sequencing Transforms Today's Biology', *Nature Methods*, pp. 16–18.

Sebat, J., B. Lakshmi, J. Troge, J. Alexander, J. Young, P.Lundin, S. Maner, H. Massa, M. Walker, M. Chi, N. Navin, R. Lucito, J. Healy, J. Hicks, K. Ye, A. Reiner, T.C. Gilliam, B. Trask, N. Patterson, A. Zetterberg, and M. Wigler (2004), 'Large-scale Copy Number Polymorphism in the Human Genome', *Science*, Vol. 305, pp. 525–8.

Semple, C.A.M. (2007), 'Bioinformatics for Geneticists', *Assembling a View of the Human Genome*, pp. 59–84, Wiley.

Shringarpure, S. and E.P. Xing (2009), 'mStruct: Inference of Population Structure in Light of both Genetic Admixing and Allele Mutations', *Genetics*, Vol. 182, pp. 575–93.

Sommer, D., A. Delcher, S. Salzberg, and M. Pop (2007), 'Minimus: A Fast, Lightweight Genome Assembler', *BMC Bioinformatics*, Vol. 8, No. 1, p. 64

Suppes, P. (1970), *A Probabilistic Theory of Causality*, Amsterdam: North-Holland Publsihing Co.

Sutton, G.G., O. White, M.D. Adams, and A.R. Kerlavage (1995), 'TIGR Assembler: A New Tool for Assembling Large Shotgun Sequencing Projects', *Genome Science and Technology*, Vol. 1, No. 1, pp. 9–19.

West, J., J. Healy, M. Wigler, W. Casey, and B. Mishra (2006), 'Validation of S. pombe Sequence Assembly by Micro-array Hybridization', *Journal of Computational Biology*, Vol. 13, pp. 1–20.

Zerbino, D.R., and E. Birney (2008), 'Velvet: Algorithms for de novo Short Read Assembly using de Bruijn graphs', *Genome Research*, Vol. 18, No. 5, pp. 821–9.

JAY GIRI

19 System-wide Computerization of India's Grid Operations

Electricity is invisible, but it is everywhere. Its energy is harnessed and brought to people around the world—at home and at work, throughout their daily lives. Many take it for granted: they just flip a switch or plug into an outlet, and electricity works for them, instantaneously.

In 1881, Edison created the first electric power company to generate and supply power to customers. Power was transmitted as direct current (DC). This was essentially what we would today call a 'micro-grid'—a small, self-contained system of generation, transmission, and consumption. By the 1930s, power transmission evolved to alternating current (AC) interconnected systems. By the 1950s, interconnection pools were created across a larger geographical footprint in order to economically share generation capacity.

In 2000, according to the US National Academy of Engineers (NAE), 'Electrification' was voted as the 'most significant engineering achievement of the last century' followed by automobiles, airplanes, and the internet which was ranked at thirteenth place. Though hydro, fossil fuels, and nuclear energy form the primary source now, there is a distinct trend towards moving to green technologies such as solar, wind and bio mass in the future.

THE ELECTRICITY SUPPLY CHAIN

Electricity has a supply chain of its own, and has an infrastructure that covers vast geographical areas. The transmission towers and overhead distribution lines carry the energy over long distances. The generators which are generally remote from the point of usage are now being supplemented by newer forms of energy sources such as wind, solar fuel cells, and bio mass which are typically closer to the actual usage points. Still many may not realize the vast complexity of this engineering infrastructure that transfer energy from the source to the end-use. This electricity supply infrastructure called the 'power grid' is very complex and will become even more complex with the addition of a multitude of elements of communication, sensors, etc., which create a 'smarter' grid.

The supply chain begins at remote generating plants, where electricity is produced. Power is transmitted at high voltages via long lines, and is distributed to homes and industries via shorter lines at lower voltages. This picture is changing with renewable energy resources (RES) being deployed across the grid. At the distribution level there may be many distributed generation resources including RESs. The distribution level is also being impacted by customer-initiated demand response as well as impacts of future growth in plug-in hybrid and electric vehicles.

When demand for electricity (or 'load') changes, output of generation has to react almost immediately. If there is more demand, there has to be more generation, and when demand drops, generation must be reduced as well. Electricity follows the 'path of least resistance', so it cannot be intentionally routed along a specific transmission path. In addition, to routine changes in demand, events such as lightning strikes, short circuits, equipment failure, accidents, or other events sometimes disrupt the supply-demand balance and configuration of the transmission system.

Whatever the cause, if demand and supply are not matched, the frequency of electricity deviates from its normal value (50 or 60 cycles per second or Hz). Generating plants and electrical equipment are damaged when frequency is not close to normal for extended periods of time; typically damage occurs when frequency deviations beyond 0.2 Hz are sustained for more than 5 minutes. This damage could cost millions of dollars to repair and electricity supply could be lost for extended periods due to long repair and restoration times. Equipment can be protected during frequency deviations by curtailing the amount of electricity in the line or by disconnecting generation. Hence, maintaining a constant frequency in a certain range around 50 Hz or 60 Hz, as the case may be, is extremely important to ensure system integrity. In the Eastern interconnection of North America, the goal is to keep frequency within plus or minus 0.05Hz. This simple operational objective requires a vast infrastructure of protection and control equipment across the entire grid and advanced computer automation monitoring and control tools.

THE EMERGENCE OF CONTROL CENTRES

Keeping the grid at close to normal frequency, without causing any un-expected disconnections of load or generation, is known as maintaining electrical integrity, or 'normal synchronous operation.' The first central-ized control centres designed to maintain the integrity of the grid were implemented in the 1950s.

These control centres used a software and hardware system called an Energy Management System (EMS). Based on a centralized command and control paradigm, the EMS has evolved over the past six decades into much larger and more complex systems through computer automation. The newer systems have the same, original simple mission as the original system: 'Keep power available at all times.'

The figure below shows the suite of EMS functions that comprise a modern control centre.

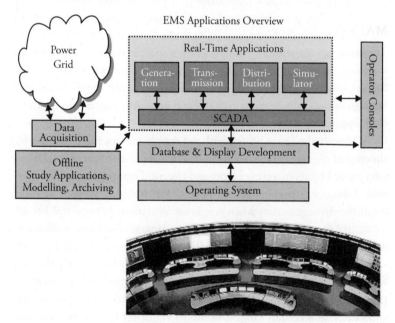

FIGURE 19.1   Energy Management System

REAL-TIME MONITORING OF GRID CONDITIONS

The first EMS application placed in control centres was known as Supervisory Control and Data Acquisition (SCADA). The objective of SCADA was to allow the operator to visually monitor grid conditions from a central location and to manually take action if adverse conditions were detected. The initial SCADA systems were hard-wired analogue systems placed in control centres across the country. They continually monitored the grid just like an electro-cardiogram monitors the heartbeat of the human body. Being hard-wired, they could not be changed without physical work, as opposed to modern technology in digital systems, which can be modified easily. At the SCADA systems, continual measurements from key locations of the grid were brought into the control centre to allow the operator to monitor grid conditions and recognize overload situations. The control centre operator could also remotely switch selected transmission components in or out of service to alleviate overloads or other adverse grid conditions. The components that could be switched included voltage support equipment, particular sections of a line, or, in the worst case, customer load.

MAINTAINING SYSTEM FREQUENCY

The next function implemented at control centres was the Load Frequency Control (LFC). The primary objective of LFC was to ensure that as load changed, system frequency would be automatically maintained close to normal by changing the generation accordingly. In the early implementations, the control centre operator visually monitored the system frequency measurement and periodically sent incremental change signals to generators via analogue wired connections or by phone calls placed to generating plant operators, to keep generation close to load. Later, as analogue systems transitioned to digital, LFC became the first 'smart grid' automation application that was implemented to 'transparently' assist the control centre operator in the mission to 'keep power available at all times'.

SHARING ELECTRICITY WITH NEIGHBOURS

The next progression was interconnecting one power utility with neighbouring utilities to allow power sharing when needed. The overall grid, therefore, became larger and more complex. The interconnections also allowed for purchase and sale of electrical energy, since some electric power companies had excess generation or could produce generation more cheaply. However, now the control centre operators had an additional responsibility to also ensure that the flows across the lines connecting the utilities—called 'tie-lines'—were maintained close to what was stipulated in purchase/sale agreements.

THE BIG BOOST TO ELECTRICITY AUTOMATION

The big northeastern US blackout of 1965 was in some sense a watershed event for the electric power industry. It alerted the industry to the concept of reliability or secure operation of the grid. Millions of dollars of lost business revenue have been attributed to this blackout as well as consumer dissatisfaction. Many postmortem analysis reports were prepared with recommendations to ensure that an event of this scale and magnitude never happened again. Electric power companies, governments, and universities were given a mandate to provide improved capabilities for grid operations. New research institutes were spawned to address this specific objective.

Around this time, digital computers were just becoming widespread in terms of speed and reliability. When mainframe digital computers became affordable, automation began to play a pivotal role in creating the modern EMS.

Hard-wired analogue EMS capabilities were quickly replaced by digital computers that received real-time measurements from the field every 4 to 10 seconds and displayed them on monitors. These digital computers performed the same functions as the earlier analogue systems, but were much faster, more reliable, and more predictable. Digital systems also facilitated fast, quick modifications via 'easy' software adjustments. The communication system was primarily power line carrier.

All these provided a greater impetus for engineering expertise in the power system industry to develop better computer applications and capabilities. This was also the beginning of the impact of control theory in the power system field. Research funding became readily available and the top electrical engineering graduates were attracted to power engineering. The ensuing research resulted in many new automation applications being built around the digital computer.

THE DIGITAL REVOLUTION OF CONTROL CENTRES

Today's advanced EMS functions were first developed on digital computers in the 1970s. Applications were designed for use in the control centre computers to assist the operator. Automatic alarming capabilities were quickly developed to alert operators to adverse system conditions only when they warranted attention and action. Furthermore, the operator did not have to manually change the multiple generation outputs to maintain frequency; a computer application did that automatically and sent out signals for generation changes every 4 to 10 seconds. Computer applications were also developed to automatically monitor tie-line flows and modify generation patterns intelligently to ensure that they were close to the contractual agreements for that time of the day.

MINIMIZING ELECTRICITY PRODUCTION COSTS IN REAL-TIME

The next step of automation was the development of an application to optimally dispatch the generators' electrical output levels, so that the total cost of all generation was minimized. For this, an application called economic load dispatch (ELD) was developed that was used in conjunction with LFC to satisfy multiple objectives simultaneously: maintain normal frequency, maintain tie-line flows to contractual values, and load generators to minimize the total generation cost.

A major benefit of these digital computer applications was in their easy redeployment and reconfiguration in other new power system grid control centres. For example, once the core applications software was written, they could easily be re-dimensioned and re-compiled for a new control centre at another utility.

SIMULATING THE ELECTRICAL NETWORK OF THE GRID

In 1968, Glenn W. Stagg and Ahmed H. El-Abiad's landmark book *Computer Methods in Power System Analysis* became the standard reference for many in the power industry to develop software applications on the computer. Prior to this, engineers solved the problem on paper or the network analyzer which was essentially an analogue device to simulate the grid of small size. In these approaches it was difficult to incorporate changes and manipulate data to study alternate, diverse system conditions that occur every hour of the day, week, month, and year. The digital computer made solving this problem much easier. Computer simulation programs were developed to calculate flows on the electrical network for different generation and load patterns. These were called Load Flow or Power Flow programs and are still actively used today.

REAL-TIME MONITORING OF NETWORK GRID CONDITIONS

Once the software for computing power system conditions for different generation and load situations matured, the next step was to implement it in a control centre in real-time. Supervisory Control and Data Acquisition measurements, generally the flows in the transmission lines that were available at the control centre, were then used to calculate the current network conditions and displayed to the operator in a more reliable and comprehensive manner. It is important to note that SCADA measurements were typically not available at all network locations.

A new application known as the State Estimator (SE) was developed using concepts from estimation theory. It used SCADA measurements with a network model to calculate the 'best guess' of system conditions across the entire network especially for network, nodes not measured by SCADA. This allowed the operator to view what was happening across the grid. The operator was alerted to overloads and adverse conditions in a more reliable and timely manner. State Estimator is typically run every minute.

WHAT-IF STUDIES

The next control centre application was called the Contingency Analysis (CA) software. Contingency Analysis used the SE solution to do a series of 'what-if' studies. Contingencies were loss of key grid components such as a transmission line, transformer, generator, or load. A list of predefined contingencies was processed to assess what overloads or problems might result if a contingency were to occur. In today's control centre this application is one of the most important one to an operator. Typically, an operator has a whole monitor screen dedicated to displaying these results. It is like a radar screen looking into the immediate future which shows what might happen if a sudden unexpected event were to occur. Contingency Analysis is typically run after every other SE run.

OPTIMIZATION OF GRID OPERATING CONDITIONS

The next step was to develop other advanced network analysis applications. They all use the SE solution as the starting point. These advanced functions include optimization techniques to minimize transmission system losses, and corrective and preventive control recommendations to alleviate the impacts of potential harmful contingencies. These applications employed advanced algorithms such as linear programming, and and mixed integer programming on very large-scale matrix systems. Without the help of powerful digital computers, these applications would not have been possible. The reliable and efficient operation of a modern grid covering a large area, therefore, depends on fast computers and reliable communication.

DYNAMICS OF THE GRID

More recently, computer solutions have been developed to simulate the dynamics of the grid when a fault or an unplanned event occurs. These are called stability applications. They offer mathematical challenges in terms of computation since they involve the iterative solution of a large number of nonlinear differential equations (the generator dynamic models) with the solution of a large number of nonlinear algebraic equations (the electrical network). With the older digital computers these simulations used to take hours to complete. With today's advances in computer technology and computational speeds, these simulations can be done quickly in real time. Stability applications have thus become an additional tool to the control centre operator to provide alerts to potential or imminent adverse situations caused by the dynamic behaviour of the grid. The ultimate goal is to provide reliable electric power to the customer.

ELECTRICITY MARKETS

Over the past decade, electricity market systems have been introduced into the control centre. The objective is to allow participants to bid generation ahead of time so that the market operator can select and decide on the most cost-effective generation portfolio in order to supply the projected system load. These market systems involve complex computer applications for supplying bids, accepting bids, ancillary services, market clearing, and final market settlements. Trading in power, therefore, has become an accepted fact all over the world; electricity is being treated like just another commodity.

TODAY'S CONTROL CENTRE

The EMS has evolved into a vast, diverse conglomeration of monitoring devices, advanced computers, and communications technology that measures power system field conditions every few seconds and automatically issues controls, as needed. Control centres are the vital 'nerve centres' of the utility. Measurements are received from devices across the wide geographical area of the grid; they are analysed and correlated to recommend protective or corrective actions to maintain the electrical integrity of the interconnected grid.

An AREVA EMS in Indiana in the United States today runs SE for over 30,000 buses every 90 seconds and processes over 7000 contingencies every three minutes. This indicates the power of computer automation that benefits the country and the consumer.

In the 1990s one could only handle around 5000 buses and a few hundred contingencies in real-time.

AUTOMATION OF THE INDIAN POWER GRID

When independence was achieved in 1947, the Indian power system consisted of around 1400 megawatts (MW) of generation capacity. Today the power system has an installed generation capacity of over 150 gigawatts (GW) (where 1 GW=1000 MW) and is growing at a fast pace. The system serves a peak load demand of around 98 GW.

The Power Grid Corporation of India Ltd. (PGCIL), which oversees operation of the national grid, is one of the premier power transmission utilities in the world. It is a also a member of the elite Very Large Power Grid Operators (VLPGO) group which has a dozen members worldwide. Membership to this group is limited to utilities which have at least 50 GW of generation capacity. Most members, like India, have over 100 GW capacity.

The Indian power system grid is divided into five electrical regions: Northern, Eastern, Western, Southern, and Northeastern. The Eastern, Western, Northern, and Northeastern regions operate as a synchronous grid with 90 GW of generation capacity, and are spread over about

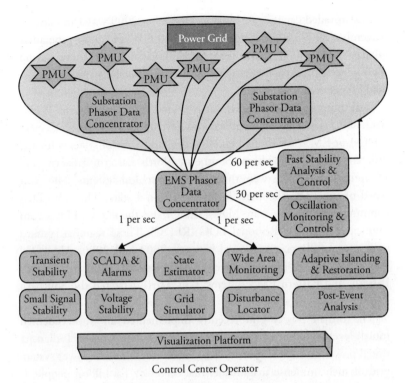

FIGURE 19.2 Control Centre Application

2.6 million sq. km. The Southern region, with 37 GW of generation capacity, is a separate independent synchronous electrical grid. By 2012, it is estimated that peak demand in all of India will be about 157 GW, and will be met by a fully interconnected, nationwide synchronous grid. To meet this demand, an installed capacity of about 210 GW is necessary. Excess generation capacity is necessary in order to provide spare capacity to allow generators to be taken off line for routine annual maintenance or for other unforeseen reasons. This peak demand is expected to increase further, to over 500 GW, by 2027, which would require total installed capacity of about 700 GW. Various large-capacity power plant clusters of about 4,000 MW each, called the Ultra Mega Power Projects (UMPP) will be set up in the next four to five years. Most of the additional generation capacity will be confined to a few areas. Therefore, large amounts of power will need to be transmitted across long distances.

The installed capacity in India in December 2009 was 156 GW. In November 2009 the peak demand was 110 GW and peak generation capacity was 96 GW. Since peak demand was not met, there was no spare generation capacity margin. The average availability index was less than 70 per cent.

Beginning in 1993, PGCIL was provided with funds by the World Bank and Asian Development Bank to develop Load Dispatch Centres (LDCs) or EMSs for unified coordination and control systems for the different regions: Northern, Southern, North Eastern, Eastern, and Western. These LDCs were three-level hierarchical systems. They consisted of sub-LDCs at many locations within a state. The sub-LDCs communicated with a State LDC (SLDC) and the many SLDCs communicated with the Regional LDC (RLDC). These regional systems were successfully commissioned between 2002 and 2006. ALSTOM T&D was responsible for delivering the National, Northern, North-Eastern, and Eastern EMS systems. GE-Harris delivered the Southern EMS.

The Indian power grid recently implemented an unprecedented fourth-level National LDC that covers the entire expanse of Indian national power grid. This four-level EMS for a nationwide power system grid of such immense magnitude, that serves over a billion people, is considered the first of its kind in the world. Today the Indian EMS systems consist of around 100 computers communicating with other computers in a hierarchical manner, gathering data from various diverse locations of the grid every few seconds to assess current grid status and vulnerability to a potential blackout.

A senior official of PGCIL was quoted in a 2004 newspaper article as saying that the deployment of the northern regional load dispatch centre (NRLDC) prevented a blackout that would otherwise have cost millions of rupees—quite an accolade for the success of power grid automation in India.

CONTROL CENTRES OF THE FUTURE

Automation of the grid will evolve toward more decentralized, intelligent, and localized control. Evolution toward a self-healing power system grid is imminent. This self-healing system will work as the human body does when it quickly identifies an intrusion and deals with

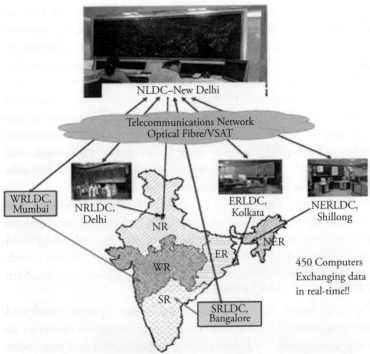

National LDC India—Managing Electricity Supply—For over 1 billion People

FIGURE 19.3   National Load Dispatch Centre

it locally by coagulating blood at wounds or engulfing foreign pathogens to preserve the integrity of the rest of the body.

The future will likely see more generation sources closer to the load centres. Residential subdivisions could have their own local fuel cell supplying power to 20 or 30 households; this will result in creation of local micro-grids that will attempt to optimize benefits for that local area. This would reduce the dependence on the transmission grid to transfer power from remote locations to populated load centres. As renewable energy sources costs become more competitive, there will be a growth in generation sources such as wind power, solar cells, and, possibly, geo-thermal, tidal, and ocean power. Customers will be able to monitor the current price of electricity and decide whether to turn on the dishwasher or not using the 'smart metering' scheme. This will tend to flatten the utility's load demand profile and make generation dispatch more predictable.

In addition to more local generation, use of renewable sources, and increased customer control, new types of measurements will be deployed aggressively worldwide. Already, globally synchronized measurements (in the sub-second range) are being used in control centres to facilitate early faster detection of problems and to make it easier to assess conditions across the expanse of the grid.

New control centre applications will be developed to use this new type of synchronized measurement technology to further improve the ability to maintain the integrity of the power system. These applications will also be able to identify contingencies, unplanned events, and stability problems at a much faster rate, at the sub-second level.

There is need for continual innovation of control centre and substation applications and tools to ensure a high degree of grid reliability. This involves creative innovation in automation and technology across the entire electricity supply chain.

CURRENT CHALLENGES

Electricity supply faces many challenges today. Existing power grids are aging across the globe—on average, they are almost fifty years old. Hence, equipment and devices tend to fail more often than before. Replacing this aging equipment with modern technology will cost trillions of dollars. In addition, it is estimated that 50 per cent of electric utility staff in North America are eligible to retire in the next five to ten years. Another issue is the recent industry mandate to increase deployment of 'green' renewable generation sources, which will produce less predictable, variable generation outputs that cannot be controlled. Hence, intense research is going on to develop improved energy storage capabilities such as batteries and flywheels. All these issues create new challenges for the EMS automation tools and accelerate the need for continued advancements in automation and control technology.

The widespread blackout of August 2003 in North America was another resounding reminder of the vulnerability of the power grid. This event identified 'situational awareness' as a key priority to improve upon. It subsequently focused the industry once again back on enhancing reliability of the grid infrastructure and its component protective mechanisms such as relaying equipment.

SMART GRID INITIATIVES

In 2009, 'Smart Grid' became the hot, new buzzword in the worldwide electric utility industry as governments around the world placed a higher priority on ensuring that the grid is reinforced to make it more reliable, resilient and secure to external threats. There are almost as many definitions of smart grid as there are entities interested in defining it. A precise definition of the Smart Grid remains elusive. Nonetheless, there are three common focus themes—efficiency, technology, and reliability. Smart Grid initiatives are focused on improving grid efficiency, deploying technology to facilitate customer involvement and decision-making, and enhancing overall grid reliability.

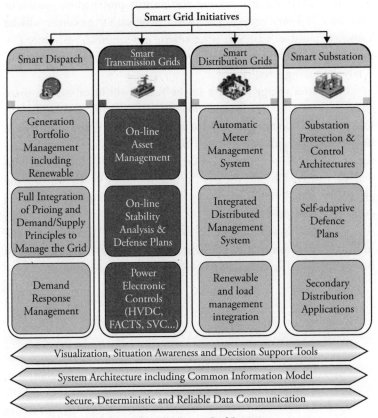

FIGURE 19.4   Smart Grid Initiative

Smart Grid initiatives include deployment of smart meters in residences as well as advanced software and measurement technologies that monitor and control the grid. Home area networks will be implemented along with 'smart' appliances and 'smart' meters to optimize a residence's electricity consumption by utilizing energy when it is most economical. Improving computer automation and control of the grid—making the grid smarter—is another key priority that provides exciting opportunities for innovation and creativity.

Smart Grid initiatives are being pursued at various levels of the electricity grid. The figure below shows ongoing activities related to making smarter decisions for dispatching generation, making the transmission and distribution grids smarter, and creating smarter substations.

In July 2001, *Wired* magazine, fortuitously proposed this vision of the grid: '... Every node in the power network of the future will be awake, responsive, adaptive, price-smart, eco-sensitive, real-time, flexible, humming—and interconnected with everything else.' This vision is now becoming a reality.

The smarter energy network of the future will incorporate a diversified pool of resources located closer to the consumer, pumping out low- or zero-emissions power in backyards, driveways, downscaled local power stations, and even in automobiles, while giving electricity users the option to become energy vendors. The front end of this new system will be managed by third-party 'virtual utilities', which will bundle electricity, gas, internet access, broadband entertainment, and other customized energy services.

This vision is reminiscent of Edison's original ambition for the industry, which was not to sell light bulbs, but to create a network of technologies and services that reliably provided illumination.

PRAVIN VARAIYA AND
ALEX A. KURZHANSKIY*

20 Active Traffic Management

Active Traffic Management (ATM) is an approach to dynamic management of vehicular traffic, based on measurement of prevailing traffic conditions, in order to maximize the efficiency of a road network. It is a continuous process of (a) obtaining and analysing traffic measurement data; (b) operations planning—simulating various scenarios and control strategies; (c) implementing the most promising control strategies in the field; and (d) maintaining a real-time decision support system that filters current traffic measurements to predict the traffic state in the near future, and to suggest the best available control strategy for the predicted situation. Active Traffic Management relies on a fast and trusted traffic simulator for the rapid quantitative assessment of a large number of control strategies for the road network under various scenarios, in a matter of minutes.

The essay describes three key components of an ATM system: the simulation model and its use for evaluating performance under various scenarios and control strategies; the database system used to calibrate the simulation model; and the traffic sensor system needed to collect traffic measurements that are input to the database.

An Active Traffic Management system enables dynamic management of vehicular traffic, based on measurements of prevailing traffic conditions.

* Research supported by National Science Foundation Award CMMI-0941326 and California Department of Transportation.

It combines automated control systems with strategic human intervention to manage traffic in order to maximize the efficiency of road networks. This essay presents a particular structure of ATM and focuses on its key components. The essay reflects the authors' engagement in the Tools for Operations Planning (TOPL) project since 2006;[†] the California Freeway Performance Measurement System (PeMS) project since 2001;[‡] and the development of a new generation of wireless vehicle sensing systems at Sensys Networks, Inc. since 2005.[§]

Active Traffic Management is a feedback process comprising (a) continuous traffic measurement and measurement data analysis, without which attempts to manage a road network are blind; (b) operations planning, which includes evaluating the road network performance under various scenarios, such as demand increase, lane closures, special events, etc., developing control strategies that improve performance, and testing these strategies in terms of their cost and the benefits they bring under these scenarios; (c) implementing the most effective of these control strategies by installing necessary hardware and software in the field; and (d) running the decision support system in real time, which includes filtering the measurement data, providing short-term prediction of the traffic state, and selecting the best available control strategy for the next one or two hours.

The process relies on a two-way communication network that feeds real-time measurements from the road network's traffic surveillance system to the traffic control centre database and transfers commands generated by the control software (and human operators) to the control actuators in the field.

The procedures in the ATM workflow process rely on an underlying macroscopic model of traffic. That model and how it is built from data are described in next section. Model construction is facilitated by the Aurora Road Networks Modeller (RNM),[¶] an open-source tool set for modelling road networks that include freeways and arterials with signalized intersections. The model simulator and its use for predicting the traffic system's performance of various control strategies under different scenarios is described in section 'Operations Planning'.

[†] http://path.berkeley.edu/topl
[‡] http://pems.eecs.berkeley.edu
[§] http://www.sensysnetworks.com
[¶] http://code.google.com/p/aurorarnm

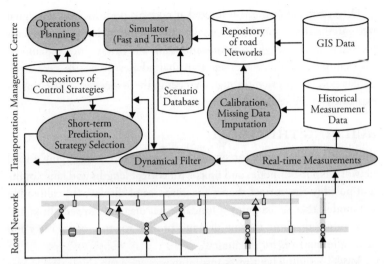

FIGURE 20.1   ATM Workflow Diagram

Active Traffic Management relies on a database of historical and real-time data. The California freeway performance measurement system or PeMS provides a database that stores detector data and allows the user to conduct a wide range of performance analyses. A brief description of PeMS is provided in the section 'Database'. Ultimately, traffic measurements are made by vehicle detectors. A new generation wireless vehicle detection system offers a uniform, flexible platform for traffic measurement. This system is described in the section 'Measurement'.

MODEL

Aurora RNM is based on the macroscopic Cell Transmission Model (Daganzo 1994, 1995). In Aurora, the road network consists of directed links and nodes. Links represent stretches of roads connected by nodes or junctions.

A link is specified by its length and number of lanes. Behaviour of traffic on the link is characterized by its fundamental diagram parameterized by its capacity, free flow speed and congestion wave speed (or, equivalently, the jam density). In the CTM model the state of the road network at any time is given by the vehicle density in each link.

Demand is expressed by vehicles entering the network through source links and departing through sink links. Routing of vehicles through the network is governed by split ratios associated with nodes.

Direct control of traffic is located at nodes: a node located at a signalized intersection controls the signal phase; a ramp metering controller is located at the node where an on-ramp joins a highway. Indirect control, for example, a variable message sign that advises drivers to take a particular exit, is expressed through changes in the associated split-ratios, as explained in the section 'Scenario Design'.

BUILDING THE MODEL

Building a model ready for simulation consists in (a) specifying a road network as a list of nodes and links with correct lengths and lane counts, and possibly the correct shapes for purposes of display; (b) calibrating the model, that is, assigning a fundamental diagrams to each link; and (c) defining the time-varying demand profiles for the source links and split ratio matrices for the nodes.

Model-building is a time-consuming process, as no single data source provides the information necessary for all three tasks.

The network is typically specified using Geographic Information System (GIS) data. Figure 20.2 shows an example of a nine-node urban network constructed in this way. The application allows the network builder to select nodes on the map and indicate which pairs of nodes are connected by links. The application automatically constructs the network graph, including link length, as well as link shapes for visualization.

Measurement data from freeway detectors archived in systems such as PeMS or PORTAL** allow the use of Aurora statistical procedures to estimate the parameters of the fundamental diagrams for the freeway links. The full description of the procedures with applications, is found in Dervisoglu et al. (2008). Calibrated models of several California freeways are available.

The most difficult part of calibrating urban streets or arterials is to estimate their capacities. The capacity of an arterial link is determined from available measurements or assigned by guess, the free flow speed can be set to the speed limit assigned on that street, and the jam density can be set as the number of vehicles this link can store divided by the link length.

Lastly, it remains to define the demand profiles for the sources and split-ratio matrices for the nodes. For highways, database systems like

** http://portal.its.pdx.edu

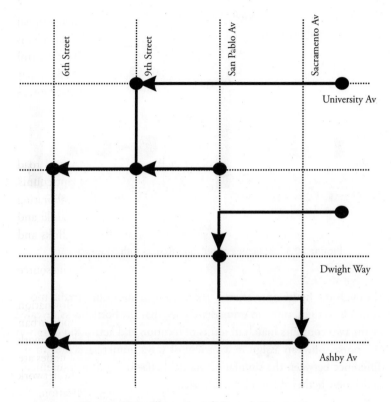

FIGURE 20.2   Illustration of Network Construction

PeMS and PORTAL may provide on-ramp flow data from which to construct the demand profiles. Split ratios could be computed from measurements of mainline and off-ramp flows. In practice, however, on- and off-ramp flows may not be available, as is today the case for several California highways. The demands and split ratios must then be imputed so that when used in the model, the model produces mainline flows that match the measurements (see Muralidharan Horowitz 2009). Sources of demand and split ratio data for arterials vary from city to city.

Once the model is built one or several base case scenarios can be run to check whether simulation results match with measurement, see Figure 20.3. The measured speed contour for the 24 hours of 19 February 2009 and a 21-mile section of I-80 East (from postmile 10 to postmile 31) is placed next to the speed contour obtained from the calibrated model.

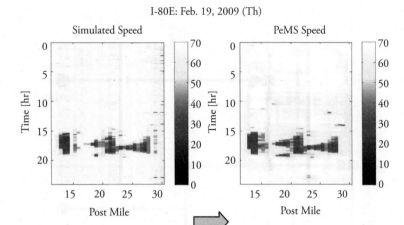

FIGURE 20.3   Matching Simulation Results with Measurement

Although the figure only offers a visual comparison, since traffic moves from left to right, one can immediately see that the bottlenecks revealed by the two contours match in terms of location and activation duration. Of course, one can assign in a variety of ways numerical scores to the difference between the simulation model behaviour and measurements to decide whether the model is reliable.

Simulator

Central to the ATM workflow is the 'fast and trusted simulator'. The Aurora macroscopic simulator is fast: it simulates several 24-hour-long scenarios in a few minutes. It is trusted because it is founded on a sound theory of traffic flow; it is parsimonious, only including parameters that can be estimated; and it is tested for reliability (Gomes et al. 2008).

The simulator has three modes of operation. In the operations planning mode, many simulations are run to model scenarios and test potential control strategies for improving road network performance. Scenarios incorporate known past events such as a festival or an accident, or future events considered plausible on the basis of statistical learning techniques that combine historical data with the current estimate of the state of the system (for example, high likelihood of an accident occurring at a specific location, conditional on the current traffic state and weather conditions [Kwon et al. 2006]). The configurations for the implemented control strategies are stored in the repository, readily accessed by the real time decision support system.

The second mode of operation is the dynamical filter: the simulation, with some uncertainty in system parameters and inputs, runs in real time as the noisy measurements arrive from the traffic sensors. By filtering the measurement data through the simulation, the traffic state is estimated and fed back into the traffic responsive control algorithms (Kurzhanskiy 2009).

The third mode of operation is the short-term prediction and strategy selection: with the initial conditions coming from the filtered real-time measurements and predicted with some uncertainty in short-term future inputs, the simulator runs a number of plausible near-term scenarios with available control strategies and calculates the resulting congestion and potentially serious stresses on the road network. The strategy promising the greatest benefits is deployed by sending the corresponding commands to the actuators in the field. Only the operations planning mode is described in some detail. A highway example is then presented to illustrate how all three modes are used together.

OPERATIONS PLANNING

The objective of the operations planning is to develop traffic control strategies that improve road network performance. Historical data may pinpoint weaknesses in road network operations, for example, by locating bottlenecks and accident hot spots. With a reliable simulation model, weaknesses are revealed in more detail since a variety of scenarios can be considered. Operational strategies can be designed and simulated under these scenarios to determine which strategy is well suited to each scenario.

The devised strategies may temporarily expand capacity at the bottleneck (for example, by permitting traffic in a shoulder lane that is otherwise restricted to emergency vehicles, or techniques of demand management that focus on reducing the excess demand during peak hours (for example, by increasing toll charges); incident management, which targets resources to reduce incident clearance times at 'hot spots'; providing traveller information, so travellers may plan trips to ensure on-time arrival; and direct traffic flow control through ramp metering at highway on-ramps and signal timing plans at signalized intersections. An operations planning needs quick quantitative assessment of the performance benefits that can be gained from these strategies, so that, in conjunction with a separate estimate of their deployment costs, promising strategies may be selected.

General link performance measures are: Traffic speed, measured in miles per hour (mph); Travel Time, measured in hours for each start time; Vehicle Miles Travelled (VMT), a measure of the 'output' of the link in a particular time period; Vehicle Hours Travelled (VHT), a measure of the 'input' to the link in a particular time period; Delay, measured in vehicle-hours, indicating the additional time spent driving below some reference speed; and Productivity Loss, in lane-mile-hours (lmh)—the degree of under-utilization of the link due to congestion. From the travel time, VMT, VHT, delay and productivity loss for each individual link, one can compute the same quantities for any specified route in the network.

Arterial links whose end nodes are signalized intersections have additional performance measures: delay per cycle, the number of vehicle-hours spent waiting at the signal; queue size, the number of vehicles in the link; phase utilization, the per cent of the green phase time used during cycle; cycle failure, the per cent of vehicles waiting for more than one red light; volume to capacity ratio, which characterizes the utilization of the available capacity; progression quality, the per cent of vehicles arriving during the green phase; and level of service, a performance measure favoured by the Highway Capacity Manual. Knowing these performance measures for each incoming link of an intersection, one can assess the overall efficiency of the intersection, and, indeed, for a network of intersections.

Scenario Design

To evaluate road network performance under different scenarios characterized by incidents, lane closures, special events, or demand fluctuations, Aurora provides 'switches' in the macroscopic model parameters (fundamental diagrams at links and split-ratio matrices at nodes) or inputs (demands at source links). The switches can be set at specified times.

Switches in fundamental diagrams can model incidents and lane closures. For example, suppose the original fundamental diagram of some link has capacity of 4000 vehicles per hour (VPH), and an accident blocking half of the lanes occurs at 10 am and lasts until 10.30 am at which time the road is cleared. To model this accident one sets two switches in the fundamental diagram—2000 representing the capacity drop at 10.00 am, and 4000 representing the return to normal operation thirty minutes later. Evaluating the impact of faster reaction times (how much better would the system perform if the accident were cleared in twenty minutes instead of thirty?) can help allocate resources for incident management. Special events and the impact of providing traveller information are modelled by switches in the split-ratio matrices at given nodes.

In Aurora these switches in parameters and inputs are implemented as events that can be generated by the user and triggered at user-specified times during the simulation. The impact of each scenario can be quickly assessed, as the simulator computes the general performance measures for links and routes.

Traffic Control

Aurora provides a facility to model three types of direct traffic control, as indicated in Figure 20.4. The facility can be used to design sophisticated control strategies. The effectiveness of these strategies is evaluated by simulating them in various scenarios.

- Local controller is assigned to a particular input link of a node and controls only the flow coming from that link. An example is a ramp meter shown in Figure 20.4a. Here, the node has two input links, uncontrolled highway link 1 and controlled on-ramp 2.
- Node controller is assigned to a node and controls the flows coming from all the input links of that node. An example is a signalized intersection shown in Figure 20.4b. Here, only two non-conflicting input flows (1 and 5, 2 and 6, 3 and 7, or 4 and 8) are allowed at any one time, while the others are blocked. The individual input flows are still controlled each by its own local controller, but the local controllers are synchronized by the centralized node control.
- Complex controller operates on multiple local node, or even other complex controllers coordinating their action toward some common objective. An example is a coordinated ramp metering system shown in Figure 20.4c. This is a highway with two identified bottlenecks, which divide the highway into zone 1 and zone 2, each ending at the corresponding bottleneck. Bottlenecks are expected to move throughout the day. Zone controllers are responsible for coordinating local ramp meters at the on-ramps within their respective zones, whereas the main

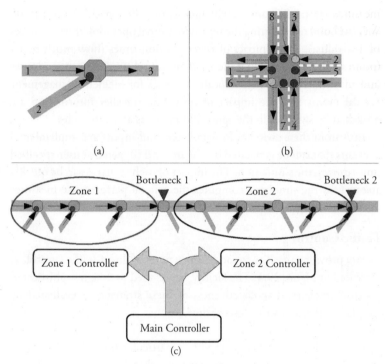

FIGURE 20.4   Controller Hierarchy

Notes: (a) local controller (ramp metre); (b) node controller (signalized intersection); (c) complex controller (coordinated ramp metering)

controller keeps track of the bottleneck locations and zone configuration. Main and zone controllers are both complex controllers.

Traffic responsive Urban Control (TUC) is an example of a closed-loop complex controller that coordinates multiple node controllers operating on signalized arterial intersections (Diakaki et al. 2000). Users can design and implement their own control strategies, but Aurora also provides several pre-designed classes of controllers. For ramp metering there are time of day, ALINEA and a coordinated version of ALINEA, known as HERO (Papageorgiou et al. 1991; Papamichail et al. 2010). For intersection signal control there are fixed-time and several traffic-responsive controllers.

Illustration

In this section we briefly consider a plausible future scenario that may lead to poor performance, and consider control strategies as counter-measures. The main case is represented by a model of highway I-210 West in Los Angeles using measurements for 25 July 2009, for 25 miles of I-210 from Baseline Road (postmile 52) to junction with I-710 (postmile 27). The scenario is as follows. Current time is taken as 6 am and measurements up to that time are available. Demand is forecast for the next two hours, until 8 am. This forecast is uncertain, with a ±5 per cent stochastic variation around the mean. The result is a stochastic simulation. Aurora can carry out stochastic simulations, but it also gives a much more revealing computation that provides an upper and lower bound of the evolution of the state (link densities) of the highway.

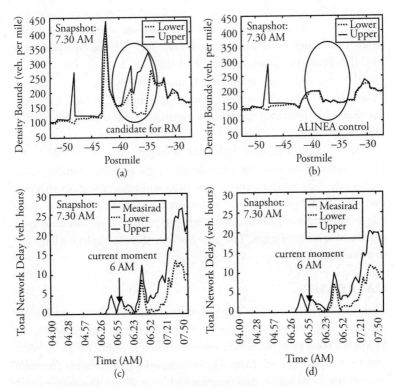

FIGURE 20.5   Short-term Prediction from 6 to 8 a.m. for I-210

Note: West (top): (a) projected density bounds for 7.30 am without ramp metering; (b) projected density bounds for 7.30 a.m. with ALINEA ramp control; (c) projected bounds for total network delay without ramp metering; and (d) projected bounds for total network delay with ALINEA ramp control

Figure 20.5a is a snapshot of the projected density bounds (lower bound in green, upper bound in red) along the highway at 7.30 am (1.5 hours into the future) computed with no traffic flow control at nodes. At the location marked by the ellipse (between postmiles 40 and 35) the projected density uncertainty interval is large, with its upper bound exceeding critical density and lower bound staying in the free flow state, indicating that the system may develop congestion if left to its own devices, or stay in free flow if managed properly. Such locations are primary candidates for aggressive ramp metering (RM).

Figure 20.5b is a snapshot of projected density bounds at the same time if ALINEA ramp metering were applied within the marked highway segment. The size of the projected density interval is significantly reduced: the controlled system is more predictable than the uncontrolled one. Figures 20.5c and 20.5d show the evolution of the total network delay (including on-ramp queue delay) for the uncontrolled and ALINEA-controlled cases respectively. From 4 to 6 am the delay is computed from the measurements (blue), and from 6 to 8 am the predicted delay bounds (lower bound in green, upper bound in red). One can see that ALINEA ramp metering potentially yields a noticeable delay reduction.

This example evaluates only one strategy, namely ALINEA. In practice, the traffic operator should test several potential control strategies, study their relative benefits and costs and apply the most effective one. A macroscopic traffic simulator such as Aurora RNM is able to run a hundred such simulations with pre-programmed scenarios in a matter of several minutes. The operator can thereby explore a large set of strategies.

DATABASE

The ATM system must be supported by a database that keeps historical data. The California freeway Performance Measurement System or PeMS is a good example, which was established in 2000. PeMS archives real time measurements from 24,000 detectors in California freeways, amounting to 50 billion data samples each year. PeMS also receives and stores event data such as incidents reported by the California Highway Patrol and lane-closure data reported by the California Department of Transportation (Caltrans). Today PeMS holds 10 TB of original and derived data.

As sensor samples arrive, PeMS subjects them to statistical tests to determine whether the measurements are valid or erroneous. If a measurement is judged to be in error, it is replaced by an imputed value. The data are processed to produce a wide range of freeway performance metrics in real time (delay, travel time, bottleneck locations, etc.) as well as metrics that cover longer periods (annual congestion, average peak period VMT) and larger regions (Bay Area, Southern California). The variety of performance metrics computed routinely in PeMS has grown over time in response to the need of different user groups.

The entire PeMS database and all performance metrics are online, so traffic engineers can gain a quick appreciation of what is happening at the moment as in Figure 20.6, which is a screen shot of the real-time dashboard, showing current and projected performance metrics of aggregate VMT, VHT, and Q (a measure of speed); the previous day's worst bottlenecks; the current day's worst incidents; and, for specific

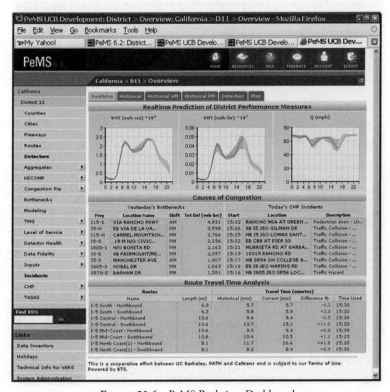

FIGURE 20.6   PeMS Real-time Dashboard

routes, a comparison of their current travel time with their historical average. Because PeMS keeps all past data online, it also provides transportation planners, consultants, and researchers the tools for retrospective studies. Figure 20.7 gives an example. It plots the 25th, 50th and 75th percentile of travel time for trips on the I-50 freeway near Hodges Lake for each month from January 2007 to May 2008. As is evident, there is a dramatic and sustained drop in travel time after August 2007, when an additional lane was opened. Planners could compare the actual benefit in travel time with what was predicted when the lane construction was approved.

MEASUREMENT

An archive of historical and real-time traffic measurement data is needed for ATM. The measurement data are generated by vehicle detection

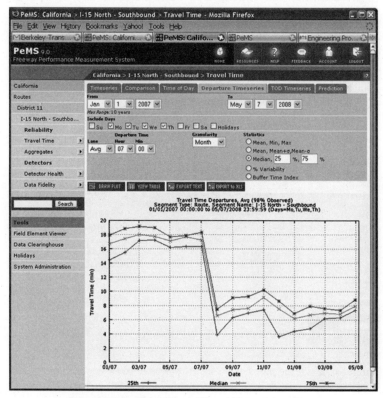

FIGURE 20.7   PeMS Plot of Travel Time Over a Route

systems and transmitted to the database in the Traffic Management Centre. Effective traffic management requires a geographically extensive network of reliable and accurate vehicle detection systems, together with a communication network over which these measurements are forwarded to the Traffic Management Centre as indicated in Figure 20.1.

Today the overwhelming proportion of these systems rely on inductive loop sensors. These loop detector systems are technologically obsolete: they have a high failure rate (for example, at any time up to 30 per cent of loop detectors in California have failed); require frequent re-calibration in the field, which is rarely undertaken, so their measurements are not accurate; they are very expensive to maintain. Lastly, installing new loop detectors is disruptive, requiring closure of a lane for several hours or days.

A new generation of wireless magnetic sensors is briefly described in this section (Haoui et al. 2008). Each sensor is housed in a 3-inch cube containing a magnetic sensor, microprocessor, radio, antenna and a battery with a ten-year lifetime. The cube is buried in a 4-inch diameter drilled hole in the middle of a lane. The sensor detects the change in the earth's magnetic field caused by the passage of a vehicle over it, and, transmits the detection to a 6-inch Access Point (AP) on the side of the road. The AP sends the detection signal to the local signal controller and, via GSM cellular modem, to the Traffic Management Centre's database server. Installation of the wireless detector station takes a few minutes.[††] Once installed the sensors immediately begin to deliver data. These sensors may be used to replace broken loop detectors and to augment the existing detector network. They are currently deployed in more than 150 cities in the US. An effective ATM system for a city should be supplied by data from sensors that serve all the functions suggested in Figure 20.8.

An array of magnetic sensors placed across a lane generates a signal from which a vehicle-specific signature can be extracted. If such arrays are placed in successive links across an arterial, these signatures can be matched to provide an accurate measurement of vehicle travel time in each link. The travel times, together with volume, occupancy, and speed measurements provided by the sensors can be processed to produce a range of performance metrics (Kwong et al. 2009). The travel time

[††] http://www.sensysnetworks.com

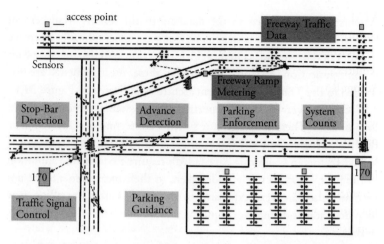

access point

Freeway Traffic Data

Sensors

Stop-Bar Detection

Advance Detection

Freeway Ramp Metering

Parking Enforcement

System Counts

170

170

Traffic Signal Control

Parking Guidance

FIGURE 20.8   Network of Sensors for Urban Traffic Measurement

measurement system was installed on approaches to Dodgers Stadium in Los Angeles. During game events, queues of vehicles form at these approaches and signs are posted telling drivers the time they will take to get to the entrances to the stadium.

A reliable, spatially dense network of detectors is essential for the data needed for any effective traffic management system. Wireless magnetic sensors offer a flexible means for building such a traffic surveillance network. The network can be incrementally expanded. Data from such a network must be archived to be of use.

Archived data are needed for an ATM system. The data are used to estimate and validate dynamic macroscopic models of the road network, and reveal weaknesses and stress points. The model has to be macroscopic for it to be fast enough for the ATM system operator to run scores of simulations in an operational setting. As advocated here, ATM provides tactical decision support to the operator by evaluating a large range of control strategies in the context of plausible near term future scenarios. In this view, ATM is proactive: it asks what adverse events are more or less likely to occur, and what countermeasures can an operator take to prevent or mitigate their ill effects. Thus, ATM enables risk management. As transportation systems experience greater stress (growing demand without corresponding capacity increase), proactive risk management becomes more important. This is a different view of

ATM than a frequently expressed view of ATM as a set of 'advanced' control strategies such as 'variable speed limit' and 'lane management'. Risk management needs a capability to assess risk. Such a capability requires a fast simulator that can rapidly assess scores of possibilities. The Aurora Road Network Modeller appears to fulfil this need. It comprises a collection of software tools for building a model and a disciplined way of specifying scenarios and control strategies, together with a set of performance metrics that can be used for a comparative evaluation of system performance. Its simulation model is austere, characterized by a few parameters, so estimation provides statistical guarantees, and each parameter has an understandable impact. This is in contrast to slow microsimulation models, which with their abundant parameters are impossible to estimate with any statistical precision and whose influence in traffic behaviour is difficult to trace, even though the visuals that microsimulation packages offer lend a deceptive air of verisimilitude.

REFERENCES

Daganzo, C.F. (1994), 'The Cell Transmission Model: A Dynamic Representation of Highway Traffic Consistent with the Hydrodynamic Theory', *Transportation Research*, Part B, 28(4): 269–87.

_____ (1995) 'The Cell Transmission Model II: Network Traffic', *Transportation Research*, Part B, 29(2): 79–93.

Dervisoglu, G., G. Gomes, J. Kwon, A. Muralidharan, and P. Varaiya (2008), 'Automatic Calibration of the Fundamental Diagram and Empirical Observations on Capacity', 88th Annual Meeting of the Transportation Research Board, Washington, D.C., USA.

Diakaki, C., M. Papageorgiou, and T. McLean (2000), 'Integrated Traffic-responsive Urban Corridor Control Strategy in Glasgo, Scotland', *Transportation Research Record*, 1727: 101–11.

Gomes, G., R.R. Horowitz, A.A. Kurzhanskiy, J. Kwon, and P.Varaiya (2008), 'Behavior of the Cell Transmission Model and Effectiveness of Ramp Metering', *Transportation Research*, Part C, 16(4): 485–513 (August).

Haoui, A., R. Kavaler, and P. Varaiya (2008), 'Wireless Magnetic Sensors for Traffic Surveillance', *Transportation Research*, Part C, 16(3): 294–306.

Kurzhanskiy, A.A. (2009), 'Set-valued Estimation of Freeway Traffic Density', *Proceedings of the 12th IFAC Symposium on Control in Transportation Systems.*

Kwon, J., M. Mauch, and P. Varaiya (2006), 'Components of Congestion: Delay from Incidents, Special Events, Lane Closures, Weather, Potential Ramp Metering Gain, and Excess Demand', *Transportation Research Record*, 1959: 84–91.

Kwong, K., R. Kavaler, R. Rajagopal, and P. Varaiya (2009), 'Arterial Travel Time Estimation based on Vehicle Re-identification using Wireless Sensors', *Transportation Research*, Part C, 17(6): 586–606 (December).

Muralidharan, A. and R. Horowitz (2009), 'Imputation of Ramp Data Fow for Freeway Traffic Simulation', *Transportation Research Record*. 2099: 58–64.

Papageorgiou, M., H. Hadj-Salem, and J. Blosseville (1991), 'ALINEA: A Local Feedback Control Law for on-ramp Metering', *Transportation Research Record*, 1320: 58–64.

Papamichail, I., M. Papageorgiou, V. Vong, and J. Gaffney (2010), 'HERO Coordinated Ramp Metering Implemented at Monash Freeway, Australia', 89th Annual Meeting of the Transportation Research Board, Washington, D.C., USA.

Appendix

R. NARASIMHAN

On the System and Engineering Design of the General Purpose Electronic Digital Computer at TIFR*

Since 1955, the Computer Section of the Tata Institute of Fundamental Research has been engaged in the development and construction of a large scale electronic digital computer for doing scientific computations. As a preliminary to this, a pilot digital calculator was designed and completed in September 1956 and was kept in operation for about a year (Newsletter 1957). The design of the full-scale machine was started early in 1957 and its final assemblycompleted in February 1959. Unfortunately, owing to the lack of air-conditioning facilities, the work had to be suspended till almost the end of 1959. The actual testing was begun in mid-November 1959 with an auxiliary air-conditioning system and the computer was commissioned for routine work in the third week of February 1960. This essay describes briefly the main features of the system and engineering design of this digital computer. In a companion essay, some aspects of the circuitry will be dealt with.

* Originally published in *Proceedings of Indian Academy of Sciences*, Section A, vol. 52 (August 1960), pp. 45–57. This essay is reproduced with permission from Indian Academy of Sciences.

The TIFR computer is a parallel, binary, asynchronous machine. It is controlled by a stored programme of single-address instructions and has a fast access ferrite-core memory consisting of 1,024 locations. The input to the computer is by means of a punched paper tape (5-hole commercial teletype tape) and the output can be either printed out directly or punched on a paper tape again. Both in the system and engineering design, the principal emphasis has been on reliability of operation and ease in maintenance. With this in view, the logical circuit types have been kept to the minimum consistent with flexibility and the wired circuits were put through a rigid acceptance test to check their performance under extreme operating conditions. For rapid fault localization and servicing, a large part of the computer has been assembled in terms of functionally self-contained packaged units. Separate testing facilities have been set up for routine checking of these plug-in units. The main computer assembly has 2,700 tubes (almost all of them double triodes), 1,700 crystal diodes (germanium) and approximately 12,500 resistors. Since the computer is DC coupled throughout, few condensers are used and except in the case of two bias supplies, no circuit is transistorized. The total power consumption is about 18 kW.

THE ARITHMETIC AND CONTROL LOGIC

In the TIFR computer, all the internal operations take place in the binary notation and numbers are stored in the main memory assigned binary fractions restricted to the range $(-1, 1)$. A number in its normal form consists of a sign (which is a 0 for positive numbers and a 1 for negative numbers) followed by 39 binary digits (bits, for short) which give its absolute value as a binary fraction. The binary point is understood to be fixed immediately after the sign bit (see Figure A.1). The complement form of a number is obtained by changing all its 1's to 0's and *vice-versa*; the sign bit is left unaltered, however, in this process.

A schematic diagram of the arithmetic unit is shown in Figure A.2. It consists of an adder, a memory register and two (double rank) shift registers (the accumulator and MQ-register, respectively), and a pair of true/complement gates. The adder is of the fast logical type and incorporates in itself special carry by-pass facilities to speed up the carry propagation time (Rao and Basu 1952). These cut down the addition time to about one-third of what it would otherwise have been. The contents of the accumulator are presented to the adder either in the true

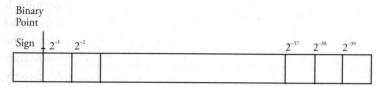

Binary
Point

Sign 2^{-1} 2^{-2} 2^{-37} 2^{-38} 2^{-39}

FIGURE A.1   Number Representation (Binary Fraction)

or the complement form depending on whether the operation called for is addition (multiplication) or subtraction (division) respectively. In some cases the result of a subtraction needs to be recomplemented to obtain the number in its true form. To simplify this procedure, facilities have been built into the adder so that its output can be gated into the accumulator either in its true or complement form. Also the particular design of the adder used makes it especially simple to obtain the logical product of the adder inputs and this is taken advantage of in the Collate order.

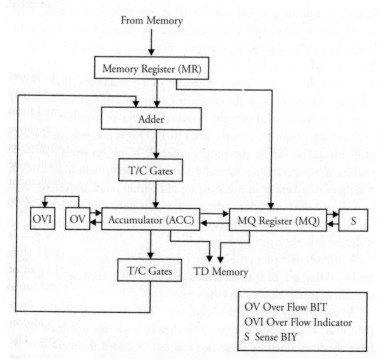

From Memory

Memory Register (MR)

Adder

T/C Gates

OVI   OV   Accumulator (ACC)   MQ Register (MQ)   S

T/C Gates   TD Memory

OV Over Flow BIT
OVI Over Flow Indicator
S Sense BIY

FIGURE A.2   Schematic of Arithmetic Unit

The absolute value representation of numbers makes the multiplication and division logic very simple and straightforward. In both cases, the operation is carried out treating the numbers as positive quantities. The proper signs are written into the accumulator and MQ-register in the end. The incorporation of an extra bit, called the *Sense bit* (2^{-40} stage of MQ) is believed to be a unique feature of this computer. In multiplication, the discrimination for add-shift/shift is obtained from this sense bit rather than from Q^{-39} as is normally done. Similarly, in division the quotient bits are written into the sense bit rather than into Q^{-39}. Thus both multiplication and division involve 40 shifts (instead of the usual 39). This has the major advantage that normal division is unrounded (that is, correct up to and including the 2^{-39} stage). It is expected that this feature will have special advantages in multiple precision work. In shift operations, the sense bit functions like an extension to the MQ-register on its right end.

All *proper* arithmetic operations should result in numbers which again fall within the range $(-1, 1)$. But there are no built-in checks to detect improper arithmetic operations. It is, in the main, the responsibility of the programmer to see that numbers are confined to the admissible range, by proper scaling, all the time. However, to help him in doing this, an extra bit, called the overflow bit, has been provided at the left end of the accumulator. In the case of a genuine overflow (that is, addition of numbers with the same signs, or subtraction of numbers with opposite signs) it is fed into the overflow bit and an overflow indicator, OVI (which normally stays 0), is set to 1. This is not reset to 0 unless explicitly called for by the programmer. A 'jump on overflow' order enables the programmer to make use of this information in variable scaling of numbers or in normalizing in floating point arithmetic. Also, in ordinary shift operations, the overflow bit functions as an extension to the accumulator on the left and the OVI becomes operative when a I is shifted into the overflow bit.

A 'round-off' order enables the accumulator content to be rounded off by adding a 1 or 0 to its least significant bit according as the MQ content is greater than or less than ½.

As has already been mentioned, the TIFR computer is of the asynchronous, single address type. The details of its control logic are effectively determined by these two features. A coded instruction in the machine requires 20 bits for its specification: (the first 9 bits for its *order* part and last 11 bits for its *address* part). Because the word length in the memory is 40 bits, instructions are stored in pairs in each memory location. They are identified as the left-hand (LHI) and right-hand (RHI) instructions in that location (see Figure A.3). A complete control cycle consists of 3 parts: (a) an *instruction cycle,* where a (next) pair of instructions is brought from the memory to the instruction register; (b) an *execution cycle A,* where the left-hand instruction is executed; and (c) an *execution cycle B* where the right-hand instruction is executed. The sequencing within the cycles is effected by means of 4-state sequencing units similar to the ones used in ORDVAC type machines (ORDVAC 1952). The static control levels are obtained by partial decoding of the order bits of an instruction. As far as possible, the micro-operations are done in parallel so as to minimize the number of sequencing steps required.

One built-in B-register (of 11-bit length) is available for address modifications. The shift counter is also similar to the one used in ORDVAC but an improved gating logic has enabled its speed to be increased appreciably (Basu and Rao 1957).

In addition to the unconditional jump order, 6 types of conditional jump orders are available, viz., jump if accumulator sign bit is 0/1; jump if MQ sign bit is 0/1; jump if the overflow indicator is 0/1. In the case of the last order, the control resets the overflow indicator to 0.

Table A.1 gives a summary of the order types and variants built into the computer.

THE MEMORY

The internal memory of the TIFR computer consists of a 3-dimensional ferrite-core matrix (made up of 40 planes), 40 output amplifiers, diode

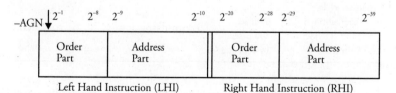

	Order Part	Address Part		Order Part	Address Part	

Left Hand Instruction (LHI)   Right Hand Instruction (RHI)

$-\text{AGN}\downarrow 2^{-1}$ 2^{-8} 2^{-9} 2^{-10} 2^{-20} 2^{-28} 2^{-29} 2^{-39}

FIGURE A.3   Allocation of bits in a pair of Instructions

TABLE A.1   Order Types and their Variants

	Type	Variants	
1. Arithmetic orders	Add	Holds Acc.	Clear Acc.
		Signed/Abs. Val.	Signed/Abs. Val
	Subtract	—id—	—id—
	Multiply Unround	—id—	—id—
	Multiply Round	—id—	—id—
	Divide	—id—	—id—
	Collate	—id—	—id—
	Round off	—id—	—id—
2. Shift orders	Shift Rt. Ace.	Hold Acc.	Clear Acc.
	Shift Lt. Ace.	—id—	—id—
	Shift Rt. Acc.-MQ	—id—	—id—
	Shift Lt. Acc.-MQ	—id—	—id—
	Shift Lt. Acc.-MQ	—id—	—id—
	(also Q°)		
3. Store orders	Store Ace.	Hold Acc-MQ	Clear Acc.
	Store LHA Acc.	—id—	—id—
	Store RHA Ace.	—id—	—id—
	Store LHA-RHA Ace.	—id—	—id—
	Store MQ	—id—	—id—
	Transfer to MQ	—id—	—id—
	Transfer to B-Reg.	—id—	—id—
4. Jump orders	If A° = 0	To LHI	To RHI
	If A° = 1	—id—	—id—
	If Q° = 0	—id—	—id—
	If Q° = 1	—id—	—id—
	If OVI = 0	—id—	—id—
	If OVI = 1	—id—	—id—
	Unconditional	—id—	—id—
5. Miscellaneous	Conditional	Stop	
	Orders	Stop	
	Input	Tape/Drum	
	Output	Punch/CRT/Drum	
Instruction cycle:	20 μ-sec.		
Execution cycle-			
Add/subtract:	45 μ-sec.		
Mult./Divide:	500 μ-sec.		
Shift n :	14 + 11 n μ -sec.		

decoding nets for address selection and drive circuits for reading and writing. The matrix assembly was purchased from Mullard and Co., England. The read-rewrite logic is essentially the same as that described by

Papian originally for the MIT computer (Papian 1953). Both amplitude and time discrimination (Strobing) is used at the output end to increase the signal/noise ratio. The read output is gated into a set of memory flip-flops which also function as the memory register of the arithmetic unit. The input to the memory can be either from the accumulator or the MQ-register. While storing from the accumulator, either the entire content of the register or only the address part (either the left-hand or right-hand address alone or both) can be written in. Except for the initiating trigger, the memory sequencing is completely independent of the rest of the computer control. The duration of a single memory read-write cycle is approximately 15 μ-seconds. Provision has been made for incorporating a second core-matrix of equal capacity at a later stage thus doubling the internal store.

THE POWER SUPPLY

The power requirements of a large-scale parallel electronic digital computer pose some severe problems normally not encountered in conventional electronic systems of a similar size. The power supply system, whilelarge in capacity (usually of the order of 20 kW.), has to be at the same time (a) very highly reliable and rugged; (b) well stabilised for not only the usual line voltage fluctuations but for load switchings at very high repetition rates (calling for a response time of the order of a few rc-seconds on the part of the regulator for almost 0 to full-load switching); and (c) fully protected against partial failures by effectively fool-proof protective interlocks. The power supply for the TIFR computer has been designed and constructed to satisfy all the above requirements and has been under satisfactory operation for several months.

The input to the power supply is from 3-phase, 4 wire, 50 cycles, 230 volt mains with a nominal rating of 40 kVA. Two regulators are provided, one an electromechanical unit capable of handling up to 20 kVA and is intended principally for the tube heater supplies. The other is an electronic stabilizer for the high tension busbars in the computer. The filament transformers are single-phase units, each capable of supplying 200 amps. at 6.3 volts. Ten such transformers are used in all to supply the heater power for the various units of the computer. A relay controlled system allows gradual application of filament voltages to the tubes and provides the necessary delay before the application of plate voltages.

The DC high tension levels used in the computer together with their full-load currents are as follows:

$$-300 \text{ V} : 18 \text{ amps.}$$
$$-150 \text{ V} : 45 \text{ amps.}$$
$$+110 \text{ V} : 10 \text{ amps.}$$
$$+150 \text{ V} : 5 \text{ amps.}$$
$$+200 \text{ V} : 7 \text{ amps.}$$
$$+300 \text{ V} : 2 \text{ amps.}$$

These voltages are stabilized to within 1 per cent for line voltage fluctuations and to within 2 per cent for 0 to 100 per cent load switching with a recovery time of the order of a few μ-seconds. The electronic regulator consists of grid controlled thyratrons used in a 3-phase half-wave circuit and a 'stiff' filter with a large output capacitance (of the order of a few hundredths of a farad for each level) to provide the necessary recovery time. A specially developed pulse-shifting circuit fires the thyratrons.

ENGINEERING DESIGN

Figures 4[*] and 5[†] show an overall view of the computer assembly and power supply units. The main computer assembly is housed in a steel rack 18'×23' 6'×8' which has been fabricated out of modules of size 4'×2j'×8'. Each module has a pair of steel doors (of size 2'×6') on either face to provide accessibility to the circuits. For ease in maintenance, single layer mounting has been adopted for the wired panels except in a few instances where a second layer has been wired on swing-out panels. The information flow is along the horizontal with the arithmetic unit in the centre flanked on either side by the control and the memory units. The bits in each functional unit occupy the modules from top to bottom. The lower 18' of the entire assembly house the filament transformers and some of the output capacitors while also serving as an air plenum for the forced-air-cooling system. Cool air (at approximately 20°C and a total flow of 6,000 c.ft./min.) is fed into the computer at the two ends, channelled through the various modules and exhausted into the room from the top. Exhaust fans mounted along the length of the

---

[*] See Chapter 1, Figure 1.2.
[†] See Chapter 1, Figure 1.3.

computer on top help to maintain uniform distribution of the cold air inside the computer assembly.

The power unit is housed in two independent racks, one containing the contactors, AC regulators, variacs, transformers and output capacitors, and the other containing the thyratrons, pulse control units, control and voltage monitoring relays. The electronic circuitry is mounted on pull-out chassis to facilitate servicing.

AUXILIARY EQUIPMENT

As has already been mentioned, the information input into the computer is by means of punched paper tapes and the output from the machine can again be either punched on tapes or directly printed out. Currently, commercial Olivetti Type T2Pr/T2CN reperforators and page printers are being used for this purpose. A Ferranti Mark II tape reader has been tried out but a much faster servo-controlled Potter Model 903 tape reader is in an advanced stage of testing and is expected to be available for use very soon. A high speed Creed Model 75-page printer/reperforator has also been acquired with a specially built-in code to facilitate direct binary to decimal conversion. This, together with the Potter tape reader, it is expected, will provide very adequate input-output facilities for the computer.

A manual control console has been set up to serve as a very flexible input/output/control unit to regulate and monitor the operation of the computer. Facilities are available for single shot operation; for slow external triggering at approximately one cycle per second and for manual hexadecimal input into the MQ-register with the help of a diode decoding net operated from a keyboard. Neon indicators enable visual monitoring of the contents of all the registers.

For routine maintenance checking and also for servicing of the various plug-in units used in the computer, a comprehensive test rack has been built. Detailed and systematic DC checking of the units can be carried out with great ease with the help of the test rack and complete test schedules have been worked out for each unit to systematise the test procedures.

A cathode ray tube (CRT) display system has been developed to serve as an auxiliary output to the computer for fast analogue and digital display of both graphs and alpha-numeric symbols. A pilot version has already been built and successfully operated (Rao 1959). The more elaborate final unit is under assembly and is expected to be available for routine use in a few months' time.

Work on the development of a magnetic drum to serve as a large capacity back-up storage has been going on concurrently with the assembly of the main computer. The final specifications of the drum have been drawn up and the mechanical assembly is under fabrication. Logical design of the drum control and read-write circuits are being finalized. When this facility is made available, the total computer storage capacity will increase eight-fold.

OPERATIONAL EXPERIENCE

Since the completion of the computer assembly early in 1959, the various parts of the machine have been under operation for almost a year now. The operational and maintenance experience gained over this period indicate that with adequate *routine* maintenance, the computer should give reliable, trouble free operation over long periods of time continuously. It has not been possible so far to collect systematic statistics of failure rates, of types of faults and of time lost in unscheduled servicing. However, it may be mentioned that in general the component failures have been remarkably few in number. Less than 5 per cent of the tubes have had to be changed (and this mostly for loss in emission) and there have been resistance failures only in the case of 2 or 3 types of resistors.

Comprehensive test programmes have been designed to check each of the functional units under a variety of input-internal state configurations. These have proved to be of invaluable aid in fault location and in routine checking. By means of test programmes every single core in the memory matrix has been tested for reading and writing under the most adverse operating conditions.

It is proposed to operate the computer, at the first instance, on an 8-hour shift daily. The first 3 hours will be devoted to scheduled maintenance and the remaining 5 for useful computing. A programming manual has been prepared to assist machine users in programming their own problems.

SUMMARY

This essay gives a brief description of the system and engineering design of the general purpose electronic digital computer that has been developed and built in TIFR, Bombay. This computer is a parallel, binary, asynchronous machine with a ferrite-core matrix fast memory of 1,024 words. The arithmetic is in the fixed point binary system with a number length of 40 bits. The computer incorporates one B-register for address modification and several other special features such as overflow indication, carry bypass, etc., Input-output is by means of punched paper tape. An auxiliary output in the form of a CRT display has been developed and a magnetic drum to serve as a back-up store is being designed.

ACKNOWLEDGMENTS

A large-scale general purpose digital computer is perhaps the most complex electronic equipment designed so far to function as one integrated centrally controlled unit. Needless to say, the development, design and construction of such a system calls for a very high degree of organization and planning and for the co-ordinated efforts of a large group of individuals. For the successful completion of the TIFR computer the following have been responsible: The overall logic and engineering system design as well as the planning and co-ordinating of the project was the principal responsibility of the author. The detailed design of the control and arithmetic logic and its physical realization in terms of circuitry as well as the design and construction of the auxiliary control and test equipments were entirely carried out by B.K. Basu, assisted by K. Bakhru, M.M. Dosabhai, Miss V.K. Joglekar, B.B. Kalia, R.R. Nargundkar, S.V. Rangaswamy, P.V.S. Rao, and V.M. Vengurlekar. For the memory assembly and associated circuits, S.P. Srivastava was responsible, assisted by C.V. Srinivasan and T.R.N. Rao. The entire development, design and construction of the power supply system was carried out by M.M. Farooqui, assisted by D.F. Cooper, R.Y.N. Iyengar, and R.K. Shah. Special acknowledgment is made here of the help rendered by the Development and Production Unit of the Atomic Energy. Establishment, Trombay, in wiring the plug-in units and in the fabrication of some of the pulse transformers. Also, the co-operation of the Institute workshop personnel at the various stages of the computer fabrication is gratefully acknowledged. Special mention should be made of the untiring and enthusiastic co-operation of Junior Mechanic, R.P. Thosar, over the past 5 years. Grateful acknowledgment is also made of the keen interest shown by Dr D.Y. Phadke in the project.

REFERENCES

'The Pilot Digital Calculator at TIFR, Bombay' (1957) in *The Digital Computer Newsletter,* January.

Basu, B.K. and K. Bakhru, (1957), 'The Input-output System of the TIFR Computer', in *Proceedings of Indian Academy of Sciences,* 45, 231–39.

Basu, B.K. and P.V.S. Rao (1957), 'A Modified Gating Logic to Improve the Speed of Operation of Double Rank Counters', in *Proceedings of Indian Academy of Sciences,* 46, 354–59.

ORDVAC Manual (1952), University of Illinois.

Papian, W.N. (1953) [1954], 'The MIT Magnetic Core Memory', in *Proc. Eastern Joint Comp. Conf,* December p. 37.

Rao, P.V.S. (1959) 'A Character Display System for Use as a Digital Computer Output', *Note, Rev. Sci. Inst.,* 30, 749—50.

Rao, P.V.S. and Basu, B.K. 'A Fast Logical Adder', *Tech. Report* (unpublished).

Contributors

Jay Giri, Director, Applications Engineering, ALSTOM ESCA, Bellevue, Washington, is co-founder of ALSTOM ESCA. He has worked extensively on Information and Communication Technologies (ICT) applications for powers systems and smart grid.

H. Peter Hofstee is a distinguished engineer and works at the IBM Austin Research Laboratory on hybrid and workload-optimized systems. Popularly known as the chief architect of the synergistic processor elements in the cell broadband engine, he is an authority on computer architectures.

Rahul Jain is Assistant Professor, Department of Computer Science, National University of Singapore, Singapore. His focus areas include information theory, quantum computation, communication complexity, complexity theory, and cryptography.

F.C. Kohli, Padma Bhushan, is regarded as the father of Indian software industry. Former Deputy Chairman and the first CEO of Tata Consultancy Services (TCS), he has special interest in Information and Communication Technologies (ICT) applications for society and business.

Alex A. Kurzhanskiy is Postdoctoral Research Fellow at the Department of Electrical Engineering and Computer Science, University of California, Berkeley. His primary research interests are dynamical systems-estimation, verification, and control.

Y.S. Mayya is Chairman and Managing Director of Electronics Corporation of India Ltd. (ECIL), Hyderabad. His focus areas include automation and control systems.

M.G.K. Menon, Padma Vibhushan, is an advisor, Department of Space, Indian Space Research Organisation (ISRO). President of Indian Statistical Institute, Kolkata and Chancellor, North-Eastern Hill University (NEHU), Shillong, he is a Fellow of Royal Society and former Director of Tata Institute of Fundamental Research (TIFR), Mumbai. His focus areas include physics, science, and technology policy.

Bud Mishra is Professor of Computer Science and Mathematics, Courant Institute of Mathematical Sciences, New York University. A Fellow of the Institute of Electrical and Electronics Engineers (IEEE) and the Association for Computing Machinery (ACM), he is an authority on computational biology.

N.R. Narayana Murthy, Padma Vibhushan, is the founder Chairman and Chief Mentor, Infosys Technologies Ltd. Pioneer of the Global Delivery Model that has become the foundation for the overwhelming success of offshore IT services provided by India, he is an IT advisor to several Asian countries.

Nandan Nilekani, Padma Bhushan, is the Chairman of Unique Identification Authority of India (UIDAI). Former CEO and Managing Director of Infosys Technologies Ltd., he co-founded India's National Association of Software and Service Companies (NASSCOM), as well as the Bengaluru chapter of The IndUS Entrepreneurs (TiE).

M.A. Pai is Professor Emeritus, Department of Electrical and Computer Engineering, University of Illinois, Urbana-Champaign. Recipient of the Shanti Swarup Bhatnagar award in 1974, he has research interest in energy systems and technical education in India.

A. Paulraj, Padma Bhushan, is Professor Emeritus, Department of Electrical Engineering, Stanford University, and Fellow, US National Academy of Engineering (NAE). He pioneered the MIMO (Multiple Input Multiple Output) technology—an essential component of all modern wireless systems. He received the IEEE Alexander Graham Bell Medal for MIMO technology.

M.V. PITKE, former Director, Centre for Development of Telematics (C-DOT), was Professor at the Tata Institute of Fundamental Research (TIFR), Mumbai. He pioneered the development of a switching system for a mobile network that was forerunner to the current ad-hoc networks. His focus areas include computer and telecommunication systems.

SAM PITRODA, Padma Bhushan, is advisor to the Prime Minster of India on Public Information Infrastructures and Innovation. Founder of the Centre for Development of Telematics (C-DOT), he is deeply interested in telecommunication and Information and Communication Technologies (ICT) for society.

JAIKUMAR RADHAKRISHNAN is Professor and Dean, School of Technology and Computer Science, Tata Institute of Fundamental Research (TIFR), Mumbai. Recipient of the Shanti Swarup Bhatnagar award in 2008, he has done original research in the areas of Computational Complexity Theory and Quantum Information and Computation.

V. RAJARAMAN, Padma Bhushan, is honorary professor, Supercomputer Education and Research Centre, Indian Institute of Science (IISc), Bangalore. Recipient of the Shanti Swarup Bhatnagar award in 1976, his focus areas include computer science and technical education.

S. RAMADORAI, Vice Chairman of Tata Consultancy Services (TCS), has been instrumental in building TCS to a USD 6.3 billion global software and services company. He is deeply interested in Information and Communication Technologies (ICT) applications for society and business.

S. RAMANI, Professor, International Institute of Information Technology (IIIT), Bangalore, is the founder director of the National Centre for Software Technology (NCST) and former director of HP Labs India. His is interested in technology in education.

P.V.S. RAO, Padma Shri, was Senior Professor at the Tata Institute of Fundamental Research (TIFR), Mumbai. Former President of the Computer Society of India, Rao was a key member of the TIFRAC team. His main research interests include speech and signal processing.

U.R. RAO, Padma Bhushan, is the Chairman of the governing council of Physical Research Laboratory (PRL). Former Chairman of Indian Space Research Organisation (ISRO) and Secretary, Department of Space (DoS), and the Chairman of Space Commission, he is an authority on space science technology and applications.

PRANAB SEN is Reader, School of Technology and Computer Science, Tata Institute of Fundamental Research (TIFR). He has done extensive research on quantum computing, and has an active interest in computational complexity theory.

N. SESHAGIRI, Padma Bhushan, is the founder Director-General of National Informatics Centre (NIC). He was formerly Special Secretary at the Planning Commission of India, and has worked extensively on IT for societal applications.

R.K. SHYAMASUNDAR, Senior Professor and J.C. Bose National Fellow, School of Technology and Computer Science, Tata Institute of Fundamental Research (TIFR), Mumbai. A Fellow of the Institute of Electrical and Electronics Engineers (IEEE) and the Association for Computing Machinery (ACM), he has made original contributions to real-time distributed computing, concurrent programming languages, logic programming, and information security.

PRAVIN VARAIYA is Professor, Graduate School, Electrical Engineering and Computer Science (EECS), University of California, Berkeley, and Fellow, US National Academy of Engineering (NAE). He has done extensive research on control and computer science.

S.R. VIJAYAKAR is former Chairman and Managing Director, Electronics Corporation of India Ltd. (ECIL), Hyderabad. His focus areas of interest include electronics and instrumentation.